Australia
A Complete Guide

© Little Hills Press, November 2004

© Photographs, see Acknowledgements page 330

© Text, Little Hills Press, 2004

Cover design by Darren Holt
Design by Dan Hormillosa, assisted by Aron Vella
Original text by Chris Baker.
This text updated and developed by Angus Paterson

Little Hills Press Pty Ltd
Atf Burfitt Family Trust
Unit 3, 18 Bearing Road
Seven Hills, NSW 2147
Australia
ABN 96 094 187 321

ISBN 1863152415

Printed in China through Colorcraft Ltd., H.K.

Disclaimer
Whilst all care has been taken by the Publisher to ensure that all the information is accurate and up to date, the publisher does not take responsibility for the information published herein. Things get better or worse, places close down, others open, so some elements of the book may be inaccurate when you get there. Please write and tell us about it so we can update in subsequent editions. If your information is used we will happily send you the new edition of the book.

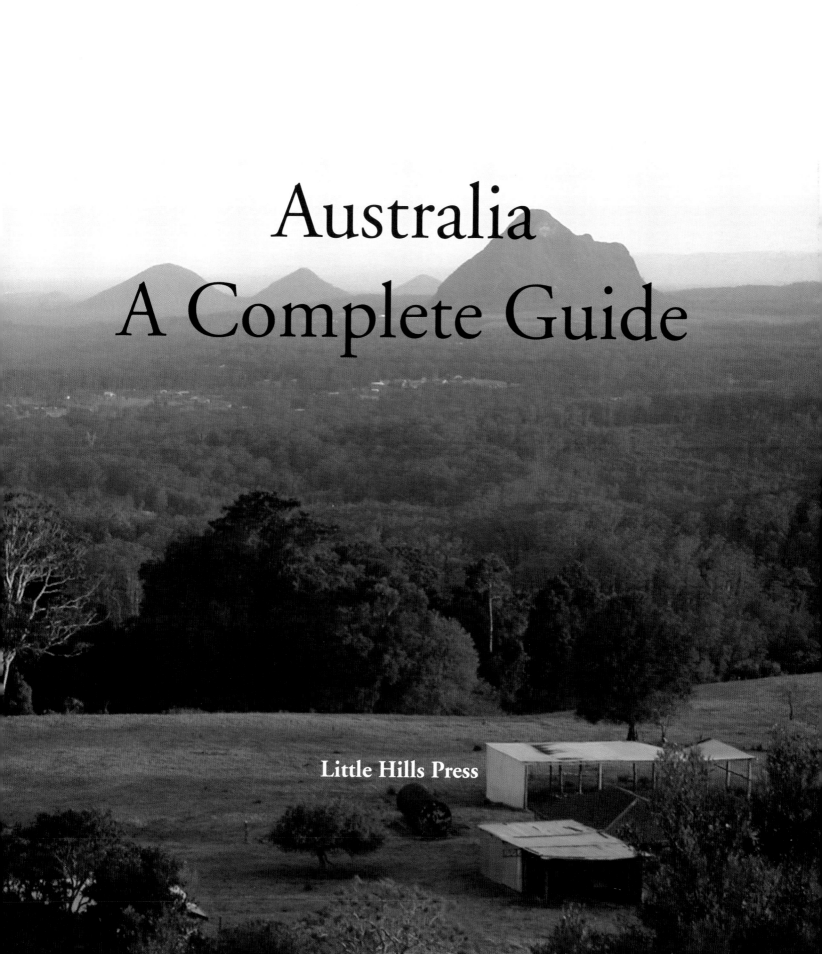

Australia
A Complete Guide

Little Hills Press

CONTENTS

INTRODUCTION
Australia An Overview 6

NEW SOUTH WALES

Sydney 10
Blue Mountains 18
Wollongong & the Illawarra 21
South Coast 24
Capital Country, Southern Highlands 28
Snowy Mountains 32
Riverina 34

The Murray Region 38
Outback New South Wales 41
Central New South Wales 47
New England, North-West 53
North Coast 56
Newcastle and the Hunter Valley 64
Central Coast 69

AUSTRALIAN CAPITAL TERRITORY
Canberra 74

VICTORIA

Greater Melbourne 80
Yarra Valley 88
Gippsland 91
Victorian Alps 96
North-East Victoria 99
Western District 103

Great Ocean Road 107
Bellarine Peninsula 111
Goldfields 113

TASMANIA

Hobart & South Tasmania 120
North-East, Launceston &
roads north from Hobart 134

North-West Tasmania 144
World Heritage Areas 152
Tasmanian Islands 154

SOUTH AUSTRALIA
Adelaide **158**
Fleurieu Peninsula & Kangaroo Island **163**
Limestone Coast **166**
Riverland **169**
The Barossa **174**

Clare Valley **179**
Yorke Peninsula **181**
Eyre Peninsula **183**
Flinders Rangers and Outback **189**

WESTERN AUSTRALIA
Perth & the South-West **194**
Goldfields **210**
Mid-West **215**

Gascoyne **220**
The Pilbara **227**
The Kimberley **231**

NORTHERN TERRITORY
Darwin and the Top End **238**
Katherine **247**

Tennant Creek **252**
Central Northern Territory **256**

QUEENSLAND
Brisbane **264**
Gold Coast **270**
Golden West **275**
Sunshine Coast **280**
Fraser Coast & South Burnett **284**
Bundaberg, Coral Coast & Country **288**

Central Queensland **291**
Mackay & The Whitsundays **298**
North Queensland **304**
Tropical North Queensland **311**
Outback Queensland **316**

MAPS **320**

ACKNOWLEDGEMENTS **330**

INDEX OF TOWNS AND CITIES **331**

Australia:
An Overview

Australia is an island continent in the South Pacific Ocean. It is the smallest continent and the largest island in the world with a coastline of 19,650km. Its nearest neighbours are New Zealand and Papua New Guinea, while East Timor and Indonesia are a little further away, off the north-western coast.

The country has an area of 7,682,300 square kilometres and is divided into six states - New South Wales, Queensland, Western Australia, South Australia ,Victoria and Tasmania - and two territories - Northern Territory and Australian Capital Territory.

The capital of Australia is Canberra in the Australian Capital Territory (ACT). The capital cities of the states are as follows:
New South Wales - Sydney
Queensland - Brisbane
Western Australia - Perth
South Australia - Adelaide
Victoria - Melbourne
Tasmania - Hobart

The capital of the Northern Territory is Darwin.

History

It was generally accepted that the continent was first settled by Aborigines around 20,000 years ago, until recent discoveries suggested that they may have arrived much earlier. They were Stone Age people, and as the country had virtually no indigenous plants that could be cultivated for crops, and no animals that could be domesticated, they neither grew nor bred their food, but survived by hunting and gathering. In the interior of the country, this necessitated a nomadic way of life, but in the coastal areas they led a more settled lifestyle because of readily available food from the sea.

The Aborigines were a peaceful race, and were deeply religious. Their mythology described the creation and explained the reasons for most human behaviour. It was passed from generation to generation in stories, songs and dances, as they had no written language. The dances were called corroborees, and there was one for every special occasion from praying for rain, to mourning death or celebrating a successful hunt.

European Discovery

Many Europeans visited Australia from the early 1600s, but the honour of discovering the continent goes to Captain James Cook, who in the ship *Endeavour* sailed into Botany Bay on April 29, 1770. Two boats went ashore, and tradition says that the first man to set foot on the land was Isaac Smith.

Cook and his party continued sailing northward, naming bays, capes, mountains and islands as they went, and reached a small island off Cape York where they went ashore on August 22, and took possession of the whole eastern coast in the name of King George III. Cook called the land New South Wales, and the island Possession Island.

European Settlement

The American War of Independence in 1783 was directly responsible for the settlement of Australia, as Britain then had nowhere to send her convicted criminals. Captain Arthur Phillip, RN, was appointed its first governor with orders to establish a penal settlement at Botany Bay, and the First Fleet sailed from England on May 13, 1787. The fleet was comprised of the *HMS Sirius*, the armed tender *Supply*, three storeships and six transports, with food clothing and other supplies sufficient for two years. They carried 1,044 people.

While Botany Bay was deemed unsuitable for settlement because of a lack of fresh water, further north Captain Phillip found the entrance to a large harbour, and decided the best spot for the new settlement was in the area he called Sydney Cove. In the afternoon of January 26, 1788, he and a party of officers and marines raised the Union Jack on the foreshore, drank toasts, fired volleys, and gave three cheers. In spite of initial problems, the settlement survived and grew. Intrepid explorers discovered new areas, and other settlements were established - Parramatta in 1788, Newcastle in 1803, Hobart in 1804, Brisbane in 1824, Perth in 1829, Melbourne in 1835, Adelaide in 1836, and so on.

Federation

The campaign to form a federation of the colonies began on October 24, 1889, with a speech by Sir Henry Parkes, known as the Father of Federation, at Tenterfield. The movement grew rapidly under his leadership, and there was a meeting of colonial leaders early in 1890 and a convention in March 1891 in Sydney. Parkes died in April, 1896, and the reins were taken over by Edmund Barton, barrister and statesman. A second convention was held at Adelaide in March 1897, and a third conference in January 1898, when a draft constitution was accepted. The next step was to hold referendums in the various colonies. The first, in 1898, was defeated. The second, in 1899, saw the five eastern colonies vote in favour of federation and Western Australia abstain.

Barton then headed a delegation to London, where various objections raised by the Colonial Office were overruled. Western Australia agreed to join in after receiving a promise that a transcontinental railway would be built to link Perth with the east coast. On July 9, 1900, Queen Victoria gave her assent to the act which would unite the six colonies into a Commonwealth.

The Commonwealth of Australia was proclaimed and the first Governor-General, the Earl of Hopetoun, was sworn in at a ceremony in Centennial Park, Sydney, on January 1, 1901. About 60,000 people were present. On May 9, in the Exhibition Hall, Melbourne, the Duke of York (later King George V) officially opened the first parliament. The first Prime Minister was Edmund Barton.

In 1910, competitive designs were invited for the federal capital, to be built on a site of 2356 sq km, about 240km south-west of Sydney. The competition was won by Walter Burley Griffin, and after much discussion, it was decided to call the capital Canberra, an Aboriginal name for 'meeting place'. The first Parliament House, which was always considered to be a temporary building, was opened by the Duke and Duchess of York (later King George VI and Queen Elizabeth) in 1927. The present Parliament House was opened by Queen Elizabeth II in 1988.

Australians fought in World Wars I and II, Korea and Vietnam. The nation has lost over 100,000 in war the twentieth century, and of these, 60,000 were casualties of the first World War.

The legal system, public service and government structure of Australia are English-based.

Population

During the 1950s and 1960s, people wishing to migrate from Europe and the United States were provided with assisted passage by the Australian government. However, it was not until the late 1960s that restricted entry to Australia from Asia was eased. In the last 40 years Australian society has undergone a tremendous change with now one in four people being a migrant or the child of a migrant.

Australia since the 1970s has become aware of its presence in South-east Asia.

Many new migrants are Asian, and society reflects this blend of European and Asian cultures.

Approximately 85 per cent of the 20 million inhabitants live in urban areas. The east coast of Australia is the most populous because of the fertile plain east of the Great Dividing Range of mountains. The major cities are the state capitals, and the most populous state is New South Wales with 6,173,000 people, followed by Victoria with 4,533,300 people.

Religion

The vast majority of Australians belong to the Christian Churches. There is only a slight margin between Roman Catholics and Anglicans, whose numbers hover around 26% each, reflecting the influence of migrating Irish and Italian Catholics, and the steady flow of English Anglicans into the country. All other religions and sects are present in Australia. Jews, Hindus, Moslems and Buddhists are all represented strongly on account of the post World War II influx and other political developments , which opened access to Australian shores. There is peaceful coexistence, and the multicultural composition of society is typically celebrated and embraced.

NEW SOUTH WALES

New South Wales was Australia's first state, and is filled with history and attractions. Travellers can explore the gorgeous coast, hike the scenic bushland, visit the outback districts or even ski the New South Wales mountains. Then there is the beauty and excitement of Sydney, the largest city in Australia and the birthplace of the nation.

NSW

Sydney

With a population of almost 4 million and a land mass that covers close to 1120 square kilometres, Sydney is the largest city in Australia. The oldest settlement in arguably the most beautiful location - Sydney Harbour (Port Jackson) - Sydney boasts of many landmarks with the Harbour Bridge and the Opera House being a sample.

Sydney Population: 4,000,000+. Climate: Sydney has a temperate climate, with a maximum in January of 26°C and a minimum of 17°C. The July maximum is 17°C, with the minimum of 8°C. The average annual rainfall is 1216mm, with the heaviest falls in the period from February to July.

Located on the south-east coast of Australia, on the shores of what is arguably the most beautiful harbour in the world, Sydney is the birthplace of modern Australia. While the tall buildings of the Central Business District fall roughly within

Sydney Tower
The AMP Centrepoint Tower is located right above the heart of Sydney's shopping district, and is the tallest building in Sydney at a height of 300m.

an area 1km wide and 3km long, Sydney is a sprawling metropolis that stretches much further than that. The seaside suburbs extend both north and south for a length of about 70km, along with the western areas of the city that takes in Parramatta up to the Blue Mountains. Possessing everything that a cosmopolitan city has to offer, Sydney's incredible landmarks like the Opera House and the Harbour Bridge are widely recognised around the globe. And thanks to the 2000 Olympic Games, Sydney has gained more international exposure than anywhere else in Australia.

While it was Captain James Cook who first sailed up the east coast of Australia in 1770 to enter Botany Bay, Captain Arthur Phillip of The First Fleet deemed the area unsuitable for settlement upon arrival in 1788. On the 26th of January Phillip led the fleet north to Sydney Harbour, and before the day was over the convicts were cutting down trees around the edge of Sydney Cove. A formal flag raising cermeony was held to to proclaim the newly formed settlement of New South Wales, and Captain Phillip made a toast to the future of the colony. While over the last two centuries Sydney has developed into the sprawling metropolis that it is today, it began its history as a struggling and empty penal colony with little to offer. While this must have been intimidating for the settlers who began construction on Australia's oldest city, gradually houses and streets were built, living spaces were constructed for the soldiers and convicts, and the surrounding countryside explored.

With the first free settlers arriving in 1793, Sydney's developing economy was hampered somewhat by a shortage of coinage. Rum, a spirit easily produced from sugar and cane, quickly came into use as an alternative currency, and slowed the settlement's development even further. In a development that was far from surprising, soldiers and convicts often found it a more attractive option to drink the rum rather than trade it for clothes, food and supplies. Ironically, it was the soldiers of the NSW Corps, formed to protect the fledgling from any threats, who had a monopoly on the endless supply of rum. Governor William Bligh was awarded with imprisonment during the infamous Rum Rebellion when he tried to stem the corruption of the NSW Corps, yet the arrival of Governor Lachlan Macquarie in 1810 saw their unchallenged reign come to an end.

The colony flourished under the leadership and vision of Macquarie, and the next several decades saw the city evolve into one where free settlers and emancipated convicts worked together. The goldrushes that began in the 1850's

Opera House

The Sydney Opera House is a unique architectural wonder that has become both a cultural centre and one of the most iconic sights in Sydney.

meant that miners and prospectors from all over the world passed through through the colony, and the city continued to expand unabaited throughout the 1870s and 1880s. Significant developments in the 20th century included the continuous growth of the suburbs of the city. Sydney grew further from the modernisation of the city centre and deployment of efficient public transport, as well as the construction of such iconic locations as the the Opera House and the Harbour Bridge.

Life in Sydney is geared to outdoor activities that take advantage of the long hours of sunshine and moderate climate, and there are so many different things to see and do that it is difficult to know where to begin. The city's beautiful harbour is perhaps the best starting point. Always busy with ferries, hydrofoils and charter cruisers, the ferry terminal located between the Harbour Bridge and the Opera House is known as Circular Quay. The area is always crowded with people arriving or departing on ferries, a variety of buskers, and culture buffs strolling towards the Opera House. One of the most beautiful walks that one can take in Sydney is the path that stretches from Circular Quay, around past the Opera House and along the Botanical Gardens. Not only is there the beauty of the Botanical Gardens on one side, on the other are the stunning views of Sydney's world famous harbour.

If shopping is the preferred activity to partake in while visiting Sydney, there are a plethora of options available to visitors. A number of large shopping areas are in the middle of the Central Business District, with the underground arcade located next to Town Hall Station being the best place to start. While one arcade of specialty shops leads to Bathurst Street near Kent Street, the other continues underneath to the famous Queen Victoria Building shopping mall. While the QVB was first built in 1898, over $75 million was invested into the building in 1982 to restore it to its original state. One of the most notable and upmarket areas for shopping in the whole city, the building's heritage is reflected by the replica of the Crown Jewels on the top level and the elaborate Royal Automata Clock that "performs" on the hour between 9am and 9pm.

Centrepoint Tower, known as the "heart of the city," is another good place for specialty shopping, with the arcade beneath the tower featuring over 170 shops on four levels,

including hairdressers, beauticians, leather shops, jewellery and accessory outlets, boutiques, and several coffee shops and takeaways. The lifts for Sydney Tower are found on the elegant Gallery Level of Centrepoint. The nearby Imperial Arcade which runs between the Pitt Street Mall and Castlereagh Street is also of interest, with over 114 specialty shops on 3 levels. If mostly interested in buying souvenirs like cuddly koalas and kangaroos, the best place to head for the would be the tourist areas such as The Rocks, Darling Harbour or Circular Quay. Also of interest for specialty shoppers are the markets that take place every weekend in the trendy inner-city suburbs of Sydney. The Rocks Market takes place every Saturday and Sunday at the end of George Street with a sail-like canopy transforming the area into a Portobello Road. The Balmain Markets are held in the grounds of the St Andrew's Congregational Church every Saturday, while the particularly trendy Glebe Markets are held in the Glebe Public School on the same day.

Sydney is also famous for its many excellent surfing and swimming locations, and most of the city's 37 beaches are located less than half an hour from the Central Business District via public transport. The most famous and popular of these beaches is no doubt Bondi, located in the eastern suburbs of Sydney. An internationally famous beach, Bondi can attract more than 40,000 people on a sunny Sunday afternoon. In the event that the surf is disappointing, there are plenty of cafes, restaurants and casual street shopping to enjoy. Bondi has its own distinct lifestyle, and the pace

Sydney Harbour Bridge

The Harbour Bridge is another of Sydney's most iconic landmarks, and is both visually stunning and an engineering triumph. The bridge links the CBD in the south to the residential areas in the north.

slows as soon as one cross into its suburban boundary. The nearby Shelley, Tamarama and Coogee beaches also make for essential visits. While Cronulla is the surfing beach of choice for those living on the southern suburbs, Manly Beach is the most famous location for swimming in Sydney's Northern Beaches area. The Northern Beaches are a delight for anyone who loves the ocean, with the friendly and relaxed atmosphere making it a top spot for visitors looking for a memorable holiday.

Visitor Information:

The Sydney Visitor Centre at The Rocks can be found at 106 George Street in The Rocks.

The Sydney Visitor Centre at Darling Harbour can be found at 33 Wheat Road, Darling Harbour behind the IMAX Theatre. Both visitor centres can be called on *(02) 9240 8788*, and their website is *www.sydneyvisitorcentre.com.au.*

The Travellers Accommodation Service can make accommodation bookings, and also has a telephone information service that can be called on *(02) 9669 5111.*

The first stop in Sydney for all visitors should be Tourism NSW at 11-31 York Street. The office has numerous brochures, and maps, etc, and a large and very helpful staff to

Bondi Beach
Bondi Beach is the most popular and famous beach in Sydney, with as many as 40,000 people visiting on a Sunday afternoon to sample the area's surf, sun and cafe culture.

---

provide information. Call them on *13 2077*.

The AMP Sydney Tower Visitors Information and Booking Service is located at the top of the tower, and can be called on *(02) 9223 0933.*

Points of Interest:

The Sydney Harbour Bridge is a famous landmark that dominates the city skyline. The bridge was completed in 1932 after nine years of construction, and is 503m long. People are free to walk over the bridge on the pedestrian walkways on either side, while the south-east pylon can be climbed for some of the best harbour views. The spectacular views of the BridgeClimb has to be one of the most spectacular activities for visiting tourists, and their offices can be found at 5 Cumberland Street in The Rocks. Their phone number is *(02) 8274 7777.*

The Opera House is a magnificent performing arts complex located next to Circular Quay, and is another one of Sydney's most famous landmarks. Recognisable everywhere

City Skyline

The skyline of the city of Sydney as seen from the harbour, with the scenic Sydney Botanic Gardens situated in the foreground.

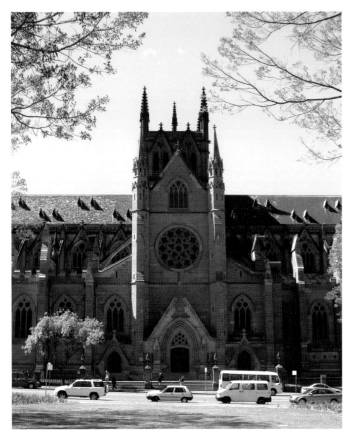

St Mary's Cathedral
The First foundation was in 1865 near the then city tip. It is now a resplendent building on the edge of Hyde Park.

for its unique architecture, the extraordinary building can only really be appreciated when acknowledged as part of its surroundings. The design encapsulates the concept of architecture mimicking its environment, with the white sails giving a vague impression that the building is a cluster of vessels on the waters of Port Jackson. The Opera House has four theatres, four restaurants and six bars, and is surrounded by wide walkways. Details of current programs are published in the daily newspapers, and the booking office can be called on *(02) 9250 7111*.

The Royal Botanical Gardens are a popular lunchtime spot for city workers, and weekends see many family picnics. Signposts point the way to Mrs Macquarie's Chair, a rock outcrop where the Governor's wife apparently sat to watch for ships arriving from England. The Royal Botanical Gardens are open daily and can be called on *(02) 9231 8125*.

Fort Denison is a small remote island in the centre of the harbour, and can be seen from Circular Quay and all the surrounding areas. For a short time it was regarded

notoriously among early convicts as the most inescapable gaol of the colony and the destination of wayward miscreants. Tours of Fort Denison leave from Wharf 6, Circular Quay, but must be booked in advance on *(02) 9247 5033*.

The Art Gallery of New South Wales is a spectacular building, housing a vast contemporary collection of Australian, European and Asian Art, and a fine collection of Aboriginal paintings and artefacts. Two statues of mounted horseman grace the patches of lawn on either side of the entrance, and both the Domain and the Botanical Gardens are also nearby. The gallery can be found on Art Gallery Road in the Botanical Gardens, facing The Domain, the contact details are *(02) 9225 1744* or *(02) 9225 1700*.

Darling Harbour, originally a shipping and storage area for the Port of Sydney, has now become one of the biggest entertainment hubs in the whole of the city. Darling Harbour is home to a wide assortment of attractions including the Conference Centre, the Exhibition Centre, the Maritime Museum, the Sydney Aquarium, the Chinese Gardens, IMAX Theatre and the giant Home nightclub. The recent upgrade of the Harbourside Festival Marketplace and construction of Cockle Bay Wharf has only raised the profile of the location even further. For information on special events phone the Darling Harbour Infoline on *1902 260 568*, or alternatively, the Sydney Visitor's Centre can be visited in Darling Harbour, near the IMAX Theatre. Phone them directly on *(02) 9240 8788*, or visit their web site is at *www.darlingharbour.com.au*.

Sydney Taronga Zoo
Taronga Zoo can boast Australia's best collection of native and exotic animals, as well as stunning harbour views that result from the zoo's location at Bradley's Head, Mosman.

Taronga Zoo has Australia's best collection of native and exotic animals, and also offers some of the finest views of the city, particularly from near the giraffe enclosure. There are seal shows, a rainforest aviary, a nocturnal house, all the usual animals, and Friendship Farm, where children can pat baby animals. Its main entrance (for car and bus access) is on Bradley's Head Road, and is only a pleasant 12 minute ferry ride from Circular Quay (leaving every half hour).

Luna Park been recently been reopened to the public, much to the delight of Sydneysiders. Situated in a prime location in Milson's Point with stunning harbour views, the Coney Island-type amusement park has been in existence since the 1930's. The venue includes a ferris wheel, merry-go-round, rollercoaster, and an assortment of other carnival rides, and initial entry is free with unlimited ride passes also available.

The Rocks are nestled on the western edge of Circular Quay, and were the initial point of colonial settlement. The architecture transports the visitor to a previous era, with even products of modern consumerism attempting to blend in with the nostalgic theme.

Kings Cross is probably one of the best known Sydney areas, its reputation stems from the many strip joints and sex shops. There are some excellent restaurants, bars and nightclubs, as well as "sleazy" venues which one would have to be brave to enter. It is a haven for backpackers because of the number of cheap hostels, Nearby **Oxford Street** stretches from corner of Hyde Park in the city through to Bondi Junction, and has a range of shops, boutiques, and fashion stores. Oxford Street is also famous for its night life with the gay and mixed night clubs. It is the site of the Gay & Lesbian Mardigras Parade every year. It is certainly a central area, though not a good place to stay there if one are travelling with children.

Darling Harbour
Darling Harbour is one of the city's main entertainment hubs, with a large assortment of exhibition centres, restaurants, pubs, nightclubs and entertainment venues located within the district.

NSW

Blue Mountains Region

Located only 110km west from Sydney and known as the city within a National Park, the Blue Mountains are comprised of 26 towns and villages which are scattered across 110 kilometres of ridgeline, the region stretching from Penrith to Mount Victoria.

Katoomba   Population: 8,544. Climate: The Blue Mountains have distinct seasons and are cooler than Sydney all year round. It occasionally snows briefly in winter.

Believed by many to be the heart of the chilly Blue Mountains, Katoomba is the principal tourist destination for the region and home to many famous attractions. The famous Three Sisters, the scenic railway and the spectacular views of the Megalong and Jamieson Valleys are all attractions that can be seen by tourists who are visiting the area. Katoomba is also the largest settlement in the Mountains, and is the administrative centre for the City of the Blue Mountains Council.

Though it is in close proximity to Sydney, it was not until twenty-five years after the arrival of the First Fleet that the Blue Mountains were crossed by explorers in search of grazing land. Blaxland, Wentworth and Lawson were the explorers who discovered the area in 1813, and three mountain towns were subsequently named after them. The region has been a large source of natural resources throughout the history of Australian settlement: George Clarke discovered coal in the area as early as 1841, while kerosene shale was discovered in Kanimbla Valley in 1870, with a coal mine subsequently opening in 1879.

While natural resources dwindled in the twentieth century and the coal mine eventually closed in the 1920's, the spectacular scenic railway that descends into the mine has remained open to become a popular tourist attraction. The decision to make the railway line electric in 1957 has been marked as the symbolic starting point when the region became a commuter zone for Greater Sydney.

No visit to Katoomba would be complete without a stop off at Echo Point. The best spot to find exceptional views of the Three Sisters, Mount Solitary, the Ruined Castle and the vast Jamison Valley, is also the location of the Blue Mountains Tourist Centre when any information is required. There are many other ways to view the spectacular scale of the bush surroundings, and the Three Sisters Walk and the Giant Stairway are both bushwalks that begin in the area.

Visitor Information:
The Echo Point Information Centre can be called on *1300 653 408*, while the Glenbrook Visitor Information Centre is located on the Great Western Highway in Glenbrook, *1300*

Three Sisters
The Three Sisters are a set of closely-spaced pillars which are the most photographed rock formation in the Blue Mountains, and they overlook the Jamison Valley which lies 300m below.

653 408. Email them on *info@blue.mountainstourism.org.au*, or visit *www.bluemountainstourism.org.au*.

Points of Interest:

The Scenic Skyway is a aerial cable car that floats approximately 275 metres above the bottom of the Jamison Valley, offering stunning views of the valley as well as Katoomba Falls and Orphan Rock. Built in 1958, it was the first horizontal passenger-carrying ropeway of its kind in the Southern Hemisphere. A new edition of the Skyway started in November 2004, with the new cable car having a glass bottom that will allow views right down into the valley. The Scenic Skyway can be called on *(02) 4782 2699*.

The Scenic Railway is located on the same site as the Scenic Skyway, and is another major tourist attraction. Claimed to be the steepest incline railway in the world, the railway has its origins in the local mining operations which used coal skips to ferry miners down the cliff face to work. Visitors descend 230 metres into the Jamison Valley via a cable car, and at the bottom is a 300-metre, wheelchair-friendly wooden boardwalk which extends into the rainforest. The Scenic Railway can be contacted at *(02) 4782 2699*.

Leura Population: 50,000

Found off the highway just east of Katoomba, Leura is a quaint and charming little town that exudes a genuine village atmosphere. A historic town full of many turn-of-the-century buildings, the main strip that extends down to the residential area is packed with quaint little tea houses, craft shops, art galleries and an excellent bookshop. It is like nothing else in the surrounding areas, and a whole day can be spent soaking up the relaxed atmosphere. It has been claimed that it is Leura's sense of exclusivity that has allowed it to retain its village atmosphere, separated from the Great Western Highway to such an extent that many travelers are unaware of the village's main street.

Exuding such a charming and relaxed beauty that it appears to have been taken straight from the 1950's, there is much

to see and do in Leura. Beyond the village atmosphere and impressive art galleries of the mains street, Leura has a wide variety of beautiful natural locations which deserve to be sampled. The Gordon Falls Reserve is a lovely picnic area that offers an excellent view of the spectacular Jamison Valley, while the Sublime Point Lookout is considered by many to offer the finest views in the whole of the Blue Mountains region. Leura Cascades on Cliff Drive is another pleasant picnic area, with a number of bushwalks starting from this point. There is also the Everglades Gardens, a property protected by National Trust which contains over 5 hectares of gardens, mixing native bushland with its displays of bluebells, daffodils, azaleas and other beautiful plants.

Visitor Information:

The Leura Visitor Centre is at shop 4, rear 208, The Mall in Leura, and they can be called on *(02) 4784 2222.*

Echo Point

The lookout at Echo Point is the best place to take in the spectacular views of the Blue Mountains, offering in this instance an exceptional view of Mount Solitary and the surrounding Jamison Valley.

Natural attractions like the Glow Worm Tunnel and Wollemi National Park are definitely worth seeing, as are a number of other tourist spots that provide evidence of Lithgow's industrial history. The Glen Davis shale mine site is one such example, as well as the Mt Piper Power Station, the Blast Furnace Park, and the Lithgow Small Arms Factory museum.

Visitor Information:

The Lithgow Tourist Information Centre can be found on the Greater Western Highway in Lithgow. Phone *(02) 6353 1859,* they canalso be emailed at *tourism@lithgow.com.*

Lithgow Population: 14,000

Situated on the western slopes of the Blue Mountains and a 2 hour drive from Sydney, the City of Lithgow is an area that contains more than a few historical, natural and scenic attractions. The area has a dense history that is heavily linked with industrialism, encapsulated no better than by the city's famous Zig Zag Railway, which to this day remains a popular tourist destination. With Thomas Brown being the one responsible for commencing the valley's first commercial zone, the Zig Zag Railway was first completed in 1869. At the time it was considered a significant engineering feat, allowing trains to descend into the valley. The combination of the effective railway service and vast reserves of coal meant that Lithgow was an ideal location for industries that relied on these resources.

Zig Zag Railway

The railway remains a popular tourist attraction in Lithgow, and was first built in 1869. Regarded as a major engineering feat of its time, the railway encapsulates perfectly the industrial history of Lithgow.

NSW

Illawarra Region

Encompassing the areas of Wollongong, Shellharbour and Kiama, the Illawarra region can boast some spectacular hills and scenery with over 85 kilometres of coastline and beaches.

Wollongong

Population: 220,000. Climate: Average temperatures: January max 27°C - min 18°C; July max 17°C - min 9°C. Average annual rainfall: 1275mm.

Wollongong lies directly between the Illawarra Escarpment and the Tasman Sea, and is only 80 km south of Sydney. The third largest city in New South Wales, the coastal stretch of Wollongong is characterised by rocky sea cliffs and pounding waves, and is dotted with tiny mining villages. While a perception exists of Wollongong as an industrial city, the windy coast of the region can match many other areas in New South Wales when it comes to aesthetic beauty. Stretching soutward from Sydney's Royal National Park for more than 30 kilometres, the coastal strip of Wollongong stretches up and down the narrow Illawarra sea line with an assortment of beautiful views such as Mount Keira and the Bulli Lookout.

The name of Wollongong was taken from Aboriginal language, with "Wol-Lon-Yuh" said to be an onomatopoeic reference to the sound made by crashing waves and surf. If not for the heavy crashing of the surf then it is possible that Captain Cook would have first landed in the Illawarra region. Instead, though he noted the attractive appearance of the narrow coastline, he continued on and landed in Botany Bay the next day. Explorers George Bass and Matthew Flinders were the first Europeans to officially set foot in the region in 1796 when their boat was landed in Port Kembla, and they were led to Lake Illawarra by members of the indigenous population. Resources were later discovered in Coal Cliff and Illawarra, though they would not come to be exploited for another 50 years.

It wasn't until the 1830's that settlers were drawn to Wollongong, and it was in 1834 that the Colonial Secretary approved a plan that would exploit the abundance of coal and other resources in the area. The region's first coal mine began operating in Mt Keira in 1849, and the demand for steam power led to 10 mines being established along the Illawarra headland by 1880. A number of mining villages popped up in the wake of these mines, and remain to this day as the northern suburbs of Wollongong. Work commenced at Port Kembla in 1898 and a number of industries established themselves in the early 20th century, yet it was the decision of Hoskins Iron and Steel to transfer their operations to Port Lithgow in 1928 that proved to be the most significant occurence in Wollongong's industrial history. The project was purchased by BHP in 1935, and came to be the largest steelworks owned by the company anywhere in the world.

Situated so closely to Sydney, Wollongong is a regional commercial centre for the Illawara. The area's focus is still heavy industries and the recreational activities that stem from the city's ethereal coastal location. The juxtoposition existing between Wollongong's beautiful coastline and the city's industrial presence can be seen when one visits the main beach. On one side there is the beautiful view of the lighthouse on Flagstaff Hill, while on the other are the factories and industries.

Visitor Information:

The Wollongong Visitor Information Centre can be found at 93 Crown Street, on the corner of Kembla Street, and their free call number is *1800 240 737*. Their web address is *www.tourismwollongong.com* and they can be emailed at *tourism@wollongong.nsw.gov.au*.

North Wollongong Beach

North Wollongong Beach is the city's most popular spot for swimming and surfing. The lighthouse on Flagstaff Hill can be seen in the background.

Points of Interest:

The Wollongong City Gallery is one of the largest regional art museums in Australia, with the collection including colonial works from the Illawarra as well as contemporary Australian and Aboriginal art. They can be found on the corner of Kembla and Burelli Street, and can be phoned on *(02) 4228 7500*.

Mount Kembla Mining Village is located 7km from Wollongong. A memorial exists to commemorates the mining disaster that occurred at the site in 1902, which left 96 men dead and a further 152 injured. It is still described as the worst mining disaster in Australian history, and a number of the original miners' cottages can be seen today, along with art and craft centres.

Bald Hill to the north is one of Wollongong's most popular lookouts, with the area also internationally known as a major centre for hang gliders. Located on the lookout is the Lawrence Hargrave Memorial, an Australian pioneer of flight.

Kiama Population: 15,100

Situated 119km South of Sydney and reached via the Princes Highway, Kiama is a popular coastal town blessed with a striking rocky coastline, beautiful beaches and the lush green pastures of the surrounding hills. The name of the town is taken from the Aboriginal word "Kiarama-a", meaning "where the sea makes a noise", and is actually a reference to the famous Blowhole. George Bass spoke of the 'tremendous noise' this 'subterraneous passage' produced when he first visited in 1797. The loud "oomph" that accompanies the spout of water occurs when large waves enter the Blowhole and compress the air, causing the retreating wave to be forced upwards in a large spray.

Visitor Information:

The Kiama Visitor Information Centre can be found at Blowhole Point Road, and can be called on either *(02) 4232 3322* or *1300 654 262*. Their email address is *tourism@kiama.com.au*, and their website can be viewed at *www.kiama.com.au*.

Kiama Blowholes

The Blowhole is the most famous attraction to be found in Kiama, and is responsible for giving the town its name – the word is taken from the Aboriginal word "Kiarama-a", meaning "where the sea makes a noise".

Shellharbour Population: 60,000

Shellharbour is around twenty minutes drive south of Wollongong on the coastal road. The town's name is derived from the many Aboriginal shell middens that are found there, and it has been listed by the Heritage Commission Register as one of the most important archaeological sites on the NSW coast. Bass Point is a popular diving area, with part of its waters forming a marine reserve. Nearby is the turnoff to Jamberoo Recreation Park, where visitors can play mini golf, go bobsledding, grass ski, or take the chairlift to the mountain top. The park can be called on *(02) 4236 0014*.

Visitor Information:

The Shellharbour Visitor Information Centre is located in Lamerton House in Lamerton Crescent, and can be called on *(02) 4221 6169*. They can be emailed at *tourism@shellharbour.nsw.gov.au*, while their web address is at *www.shellharbour.nsw.gov.au*.

NSW

South Coast Region

Beginning at Berry and stretching through the Shoalhaven, Eurobodalla Coast and the Sapphire Coast onto the Victorian border, the South Coast is one of the most attractive and vibrant tourism destinations within New South Wales.

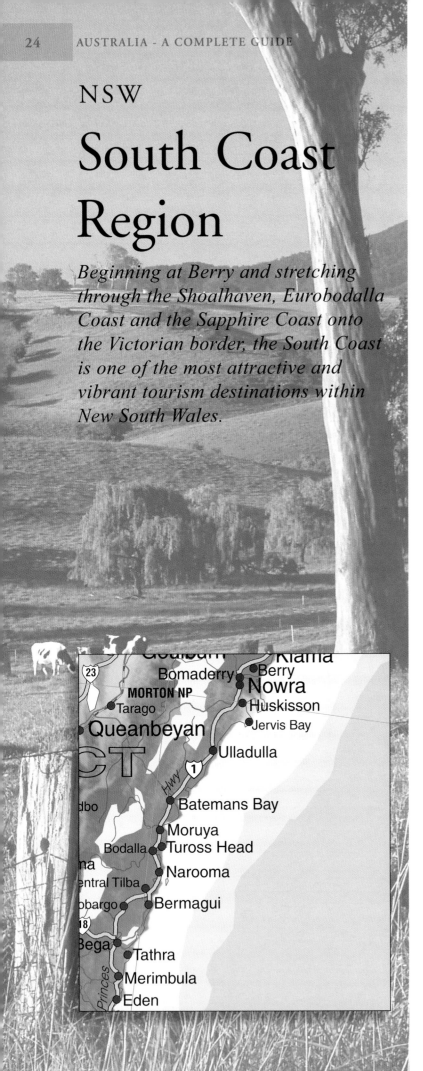

Bateman's Bay Population: 13,000. Climate: Average temperatures: January mid 30°C's; July max 16°C.

Located approximately 290 km south of Sydney and situated on the Clyde River Estuary, at the foot of Clyde Mountain, the town of Bateman's Bay is the largest in the Eurobodalla area. But while it may have a larger population than other nearby townships, Batemans Bay has maintained a distinct small-town atmosphere that compliments the beautiful coastal surroundings. A popular getaway destination for those who live in the national capital of Canberra, Batemans Bay has all of the necessary tourist facilities for those wishing to visit. It also enjoys the added advantage of being in close promiximity to other nearby towns such as Moroya and Mogo, and a number of spectacular beaches.

It was Captain James Cook himself in 1770 who discovered the expansive waterway at the mouth of the Clyde River, naming it after his superior Nathaniel Bateman who was exploring the coasts of Nova Scotia and Newfoundland. The first Europeans to later explore the area in 1797 were the survivors from the wreck of the Sydney Cove, nine of which eventually died in the area. Yet it wasn't until 1859 that the township of Bateman's Bay was eventually formed, with the postal service commencing operations in that same year.

For those wishing to visit the town, Bateman's Bay offers local seafood restaurants, casual cafes, art galleries and studios. A close encounter with the native fauna can be found at the Birdland Animal Park, while a number of endangered and exotic species can be seen further south at Mogo Zoo. Those wishing to plan a fishing trip would also be advised to gravitate towards Bateman's Bay, with an experienced group of charter operators available throughout the year.

Visitor Information:
The Bateman's Bay Visitors Centre can be found at the corner of the Princes Highway and Beach Road and their phone number is *(02) 4472 6900*. Email them at *info@naturecoast-tourism.com.au*, or visit their website located at *www.naturecoast-tourism.com.au*.

Points of Interest:
McKenzie's Beach is an unspoilt beach that has consistent small to medium waves, whilst the better surfing beach is found at the patrolled waters of Malua Bay. There are several

good beaches to the north including South Durras near Wasp Head. Altogether Batemans Bay has 16 golden beaches.

The **MV Merinda** offers a great way to see the Clyde River, which has been recognised as the 6th most scenic coastal waterway in Australia. For a cruise on the *MV Merinda*, call *(02) 4472 4052*. Other options include hiring a boat and using it to explore the extensive mangrove and estuary systems.

Malua Bay and **Pretty Point** are considered the most popular fishing spots around Batemans Bay for experienced rock hoppers. The waters near the oyster beds and the mangrove flats on the Clyde River yiled excellent catches including whiting, mulloway and bream.

The **Birdland Animal Park** is located at at 55 Beach Road and can be contacted on *(02) 4472 5364*. It includes Wombat World, snake demonstrations, an animal nursery, a koala exhibit, and a scale model train (popular with children).

The **Mogo Zoo** is a very popular attraction for everyone, and should not be missed by those visiting Bateman's Bay. An organisation committed to the survival of endangered animals, they provide housing for no less than 100 animals including 35 endangered and exotic species. Situated 10km south of Batemans Bay in the historic gold mining village of Mogo, the zoo can be contacted on *(02) 4474 4930*.

Berry

Berry is a quaint little town with a classic English feel. The fashionable main street contains many antique and craft stores, trendy cafes and restaurants, and other opportunites for shopping.

Berry Population: 1600.

Located 16km north of Nowra, the town of Berry is a quaint and fashionable spot on the south coast with a classic English feel. Named "The Town of Trees" by the local Chamber of Commerce in 1975, the streets of Berry are lined with an extensive collection of English oaks, elms and other examples. With the main street full of antique and craft stores along with trendy cafes and restaurants, Berry has in recent years become a fashionable visiting place for many city-dwellers wishing to get away for the weekend.

One of Berry's main characteristics is a sense of style - shopping is one of the activities that keeps tourists coming back time and time again, and the Berry Country Fair is a popular fixture on the first Sunday of every month. For a taste of the town's history, the Berry Historical Museum is open every weekend, and they are able to point out the other buildings classified by the National Trust, such as the Court House and National Bank.

Visitor Information:

Local information can be obtained from Pottering Around, on the corner of Queen and Alexandra Streets, phone them on *(02) 4464 2177*.

Nowra **Population: 25,000 (including Bomaderry)**
Situated 160km from Sydney on the banks of the Shoalhaven River, Nowra is the central hub of the City of Shoalhaven. The major service centre to the agricultural industries and coastal resorts of the surrounding areas, particularly Jarvis Bay, the population of Nowra is rapidly expanding. The town's name was originally spelt Nou-woo-ro, with the Aboriginal meaning of "camping place or "black cockatoo".

Intriguingly, the town was responsible for producing two Melbourne Cup winners - Arwon (Nowra spelt backwards) and Archer. There are a number of special attractions to be seen at Nowra: the Historic Meroogal Home was built by Robert Taylor-Thorburn in 1886, and is now owned by the Historic Houses Trust of New South Wales. They can be contacted on *(02) 4421 8150*. There is also Australia's Museum of Flight at 489A Albatross Road, which is one of the finest collections of military and civilian aircraft in the whole of Australia.

Visitor Information:
The Shoalhaven Visitors Centre can be found at the corner of Princes Highway & Pleasant Way, phone them on *(02) 4421 0778* or *1300 662 808.*
The website *www.shoalhaven.nsw.gov.au* has comprehensive information and the centre may also be contacted by email at *tourism@shoalhaven.nsw.gov.au.*

Outlying Towns in the Region

Moruya

The town of Moruya is 27km south of Batemans Bay on the Princes Highway. It has some fine old buildings, though accommodation is not plentiful in the area. The area has excellent fishing in the Deua River with its mangrove swamps, and along the various coastal headlands. Surfing is great from Moruya Heads to Congo, North Head, Broulee South, North Broulee, Pink Rocks (off the north face of Broulee Island - experienced riders only, 6m waves) and Mossy Point near the mouth of the Tomago River.

Bodalla

24km south along the Princes Highway is the town of Bodalla, made famous by Bega cheese which uses it as a brand name. The All Saints Church is one of several photogenic buildings in this attractive little town. Just before Bodalla is the turnoff to Tuross Head, where boats can be hired for fishing and boating on the lake of the same name.

Narooma

This town is 44km south of Moruya, on the estuary of the Wagonga Inlet. It is another popular fishing resort with excellent beaches for surfing (Mystery Bay, Handkerchief Beach, Narooma Main Beach, Bar Beach, Dalmeny Point, Potato Point, Blackfellows Point and Tuross Head). It has a narrow channel that leads to a small harbour. Contact the Narooma Visitors Centre on *(02) 4476 2881* with any queries, or email them at *narooma@naturecoast-tourism.com.au.*

Central Tilba

21km south is Central Tilba, which neighbours Tilba Tilba. Both of these artisitic settlements are in the shadow of an ancient volcano, Mount Dromedary. Situated in rather pleasant hilly country at the base of Mt Dromedary (Gulaga Mountain), Central Tilba has become a tourist spot with art and craft shops, an old wooden general store, a cobblers cottage, a pub, and a quaint restaurant with displays of the traditional crafts. A pleasant day excursion from Narooma.

Cobargo

This village is 19km from Central Tilba. It has various cottage industries of pottery and leather, art and craft galleries, and a pub. One can turn off here for Bermagui, or it can be reached by turning off at Tilba Tilba and going along the coast road and crossing Wallaga Lake.

Bermagui
Typical farm land on the South Coast

Bermagui

Located on the coast 18km from Cobargo, Bermagui is the mecca for big game fishing in New South Wales, and was made famous in the 1930s by the novelist Zane Grey. Today a large fishing fleet operates out of Bermagui, and game fishermen from all over come for the sport between November and May. Charter boats are available for pleasure cruising or game fishing, and the harbour has a boat ramp and provision for trailer parking. Swimming and surfing are again the other main diversions - at Blue Pool, Horseshoe Bay and Wallaga Lake. Water skiing is the go on Wallaga Lake.

Bega

The town of Bega is 170km south of Batemans Bay, and 80km south of Narooma. It is the commercial centre of the district with a population above 4000. The district is famous for its dairy industry and cheeses. The Bega Cheese Heritage Centre is open daily for inspection and tasting, and can be found on the northern side of the Bega River, Lagoon Street, *(02) 6491 7777*. The Sapphire Coast Tourist Information Centre is at 163 Auckland Street, and can be called on *(02) 6492 3313* or *1800 150 457* and emailed at *info@ sapphirecoast.com.au*.

Tathra

Tathra is a quiet seaside village 18km east of Bega, with a beautiful beach and great fishing spots. Tathra offers the best of both worlds: beautiful beaches with ocean activities, as well as the opportunity to explore the wildlife of nearby Mimosa

Bega Valley

The town of Bega is the rural centre of the surrounding district, and is set at the gateway to the rolling pastures of the lush Bega Valley. The area is famous for its dairy industry and cheeses.

and Bournda National Parks. Tathra Tourist Centre on Tathra Wharf, Wharf Road, *(02) 6494 4062*, is the best place to find any necessary information. The local people are very friendly and helpful.

Merimbula

This flourishing resort town on Lake Merimbula is 26km south of Bega. Merimbula is an activity-based centre, with surfing on Main Beach, Short Point and Tura Beach, sailboarding and water skiing on Lake Merimbula, golf at the 27-hole Pambula-Merimbula golf course, lawn bowls at the ubiquitous bowling clubs and a variety of other activities - tennis, canoeing, horseriding and cycling. Contact the Tourist Information Centre on Beach Street, *(02) 6495 1129*.

Eden

Eden is situated some 61km south of Bega, on Twofold Bay. A former whaling station, it is now a deep water fishing port, and the fishing and timber industries are of utmost importance to the survival of the town. The town's Killer Whale Museum gives an overview of Eden's history, and houses the skeleton of 'Old Tom' a legendary whale from the area. They can be found at 94 Imlay Street, and can be called on *(02) 6496 2094*. For more information, contact the Eden Tourist Information Office on *(02) 6496 1953*.

NSW

Capital Country Region

The Capital Country region is the area of New South Wales that the Australian Capital Territory is contained within. The area also contains the area of Southern Highlands which includes Bowral, as well as the cities of Goulburn and Queanbeyan in the Southern Tablelands.

Bowral Population:10,402

Located 126 kilometres from Sydney, Bowral is the commercial centre for the Southern Highlands district beneath Mount Gibraltar. The upmarket streets of Bowral have many obvious attractions for tourists, and the town is full of galleries, bookshops, antique stores and cafes. Bowral was home to Australia's most famous sportsman Sir Donald Bradman, and the town has a museum dedicated to the cricketing legend, call *(02) 4862 1247,*

Visitor Information:

For information on the area visit the Vistors Centre at 62-70 Main Street in Mittagong, call *(02) 4871 2888.*

Goulburn Population: 22,500

Situated 197km south-west of Sydney and 94km north-east of Canberra, Goulburn is Australia's oldest inland city (1863). Many of the buildings in the town have beautiful cast iron lace work, amd Goulburn remains an administrative centre for several State Government departments. Nearby is Bungonia State Recreation Area, the largest State Recreation Area in New South Wales. The Wombeyan Caves can also be found not far north-east, *(02) 4843 5976.*

Visitor Information:

The Visitor Centre is at 201 Sloane Street, *(02) 4823 4492.* Email them at *visitor@goulburn.nsw.gov.au.*

Mittagong

The area was one of the first settled by Europeans when the government allowed settlement south of the Cowpastures (now Camden). Many gracious sandstone buildings were constructed in the town in the 1860's, not only public buildings, but small cottages.

Moss Vale

The town of Moss Vale stands on part of the original grant made to the district's first European settler, Charles Throsby. Throsby Park is open by arrangement and guided tours are available, contact the National Parks and Wildlife Service for information, *(02) 4887 7270.* Scenic attractions in the area include Belmore and Fitzroy Falls (82m), and Morton National Park, (154,000 hectares) with its 55km of river frontages and virgin bushland.

Berrima

Situated 14km south of Mittagong on the old Hume Highway, Berrima is considered the best remaining example of a1930's small Australian town. The town was founded in 1829 by Surveyor-General Sir Thomas Mitchell in 1829, and many of the original buildings have been restored. The Surveyor General Inn built in 1835 is the oldest continuously licensed inn in Australia still trading within its original walls.

Robertson

The town was named in honour of John Robertson, who was responsible for the Land Act of 1861. The Robertson Nature Reserve south of the town is an important conservation area, containing about 5 hectares of the Yarrawa Brush vegetation. The area is one of the most beautiful to be found anywhere, with its rolling red soil country and rugged bushland.

Bundanoon

The town of Bundanoon has been a holiday spot for decades and is a bushwalker's paradise, with walks going to Glow Worm Glen, Fern Glen, Fairy Bower Falls, and the Amphitheatre, amongst other places.

Bywong

The Historic Bywong Mining Town is 33km north of Canberra, off the Federal Highway, Millyn Road, Gearys Gap. It is a gold mining village with areas classified by the Heritage Council. Guided tours of the village are available and panning tools can be hired. There is a kiosk, barbecue and picnic areas. Call *(02) 6236 9183* for further details.

Queanbeyan

Although in New South Wales, Queanbeyan is virtually a suburb of Canberra. Accommodation is plentiful and generally the prices are lower than in Canberra. Lookouts in the area include Bungendore Hill, 4km east of the city, and Jerrabomberra, 5km west. The Googong Dam area is open 8am-5pm. (02) 6207 2779. Activities include canoeing, sailing, fishing and walking. Points of interest include London Bridge Homestead, a woolshed and shearer's quarters. The turnoff to the dam is about 10km along the Cooma Road.

Visitor Information:

Contact the Visitor Information Centre on *(02) 6298 0241* or *1800 026 192*, or email them at *tourist@qcc.nsw.gov.au*. The web site is *www.queanbeyan.nsw.gov.au*.

Berrima
A typical scene in this historical Southern Highlands town, with the boutique cafes, stores and old world pubs making it a mecca for visitors.

South Coast farmland

NSW

Snowy Mountains Region

Found in the south-east corner of New South Wales with the highest peak being Mt Kosciuszko, the Snowy Mountains are home to the ski fields of New South Wales. While the region conjures up images of skiers hurtling down ski slopes, that is only one facet of the mountains. The mountains are a carpet of wildflowers in summer and there are numerous trails for bushwalkers. Lake Jindabyne (three times the size of Sydney Harbour) is ablaze with sailboard and catamaran sails, and the lakes and rivers abound with trout.

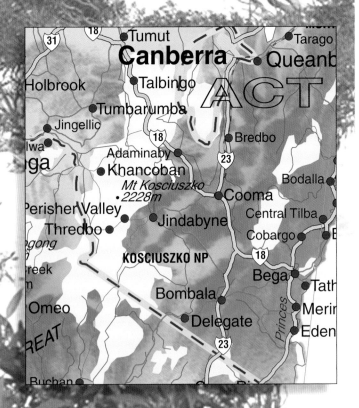

Cooma

Cooma Population: 9,000. Climate: Average temperatures: January max 26°C - min 11°C; July max 9°C - min 1°C. Annual rainfall 450mm.

Located 420km from Sydney near the New South Wales-Victorian Border, Cooma is where the Snowy Mountains begins. It remains the main town in the Snowy Mountains region, and is the gateway to all of the surrounding areas.

The name of the town is derived from the Aboriginal word 'coombah' which means either 'big lake' or 'open country', Captain Currie and Major Ovens were the first Europeans to lead an expedition in the area in 1823. Cooma remained a small settlement over the next several decades, but the discovery of gold in nearby Kiandra in 1859 caused its population to skyrocket, with over 15,000 miners and prospectors passing through in less than 12 months.

While things gradually returned to normal in the decades that followed, the railway link that was built to Cooma in 1889 opened up access to the snowfields for the rest of Australia. The population soared again in the 1950s when the Snowy Mountains Hydro Electric Scheme established their base in Cooma. Today, tourism, rural industry and the Snowy Hydro are still major influences in the town.

Visitor Information:

The Cooma Visitors Centre is at 119 Sharp Street, and can be contacted on *1800 636 525*. Email them at *info@visitcooma.com.au*, or visit the website at *www.snowymountains.com.au* or *www.visitcooma.com.au*.

Points of Interest:

The Snowy Hydro Authority Information and Education Centre has displays and models of the Snowy Mountains Scheme, a project which captures the water from the melting snow and redirects it through mountain channels to the interior. Call *1800 623 776* or visit *www.snowyhydro.com.au* for more details.

The Cooma Monaro Railway runs a vintage rail motor from Cooma's historic railway station. The service travels to Chakola on the banks of the Umeralla River, and they can be called on *(02) 6452 7791*.

Mount Gladstone affords an uninterrupted view across the open plains of Monaro to the peaks of the Snowy Mountains, and it can be found on the edge of town.

Thredbo Population: 150

Situated 97km from Cooma, is Thredbo nestled within the beautiful confines of the Kosciuszko National Park, While it is a popular resort during all four of the seasons, Thredbo is one of the most popular locations for skiing in the region and has suitable slopes for both beginners and professionals. Experienced skiers can tackle the 4 km long Crackenback Supertrail off the Kosciuszko Express chairlift, while Friday Flat offers an easier way for beginners and families to enjoy the snow.

Visitor Information:

The Thredbo Information Centre is found at Friday Flat Drive, and can be called on *(02) 6459 4197*. Their website is at *www.thredbo.com.au*.

Jindabyne Population: 1,800

Situated at the edge of Lake Jindabyne and 40km from Cooma, Jindabyne thrives on its close proximity to the ski fields. Many people choose to stay in the town and drive to the fields each day, and Lake Jindabyne remains an attraction during the summertime. There are a number of travel companies in Jindabyne which specialise in such activities as white water rafting, mountain biking, horse riding, canoeing and walking treks. Interestingly, the new town of Jindabyne was created in the 1960's after the original settlement was drowned by the Snowy Mountains Hydro-electricity Authority's creation of Lake Jindabyne.

Visitor Information:

The Snowy Region Visitor Information Centre is on Kosciusko Road and can be called on *(02) 6450 5600*. They can be contacted by email at *srvc@npws.nsw.gov.au*, and their website is *www.kos.com.au*.

Adaminaby

The town of Adaminaby is 51km from Cooma, and is the home of The World's Largest Trout. The town was moved to its present site in 1956-57 to allow for the filling of Lake Eucumbene. Facilities include boating, fishing, sailing, snow skiing, tennis and water skiing, and the town has a population of 300.

Thredbo Creek

NSW

Riverina Region

The Riverina region of New South Wales is a 500km stretch that extends from the alpine peaks of Kosciuszko National Park in Tumut Shire to the South West Slopes and the riverine plains, encompassing the middle and lower reaches of the Murrumbidgee River Valley of South-Eastern Australia.

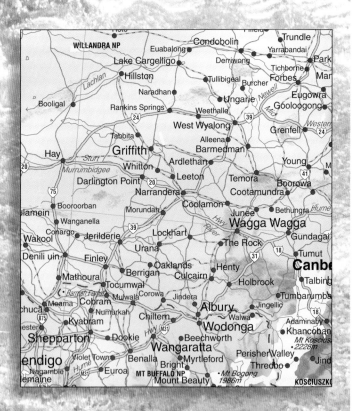

Wagga Wagga Population: 57,000. Climate: Average temperatures: January max 31.4°C - min 16.1°C; July max 12.6°C - min 2.6°C Average annual rainfall: 584.1mm.

Located 451km south-west of Sydney on the banks of the Murrumbidgee River, the city of Wagga Wagga is well known as one of Australia's most prosperous regional areas. First explored by Captain Charles Sturt in 1829 on an expedition that discovered the Murrumbidgee and Murray River systems, settlement swiftly followed and Wagga Wagga was proclaimed a town in 1849. It became a city in 1946, and is now the largest inland city in New South Wales.

The major centre for industry and retail in the Riverina region, Wagga Wagga can boast excellent educational facilities to compliment their already significant sporting and cultural achievements. In addition to being home to the Charles Sturt University, the Forest Hill RAAF base and the Kapooka Australian Army Base, the city of Wagga Wagga can also boast another 22 primary schools, 8 secondary schools, a regional TAFE centre as well as several community colleges. Wagga Wagga is also known as the place of origin for a significant number of Australian sporting heroes, with some of the familiar names including Wayne Carey, Mark Taylor, Steve Elkington, Michael Slater, Peter Sterling, Paul Kelly, Tony Roche, Greg Brentnall and Scobie Breasley. A brief snapshot of this history can be viewed at the Wagga Wagga Sporting Hall of Fame, *(02) 6925 2934*.

Visitor Information:
The Visitors Information Centre is located in Tarcutta Street, and can be called on *(02) 6926 9621*. They have a website at *www.tourismwaggawagga.com.au*, or can emailed at *visitors@wagga.nsw.gov.au*.

Points of Interest:
The Wiradjuri Walking Track follows a 30 km perimeter route along the Murrimbidgee River, taking in bushland, lagoons as well as the city streets and recreation reserves.

The Civic Centre offers an interesting reflection on the civic history of Wagga Wagga, and contains the Wagga Wagga Art Gallery and Community Gallery, the National Art Glass Gallery, the Museum of the Riverina and the Wagga Wagga City Library. Customer Service is *(02) 6926 9100*.

Riverina Scene
Farms in the Riverina show the effects of efficient agricultural practices and the influence of effective irrigation on fertile soil.

Murrumbidgee River Cruises allow visitors to sit back and relax on one hour cruises, *(02) 6925 8700.*

The Charles Sturt University Winery can be visited for wine and cheese tastings and sales, and they can be called on *(02) 6933 2435* for information.

The Farmers Market is held on the banks of the Wollundry Lagoon on the second Saturday of every month, offering a huge range of food and produce. The Sunday Markets are held every Sunday until noon in the Myers Car Park.

Griffith Population: 25,000.

Located 196km North West of Wagga Wagga, Griffith is worth considering for a day trip or overnight stay. Part of the Riverina district, the soil has been made rich and fertile from the efforts of the farmers and irrigation scheme which brings water all the way from the Snowy Mountains. Wine, fruits, vegetables, rice, and poultry products are grown and cultivated here. There are a number of attractions, including the extensive Pioneer Park museum, the Regional Art Gallery, Catania Fruit Farm, and the natural wonders of Lake Wyangan and Cocoparra National Park.

Interestingly, the town of Griffith was designed by Walter Burley Griffin, the same man who designed the streets of our nation's capital Canberra. So similarly, the streets are wide and lined with trees and complimented by ring roads and parks. The Hermit Cave is a charming local oddity that may interest those visiting Griffith, a personal utopia built by Italian immigrant Valerio Recitti and full of massive stone galleries, cliffside gardens and floral painted rock walls. The various festivals are also of interest: the local Wine and Food Festival is held annually during Easter, while a number of private gardens are opened up during the Festival of Gardens and Agricultural Show in October.

Visitors Information:

The Griffith Visitor Information Centre, corner of Banna & Jondaryan Avenue, can be freecalled at *1800 681 141*. They can be emailed at *griffithvc@griffith.nsw.gov.au.*

Dog on the Tucker Box, Gundagai

Gundagai Population: 4,000.

Situated on the Murrumbidgee River and 387 km south-west of Sydney, the town of Gundagai is one that has entered Australian folklore. The famous Dog on the Tucker Box is, as every Australian knows, 5 miles from Gundagai. The monument was built in 1932 to celebrate the deeds and courage of Australia's pioneers. Opposite the memorial to mateship between man and dog are copper representations of the Dog, and Dad, Dave, Mum and Mabel of Snake Gully, the characters of Steele Rudd.

The walking tour, devised by the Tourist Centre, takes in: the Dr Gabriel Gallery; the Court House built in 1859, where Moonlight the Bushranger was tried; the Gundagai Historic Museum; the Old Flour Mill constructed in 1849; and the two bridges, Railway Bridge, 1901, and Prince Alfred Bridge, 1866, the longest timber viaduct in Australia. The Tourist Centre also has details of the Mount Parnassus Walking Tour, and can arrange coach tours and canoe tours of the Murrumbidgee and Tumut Rivers.

Visitor Information:

The Visitors Information Centre is at 294 Sheridan Street, *(02) 6944 0250*. Email: *travel@gundagaishire.nsw.gov.au*

Outlying Towns of the Riverina Region

The Rock

Proceed south from Wagga Wagga along the Olympic Way to The Rock and then turn left, with Lockhart being 42km further on. Originally named Kingston, the town of The Rock is located 6km east of craggy outcrops which rise more than 360m above the surrounding districts. The peak of the Rock Hill Nature Reserve is the only place in Australia where the Senecio wildflower is found.

Lockhart

The centre of the town has been classified by the National Trust, as has been the Old Urangeline Woolshed. Approximately 16km north of Lockhart is the Galore Hill Recreation Reserve. The reserve comprises 510 hectares of natural bushland, rising 215 metres above the countryside.

Coolamon Shire

The shire includes the townships of Coolamon, Ardlethan, Ganmain, Beckom, Grong Grong, Matong and Marrar, and is the agricultural centre of the Riverina. Ganmain, situated between Junee and Narrandera, is the centre of the chaff industry of Australia. Coolamon is 39km (24 miles) north-west of Wagga Wagga, and has many antique shops.

Junee

The town of Junee is built to an unusual plan with the railway running down the middle of the central business district. The railway has been important to the town as is shown by the impressive railway station, built in 1883.

Temora

Temora is a centre for Harness Racing, and was established after the 1880 gold rush when the famous 258 ounce Mother Shipton nugget was discovered. The decline of gold saw the town become a major wheat growing district. The Temora Visitor Information Centre is at 294 -296 Hoskins Street, *(02) 6977 1511*.

Cootamundra

The town has a population of 7,100, is the home of the Cootamundra Wattle (Acacia Baileyana) and the birthplace of the late Sir Donald Bradman, Australia's famous cricketer. The cottage where he was born has been restored and now contains his memorabilia and Australian cricketing history (89 Adams Street). A leisurely stroll can be taken through Jubilee Park, which features many bronze sculptures of Australian Test Cricketers, including a life-size sculpture of Sir Donald Bradman. The Visitor Information Centre is in Hovell Street and can be contacted on *1800 350 203*.

Roxy Theatre, Leeton

Tumut

Tumut is now a town of around 6,000 people, and the Festival of the Falling Leaf is held there every year in April-May. There are street parades, band recitals, Plaza Night and a Family Fun Day at the Sports Club. Tumut is 128km (80 miles) west of Canberra, about midway between Sydney and Melbourne, and is the gateway to the giant Snowy Mountains Scheme. The town is surrounded very picturesque countryside, and the rivers and mountain streams within easy access are stocked with trout. The Visitor Information Centre is at the Old Butter Factory on Adelong Road, *(02) 6947 7025.*

Hay

Located on the Murrumbidgee River halfway between Adelaide and Sydney amidst a vast plain, this town has become known in recent years for the Shear Outback museum. Showcasing the stories, artefacts, technology and culture of the Australian shearing industry, the facility comprises an iconic purpose built interpretative centre and an historic woolshed. The buiding won an Australian Architecture award and is worth a visit.

Deniliquin

Deniliquin is situated on the Edward River, in the centre of Riverina sheep station country and on the fringe of Australia's largest redgum forest, where bird and wildlife abound. The Peppin Heritage Centre, which incorporates both the Visitor Information Centre and a regional museum, is an ideal starting point when arriving in Deniliquin and can be called on *1800 650 712.* A good selection of restaurants and historic hotels are available in the town.

Conargo

To the north of Deniliquin is the village of Conargo, the home of the world famous Conargo Pub. Between the village of Conargo and Deniliquin is Clancy's of Conargo Winery, where visitors can enjoy cellar door tastings, picnic facilities and winery tours. Some of the annual events in the town include the Conargo Open Hang Gliding Championships, and the Conargo Legendary New Years Eve Ball.

Leeton

Another significant town in the Riverina region with a population of 12,000, the history of Leeton dates back to the early 1900's when the Irish landholder Sir Samuel McCaughey demonstrated that irrigation was possible in the relatively arid area. Australia's first commercial rice crop was grown in Leeton in 1924, and the town is now the headquarters of SunRice, one of Australia'a most successful, vertically intergrated agribusinesses. The Leeton Visitors Information Centre can be called on *(02) 6953 6481.*

Historic Hotel, Narrandera

Narrandera

With a population of 5000, Narrandera is located in the heart of the Riverina district on the banks of the Murrumbidgee River. Lake Talbot is one of the town's main attractions and is a focus for water sports during summer. Swimming pools and several walking tracks flank the Lake, while the Lookout at the head of the track provides a great view over the water. Narrandera is also home to the John O'Brien Bush Festival, which celebrates the Irish-Australian pioneering tradition through bush poetry, bush music, dance, art and craft.

NSW

The Murray Region

Winding all the way to the Southern Ocean in South Australia, the Murray River has played a special part in the heritage of our nation. While Aboriginal tribes took advantage of the river's healthy fish population in ancient times, it later became a vital transport system for European settlers that linked the inland to the coast.

Albury-Wodonga Population: 77,000. Climate: Average temperatures in January are a max of 32°C and a minimum of 15°C, while the June max is 14°C and the minimum 2°C. Average annual rainfall is 796mm, with the wettest month being August.

Although they are located 7km apart on the opposite sides of the Murray River, Albury and Wodonga are considered twin towns and make up the large urban area on the border of New South Wales and Victoria. The two towns are often referred to as Albury Wodonga, and are responsible for servicing the agricultural, dairying and pastoral industries in the surrounding areas. Wodonga is located on the Victorian side of the Murray River, and while it used to be one of the largest stock centres in the whole of Australia, it is now more of a suburb that houses those who work in the surrounding areas. Located on the New South Wales side of the Murray River is Albury, which in contrast is the centre for business, industry and administration in the region.

With the area around the Murray once inhabited by the Wiradjuri Aboriginal tribe, Hume and Hovell were the first Europeans to cross over into the region in 1824. Arriving at

what would later be called Albury, Hume and Hovell both preceeded to carve comments into the trunks of several trees. While Hume's graffiti was later removed by a campfire accident, Hovell's apprently still remains. Charles Sturt later named the Murray River, and the land was first taken up in 1835 when William Wyse established the Mungabareena station. While Wodonga was first established itself with the arrival of Paul Huon in 1837, Albury ironically found its origins in an attempt by the police to crush black resistance. Upset that European stock was effectively displacing their traditional sources of food, the local Aborigines had been killing sheep and other livestock. A settlement was established with the intention of securing inland settlements from their interference.

Visitor Information:

The Albury-Wodonga Gateway Visitor Information Centre is at the Lincoln Causeway on the Hume Highway, and their freecall number is *1300 796 222*. They can be emailed at *gateway1@destinationalburywodonga.com.au*, while their web address is *www.destinationalburywodonga.com.au*.

Points of Interest:

The Albany Regional Art Gallery is one of the best regional galleries in Australia, and has a diverse program of exhibitions, lectures and workshops for inspection. Included in the gallery are a number of specialist collections of photography, 17th & 19th century prints, painting by Russell Drysdale, as well as Chinese, Tibetan and Pacific Basin artifacts. Located at 546 Dean Street, the gallery can be called on *(02) 6051 3480* and emailed on *alburygallery@alburycity.nsw.gov.au*.

The Albury Regional Museum features a diverse program of static displays and travelling exhibitions. The museum is also home to the "Bonegilla Collection," a reflection on the Bonegilla Migrant Reception and Training Centre in the Wodonga district, were migrants were sent initially after relocating to Australia post World War II.

The PS Cumberoona is a classic wood-fired steam driven paddlesteamer that allows visitors to cruise the River Murray, and can be called on *1300 796 222* to organise bookings.

The Junction of the Murray and Darling Rivers
A landmark in Australia where both these grand rivers, who giving life to an otherwise parched land, meet.

The Albury Region Heritage Trail allows visitors to learn about the history of the area, and takes in such historic locations as the Albury Railway Station, the Botanic Gardens, Hume Dam, the War Memorial on Monument Hill, the Hovell Tree, Saint Matthew's Church, the Albury Pioneer Cemetery, and the former Farmers and Graziers Woolstore.

Corowa Population: 5,400

Located 56km west of Albury with a wide main street that stretches to the banks of the Murray River, Corowa is known as the birthplace of Australian federation. In memory of the important role that Cowra played in this momentous change, a week-long Federation Festival is held every January with a grand parade, floats, pipe bands and brass bands.

Corowa lies at the centre of a prosperous district devoted mainly to the cultivation of wool, cereals, wine grapes and fat lamb stock, and is supported by various industries such as a piggery, an abattoir, timber-milling and wine-making. Anyone interested in Australian history should visit Corowa's Federation Museum in Queen Street, *(02) 6033 1568.*

Visitor Information:

The Corowa Visitor Information Centre is in Sanger Street and their phone number is *(02) 6033 3221.* They can be emailed at *corinfo@dragnet.com.au*, with internet info available at *www.corowa.nsw.gov.au.*

Outlying Towns in the Region

Mulwala

The town of Mulwala is 40km west of Corowa, and is renowned for its year-round mild climate. Nearby Lake Mulwala offers swimming, sailing and cruising. Mulwala is often linked with Yarrawonga, on the other side of the river, and the Tourist Information is on the corner of Irvine & Blemore Streets, their phone number *1800 062 260.*

Jindera

Only about 20km north-west of Albury, Jindera has a Pioneer Museum that is rated a world-class attraction. It is housed in an old store and home that belonged to the pioneering Wagner family, and the store is stocked with authentic goods of the 19th century. Call *(02) 6026 3622* for information.

Culcairn

Culcairn is 53km north of Albury-Wodonga, in the heart of 'Morgan' country. Other towns in the area are Henty, Walla, Jindera, Gerogery, Cookardinia, Morven and Walbundrie.

Bushranger Dan Morgan began his criminal career at Round Hill at Culcairn in June, 1864. Events surrounding the incident can be read at a site overlooking Round Hill, about 3km east on the Holbrook Road. A life-sized effigy of Dan Morgan is displayed in the Billabong Art and Crafts Centre's 'Mad Dog Morgan' art cellar. It was made for the movie of the same name, filmed in the district in 1975. The first Australian film to win an award at the Cannes Film Festival.

Holbrook

The Tourist Information Office is in the Woolpack Inn Museum, and can be called on *(02) 6036 2131.* The museum also has a section devoted to the exploits of Commander Norman Holbrook, after whom the town was named. In December, 1914, British submarine commander Lt Norman Holbrook guided a B11 submarine below a minefield to torpedo an enemy Turkish battleship, the *Messudiya.* The submarine was immediately attacked, and during the trip back Holbrook and his crew were forced to stay submerged for nine hours, an incredible feat in 1914.

Albury
The historic Railway Station has been an important administration and commercial junction between New South Wales and Victoria.

NSW
Outback New South Wales Region

The most desolate and uninhabited region in the whole of New South Wales, the outback offers wilderness, wildlife and wide open spaces. The region is at the rural heart of Australia and has a memorable history, full of woodsheds, mineshafts and aboriginal heritage.

A portion of Broken Hill
The inland mining town as seen from the air.

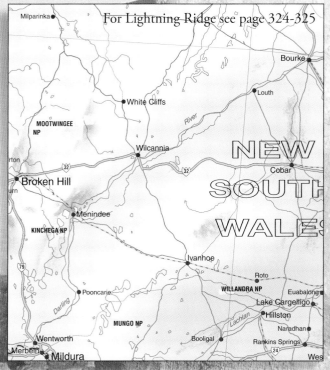

For Lightning Ridge see page 324-325

Broken Hill Population: 21,500. Climate: The rainfall average is 235mm and spread evenly throughout the year, with the temperature only climbing above 38°C eight or nine times a year. Maximum summer temperatures are generally in the low 30's with low humidity, while nights are cold throughout the year.

Lying near the South Australian border in the Barrier Ranges of outback New South Wales, the town of Broken Hill is a long way from anywhere - 1170km from Sydney, 882km from Melbourne, and 510km from Adelaide. "The Silver City" is first and foremost a mining town, possessing one of the richest silver and lead deposits found anywhere in the world. As a reflection of this, all of the streets are named after metals, minerals and compounds. People who have never visited the outback of New South Wales will be amazed by the aridity of the region. If continuing on through the nearby Mundi Mundi Plain, the vastness of the desert continues to stretch out around until the West Australian coast has been reached. It is this remoteness that has meant the area has been used to film such classic cinematic moments as Mad Max 2 and Priscilla Queen of the Desert. Broken Hill, however,

Broken Hill Trades Hall

stands out from the endless outback that surround it: the city is a refuge in the middle of the desert, with plenty of green parks and gardens.

Willyama Aborigines were known to have inhabited the areas surrounding Broken Hill prior to European settlement, yet afterwards their presence was not considered welcome. Forcibly driven from the land by the new settlers, they were also quashed in large numbers by introduced diseases. When exploring the region in 1844, Charles Sturt described Outback New South Wales as some of the most barren and desolate land he had ever laid eyes upon, referring in his diary to a "broken hill". Burke and Wills were the next to encounter the area in their trek during the early 1860's, yet it wasn't until 1863 that boundary rider Charles Wasp discovered tin deposits in the "broken hill." And later in January 1885, a group of seven discovered what turned out to be one of the largest deposits of silver, lead and zinc in the entire world. Shares were immediately formed and floated in the The Broken Hill Proprietary Company (BHP), which now holds the title of being the largest diversified resources company in the world.

Recognised as a municipality in the late 1880's and declared a city in 1907, Broken Hill was known for the shocking working and living conditions exisitng in the early days of

settlement. Disease and lead poisoning were common and over 350 men died in the mines between 1894 and 1913, with this number not even taking into account the others who later died of lung disease. Because of this, industrial unrest was never far away: a strong trade union movement led to protracted strikes throughout the 1890's, with unrest continuing sporadically until the "Big Strike" in 1920. Dust storms appeared insurmountable in the early days of the town, but were overcome when a protectionist reserve was built around the area in the 1930's. While BHP ceased operations in Broken Hill in 1940, a company named Perilya remains operating in the area. The ore is now mined, extracted, brought to the surface and treated at Broken Hill, after which it is smelted at Port Pirie.

Visitor Information:

The Broken Hill Visitor Information Centre is at the corner of Blende and Bromide Streets, and can be called on *(08) 8088 9700*. Their email address is *tourist@pbrokenhill.nsw .gov.au*, while their website is *www.visitbrokenhill.com.au*.

Points of Interest:

The Symposia Sculptures are a collection of stone statues located in the desert just north of Broken Hill, and are visible for over 100 kilometres. Worked on by 12 of the finest sculptors from around the world, the hand crafted statues were supported by the Broken Hill City Council and local businesses. Providing one of the most spectacular views in the area, the Horse Head, the Moon Goddess, the Thomasina and the Bajo El Sol Jaguar are all a wonder to behold.

The Broken Hill Regional Gallery is found at the Civic Centre at the corner of Blende and Chlorine Street, and the fact that it was opened in 1904 makes it the second oldest art gallery in Australia. The gallery includes the "Silver Tree" which was commissioned by Charles Rasp, as well as a number of modern, traditional and Aboriginal works.

The Delprats Underground Tourist Mine offers a great way to experience the mining history of the city of Broken Hill, and is only a five minute drive from the Visitor Information Centre. The tour explores one of the old mines operated by BHP, and they can be called on *(08) 8088 1604*.

The Line of Lode Miners Memorial is an informative mining centre that shows the past and future of mining in Broken Hill. The project is composed of a memorial and a visitors centre that commemorates the hundreds of miners who have died in the town since 1883. Recognised as a rich and powerful example of urban design, it has been claimed the structure has established an identity for the town simillar to that which Sydney has with the Opera House. The memorial can be called on *(08) 8088 6000*.

Silverton Population: 50

On a sealed road 25km north-west of Broken Hill, Silverton's population has dwindled from what was once a number of over 3000. With a population now around only 50 inhabitants, it could be adequately described as a ghost town. Silverton is a place where donkeys have been known to wander aimlessly down the main street, dilapidated old VWs are parked defiantly on the side of the road like rusty antiques, while the infamous "Dunny of Singleton" stands shakily on the side of the hill while all else crumbles around. Yet it is this desolate emptiness that has captured the imagination of many a filmmaker: Mad Max 2, Priscilla: Queen of the Desert, A Town Like Alice and Razorback are among the 45 movies that have been shot in Singeton, earning the town the reputation of an "Outback Hollywood".

The Silverton Pioneer Museum features an outdoor display with a garden setting, featuring farm equipment and machinery from the old sheep stations. The indoor collection includes minerals, shells and Aboriginal rock carvings, and is also home to the Opal Shop. At the corner of Burke and Loftus Street is the second gaol that was built in Silverton, erected in 1889 when the NSW Chief Justice Sir Frederick Darley was appalled at the conditions which the inmates had to suffer. The site was restored by the local historical society and reopened as a museum in the 1960s, and now displays historic items such as photographs, documents, household items and pastoral and mining equipment. The lookout just west of Silverton offers a remarkable view of the deserted outback which stretches in all directions towards the horizon.

Rust & History, Silverton

A country lane near Cowra

Menindee Lakes

Menindee

Situated 110km south-east of Broken Hill, there is a series of natural lakes stretching 50km north and 35km south of the town of Menindee, and areas have been developed for caravan parks and weekend cottages. Activities on the lakes includes speedboats, water skiing, sailing, safe swimming and good fishing.

The Kinchega National Park, on the western bank of the Darling River adjacent to Menindee, is an example of one of the major landscape categories of the arid and semi-arid regions of New South Wales. The Menindee Regional Tourist Association is on Menindee Street, *(08) 8091 4274.*

White Cliffs

The well-known opal field and township of White Cliffs is 295km north-east of Broken Hill. There visitors can try their luck at fossicking, see the superb opalised Plesiosaur skeleton, and the dugouts where many of the residents live. Facilities include a hotel, motel, general store and cafe. Fossicker's Licences are available from the Whitecliffs Store and Tourist Information in Karara Road, *(08) 8091 6611.*

Wilcannia

Wilcannia is a small junction town situated on the banks of the Darling River. The Barkindji people have been in the area for 40,000 years. The Visitor Information Centre is at 37 Reid Street, *(08) 8091 5333.*

Cobar

Cobar is a major mining centre that is situated between Dubbo and Broken Hill, and can boast an excellent mining museum with tours of underground mines. The museum is located within the Great Cobar Outback Heritage Centre on Marshall Street, call *(02) 6836 2448.*

North West of Outback Region

Bourke Population: 3000

Bourke is a town with its own folklore. Situated on the upper banks of the Darling River the area produces wool, beef, cotton and citrus fruits. In days gone by the boats would travel up and down the Darling transporting goods and produce, and the Post Office still flies the pennant indicating the town is a port. As the town is the last spot before the vast empty centre of the outback, the expression "out the back of Bourke" has come into popular usage in Australian culture, describing the loneliness and emptiness of the centre of Australia. The town derived its name from NSW Governor Sir Richard Bourke, and was built mainly to protect Mitchell from his poor relationship with the local Aboriginal population. The location on the Darling River meant it was to eventually become the transport centre for western NSW and south west Queensland. The port at Bourke was an efficient way of transporting wool to coastal markets however the last commercial riverboat sailed in 1931.

The famous Australian poet, Henry Lawson who lived in the town for a number of years, is quoted as saying that "if you know Bourke, you know Australia." The Back O'Bourke Exhibition Centre once completed will cover the colourful history of the area. The Bourke Cemetary also contains graves of historical interest, the most notable being that of Fred Hollows, along with bush poet Francis Brown. The Visitor Information Centre is in Anson Street. *(02) 6872 2280,* email *tourinfo@ozemail.com.au.*

Lightning Ridge

The old fashioned and carefree 'tomorrow will do if it can't be done today' atmosphere of Lightning Hill is treasured and preserved by local residents as a valuable way of life. It is the only place in the world where a wet pudding can be seen (the operation which is used to separate opal nobbies from the clay in which they are found). This area is world famous for its black and blue opals, and attracts many tourists.

Walgett

Walgett is near the junction of the Namoi and Barwon rivers and a little over 100km from Lightning Ridge. It is surrounded by pastoral properties stretching far in each direction. Irrigation has opened up large new areas to cotton, sorghum, maize and other crops.

NSW

Central New South Wales Region

Central New South Wales offers an ideal way to experience the rural and bush aspects of Australia, with all of the smaller and more isolated towns adjoined to inland cities like Dubbo, Orange and Bathurst. The area is rich in history and towns such as Ophir and Gulgong offer a view of our pioneering past, while the City of Dubbo has a history that stretches right back to the beginnings of our settlement. There are over 14 National Parks to visit in the region.

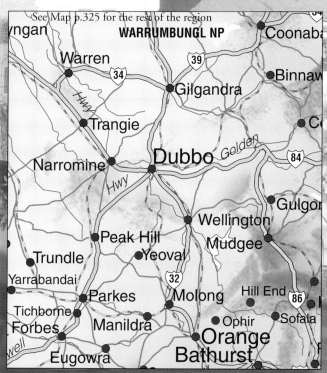

See Map p.325 for the rest of the region

Dubbo Population: 38,000. Climate: Average temperatures: January max 32°C - min 18°C; July max 15°C - min 3°C. Average annual rainfall - 584mm; height above sea level - 262m; average number of rainy days per year - 74.

Situated on the Macquarie River in mid-western New South Wales, 416km from Sydney, the city of Dubbo is known as the Hub of the West. One of the fastest growing cities in inland Australia, Dubbo is a thriving service centre for the fertile farmlands that surround it. The city is responsible for

Dubbo
The clocktower in the centre of Dubbo. The town is a commercial and administrative centre. People from outlying towns and properties come here to shop.

providing commercial, industrial and administrative duties to almost a third of New South Wales. The Area is known for its wheat and wool production, its diverse agricultural industries and The city is home to a campus of the Charles Sturt University.

The City of Dubbo is a much-visited destination for tourists due to the fact that it lies at the halfway point between Brisbane and Melbourne. While it has all the necessary facilities that one would expect from such a location, it also has a lot to offer those who wish to sample the bush atmosphere of Central New South Wales. While Dubbo is known for attractions such as the world class Western Plains Zoo, it is also in close proximity to the wine growing township of Mudgee and the historical site of Gulgong, as well as being only a 2 hour drive from the Warrumbungle National Park.

Central NSW was originally stumbled upon by explorers Blaxland, Wentworth and Lawson, after they finally managed to cut a path through the unforgiving bush of the Blue Mountains. The Aboriginal Wiradjuri tribe were said to be in occupation of the land, and John Oxley was the first European to pass through the area of Dubbo in 1818. He noted the quality of the soil and the abundance of water supply, and several squatters were allowed to set up large sheep and cattle properties near the Macquarie River shortly after in 1824. One of Australia's wealthiest settlers, Robert Dulhunty, embarked on an expedition with

a party of 40 Aboriginal guides in the early 1830's, and he used the Aboriginal term "Dubbo" to name the grazing area he chose near the town's current location. Much to Dulhunty's frustration, the government decided to erect a law enforcement institution only 5km downstream from his property in 1847, and both a courthouse and post office were established within a year's time. The most interesting figure to later be held in the newly established lockhouse was the infamous bushranger Johnny Dunn, who escaped from his confines only to later be recaptured and hung in Sydney.

Not long after 1847, Dulhunty began negotiations with a Sydney lawyer to establish a store and inn near his property, and so began Dubbo's growth into the thriving regional centre it is today. The village of Dubbo was proclaimed in 1849 with the first land sales taking place the following year, and before long stockmen from NSW and Queensland found themselves drawn to the area. While development was initially slow, by the time a bridge had been built over the Macquarie River in 1866 the village was full of shops, boasting five hotels and a mill under construction, as well as a court house and

Western Plains Zoo
One of the giraffes at the Western Plains Zoo which is situated just outside of Dubbo.

lock-up. By the time Dubbo had become a municipality in 1872 it had grown to a population of 850 people, developing into the major manufacturing and service centre for western New South Wales. Dubbo experienced a further explosion in population following World War II in the tweintieth century, and was finally declared a city in 1966.

Visitor Information:

The Dubbo Visitors Centre and Events Bureau is on the corner of Macquarie and Erskine Streets, and can be called on *(02) 6884 1422*. They can be emailed at *tourism@dubbo.nsw.gov.au*, while their website address is *www.dubbotourism.com.au*.

Points of Interest:

The Western Plains Zoo is easily one of the most persuasive reasons to visit Dubbo. Cited around the world as one of the most humane examples of how animals can be kept in captivity, the Western Plains Zoo is home to over 1,000 animals, many of them endangered species. Some of the more rare examples that can be viewed in the Zoo include the African Black Rhinocerous, the African Elephant and

the Greater Bilby. Yet instead of keeping them locked up in constrictive cages, all the animals are allowed to roam free across the 300 hectares of open ranges in reconstructions of their natural environments. Visitors are allowed to cycle or drive through the zoo, and they can be phoned for bookings on *(02) 6882 5888*.

The Dubbo Museum offers an effective way for visitors to peruse the extensive history of the city, and is located at the former site of the Bank of NSW. Colonial, farm, domestic, Aboriginal and commercial artefacts are all on display. While the museum is currently undergoing renovations it is due to be reopened at the end of 2005, and in the meantime they can still be called on *(02) 6882 5359*.

The Old Dubbo Gaol offers another window into the extensive history of the city. Originally built in 1871 before finally being closed in 1966, the old gaol has since been converted into a museum and offers visitors an opportunity to see how Dubbo's judicial system once operated. Highlights include a collection of animatronic models which tell of the

Orange

Duntryleague Guesthouse with the golf course in the foreground.

experiences of the inmates and keepers, as well as a gallow's pole with the equipment that was used to hang eight men in the gaol. The museum is located at Macquarie Street, and they can be called on *(02) 6882 8122.*

Orange Population: 38,000

Located 261 km west of Sydney on the Western side of the Great Dividing Range, Orange is a large and highly developed rural service centre. The city of Orange lies at the centre of some of the most important agricultural land in the region. Its name is derived from William Prince of Orange, a man who later went on to become the Prince of Denmark. Orange does however specialise in the growing of fruit: but rather than citrus, they are responsible for supplying 10% of the country's apples, along with grapes, berries and olives. The city prides itself on being one of Australian best suppliers of food, as it is a prolific supplier of fine lamb and beef.

With the four distinct seasons showering the city streets with a kaleidoscope of colours at any given time of the year, Orange has become known as Australia's "Colour City". Autumn sees a wealth of reds and oranges splashed through the city; the snow of winter brings a sharp and pristine white; spring sees the proliferation of a rich velvet green; while the

The Orange area with its orchards.

summer brings a splash of warm, golden sunshine. Orange's abundance of natural colour can be sampled at any of the city's popular parks or gardens, with the Cook Park at the western end of the main street being the main attraction. A great place to have a picnic lunch at any time of the year, the garden is memorable for the 100 year old trees found within, along with a number of ponds, walkways and fountains, along with an aviary and a begonia house.

Orange is notable for being the birthplace of Australia's most famous poet Banjo Patterson, who wrote 'Waltzing Matilda'. A white monument can be visited which commemorates where he was born.

Visitor Information:

The Information Centre is located at Civic Square, Byng Street. *1800 069 466.* Visit the website at *www.orange.nsw.gov.au*, or email *tourism@orange.nsw.gov.au.*

Bathurst Population: 31,300

With a historical significance that extends from being Australia's first site of government settlement, Bathurst is one of our nation's oldest inland cities, and is full of many historical buildings. While the practice of raising sheep, cattle and horses common during European settlement still takes place in areas near the city, in recent times Bathurst has a reputation for its impressive educational facilities. Most notable is the Charles Sturt University. The young people have given the city a diverse sense of contemporary culture.

A good place to start a sightseeing tour is the Victorian Renaissance Court House. Facing Kings Square with double-storey portico and large octagonal central dome, it was originally built as a telegraph office. The Bathurst Regional Art Gallery and Abercrombie House are both open for inspection, as is Ben Chifley's Cottage, the home of the former Prime Minister. The nearby Mt Panorama is one of Australia's premier sporting locations, with the Bathurst 1000 Touring Car Race and the Australian 1000 Classic held there every October. The Bathurst 1000 was first held in 1960, and is now attended by 40,000 spectators.

Visitor Information:

The Bathurst Visitors Information Centre is located at 28 William Street, and can be called on *(02) 6332 1444*, or toll-free on *1800 681 000.*

Outlying Towns in the Region

Parkes

Parkes is 121km south-west of Dubbo, and is the major centre of the Lachlan Valley, servicing the towns of Peak Hill, Alectown, Bogan Gate, Trundle and Tullamore. Parkes has a town population of 10,100, and the Parkes Visitor Information Centre is on the Newell Highway and can be called on *(02)*

Bathurst's Historic Courthouse

6862 4365 or emailed on *tourism@parkes.nsw.gov.au*. The main attraction in the area is the Radio Telescope, and to get there travel north on the Newell Highway for 20km, turn off the highway and follow Telescope Road for 6km and then follow the signs.

Forbes

35km south-west of Parkes on the Newell Highway, is Forbes, which has many well attended parks and gardens and historic buildings. Forbes Railway Arts and Tourist Centre, Union St, can be contacted on *(02) 6852 4155*.

Forbes is Ben Hall country. The famous bushranger was part of the notorious Gardiner Gang who carried out a gold escort robbery at nearby Eugowra. He met his death in a hail of bullets at the age of 28 and is buried in the Forbes Cemetery. The Forbes Museum, in an old Music Hall which once formed part of the Osborn Hotel, houses an interesting collection of relics of the bushrangers, and outside of Forbes a plaque marks the spot where Ben Hall was killed.

Wellington

Situated on the Mitchell Highway, 50km south-east of Dubbo, Wellington is famous for the Wellington Caves, 8km south of the town. The Wellington Tourist Information Centre is at Cameron Park, *(02) 6845 1733*, and they have information on attractions in the town, which include a clock museum, a winery, and arts and crafts galleries.

The Burrendong Dam is 32km upstream from Wellington, and there one can waterski, sail, swim, fish, or relax in the sun. Burrendong's arboretum covers an area of nearly 160 hectares, set aside for the cultivation and preservation of plant life native to Australia. Mookerawa, another section of the Burrendong State Recreation Park, and Burrendong offer great facilities for visitors who love to camp.

Gilgandra

The town of Gilgandra is on the Newell Highway, 66km north of Dubbo, on the western side of the Warrumbungles. It was known originally as the town of windmills, and is home to one of the country's best privately owned observatories. The Gilgandra Visitor Information Centre is on the Newell Highway, call on *(02) 6847 2045* or email at email *gilinfo@tpg.com.au*. Drop in here for information on the attractions in the town, and available accommodation.

Coonabarabran

Situated 95km north-east of Gilgandra, Coonabarabran has a population of around 4000. The town name means 'Inquisitive Person' and the Tourist Centre is on the Newell Highway at the southern end of town, call on *(02) 6842 1441* or email *coonavic@lisp.com.au*. The main attraction is the Anglo-Australian Observatory in Siding Spring, whose visitor's gallery allows visitors to view some of the workings of this immense piece of equipment. The Observatory is 28km west of the town, and can be called on *(02) 6842 6291*.

35km from town is the Warrumbungle National Park, covering 21,004 hectares and containing magnificent scenery and prolific fauna and flora. For further information visit *www.npws.nsw.gov.au*. Between the Warrumbungle Mountains and the Namoi River is the Pilliga Forest and Nature Reserve, a vast flat area covering approximately 5400 sq km of natural wild forest and scrublands known as the Pilliga Scrub. The town of Baradine is the heart of the Pilliga. Visit the Baradine Forest Centre, Lachlan Street, *(02) 6843 1607,* and find out details of the many forest drives, and the location of the numerous sandstone caves.

Ophir

Gold was first discovered in Australia in 1851 at Ophir, approximately 40km from Orange. Today the area is a reserve, with trails leading to old tunnels, sluices and other relics among the hills. The reserve is popular with fossickers.

Sofala

Set amongst the steep hills of Turon Valley, Sofala is one of the old gold rush towns. It has a quaint store and faded old-time buildings. The Royal Hotel is the only hotel remaining of the forty which were operating during the gold rush era.

Hill End

The Parks and Wildlife Service have declared Hill End an historic site. They publish an excellent information sheet 'Exploring Hill End Historic Site'. Only a small community remains today. Miners dug up 701,000 ounces of gold here. Panning and fossicking are still popular, and gold pans may be hired in town. Hill End is 84km from Bathurst.

Mudgee

Situated 69km north of Hill End, Mudgee is the second oldest town west of the Blue Mountains, and was laid out in 1838. A score of handsome buildings (classified by the National Trust) dot the town, the oldest being the Catholic Presbytery, built in 1852. Mudgee is renowned for its honey, and visitors are able to watch honey processing at two factories. There are also many wineries in the district, and all have cellar door sales. Mudgee is well known for its fine wines, and is gaining fame for its beautiful rose gardens. There is a Days of Wine and Roses Festival each year in September/October. Mudgee Gulgong Tourism is at 84 Market Street, call on *(02) 6372 1020* or email *info@mudgee.org*.

Gulgong

Gulgong, 29km from Mudgee was, until the advent of plastic currency, the 'Town on the Ten Dollar Note'. It has narrow streets which wind between quaint clapboard and iron buildings, complete with verandahs and iron lace.

The township of Sofala

NSW

New England North West Region

An area that stretches right along the Great Dividing Range near Newcastle to the Queensland border, the "Big Sky Country" of the New England North West Region is home to thriving towns such as Tamworth, Armidale, and Moree

Tamworth Population: 32,543. Climate: Average temperatures: January max 35°C - min 17°C; July max 16°C - min 2°C.

Situated on the banks of the Peel River and 411km from Sydney, Tamworth is familliar around Australia as the nation's Country Music Capital. With the city lying in the centre of the largest gemstone fossicking region in NSW and surrounded by picturesque countryside, Tamworth is also the commercial and administrative capital of the New England region. The city services all of the surrounding districts, who are responsible for producing wool, dairy products, eggs, poultry, wheat, tobacco, honey, as well as various livestock.

John Oxley was the first to be impressed by the area when he entered the Peel River Valley in 1818, commenting that "it would be impossible to find a finer or more luxuriant country than its waters...No place in this world can afford more advantages to the industrious settler than this extensive vale." While settlers arrived to take advantage of Oxley's discovery in 1830, it was not long before they were booted out by the

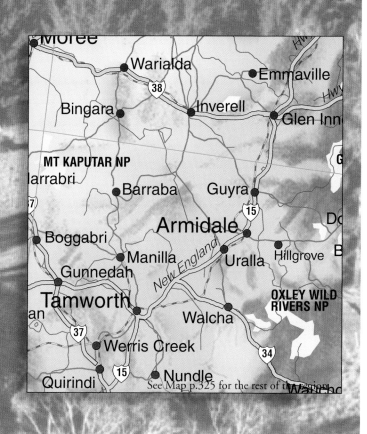

Giant Golden Guitar, Tamworth

Tamworth District

Australian Agricultural Company (AAC), who arrived with 6000 sheep in 1834. The AAC established their company headquarters in the region, and before long a private village began to develop on the banks of the Peel River.

The growing population of Tamworth benefited by this development into a major coaching station and milling centre in the 1860's, and were connected by rail to Newcastle in 1878. It wasn't until the 1960's that Tamworth began its famous association with country music: a local radio station 1287 2TM began to broadcast a program that specialised in country music, and Tamworth hasn't looked back since.

The **Big Golden Guitar** at Tamworth is evidence of how happy the city is to associate itself with country music, and the area is thought of as the Australian equivalent to Nashville in the US. The Australasian Country Music Festival is one of the best ways to sample the country culture in Tamworth, and it attracts over 50,000 visiting fans every January.

Visitor Information:
The Tamworth Visitor Information Centre can be found on the corner of Peel and Murray Streets, call *(02) 6755 4300*. Their email address is *tourism@tamworth.nsw.gov.au*.
Points of Interest:
The **Australian Country Music Foundation Museum** is located at 93 Brisbane Street, and the Legends of Australian Country Music Exhibition features profiles on Slim Dusty, Smoky Dawson, Tex Morton and Buddy Williams among others. They can be telephoned on *(02) 6766 1577*.

The **Golden Guitar Tourist Centre** is located just behind the 12 metre Giant Golden Guitar in Quartpot Lane, which features a wax model collection of country music stars such as Slim Dusty, Smoky Dawson, Tex Morton, Buddy Williams, Beccy Coles and Shirley Williams among others. They can be called on *(02) 6765 2688*.

Walk a Country Mile is an Interpretive Exhibition Centre depicting the story of Australian Country Music. Located at the Tamworth Tourism Information Centre, the exhibition is a must see attraction in Tamworth. *(02) 6755 4300*.

Armidale Population: 25,000
Located halfway between Brisbane and Sydney and part of the Great Dividing Range, the city of Armidale can boast a great deal of impressive scenery. Surrounded by National Parks, the beautiful trees and flora which fill the streets mean the town is full of colour all year round. Grazing and high-grade fine wool production are the biggest sources of income in the area, with other industries including dairying, the growing of potatoes and stone fruits, as well as timber processing, contributing.

Armidale is surrounded on all sides by the natural beauty

of the bush: the impressive scenery of Oxley Wild Rivers National Park, New England National Park, and Cathedral Rock National Park are all within close proximity. Armidale is also recognised as the best place for education in the New England Region, and the presence of the New England University contributes a great deal towards the presence of arts and culture in the city.

Visitor Information:
The Armidale Visitor Information Centre can be found at 82 Marsh Street. They can be contacted on *(02) 6772 4655.* Their email address is *armvisit@northnet.com.au.*

Outlying towns in New England

Manilla
On the Namoi River, it is known for Dutton's Meadery in Barraba Street, where their honey-based alcoholic drink can be tasted, which is reputedly mans' oldest liquor.

Nundle
If visitors want to try their luck fossicking then try the 'Hills of Gold' area, after visiting Hanging Rock, and asking one of the locals for advice. The Nundle Historical Museum is in Jenkins Street, *(02) 6769 3292.*

Hillgrove
An old ghost town about 27km east of Armidale, Hillgrove has been carefully restored to serve as an uncanny reminder of its vibrant and colourful past.

Wollomombi Falls
The highest falls in Australia, Wollomombi Falls have a drop of 460 metres. For rockhounds and gem fossickers, the area has numerous little pockets which contain precious stones. Inverell, to the north-west, is one of the more popular fossicking towns.

Uralla
A little less than 22 kilometres south of Armidale, Uralla is famous in folklore for being the resting place of the bushranger Captain Thunderbolt. It has many historic buildings, three museums and several pubs. Contact the Uralla Visitor Information Centre *(02) 6778 4496.*

Guyra, Glen Innis, Tenterfield, Inverell
Leaving Armidale on the New England Highway and bypassing the village of Ben Lommond, one encounters Guyra , the highest sheep country in Australia. Further along the Highway is Glen Innis (Visitor Centre: *02 6732 2397*), with some monumental buildings, and Tenterfield (Visitor Centre: *02 6736 1082*), remembered for its participation in the history of Federation. Turn off from Guyra and travel through Tinga to Inverell (Visitor Centre: *02 6728 8161*), a town that services the local farming and grazing district.

The North West

Moree Population: 10,000
An affluent little town found 628km North-West of Sydney, Moree is blessed by the rich plains of black soil that it uses to cultivate produce. Moree straddles the Gwyder River and so it has suffered regularly from floods over the years. This provides an explanation for a relative lack of historical buildings in the town: Moree has been completely submerged in water on more than a few occasions.

The hot artesian spa complex in the town evolved from the Moree bore and has been championed as a healthy source of relaxation and enjoyment. Moree actually promotes itself as the "Artesian Spa Capital", and the spas can be called on *(02) 6757 3450.*

Visitor Information:
Located at the corner of the Newell and Gwydir Highways, and can be phones on *(02) 6757 3350.*

Saumarez Homestead, Armidale

NSW
North Coast Region

The North Coast region offers a literal smorgasboard of beautiful beaches and coastal areas for travellers passing through to either Brisbane or Sydney. Stretching from the definitive coastal New South Wales town of Port Macquarie right along to Coffs Harbour, tourists will not be disappointed when exploring the areas of the north coast.

Lighthouse Beach
Port Macquarie has many beautiful beaches to its south and also beyond the harbour , to the north. Many surf carnivals are held here at this beach.

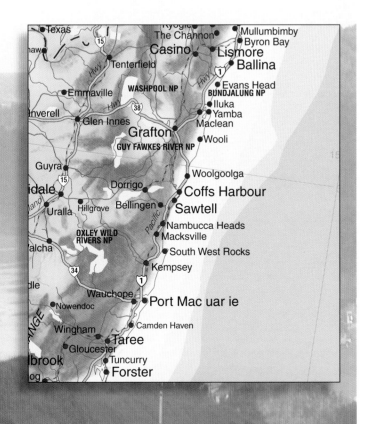

Greater Port Macquarie Population: 70,000. Climate: Average temperatures: January max 28C - min 18°C; July max 18°C - min 7°C. Average annual rainfall: 1563mm. The CSIRO suggests that Port Macquarie has the most ideal climate in Australia.

Situated 423km north of Sydney at the mouth of the Hastings River, Greater Port Macquarie is one of the most popular tourist destinations in the state. Perhaps the most definitive coastal town in New South Wales, Port Macquarie is reknown for offering an enviable lifestyle of coastal leisure and possesses some of the most magnificent waterways and beaches in the whole of the country. Located at an almost equal distance Sydney and Brisbane, Port Macquarie offers road travellers plenty of options to indulge in during a scheduled stopover.

An area that has impressed with its natural beauty overtime, John Oxley described the area in 1818 as "... a beautiful point of land, having plenty of good water and grass, and commanding a fine view of the interior of the port and the surrounding country". With Oxley naming the inlet Port Macquarie in honour of the Governor of the Colony of New South Wales, the settlement was established in 1821 by a pioneering party of soldiers and convicts.

Visitor Information:

The Information Centre is on the corner of Clarence and Hay Streets, *(02) 6581 8000* or *1300 303 155*. Their web page is at *www.portmacquarieinfo.com.au* and emails can be sent to *tourism@hastings.nsw.gov.au.*

Points of Interest:

The **Sea Acres Rainforest Centre** can be found at Pacific Drive, their contact number is *(02) 6582 3355*. The centre has a 1.3km boardwalk within 6.2 hectares of coastal rainforest, and there are guided tours at regular intervals.

Timber Town is a must see attraction, and is located on the Oxley Highway near the village of Wauchope. A heritage theme park that allows visitors to experience the oldworld charm of yesteryear, there are literally dozens of houses which recreate an old timber town of the 1880's. The park is open every day and admittance is free, *(02) 6581 8511.*

The **Billabong Koala and Aussie Wildlife Park** is a place where visitors can have a hands-on experience with some of Australia's much loved animals - koalas, kangaroos, wallabies, wombats and more. The park is located near the intersection of the Pacific and Oxley Highways, and their phone number is *(02) 6585 1060.*

The **Hastings District Historical Museum**, in Clarence Street near the corner of Hay Street, *(02) 6583 1108*, won the Museum of the Year Award in 1981 and 1982. Its 14 rooms are open 7 days a week.

The **Harvest Picnic and Cultural Festival** is held in November and celebrates the arts, culture and fine produce of the region. Other events on the annual calendar include the Heritage Festival and the Camden Music Festival in April.

Taree Population: 16,200

Located only 310km north of Sydney, Taree has become known as the "River City" due to its prime location on the banks of the beautiful Manning River. The surrounding coastal and hinterland areas of Taree offer an abundance of natural attractions, including scenic lookouts, waterfalls, and some of the cleanest, whitest beaches to be found in New South Wales. In fact, Taree is home to Black Head Beach, named last year as "Australia's Friendliest Beach" as part of the "Keep Australia Beautiful Clean Beach Challenge," and receiving the runner-up title for Australia's cleanest beach in 2004.

The commercial hub of the Manning Valley, Taree is a large and modern town that sevices many of the rural industries in the surrounding areas. It is also a popular destination for tourists. A cruise on the Manning River offers a great way to take in the town's main waterway and the beautiful landscape of the banks, while Fotheringham Park, Queen Elizabeth

A lone Pelican
The lakes and waterways around Taree and Foster/Tuncurry are a haven for pelicans.

Park and Kendall Reserve are some of the beautiful riverside parks that can be enjoyed.

Visitor Information:

The Manning Valley Visitor Information Centre is located on Manning River Drive, and can be phoned on *(02) 6592 5444* or *1800 801 522*. Web address is *www.manningvalley.info*, and email *manningvic@gtcc.nsw.gov.au*.

Forster & Tuncurry

Located around 161km north of Newcastle are the twin towns of Forster and Tuncurry, both major tourist spots of the Great Lakes area. Both Foster and Tuncurry are renowned for their beaches, fishing, seafoods and temperate climate all year round. On land there is the Booti Booti National Park to explore, and the Cape Hawke Bicentennial Walk with its panoramic viewing platform. The popular beaches and lakes provide ample opportunites for swimming, fishing and sailing.

Visitor Information:

Forster has the Great Lakes Visitor Centre located in Little Street, *(02) 6554 8799* or *1800 802 692*. They have a web page located at the *www.greatlakes.org.au* and their email address is *tourglc@tpgi.com.au*.

Coffs Harbour Population: 22,000

Situated 578km north of Sydney and 427km south of Brisbane, Coffs Harbour is a popular destination all year round. Surrounded on either side by both the blue waters of the Pacific Ocean and the western border of the Great Dividing Range, the area sprawls for miles up and down the coast. The scenery is characterised by a combination of golden sands, high mountains, dense luxuriant rainforests and clear rivers and streams, making it a superb holiday area.

One of the destination's most popular tourist attractions is the giant man-made banana located at the northern end of the town, indicating the importance of bannana growing in the area. The 33 year old giant structure is perhaps one of Australia's most photographed icons, and the Big Banana can be called on *(02) 6652 4355*. The Coffs Creek Walk offers visitors an effective way to appreciate the beauty of the area, and is a well signposted 9km track that winds through the bushland and the wetlands of the Coffs Creek Reserves.

Visitor Information:

The Coffs Harbour Tourism Holiday Coast Information Centre is located at the corner of Rose Avenue & Marcia Street, and can be called on *(02) 6652 1522* or *1300 369 070*. Email them at *tourism@coffscoast.com.au* or check out the website at *www.visitcoffsharbour.com*.

Grafton Population: 15,500

Situated on a bend of the Clarence River, 660km north of Sydney and 320km south of Brisbane, Grafton is known widely as the "Jacaranda City". The streets of Grafton are lined with trees and graceful old buildings, further complimented by no less than twenty-four council maintained parks. The district was originally discovered by escaped convict Richard Craig in 1831, and before long stories of the 'red gold' had spread, with John Small arriving in 1838 to occupy the land on Woodford Island. The settlement was established shortly after and was proclaimed a town in 1885, with Governor Fitzroy officially naming the town after his grandfather, the Duke of Grafton.

With the fertile river flats having encouraged dairying, sugarcane plantations and mixed farming, Grafton is the commercial centre of an extensive agricultural and pastoral district. The town is also home to Australia's longest running floral festival, with the Jacaranda Festival first held in Grafton in 1935. Crowds flock to Grafton during the festival to view the trees and enjoy the many other exhibitions and events, with a queen crowning ceremony held on the last Saturday in October and the first weekend in November featuring a spectacular street parade.

Grafton
A famed Jacaranda Tree on the Clarence River.

View from Clunes
Inland from Byron Bay and Ballina the countryside consists of rolling hills and valleys with rich soil.

Visitor Information:
The Clarence River Tourist Association is on the corner of Spring Street and the Pacific Highway, and can be phoned on *(02) 6642 4677*. Their website can be found at *www.clarencetourism.com*, and can be emailed at *contactus @clarencetourism.com*.

Lismore Population: 41,883

Situated inland from Ballina on the Bruxner Highway between rainforest and the sea, Lismore is an area that only continues to grow in importance. Not only the commercial, cultural and sporting capital of the North Coast region for over 100 years, Lismore is also the administrative centre for Federal and State Government departments for all of the surrounding areas. In addition, the local university attracts many students to the area.

Known by locals as the "Rainbow Region," all types of agriculture and tropical fruits can be found in the extremely fertile countryside. The area of Lismore has become popular for those engaged in arts and culture, with many artists, painters filmmakers and musicians making the town their home in recent years. The many galleries, studios and theatres are a reflection of this. A major community celebration known as the Lantern Parade is held every June, as well as the North Coast National Show every October.

Visitor Information:
The Rainbow Region Visitor Information Centre can be found on the corner of Ballina & Molesworth Street, and their phone number is either *(02) 6622 0122* or *1300 369 795*. Online references include the website at www.lismore.nsw.gov.au, and email at tourism@lismore.nsw.gov.au.

Ballina Population: 20,000

Ballina is major service centre for the New South Wales North Coast and popular with tourists passing through on the way to Queensland. The town is reknowned for being home to the Big Prawn, an object that can be seen from kilometres away, above the sugar cane crops that surround it. The urban town centre of Ballina contains many of the necessary facilities, and the main street is packed with an assortment of cafes, restaurants, pubs and clubs.

The beaches to the east of Ballina are of a fantastic quality and deserve a visit from anyone passing through the area. Lighthouse Beach, Shelly Beach and Angels Beach all stand out, while the Ballina Lighthouse is among the smallest on the Australian coast and is located in a park near the water.

Visitors Information:
The Ballina Visitor Information Centre is on the corner of La Balsa Plaza & River Street, phone them on *(02) 6686 3484* or email them at *balinainfo@balshire.org.au*.

Byron Bay Population: 10,000

An area perhaps more famous for its physical beauty than any other spot in Australia, Byron Bay is legendary for its relaxed and peaceful atmosphere. Tourism (along with agriculture) is where much of the town's income is derived, and it is estimated that 1.7 million tourists visit the town each year. While the development of urban sprawl has been kept to a minimum by council-led initiatives, other home-based businesses have managed to thrive with a focus on alternative, cultural and knowledge industries. A growing population of artists, writers and filmmakers are choosing to make the beautiful town their home.

While associated often with an alternative or "hippy" lifestyle, the appeal of Byron Bay has spread much further than any such limited definition, and has even been referred to as New South Wales's "worst kept secret". It's no understatment to say that the beaches in Byron Bay are stunning: Main Beach is located at the end of Johnson Street, and is the most popular destination for those exploring the town area. Belongil Beach

Byron Bay

is a little quieter, and is located north of the town centre. Additionally, Cape Byron is the most easterly point of Australia, topped by an extremely powerful lighthouse that offers magnificent views of the surrounding coastal areas.

Though tourism continues to thrive in Byron, the residents have fought to protect the environment and retain the natural beauty of the area. The locals have protected local businesses from the opening of big business franchises like McDonalds, as well as keeping out high-rise buildings and traffic lights. A reflection of the town's thriving culture is the many festivals and associated events held in Byron Bay every year. These include the famous Blues and Roots Festival every March, the Byron Bay Writers Festival in the middle of the year, as well as the Splendour In The Grass music festival every July.

Visitor Information:
The Byron Bay Visitor Information Centre is located at the Old Railway Cottage, on Johnson Street, and can be phoned on *(02) 6685 8050*. Their website is located at *www.byron-bay.com/byronbay*.

Outlying Towns on the North Coast

Ulmarra
Situated 13km north of Grafton, Ulmarra is a fine example of a 19th century river port, and the township is classified by the National Trust. The Commercial Hotel is a magnificent old style country pub on the river bank. Ulmarra is also home to an assortment of bric-a-brac shops, and cosy little tearooms.

Maclean
"The Scottish Town in Australia," Maclean is 34km north of Grafton and was first settled by Scottish immigrants. The town's annual Highland Gathering is held over the Easter period, while the Free Presbyterian Church (the oldest in Australia) is a legacy of the town's past. The Clarence River is one of only two NSW rivers trawled for prawns, and the river fleet works from the Ulmarra ferry to the river mouth using Maclean as its base. The Lower Clarence Visitors Centre is in Ferry Park on the Pacific Highway, and can be called on *(02) 6645 4121* and emailed at *crta1@nor.com.au*. Attractions

include Maclean Lookout, The Pinnacle Rocks, and the Bicentennial Museum, all in Wharf Street, and a number of historic buildings. Water skiing, sailing and fishing are popular pastimes.

Yamba

Yamba is the largest coastal resort in the Clarence Valley, and is 14km off the Pacific Highway and 62km north-east of Grafton. It is primarily a holiday town with motels, caravan parks and hundreds of holiday flats and cottages. In the July school holidays the Family Fishing Festival is held, and tonnes of fish are caught.

South of Yamba is the village of Angourie, famous for its surfing, and natural freshwater swimming at the Blue Pool. Angourie marks the northern limit of the Yuraygir National Park. A daily passenger ferry service operates between Yamba and Iluka.

Iluka

The town of Iluka is situated on the opposite headland to Yamba, and is connected by the ferry service. Nearby is a rainforest that is World Heritage listed. It has excellent walking tracks, with interpretive signs for the most notable features. West of Iluka is the world's southernmost coffee plantation, and they have tours of the plantation on weekends and during school holidays. At the plantation there is an intimate coffee house, and an arts and crafts shop.

Wooli

The river and beach offer many ideal swimming and fishing spots. Wooli River is probably the most unpolluted river in Australia, as it flows completely through National Park.

From the North

Murwillumbah Region

If one wishes to visit the Murwillumbah region, drop into the World Heritage Rainforest Visitor Information Centre Murwillumbah, corner of the Pacific Highway & Alma Streets. They share a web page with Tweed Heads Information at *www.tactic.nsw.gov.au*. The 1157 metre high Mt Warning, which towers above the Tweed Valley behind Murwillumbah, dominates the scenery for miles around. The area is a National Park, and a walking track winds its way to the top through rainforest for panoramic views of the Tweed

Yamba

Valley and the coast.

The Channon

The Channon is a charming village on Terania Creek, 20km north of Lismore. Terania Creek, about which there was so much controversy in the 1970s, is now part of the Nightcap National Park, in which there are many walking tracks through tropical rainforest and to Protesters' Falls.

Nimbin

Situated inland 30km from Lismore, the town of Nimbin is in the centre of an area where the 'hippy' approach to life is very popular. One could say Nimbin was the birthplace of alternative lifestyle in Australia in the late 1960s, and the town has a unique style and character of its own. The Nimbin Needles, are unusual rock formations 3km on the Lismore side of Nimbin. They are a sacred site of the Bundjalung Aboriginal Tribe. The website at *www.nimbin. net* gives an idea of the limited facilities the town offers and a taste of the prevailing attitudes of the small rural community.

Kyogle

Kyogle is a small town 50km inland north-west of Lismore that is known as the Gateway to the Rainforest. From the township it is an easy drive to the spectacular Border Ranges National Park. The town has an Information Centre at the Shire Council in Strathedon Street, *(02) 6632 1611*.

Brunswick Head

Going back to the coast, Brunswick Heads is a fairly quiet tourist resort. It is 21km from Byron Bay, and is popular with keen fishermen and families. Apart from the attraction of the beaches, there can be found a sub-tropical Nature Reserve located near the Brunswick River. Just north of the town is an alternative route along the coast, passing many popular surfing and fishing beaches, to Kingscliff. When in town, drop into Brunswick Valley Coach and Travel, Park Street, *(02) 6685 1385*, for local information. There is a good website located at *www.tropicalnsw/brunswickheads*

Lord Howe Island

Part of New South Wales this lone island in the Pacific is stationed off the NSW coast. Their Visitor Centre can be contacted on *(02) 6563 2114* or *1800 240 937*.

Tea Gardens, Myall Lakes National Park

NSW

Newcastle and Hunter Valley Region

The Newcastle and Hunter Valley region are only a few short hours drive from Sydney. Travellers exploring this area will experience a diverse range of sights, from the bright lights and beaches of the coastal city Newcastle to the famous wineries found further inland.

See Map p.325 for the rest of the region

Newcastle Population: 137,000. Climate: Average temperatures: January max 27.2°C - min 19.5°C; July max 17.1°C - min 7.8°C. Average annual rainfall: 1123mm, and the rain falls quite evenly throughout the year.

Situated on the coast with an accessible harbour at the mouth of the Hunter River, Newcastle is located 171km north of Sydney. The second largest city in New South Wales and the sixth largest in Australia, Newcastle is a spot that enjoys international-style hotels, motels and shopping centres, and is an ideal base for those visiting the holiday areas of Lake Macquarie, Port Stephens and the Hunter Valley. While it is no doubt famous for the beautiful Hunter River that runs down the middle, Newcastle has in the past been known as an industrial city. This is changed in recent years however, with BHP no longer operating out of the Newcastle and coal exportation the only major industry that remains in the city.

Natural resources played an important part in Newcastle's history since early settlement – it was escaped convicts who first discovered coal in the region in 1791. Only six years later Lieutenant John Shortland stumbled upon what would later come to be called the Hunter River, as well as the rich resources of coal that lay nearby. Newcastle became the nation's second major European settlement before the end of the 18th century, and had already been recognised as a city by the time industrialisation developed in the 1880's. Over the twentieth century the city became both the commercial and cultural centre for the Hunter Valley and surrounding regions.

Visitor Information:

The Newcastle Visitor Information Centre is located at 363 Hunter Street, *(02) 4974 2999* or *1800 654 558*. Their email address is *tourism@ncc.nsw.gov.au*, and the website *www.visitnewcastle.com.au*.

Points of Interest:

The Honeysuckle Markets are located at the corner of Honeysuckle Drive & Merewether Street, and offer offer fresh food produce, craft and much more.

Hunter Mall became a pedestrian arcade in 1980, and is framed by fine Victorian and Edwardian buildings. In addition to the David Jones department store, it has many other specialty stores.

Bar Beach, just south of the city, Newcastle

The City Hall in King Street is the office of Newcastle's Lord Mayor, and is an impressive sandstone building with a tall clock tower. Opened in 1929, it was completely refurbished in 1970-80 and is now a Convention Centre.

The Civic Park opposite the City Hall is a large park that is a favourite place for Newcastle's business people to relax during the lunchbreak. The trees planted at the eastern and western ends are gifts from Newcastle's Sister City, Ube in Japan.

Queen's Wharf and Harbour is a pleasant attraction which cost millions to establish. The promenade can be walked along, metres away from ships from all over the world, or a Daisy Trike or bike can be hired to pedal the way around. The complex is only 50m from the Hunter Mall, and includes a fisherman's co-op, restaurants and a boatyard. From the top of the tower in the complex one has a view of the city, harbour and beaches north up to Port Stephens, and west to the Watagan Mountains.

The Newcastle Regional Art Gallery, in Laman Street , was opened in 1977 by Her Majesty, Queen Elizabeth II. It houses the city's Art Collection and features visiting exhibitions regularly. In front of the building is another gift from Ube, a stainless steel sculpture, 'Space Two'. Open Tues-Sun 10am-5pm with free entry, or the gallery can be contacted on *(02) 4974 5100.*

Supernova, Newcastle's Science and Technology Fun Centre, is housed within the Regional Museum. It is hands-on science, a museum where kids are encouraged to touch the displays. Supernova is open the same hours as the Museum, and admission is free.

Newcastle Beach offers safe swimming from the rocks at the northern end to the front of the club pavilion, and surfboard riding to the southern end. Surfest, one of the world's leading surfing events takes place here every Febuary/March. The floodlit and patrolled Ocean Baths are here also.

Bar Beach is also a great family beach, with safe swimming from the northern end (Bar area) to the front of the pavilion,

An anchorage at Nelsons Bay.

and surfboard riding from thereon to the southern end. There is plenty of parking, and the beach is patrolled and floodlit.

Port Stephens & Nelson Bay

Population: 62,000

A 45 minute coastal drive north of Newcastle, Port Stevens is regarded as one of the most attractive and unspoilt waterways existing anywhere in Australia. Proclaiming itself as the 'Dolphin Capital of Australia' with more than 140 bottlenose dolphins residing in the port, their harbour is more than twice the size of the one found in Sydney. Further upstream are the Broadwater and the Myall Lakes systems, where can be found lovely waterways, tiny uninhabited islands, abundant bird life, a national park and unpolluted beaches.

Nelson Bay is the Port Stephens service centre, with a variety of shops, a movie cinema, a supermarket, restaurants, banks, a pub, and plenty more. People flock to the scenic Marina for shopping, dining and entertainment. The area also has theme parks catering for children, including Toboggan Hill Park in Salamander Bay, (02) 4984 1022, and Oakvale Farm and Fauna World in Salt Ash, *(02) 4982 6222*.

Visitor Information: The Port Stephens Tourist Information Centre is on Victoria Parade, Nelson Bay, *(02) 4980 6900* or *1800 808 900*. Email them at *info@portstephens.org.au* or find the website at *www.portstephens.org.au*.

Maitland Population: 55,000

Maitland is located only minutes away from the Hunter Valley Wine Country, and is 33km west of Newcastle. The two national highways allow a quick 90-minute freeway drive to Sydney and a 30 minute drive to the vineyards, Newcastle and Port Stephens. Maitland's most important asset is its location on the rich alluvial flats of the Hunter and Paterson Rivers.

Visitor Information:

The Maitland Visitor Information Centre is located on the corner of the New England Highway (Les Darcy Drive) and High Street, *(02) 4931 2800*. The webpage for Maitland tourism can be found at *www.hunterrivercountry.com.au*.

Hunter Valley Wine Country

Situated in the Hunter River basin some 162km north of Sydney, the Hunter Valley Wine Country is a place where grapes have been grown and processed for over 180 years. Continuing to prosper in recent times, the Hunter Valley now finds itself home to more than a 80 wineries and cellar doors and is one of the most popular tourist destinations in New South Wales.

Afternoon light over the Vineyards.

A visit to the Hunter Valley allows the opportunity to taste wine in the very area in which it was produced. The Arrowfield Winery is located on a hill overlooking the beautiful views of the Hunter River, and wine can be purchased from the cellar doors and an onsite restaurant can be visited. The Rosemount Estate has a history that stretches back to 1864, and the cellar doors can be visited in the Upper Hunter Valley. The Wyndham Estate on the other hand has been a successful producer of wines for over 170 years, and functions, festivals and events are held there all year round.

The town of Cessnock is 52km from Newcastle and 185km from Sydney, and is the major gateway to over 30 of the wineries that are located in the area. Yet the satellite district of Pokolbin is where the best accomodation can be found, and is renown for its heritage in the local wine industry. The Hunter Valley Wine Country has a huge calendar of annual events with over 1.5 million tourists visiting the region every year, with one of the highlights being the Hunter Valley Harvest Festival held in March and April of every year.

Visitor Information:

The Hunter Valley Visitors Centre can be found at 445 Wine Country Drive in Pokolbin, *(02) 4990 4447*. Their web address can be visited at *www.winecountry.com.au*, and can be emailed at *info@winecountry.com.au*.

Singleton Population: 22,500.

Singleton is only an hour away from Newcastle on the New England Highway, and is the heart of the Hunter Valley wine producing area. The town is surrounded by rich grazing land, and the Hunter River flows right past its doorstep. Not only is the Singelton Shire home to the Wyndham Estate Winery, the oldest vintage wine producer in Australia, but the recently established Broke Fordwich wine growing area is also garnering praise for their quality produce. The nearby Lake St Clair offers boating and fishing, and maps of the waterways are available from the Information Centre.

Visitor Information:

The Hunter Heartland Visitor Information Centre is at 39 George Street in Singleton, and they can be freecalled on *1800 449 888*.

Their web address is *www.hunterheartland.com.au*, and the email address is *visitorcenrtre@singleton.nsw.gov.au*.

Muswellbrook Population: 11,500

Located in the upper Hunter Valley and approximately 130 km north-west of Newcastle, Muswellbrook has come to be known as "Blue Heeler Country." Thomas Hall was responsible for breeding the dog in 1840's, aiming to produce an animal able to withstand heat, to be a quiet worker, and be effective in the roundup of wild bush cattle. The "Blue Heeler" went on to become the international cattleman's best friend, and the thoroughbred industry remains subsrantial in Muswellbrook. The town has also benefited in recent years from the growth of the mining and power industries, as well the wine industry.

Visitor Information:

The Information Centre can be found at 87 Hill Street Muswellbrook, and can be phoned on *(02) 6541 4050.*

Scone Population: 5,000

Located at the northern end of the Hunter Valley, Scone is known widely as the "Horse Capital of Australia," with a reputation equvalent to the Kentucky Bluegrass region of the United States. The town is also a thriving commercial centre that supports a wide variety of rural industries, not the least their thoroughbred horses.

The Scone Horse Ferstival is held in the town every May, and includes over 10 days of rodeos, street parades and stock sales. The nearby Glenbawn Dam is well stocked with freshwater fish, and is ideal for boating, yachting, water skiing and swimming. The Burning Mountain between Scone and Murrurundi near Wingen has been burning for thousands of years, and is easily reached via a two kilometre walking track. The Visitor Information Centre can be found on the corner of Susan & Kelly Streets, *(02) 6545 1526.*

Murrurundi Population: 800

Located in the northern section of the Upper Hunter Valley, the Murrurundi district is a picturesque and environmentally conscious area predominantly involved with farming and grazing on fertile soils. Following the trail of Henry Dangar, early settlers brought fine merino to graze in the area, and the town now has a reputation for sheep, beef cattle and thoroughbred horse studs. While the town has traditionally stuck to their agricultural roots rather than trying to develop other industries, the many heritage-listed buildings are a reflection of the region's strong sense of history. Infamous bushranger Ben Hall spent his childhood in the town, and Murrurundi was the place were the members of the Jewboy Gang were finally brought to justice. The Bushman's Carnival is held in the town early each October.

The Visitor Information Centre is located at 113 Mayne Street, and can be phoned on *(02) 6546 6446.*

Sedgenhoe Stud, Scone.

NSW

Central Coast Region

Beginning at the Hawkesbury River and stretching northwards to the southern shores of Lake Macquarie, the Central Coast of New South Wales is an area that has a thriving population. It is well known for the pristine beaches and surf associated with the relaxed nature of Central Coast living. Fishing and sailing are also popular in the many waterways and inlets, and the State Forests and National Parks make for a great area for camping and hiking.

Gosford Population: 129,000. Climate: Average temperatures: summer max 25°C - min 18°C; winter max 17°C - min 10°C. Average annual rainfall is 1300mm.

Situated 88km north of Sydney and in close proximity to Newcastle, the city of Gosford has become associated with the relaxed living conditions of the state's Central Coast. While the area has long been known as a destination for tourists and retirees, Gosford and the surrounding areas have become an increaingly popular choice for families wishing to find an alternative to the city living of Sydney and Newcastle.

European settlement of the Gosford area began in the 1820's, with the main points of entry being a tributary of the Hawkesbury River in the West and the Brisbane Water in the east, an area that remains famous for fishing, sailing and other recreational pursuits to this day. Most of the subsequent development occurred in the eastern or coastal sector, with the Brisbane Water attractive to settlers because of the wealth of timber resources and its close proximity to Sydney.

A government township was laid out during the 1830's, and the town was named by Governor Gipps after the Earl of Gosford, with whom he had worked closely with before coming to New South Wales. Access to the Gosford district was revolutionised by the arrival of the railway in 1887, and since the 1940's the greatest developments in Gosford have been linked to the growth of urbanisation. This process has been helped along by government policies which have viewed Gosford as an expanding part of the Sydney region

Many people now visit Gosford for the surf, and the area has many beautiful beaches which are worth discovering. Pearl Beach in particular is a gorgeous little location just south of Woy Woy.

The Central Coast is also renowned for some of the rural areas that form the region's Hinterland. Places like Yarramalong are one of the Central Coast's least promoted areas, yet in fact some of the best places to visit and relax, conveniently located only minutes from suburbia.

Visitor Information:

The Gosford Visitor Information Centre is located at 200 Mann Street, and can be phoned on *1300 130 708*. Their email address is *info_thecoast@bigpond.com*, and the web address is *www.visitcentralcoast.com.au*.

Points of Interest:
The Henry Kendall Cottage & Historical Museum was built for the famous poet in 1836, and is located at 27 Henry Kendall Street in West Gosford. It is now a historical museum with displays of various items from the past, and can be called on *(02) 4325 2270*.

The Australian Reptile Park is one of the major tourist attraction on the Central Coast, and is a popular science exhibit for school students. Crocodile feeding takes place in an impressive crocodile enclosure every day, and the picnic and barbecue facilities are complemented by a large number of kangaroos who roam freely around. The park can be found on the Pacific Highway in Somersby, and can be called on *(02) 4340 1146* or visit their website at *www.reptilepark.com.au*.

The Riverboat Postman Cruise offers visitors a great way to see the Hawkesbery River, with traditional timber ferries departing daily for a four hour cruise at 9:30am. All cruises depart from the Riverboat Postman Wharf alongside the Hawkesbery River Railway Station, and bookings can be made by calling *(02) 9985 7566*.

The Mt Penang Gardens function as a reflection of the wide Australian landscape, and feature over 6 hectares of land, elaborate gardens, and waterways to explore. Free guided tours of the gardens are available daily, and bookings can be made by telephone on *1300 30 46 76*. The Mt Penang Gardens are located at Kariong, only two minutes from the Gosford exit on the Pacific Highway.

Terrigal
There is a large five star Crowne Plaza hotel located in the town, plus plenty of other forms of holiday accomodation including hotels, holiday apartments, houses and cottages. The Skillion is Terrigal's greatest natural feature, and is a narrow section of headland that offers breath taking coastal views. Located just over the hill from the main shopping strip, the headland rises quickly in an easterly direction to a considerable height, and is only a short walk fromboth a lookout and Yumbool Point.

Visitor Information:
The Terrigal Visitor Information Centre is located at Rotary

Brisbane Waters

Park on Terrigal Drive, and share contact details with the Gosford Centre.

The Entrance

Located only 99km north of Sydney via the Newcastle Freeway, The Entrance derives its name from the narrow channel that connects Tuggerah Lake to the ocean, dividing the mainland of the Central Coast region. A popular holiday resort and retirement centre, The Entrance has a lot to offer visitors. There are surf beaches, as well as an attractive foreshore parkland known as Memorial Park, a pathway that stretches from Memorial Park right around to the surf lifesaving club. Also worth visiting is the spectacular 597 hectare Wyrrabalong National Park, which contains the last significant coastal rainforest on the Central Coast.

Visitor Information:

The Visitors Centre can be flound at Memorial Park on Marine Parade, and share details with the Gosford Information Centre.

Tuggerah Lakes

The Tuggerah Lakes district has developed from a small series of fishing towns into a popular holiday spot, with first class motels, hotels, restaurants and sporting facilities. The administrative centre for the district is Wyong, 22km north of Gosford on the banks of the Wyong River. The Lake system extends from Killarney Vale in the south to the township of Lake Munmorah in the north, and consists of three lakes – Tuggerah, Budgewoi and Munmorah.

The Skillion, Terrigal

AUSTRALIAN C.
TERRITORY

PITAL

Parliament House

Staying true to the original plans of the city's designer Walter Burley Griffin, Parliament House is the central landmark of Canberra. It is situated on Capital Hill just south of Lake Burley Griffin.

ACT

Canberra

Located only three hours drive from Sydney and less than seven from Melbourne, Canberra is the capital city of Australia. The parliament house within Canberra is the location where the elected members of the Federal Government sit to govern, and the city is the political hub of the nation.

Canberra Population: 338,727. Climate: The average maximum temperature in Canberra during January is 27°C, while the average maximum temperature during July is 11°C.

Situated in the Australian Capital Territory in the southern tablelands of New South Wales, 100km from the coast and 300km from Sydney, Canberra is the capital city of Australia. Known somewhat as a home for public servants and politicians, Canberra is a unique city in that the layout was actually planned from inception in 1912. American designer Walter Burley Griffin won first prize in a world-

Telstra Tower
The Telstra Tower provides telecommunications facilities to Canberra, but is also a popular place to visit for tourists. At a height of 195 metres, the viewing gallery near the top provides an impressive 360 degree view of Canberra and the surrounding countryside.

wide competition to design the new capital, and from the outset Canberra was developed as a garden city. Thousands of trees have been planted annually since 1915, with a marked variation in the shades and colours. While some may find the precise geometric layout of Canberra's design to be a little unnerving, over half of the area is made up of parklands and open spaces, which will no doubt leave a pleasant impression on visitors.

The Canberra region has been home to the Ngunnawal Aboriginal tribe for over 21,000 years, with archaeological evidence of their occupation existing at both the Tidbinbilla Natural Reserve and the Namadgi National Park. The first Europeans to enter the Australian Capital Territory were Joseph Wild, James Vaughan and Charles Throsby Smith, who in 1820 discovered the Limestone Plains upon which modern day Canberra is situated.

Following the declaration of the Australian Federation in 1901, it was decided that Australia needed to have a national capital. While it may have seemed an obvious choice to make either Sydney or Melbourne the nation's capital and thus

integrate Federal politics into the landscape of an existing city, a compromise between the two rival states was needed. Thus it was decided that the capital city would need to lie at a roughly equal distance from Sydney and Melbourne, and it was decided in 1908 that 2,330 square kilometres of sheep grazing land in New South Wales would become the site of the capital city. In 1911 the Australian Capital Territory was handed over to the Commonwealth Government, and Walter Burley Griffin's precise designs were chosen for the city's layout. It wasn't until 1927 that the Commonwealth Parliament finally sat for session in Canberra.

It cannot be denied that the Capital City of Australia is one of great aesthetic beauty. The consistent planning of Canberra is evident in the many parks that fill the area, and the streets are spacious and filled with trees. The governmental role of the city is also obvious in the many beautifully designed buildings that can be seen everywhere. But in a trend that may surprise a lot of people, there are many who are less than

Parliament House
The Old Parliament House is situated between Parliament House and Lake Burley Griffin. Although initially it was only built as a temporary solution, it was the place of government from 1927 right up until 1988.

seduced by the structured charms of Canberra.

But while these negative perceptions exist, they are something that Canberra has attempted to move away from in recent times. This new direction can be observed in some of the new institutions that have been established in the city. While institutions like the Australian Institute of Sport offer reflection on the nation's sporting culture, the National Museum of Australia explores themes of Australian land and social history. Canberra has attempted to demonstrate that there are many different aspects in the city, all of which offer some comment on what it is like to be an Australian. And indeed, Canberra has many interesting places to see for tourists visiting the area, not only for those interested in the governmental and administration side. Canberra Day is held on the third Monday of every March, and is the culmination of a 10 day Celebrate Canberra Festival, where Canberrans are able to celebrate their love of the city. The day commemorates and celebrates the official founding of Canberra on the 12th of March in 1913, and is also the time where the Canberra Citizen of the Year is named.

Besides the Celebrate Canberra Festival, many other colourful events take place in the city throughout the year. For the city's celebration of Spring, Commonwealth Park comes alive with over one million bulbs and annuals for the Floriade Festival. And every Autumn, over 50 hot air balloons take to the skies over Canberra for the week-long Canberra Balloon Fiesta. Summernats is a huge 3 day car festival that is held every January at Canberra's Exhibition Park. Another big event on the sporting calendar is the Rally of Canberra, which is round one of the Asia-Pacific Rally Championships and is held every May in the forests surrounding Canberra.

Visitor Information:

The Canberra and Region Visitor Centre can be found at 330 Northbourne Avenue in Dickson, and can be contacted on *(02) 6205 0044* and *1300 554 114*, or by email at *crvc@act.gov.au*. Their web page can be browsed at *www.vi sitcanberra.com.au*.

Points of Interest:

Parliament House, in keeping with Walter Burley Griffin's original plan, is the central landmark of Canberra. While some might not be taken with the 81m stainless steel flagpole that dominates the city, all have to agree that the interior

of the building is magnificent. There are imposing marble columns and stairs, extravagant halls, outstanding collections of paintings, sculptures, photographs and ceramics and well-worked timber masonry. Public galleries overlook the House of Representatives Chamber at the eastern side of the building, and the Senate Chamber to the west. Details on sitting hours of either of the Houses are available at the information desk in the foyer, or call *(02) 6277 7111*.

The National Library of Australia is on the southern shores of Lake Burley Griffin, and can be found in Parkes Place. It has over 6 million books, periodicals and newspapers, thousands of paintings, maps, films, photographs, music scores, oral histories, and treasures. For further information, call *(02) 6262 1111*.

The Australian War Memorial commemorates the Australians who gave their lives for their country. The stylised Byzantine building houses a collection of relics, paintings, models, displays and records from all theatres of war. Exhibitions cover the history of Australians at war from Gallipoli up until present day, including an exhibtion on Australia's contributions in Iraq. The memorial is located at Limestone Avenue, Campbell, and can be called on *(02) 6243 4211*.

The National Gallery of Australia was opened in 1982, and houses the national art collection. Eleven galleries provide more than 7000 square metres of exhibition space spread

Dome
The central focus of the Australian War Memorial in Canberra is the Hall of Memory, with its distinctive copper-sheathed dome that adorns the room's ceiling.

over three levels. Regular lectures, film screenings and guided tours are available, and there are frequent special exhibitions, including some from overseas. The gallery can be called on *(02) 6240 6502.*

Questacon is Australia's leading interactive science centre, aiming to bring together fun and education in a combination that makes science relevant for everyone. The centre includes over 200 interactive exhibitions, seven major displays and daily science shows, and they can be called on *(02) 6270 2800.*

Cockington Green was originally opened in 1979, and is one of the premier visitor attractions in Canberra. The spot is most notable for the stunning collection of miniature building displays, taken from parts all over Britain and recreated to scale down to the smallest detail. There is also a minature steam train to ride and an expansive collection of landscaped gardens to view. Cockington Green is located at Gold Creek Village only 10 minutes from the Canberra City Centre, and they can be called for bookings on *1800 627 273.*

The Telstra Tower provides telecommunications facilities for the city of Canberra, but is also a popular place for tourists.

The Australian War Memorial

The War Memorial in Canberra commemorates the Australians who gave their lives for their country, and the building houses a collection of relics, models, displays and records from all theatres of war.

At a height of 195 metres it is located on the summit of Black Mountain, and the viewing gallery near the top provides an impressive 360 degree view of Canberra and the countryside around it. In the lower level of the entrance foyer there is the "Making Connections" exhibition, which traces the history of Australian telecommunications from early settlement.

Besides Queanbeyan, Canberra has other towns its vicinity. A number of people prefer to enjoy the country hospitality of villages like Bungendore near Lake George and commute to work. Others, have a house in Yass, a pleasant place on the Hume Highway or on the road to Yass and also commute.

Other Places

Norfolk Island

Norfolk Island is a three million year old volcanic outcrop located in the South Pacific Ocean, approximately 1000 kilometres east of the Australian coast. Call Norfolk Island Tourism on *6723 22147* for more information.

VICTORIA

Victoria is located on the south-east corner of the Australian continent, and it can boast an exciting mixture of old and new, metropolitan and regional, beautiful coastal areas along with prosperous inland communities. Melbourne is Victoria's capital city and the second largest in Australia, and is known for its love of sport and cultural pursuits.

Portion of the Twelve Apostles, Great Ocean Road

VIC

Greater Melbourne Region

With a population of just over 3 million, Melbourne is the second largest city in Australia. The combination of the pleasant location on the banks of the Yarra River and a spectacular range of culture, eating and fashion has led many to judge Melbourne as one of the most livable cities in the world.

Melbourne Population: 3,200,000. Climate: Average temperatures: January max 26°C - min 14°C; July max 13°C - min 6°C. Average annual rainfall: 656mm.

Situated on the shores of Port Phillip Bay with the Yarra River flowing through the city, Melbourne is the capital of Victoria. The nation's second largest city and often seen to be in competition with Sydney, Melbourne is considered by many to be the best place in Australia to live. Victoria is know as the "Garden State" and this is never more evident than in its capital city, with the tree lined streets and Yarra

Federation Square
With its star architecture and almost barren forecourt The Square reflets the feel of Australia's interior.

River parklands pleasantly complementing the skyscrapers of the Central Business District. Known for its trendiness and sophistication, its love of fashion and food and a healthy respect for arts and entertainment, Melbourne was voted as the world's most livable city in 2002. It is renowned as the best spot for culture in Australia, whether it be the proliferation of great restaurants and cosy cafes, sporting facilities and theatres, or the thriving pub and nightclub scene. The clever planning makes it an easy city to navigate for those who are visiting, and Melbourne has also maintained its trademark system of trams. But it is a certain indefinable element that makes those who live there rave about it so much: a certain soul, a touch of style, a sense of substance that is difficult to convey in words.

Settlers in Van Diemen's Land had known for years that there was good grazing land in the Port Phillip area, but had been refused permission to settle. Hence, the settlement of Melbourne did not begin under official circumstances. Aware that their land was becoming overstocked, a group of Tasmanian settlers formed the Port Phillip Association with the intention of procuring further pastoral land. John Batman defied the settlement ban in 1835, setting sail on the 10th of May to explore Port Phillip for land. After landing with a party, Batman 'bought' 600,000 acres of land from the local Aborigines for only a few axes and trade goods. The area encompassed both Melbourne and Geelong, and a small plaque marking the city's birth can be seen on the north side of Flinders Street between Market and William Street.

But the authorities were quick to act on the fact that Batman had not gone through the official avenues. That same year, the NSW Governor Sir Richard Bourke issued a proclamation stating that all land purchased would be dismissed as if the Aborigines were trespassers on Crown lands. Bourke proposed that a township be marked out and allotments be sold, and in 1836 he was authorised by to form a settlement. The Port Phillip district was constituted as a separate colony when the Australian Colonies Government Act was passed in 1850, and by this time the population was over 80,000. But it was the discovery of gold around Ballarat that really pushed Victoria forward: people flocked from all over the world, and by 1854 the colony's population had reached 300,000. Over £100 million worth of gold was mined from the earth during the 1850s, securing Melbourne's position as an important financial centre. It was this prosperity that continued to characterise the city throughout the twentieth century.

If looking for a place to start to take in the cosmopolitan sights that Melbourne has to offer, there is an Observation

The Yarra River at Night

The city of Melbourne straddles the Yarra River with the Victorian Arts Centre, Southbank and the Casino on the south side and the commercial and financial districts on the northside.

Deck available on the 55th level of the Rialto Towers on Collins Street. The tower is the tallest office structure in the Southern Hemisphere at 253 metres, and offers stunning 360-degree views which stretch 60km to the horizon. Showing all the Central Business District has to offer, the Observation Deck also takes in impressive views of the Yarra River, Port Phillip and the surrounding mountains and ocean. The Flinders Street Station can be found at the heart of the city, and the attractive 1899 domed building is one of the most common meeting places in Melbourne. A walk along the Yarra River also makes for a pleasant way to view the city's sights: the bridge can be crossed at Flinders Station along the banks of the river, which adjoins the Royal Botanic Gardens in the south. The gardens feature 41 hectares of lawns, trees and ornamental lakes, and are regarded as one of the finest examples of landscape gardening in the world.

Melbourne is considered the fashion capital of Australia, and has an enormous selection of clothes and accessories boutiques. Collins Street is home to a huge number of shops: there are more designer label boutiques than you could possibly afford to visit, and it is linked to Bourke Street by a network of arcades and alleys full of specialty shops. 234 Collins is a complex dedicated to fashion, while Australia on Collins is another fashion mecca that boasts an elaborate food court. The Bourke Street Mall on the other hand is in the heart of the city, between Swanston and Elizabeth Street, and offers fantastic shopping. Dominated by the David Jones and Myer Department Stores, other arcades running off the Mall include the Centrepoint Mall and The Walk. For an alternative shopping experience, head to the Queen Victoria Markets on the corner of Victoria and Elizabeth Streets. A heritage shopping institution that has been operating since 1866, a wide range of clothing and food can be purchased here.

If the aim is to gain a more definitive view of what Melbourne is like, there are a number of suburbs outside the Central Business District that deserve a visit. St Kilda is a place much loved by its residents, and its contemporary streets have featured heavily on the popular Australian drama "The Secret Life of Us". The Esplanade runs along the beach and leads to the St Kilda Pier, where a kiosk built on the corner in 1904 still remains. Luna Park can be found at Lower Esplanade, and like the equivalent in Sydney, has been entertaining the locals with amusement rides since the first half of last century. Just

to the north, Parkville is home to the Melbourne University campus, which is set amidst fashionable homes, office buildings and Victorian terraces. The suburb of Flemington is home to one of the most handsome sporting facilities in the world, the Flemington Racecourse. Every November it plays host to Australia's most popular annual sporting event, the Melbourne Cup.

Visitor Information:

The Victoria Visitor Information Centre is at Federation Square, *(03) 9658 9658*.

Their information booth in Bourke Street Mall, between Elizabeth and Swanston Street.

The Victorian Tourism Information Service can be called on *132 842*.

Points of Interest:

The Melbourne Museum was established to replace the Museum of Victoria, with the exhibitions focussing on the natural environment and new technologies. The facilities

---

Collins Street near Swanston Street.
An early morning in the city featuring the ubiquitous tram and taxi, with the Manchester Unity Building and Town Hall in the background.

Melbourne city viewed from the south.
This scene takes in Flinders Street Station, St Paul's Anglican Cathedral, Federation Square and Princes Bridge with the high rise of the financial district in the background.

include an Aboriginal Centre, a Forest Gallery, a Mind and Body Gallery, Technology Exhibitions and a Science Gallery. Nearby is the heritage Royal Exhibition Building in Carlton Gardens *(03 9270 5000)*, as well as the IMAX Theatre, *(03) 9663 5454*. The Melbourne Museum can be found at the Carlton Gardens, the phone number is *(03) 8341 7777*.

The Immigration Museum takes visitors through a cultural tour using interactive computer displays and permanent physical exhibits. Personal stories are recounted by immigrants themselves, providing insights into the emotions and memories of immigration experiences. The museum is located in the Old Customs House on the corner of 400 Flinders Street and William Street, *(03) 9927 2700*.

The Scienceworks Museum includes exhibitions which offer a detailed exploration of the human body and its mechanics (Stayin' Alive), and a 'behind-the-scenes' look at producing special effects for movies and television (The Sequel). Also included in the complex is the fascinating Melbourne Planetarium. Science-works is a short 10 minute drive from the city centre, and occupies the futuristic cylindrical building in 2 Booker Street, *(03) 9392 4800*.

The State Library was established in 1856, and is the oldest public library in Australia. It contains over one million books and periodicals, as well as overseas manuscripts, maps, microfilms, a multimedia catalogue, paintings and photographs. The State Library can be found on the corner of Swanston and La Trobe Streets, *(03) 8664 7000*.

Old Melbourne Gaol has one remaining cell block that was preserved by the National Trust as a penal museum. The museum has a unique collection which traces the story of transportation, convicts, and the development of Victoria's penal system. The gaol is located in Russell Street, near Victoria Street, and can be called on *(03) 9663 7228*.

Chinatown can be found in Little Bourke Street, and extends from Exhibition Street to Swanston Street. It contains many restaurants from the most economical to the extremely expensive. The Chinese Museum is in 22 Cohen Place, *(03) 9662 2888*.

The Parliament House is a Victorian construction through

City Skyline at dusk

A corner of Fitzroy Gardens.

which guided tours can be taken. The State Houses of Parliament were built in stages between 1856 and 1930, and have never actually been finished as the dome and facades to the side and rear were never added. The Parliament is in Spring Street at the top of Bourke Street, *(03) 9651 8911.*

The Old Treasury is a fine public building that was restored and converted to a museum, before being re-opened in 1994. There are three permanent exhibitions which encompass the past history and contemporary life of the city, its art, culture and architecture. The treasury is situated in Spring Street at the top of Collins Street, *(03) 9651 2233.*

St Patrick's Cathedral is a Gothic Revival cathedral that was constructed out of Footscray bluestone. It was completed in 1897, except for the spires, which were added in 1936. Inconguorusly, There is a statue in the churchyard of the great Irish liberator, Daniel O'Connell, which is a replica of that which stands in O'Connell Street, Dublin. The Cathedral contains many beautiful works of art, and is located at 1 Cathedral Place, which runs off Lansdowne Street in East Melbourne, *(03) 9662 2233.*

Federation Square is the first major city project to break Melbourne's traditional rectangular grid pattern, joining the CBD to the Yarra river. This complex series of structures, the winner of an international design competition, is located on the intersection of Flinders Street and Swanston Street.

La Trobe's Cottage was the colony's first Government House.

La Trobe brought the house with him in the ship *Fergusson*, along with his family and possessions. The National Trust supervised the re-creation of the buildings, and they contain many of the original furnishings. The Cottage is on the corner of Birdwood Road and Dallas Brooks Drive, in the Domain at South Yarra, call *(03) 9654 4711* for bookings.

Victorian Arts Centre Complex can be found on the banks of the Yarra River, and comprises theatres, the Melbourne Concert Hall, the Performing Arts Museum and the National Gallery of Victoria. As well as the performance and exhibition spaces, the Victorian Arts Centre has several restaurants. The George Adams Gallery has an extensive collection and can be called on *(03) 9281 8194.* The Performing Arts Museum has regularly changing exhibitions. The Victorian Arts Centre can be called on *(03) 9281 8000.*

The Princes Bridge is Melbourne's oldest and grandest, and is located at the point where Swanston Street becomes St Kilda Road. It was built around 1886, replacing a wooden bridge that had been opened by La Trobe in 1850.

The Melbourne Town Hall was built between 1867 and 1870, and the portico added in 1887. It is worth going inside

The Exhibition Centre
These ornate builidngs grace Carlton Gardens. The formal opening of Australia's First Parliament was held here.

the main hall to see the chandeliers, murals and organ and the rest of its recently restored interior. The Town Hall was one of the main venues for concerts before the advent of the Concert Hall in St Kilda Road. The Town Hall can be found on Swanston Street Walk, *(03) 9658 9779.*

The Crown Entertainment Complex is often described as 'the city under one roof', and indeed its restaurants, theatres, cinemas, Crown Towers Hotel, bars, nightclubs, showrooms, cocktail lounges, shopping boutiques and unabated gambling opportunities at the Crown Casino, do give the impression of a mini metropolis. The complex is in Southbank and the Casino is at 8 Whiteman Street, *(03) 9292 8888.*

Outlying Areas in the Greater Melbourne Region

Mornington Peninsula

The Nepean Highway follows the eastern shore of Port Phillip Bay for 97km via the city of Frankston, to the seaside resort of Portsea. On the way it passes picturesque peninsula beaches such as Dromana, Rosebud and Sorrento. At Dromana, the Arthur's Seat Scenic Chairlift ride *(03 5987 2565)* offers great views of Melbourne, Port Phillip Bay and the Mornington Peninsula. The Mornington Peninsula Visitor Information Centre can be found at Point Nepean Road in Dromana, *1800 804 009.*

Tynong

To the east of Melbourne is the town of Tynong on the Princes Highway, on the way to Melbourne from Sale. Here you will find Victoria's Farm Shed, Australia's leading farm animal theatre that features parades, milking, shearing and sheep dog displays. For more information call *(03) 5629 2840.* Also at Tynong is the Gumbuya Recreation and Leisure Park, a 174 hectare recreation park, *(03) 5629 2613.*

Bass

Bass is located on the Bass Highway, on the way to Phillip Island from Melbourne. The Giant Worm Museum, on the Bass Highway, is a unique attraction and education facility. They do actually have giant worms and many other historical and hands-on displays, *(03) 5678 2222.*

Dandenong Ranges

The Dandenongs are only 35km east of Melbourne, and the

Bridges in Frankston, Mornington Peninsula

area is ideal for picnics, bushwalks and wildlife observation. It is an extremely popular destination with Melbournians and tourists for both daytrips and weekend escapes. The 630 metre high Mt Dandenong offers a panoramic view of Melbourne from its strategic lookout points. It is also home to the Puffing Billy (see below).

VIC

Yarra Valley Region

The Yarra Valley is an area renowned for its natural beauty, full of mountains, forests, national parks and wineries.

Healesville

Population: 8,150. Climate: The climate can be brisk in winter, with snow on the higher peaks. Average temperatures: January max 26°C - min 11.2°C; July max 12.2°C - min 4.2°C.

Situated 60 km east of Melbourne at the junction of Watts River and Grace Burn Creek, Healesville is the commercial centre of the surrounding Yarra Valley. A gateway to towering ash forests, waterfalls and fern bowers, the town is surrounded on all sides by an extravagant series of mountain ranges. One of Victoria's most picturesque mountain highway climbs can be found in Healesville, extending to Marysville over the Black Spur through forests of mountain ash, beech and wattle. The rolling hills of Healesville are also dotted with vineyards, and recent times have seen winemaking take on a greater role in the region.

Healesville and the surrounding areas were originally settled by the Wurrundjeri Aboriginal group, also known as the Yarra Yarra, who lived in the Coranderrk Aboriginal Reservation on Badger Creek from 1863. Unfortunately the settlement earned a name for itself, not for any positive reasons, but because of the large amount of Aboriginals who had died from disease and maltreatment. The numbers of the Yarra Yarra people had been severely depleted by 1922, at which time the mission was closed for good. Following the closure of the mission, the land was divided up and settled by a large proportion of ex-diggers from World War I.

The business centre of Healesville is situated along an attractive boulevard that is lined with trees, the strip dominated by the historic Grand Hotel. The Maroondah Reservoir lies at a close distance from the business district, and is set in a landscaped park of trees, shrubs and flowers. One of the main tourist attractions of the area is the Healesville Sanctuary just south of the town, and it features an impressive collection of birds, mammals and reptiles. The Yarra Valley Grape Grazing Festival in February makes for a good way to soak up the wine culture of the area.

Visitor Information:

The Yarra Valley Visitor Information Centre is in The Old Courthouse on Harker Street, *(03) 5962 2600*. Email them on *info@yarravalleytourism.asn.au*, or visit the site online at *www.yarra valleytourism.asn.au*.

Yarra Valley

Points of Interest:

The Hedgend Maze is a giant hedge carved into a maze, with cryptic messages to solve on the way to help you find your way through. The grounds make for a pleasant picnic setting. The Hedgend Maze can be found at at 163 Albert Road, and their phone number is *(03) 5962 3636.*

Badger Weir and Donnelly's Weir have bushland walks and superb picnic-barbecue areas. For the more energetic walking tracks, explore local National Parks and Forests.

Queen's Park, in the centre of the township, is ideal for picnics with its barbeque facilities, and has a sports oval, tennis courts, children's playground and swimming pool.

The Healesville Sanctuary is one of the most popular attractions in the Yarra Valley. The sanctuary is the only place where the platypus has been bred in captivity. There are also koalas, wombats, kangaroos and emus, and a Nocturnal House with some of Australia's least-seen animals such as the Leadbeater possum, kowari and sugar gliders. The Sanctuary is located on Badger Creek Road, *(03) 5957 2800.*

The Yarra Valley Tourist Railway winds between Healesville and the old historic tunnel at Tarrawarra, at a distance of 11km. Trolley rides can be taken from Healesville Station through an old 100m brick-lined tunnel. Just out of Yarra Glen is the historic Gulf Station, which is worth a visit.

Wineries

The following is a list of some of the wineries located in the Yarra Valley: **Dimension Domaine Chandon** - Maroondah Highway, Coldstream, *(03) 9739 1110.* **Yering Station** - Melba Highway, Yering Station, *(03) 9730 0100.* **Yarra Burn Winery** - Settlement Road, Yarra Junction, *(03) 5967 1428.* **McWilliams Lillydale Estate** - 45 Davross Court, Seville, *(03) 5964 2016.* **Five Oaks Vineyard** - 60 Aitken Road, Seville, *(03) 5964 3704.* **Kelly Brook Winery** - Fulford Road,

Lake Eildon

Wonga Park, *(03) 9722 1304. Bianchet Winery* - Victoria Road, Lilydale, *(03) 9739 1779*. **Warramate Vineyard** - 27 Maddens Lane, Gruyere, *(03) 5964 9219*. **St Huberts Vineyard** - St Huberts Road, Coldstream, *(03) 9739 1118*. **Fergusson's Winery** - Wills Road, Yarra Glen, *(03) 5965 2237*. **De Bortoli Winery & Restaurant** - Pinnacle Lane, Dixons Creek, *(03) 5965 2271*. **Shantell Vineyard** - Melba Highway, Dixons Creek, **(03) 5965 2155**. **Long Gully Estate** - Long Gully Road, Healesville, *(03) 9510 5798*.

Outlying Towns in the Yarra Valley Region

Marysville

Situated 36km north-east of Healesville, Marysville is high in the Great Dividing Range, 500 metres above sea level. It has great forests, tree-fern gullies and is a cool and welcome retreat. In winter, nearby Lake Mountain offers one of the best cross-country ski areas outside Scandinavia. Steavenson Falls, the tallest in Victoria, cascade 82 metres in three leaps and are floodlit at night. For more information on Marysville,

contact the Visitor Information Centre at 11 Murchison Street, *(03) 5963 4567*.

Eildon and Alexandra

These towns are the gateways to Lake Eildon and Fraser National Park. Both have facilities for bushwalking, camping and all sorts of outdoor activities. Alexandra is 69km north of Healesville, and Eildon is 26km east of Alexandra. The Visitor Centre at 36 Grant Street, Alexandra, *(03) 5772 1100* will assist with further enquiries.

Warburton

This town is a mountain retreat in the heart of the Warburton Ranges. Popular as a conference venue, attractions include the beautfiul Donna Buang Rainforest Gallery and the treetop observation deck. There are also the stunning river walks, providing a unique opportunity to enjoy the Yarra River at its best. This small town boasts six bridges, so easy to choose the length of your walk. For more information contact the Warburton Water Wheel and Visitor Centre on *(03) 5966 5996* or at: *info@warburton-ranges.net.au*

VIC

Gippsland Region

The Gippsland region stretches from the east of Bairnsdale to Phillip Island, north of Morwell and Traralgon down to Wilsons Promontory, and to the Ninety Mile Beach on the southern coast, taking in just about everything in between. It covers the beautiful landscapes of fertile countryside and is full of various natural wonders, from mountains and forests to rivers and beaches.

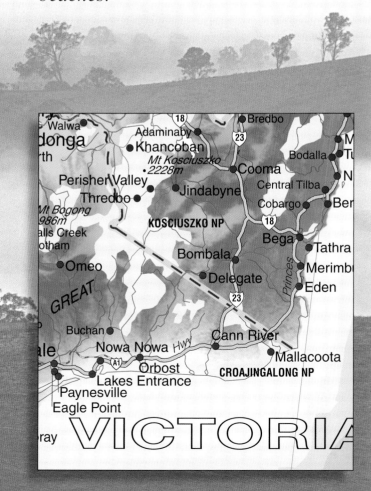

Lakes Entrance Population: 7,000. Climate: Lakes Entrance has a temperate climate. The average maximum temperature in summer is 33°C, in winter 21°C.

Located 360km east of Melbourne and the gateway to Gippsland Lakes, the town of Lakes Entrance is the largest inland water system in Australia. The Gippsland Lakes stretch 90km down the coast and cover 400 square kilometres, and are connected to five major river systems. Lakes Entrance is the largest town on Ninety Mile Beach, and possesses a spectacular hinterland with mountains, rivers and forests. Wildlife in the area includes dolphins, water birds, kangaroos, wombats, koalas and bush birds. The Lakes National Park and the Gippsland Lakes Coastal Park have both been classified as national parkland, and together they cover 17,880 hectares. Lakes Entrance is the biggest fishing port in Victoria, and the importance of the industry in the town has continued to grow over several decades. In that time it has became one of the most important deep sea fishing locations in the whole of Australia.

John Reeves was the first European to charter the lakes in 1843, and the settlement that developed over the next decade eventually led to the river being used for trade. The *Georgina Smith* was the first large vessel to sail into the lakes, and Lakes Entrance played an important role in the trade of the region over the next 100 years.

If you want to enjoy Lakes Entrance's proximity to the Gippsland waters, there are several different river cruises that can be enjoyed in the town. While sightseeing cruises and lunch cruises are available, small boats can be hired if you wish to explore the lakes on your own. For a fantastic view of the area, Jemmy's Point Lookout looks down over Lakes Entrance and the vast nearby ocean. For a closer look at the town and the beach, there is a 2.3km walking track that continues from Lakes Entrance down to the Ninety Mile Beach. Some interesting wooden statues can also be seen along the promenade: a number of tree stumps have been carved into famous images of Australia at war, and were the efforts of a local wood carver.

Visitor Information:

The Lakes Entrance Visitor Information Centre is on the corner of Marine Parade and The Esplanade, and can be called on *(03) 5155 1966*. Contact them via email at *lakesvic@egipps.vic.gov.au* or explore the web page at *www.lakesandwilderness.com.au*.

Points of Interest:

Nyerimilang Park on Lake King, Kalimna West Road, Nungurner, overlooks Rigby, Fraser and Flannagan Islands. With Nyerimilang an Aboriginal word for "Chain of Lakes," it has bullock driving demonstrations and field days, and there are bushwalks, as well as barbecue and picnic facilities. The Nyerimilang Park can be called on *(03) 5156 3253*.

Griffiths' Sea Shell Museum and Marine Display has over 90,000 shells on display from around the world, and there is also a model railway room for locomotive enthusiasts. The museum can be found at 125 Esplanade, *(03) 5155 1538*.

Phillip Island Population: 6,700

Situated 129km from Melbourne, Phillip Island is known as the home of the fairy penguins. At dusk the famous penguins emerge from the surf, completely ignoring the thousands of curious onlookers. The native Australian animals are the smallest of their species at only 33cm, and are the #1 tourist attraction in Victoria. The island also has the Phillip Island Nature Park, which is divided into a number of outlets for wildlife viewing and information. There are more than fifty places to stay in Cowes alone, the main tourist centre of Phillip Island, and other alternatives include the districts of Newhaven, Rhyll and San Remo.

Visitor Information:

The Phillip Island Information Centre can be found at Newhaven on Phillip Island Tourist Road, *(03) 5956 7447*. The web page at *www.phillipisland.net.au* offers comprhehensive information, or call the accommodation booking service on *1300 366 422*.

The Penguin Parade Visitors Centre can be found off Ventnor Road, and you can call them on *(03) 5956 8300*.

Outlying Towns in the Gippsland Region

Mallacoota

Reached via Genoa on the NSW/Vic border, Mallacoota is surrounded by the Croajinolong National Park. Mallacoota is situated in one of Victoria's most remote and peaceful lakeland settings, and there are many walking tracks through the Croajinolong National Park. Contact the Information Centre in nearby Cann River on *(03) 5158 6351*.

Orbost

Orbost is the railhead for East Gippsland, and is situated on the Snowy River 16km from the coast. It is the gateway to Marlo where the Snowy meets the Brodribb River, and where a sandbar allows the rivers to reach the sea. Scenic drives and walks are the main attraction of this stunning region. The Snowy River Visitor Centre in Lochiel Street can be contacted on *(03) 5154 2424*.

Omeo

Omeo is on the way to the snowfields at Mt Hotham, about one-and-a-half hours drive from Bairnsdale. The town's history lies in timber, gold and cattle, and is an ideal place to stop for a meal and to hire skis and chains during winter.

Lakes Entrance

Pinnacles, Phillip Island

It is even close enough to stay in the town and visit the snow of Alpine National Park daily. Many people visit Omeo for trout fishing, bushwalking and canoeing.

Buchan

In the foothills of Snowy River Country, 56km from Lakes Entrance, lies the town of Buchan which is well known for its limestone caves. The reserve surrounding them has picnic facilities, barbecues, and lots of kangaroos. There is also a swimming pool fed by an extremely cool underground stream. The rangers conduct tours through the caves daily. Call the Visitor Centre in Lakes Entrance, *(03) 5155 1966*.

Nowa Nowa

Situated approximately 24km from Lakes Entrance, Nowa Nowa is predominately a timber milling town. Numerous forest drives off the Princes Highway lead to delightful barbecue spots. Close by are the trestle bridge and the Mundic Creek waterfall at Cosstick Weir. The arm from Lake Tyers extends to the town, offering good fishing.

Paynesville

Known as the boating capital of the Gippsland Lakes, Paynesville is 18km south-east of Bairnsdale. McMillan Strait, Newlands Arm and canals provide sheltered moorings for boats, and from Paynesville there are many places to go by boat. There is also a ferry that runs from Paynesville to Raymond Island, which is inhabited by wildlife.

Bairnsdale

Bairnsdale, just over 30km west of Lakes Entrance, was the port for its pastoral hinterland in the days before road transport. Now it supports a number of secondary industries. The Bairnsdale Information Centre is at 240 Main Street, *(03) 5152 3444*, and they have details of all attractions.

Eagle Point

Eagle Point is only 15 kilometres from Bairnsdale. The well known Mitchell River silt jetties are found at Eagle Point. Eagle Point is also known for its fishing, both in Lake King and the Mitchell River.

Sale

Situated on the Melbourne side of Lakes Entrance, Sale is the operations centre for the nearby Bass Strait oil fields of Esso-BHP. There is also a large RAAF training base located here. Cullinen Park, off Foster Street, is the site of the historic Port of Sale where, in days of yore, steamers tied up after their long trip from Melbourne. From Sale there are roads leading to the Ninety Mile Beach. The Central Gippsland Visitor Information Centre is at 8 Foster Street, *(03) 5144 1108*.

Stratford

Stratford is a town located on the Avon River 17km north of Sale. A Shakespearean Festival is held here in April every year. For more details call *(03) 5145 6133*, or email *dmccubb@netspace.net.au*.

Mount Buller

VIC
Victorian Alps Region

Lying to the north east of Melbourne and stretching endlessly towards the New South Wales border, the Victorian Alps meet with the Snowy Mountains and the Mount Kosciuszko National Park in the neighboring state. The closest snow slopes are located only 100km away from Melbourne, while Falls Creek and Mount Hotham are 360km away.

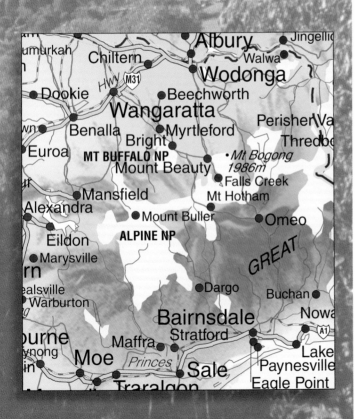

Bright Population: 3,000. Climate: Though Bright is the gateway to several ski resorts, it averages summer temperatures of 26C to 31C.

Situated on the Ovens River in the foothills of the Victorian Alps, Bright is the gateway to the ski resorts of the region. While many assume that Bright is a chilly town all year round, it is truly a place that changes with the seasons. During summer the Owens River is full of people swimming and fishing, with horseriding and bush walking also popular activities. In autumn the European and Asian trees left by the pioneers become a blaze of gold, orange, red and yellow, and the town celebrates with the Autumn Festival. Winter brings snow to the mountains surrounding Bright, and the skiers arrive in their thousands for the slopes at the nearby alpine resorts. And in Spring, the elms, poplars, wattles and fruit trees light up the town. It is the time of the Bright Festival.

First explored by pioneers Hume and Hovell in 1824, it was the discovery of gold along the Buckland River in 1853 that kick started the Victorian Alps district. The arrival of over 3000 miners, rampant disease that killed over 1000, and racists riots between chinese and european miners ending in many deaths, caused a police station to eventually be established in 1861. In 1861 the future site of Bright became the administrative centre for the Buckland Gold District. The name was later changed to honour British politician John Bright. Gold was eventually exhausted in the area, and while pine plantations helped the town through the depression,

The Village of Bright from the surrounding hills.

The Village of Bright.

tourism has been what has sustained Bright through the second half of the twentieth century.

Bright is often passed through by tourists heading for the ski slopes of the Victorian Alps, with the major ski centres including Falls Creek, Mt Buffalo and Mt Hotham. The pretty village of Bright sparkles against its backdrop of dark green-clad hills, and having welcomed visitors for more than a century is one of Australia's longest established holiday destinations. Some of the most popular walks are to the Clearspot, Huggins and Mt Porepunkah lookouts, which offer panoramic views of the village.

Visitor Information:

The Bright Tourist Information Centre can be found at 119 Gavan Street, and can be called on *1800 500 117*. Email them at *bright@dragnet.com.au*.

Points of Interest:

The Historical Museum of Bright has been established in the town's disused railway station. The link to Wangaratta was originally established in 1890, and when the line was terminated in 1952 it was converted into a museum. Including photos and interesting items from the town's past, the Tourist Information Centre can be called for information.

The Bright Art Gallery & Cultural Centre has a comprehensive art collection, as well as a number of rare minerals and gems. Over the Easter period the gallery is host to the annual national Autumn Art Exhibition, with over 800 paintings on display. The gallery also holds an exhibition to coincide with the Bright Festival in spring, and visitors so inclined can check out the oddity that is the largest cuckoo clock in Australia. The gallery can be found at 28 Mountbatten Avenue, call *(03) 5750 1660*.

Gallery 90 has original paintings, pottery, leather, handpainted clothing, jewellery, handpainted porcelain, traditional cottage crafts, and much more. Housed in a restored local granite and bluestone cottage that dates back to 1881, it can be found at 90 Gavan Street, *(03) 5755 1385*.

Walking Tracks around Bright are marked by sign posts and yellow track markers fixed to trees and posts. Maps and guides are available from the newsagent and the Tourist Information Centre for walks further afield. The climb to Mt Buffalo commences at the Park entrance and climbs through 11km of varied scenery, to arrive at the oval below the Mt Buffalo Chalet. For the less energetic, there is a wide variety of tours, both half and full day, to various attractions around Bright and the high country. Contact the Tourist Information Centre for further information.

Falls Creek

Located 62km from Bright and 356km from Melbourne, Falls Creek is a true alpine village. With a reputation as one of the most exclusive and expensive ski resorts in Victoria, the village sits in a unique Nordic bowl that allows access to both sides of the mountain via lifts. As Falls Creek is situated right next to a river, they are able to offer a "snow guarantee" to visitors with their snow making machine. The amount of facilities available easily matches Falls Creek's reputation as an exclusive holiday spot, with plenty of places to hire gear, learn how to ski, shop, grab a bite to eat, as well as bars and nightclubs. Much of the accommodation resorts are in close proximity to the ski fields.

While the ski season opens on the Queen's Birthday weekend in June, the resort is open for business all year round. The village has been drawing increasing numbers of tourists in the summer when the views are exceptional, the air is crisp and the wildflowers and snow gums are in bloom. Early January is an ideal time for walking and there are many tracks to explore. Mountain biking, canoeing, sailing, fishing, horseriding, abseiling, archery, camping, orienteering, a

The view from Mt Buffalo

ropes course, rafting, fishing, cable gliding, yoga and massage are all activities that can be enjoyed.

Visitor Information:

The Alpine Discovery Centre is located on Bogong High Plains Road at Mt Beauty, *(03) 5754 1962*. Visit the website at *www.fallscreek.com.au*.

Porepunkah

The small town of Porepunkah is 6km from Bright, at the junction of the Buckland and Ovens Rivers, and the turnoff to Mount Buffalo National Park. Originally named Port Punka, the area was part of a cattle station which reached from Eurobin to Bright. It is a quiet, peaceful spot, and has a hotel, post office, petrol station, general store, several riverside caravan parks, and a growing number of flats and motels. The two rivers provide excellent fishing for trout.

The Snow Country

Mount Buffalo

The mountain is 32km from Bright, and 320km from Melbourne. Operating only 3 poma lifts and 2 chairlifts, Mt Buffalo is a small, sheltered ski field that focuses on laid-back family enjoyment. It is comprised mainly of gentle downhill slopes. Serious skiers looking for a challenge should head elsewhere, although cross-country ski trails are available here in the Mt Buffalo National Park.

Mount Hotham

Mount Hotham is 55km from Bright, and 354km from Melbourne. It is Australia's highest alpine village at 1750m, and all accommodation is only minutes from the ski runs. The runs are classified as 27% beginner, 36% intermediate and 37% advanced, and there are over 40 marked and groomed runs on the slopes. Call the Mount Hotham Alpine Resort Management Board, Great Alpine Road, Mount Hotham, *(03) 5759 3550*.

Myrtleford

Situated 29km north-west of Bright on the Ovens Highway, Myrtleford is at the foot of Mount Buffalo. The district's main industries are timber, hops, tobacco and cattle. The town has 3 hotels, 2 motels, a caravan park, 2 camping reserves, bunkhouse and lodge accommodation. There are facilities for all types of sport, fishing (trout and redfin), horse riding, hang gliding, bush-walking, and of course, skiing.

VIC

North East Victoria Region

The North East Victoria region stretches from the high snow-covered alpine country in the east, to the Goulburn River situated in the west, and north to the Murray River and New South Wales border.

Shepparton   Population: 32,700. Climate: Shepparton is well known for its ideal climate for growing agricultural products. In Febuary 2004 the city enjoyed a maximum temperature of 32.3°C, and a minimum temperature of 14°C. Average rainfall is 26.5mm.

Situated in the Lower Goulburn Valley in the northern 'centre' of Victoria, the sunny city of Shepparton is well known as the "Food Bowl of Australia". The surrounding Goulburn Valley district is one of Australia's largest sources of fruit produce: irigation channels cross through the region, and neat rows of fruit trees are eveywhere to be seen. With the SPC Ardmona canned fruit company operating out of Shepparton, their peaches, pears, apples, plums and other fruits and vegetables are packaged and exported worldwide. A Campbell's Soup Australia factory is also located in the city, and the surrounding areas of Shepparton are responsible for a substantial amount of Australia's agricultural output, including cereal crops, grapes, wine, beef, wool and lamb. Charles Bonney and Joseph Hawdon were the first Europeans to enter Shepparton in 1838, setting up camp while shifting cattle from Albury to Adelaide. A settlement was established

A portion of the town of Shepparton from the air

by Sherbourne Sheppard in 1843, though it was the building of an irrigiation system in 1912 that began the agricultural focus that Shepparton is so famous for today. In 1917 the famous Shepparton Preserving Company (SPC) set up shop, and another major cannery named Ardmona was established in the 1920's. Shepparton's fate as a major agricultural producer was sealed when both the Cleckheaton Woollen Mill and Campbell's Soups arrived later in the century.

Situated near the Goulburn, Broken and Murray River systems, Shepparton has plenty to offer those who enjoy fishing, boating and other water activities. As a reflection of the Goulburn Valley's importance as an agricultural district, there are more than a few festivals in Shepparton that revolve around food. International Dairy Week is held in January every year, the Fruit Salad Day Market is held the following month, while the SheppARTon Festival is held in March. And as a celebration of all the food produced in and around the city, the Shepparton Agricultural Show is held in October.

Visitor Information:

The Visitor Information Centre is at Victoria Park Lake, 534 Wyndham Street, *1800 808 839*. Online at *www.greatersh epparton.com.au*, or email *visitor@shepparton.vic.gov.au*.

Points of Interest:

The Victoria Park Lake can be found near the Visitor Information Centre, and has picnic, barbecue, skate park and shared pathway facilities. It is the leisure centre of the city.

The Eastbank Centre houses the town hall, art gallery, performing arts centre and municipal offices, and can be found in Welsford Street. Call *(03) 5832 9511*.

The Shepparton Art Gallery has an extensive collection of 4000 ceramic works by well known artists, and around 400 paintings and works on paper including artworks by McCubbin. Located within the Eastbank Centre, admission is free and they can be contacted on *(03) 5832 9861*.

The Maude Street Mall is in the heart of the city and is a shopping centre with many features including entertainment areas, loads of trees and flower beds, and plenty of parking.

A Paddlesteamer on the Murray River

The **SPC-Ardmona Factory Sales Outlet** underwent large refurbishments following the merging of the two companies in 2002, and is now one of the largest food clearance centres in the country. The outlet can be found in Mooroopna, which is just 5 minutes away from Shepparton, *(03) 5825 2444.*

The **Ardmona KidsTown** is considered one of the largest outdoor playgrounds in Australia, and some of the different rides include flying foxes, giant slides, tree houses and monkey bars. KidsTown can be found on the Peter Ross Edwards Causeway, *(03) 5831 4213.*

Echuca-Moama Population: 15,000

Located 205km from Melbourne near the junction of several major rivers, the twin towns of Echuca and Moama are on opposite sides of the Murray River. Established by former convicts Henry Hopwood and James Maiden during the mid-1800's, Echuca was once the most substantial inland river port in Australia. Scores of paddlesteamers and barges sailed in and out of the port between 1860 and 1900. The town has centred upon this history for its tourism focus, and paddlesteamers have again been traveling the waters since the old port area was restored to its former greatness in 1973. Many of the old buildings in the town have also been restored, and it was the authentic look of Echuca that led the producers of the riverboat era mini-series "All The Rivers Run" to decide to shoot there.

The riverboats and barges can be boarded by visitors, with the *P.S Pevensey* that was featured in "All The Rivers Run" being one example. Other ways to enjoy the history of Echuca include a 10 minute film telling the Port story, and the Paddlesteamer Gallery. The Port of Echuca Wharf can be called on *(03) 5482 4248.* The Historical Society Museum can also be visited, and some of the items on display include original Murray River river charts and river boat photographs. The museum's phone number is *(03) 5480 1325.* The Barmuh Forest is a 20 minute drive from Moama, and is the largest Redgum Forest in the Southern Hemisphere.

Visitor Information:

The Echuca-Moama Tourism is located at 2 Heygarth Street, Echuca, *1800 804 446.* Email them at *emt@echucamoama.com*, or visit *www.echucamoama.com.*

Outlying Towns in the North East Victoria Region

Numurkah

Situated 35km north of Shepparton on Broken Creek, Numurkah is surrounded by mostly irrigated farmland with a wide range of crops and livestock. The Numurkah Information Centre is at 42 Quinn Street, *(03) 5862 3458.*

Tocumwal

This is the first New South Wales town on the Newell Highway, situated on the banks of the Murray River. It offers a blend of old with new, from Federation era buildings to modern establishments. The Visitor Information Centre is at 41-43 Deniliquin Street, *(03) 5874 2131.*

Benalla

Back in Victoria, Benalla is 61km south-east of Shepparton, at the junction of the Hume and Midland Highways. Benalla is famous for its roses, and from October until April the Benalla Gardens provide the finest display of that bloom. The Rose Festival is held each November. The Visitor Information Centre is at 14 Mair Street, *(03) 5762 1749.*

The Old Courthouse, Benalla

Mansfield

Situated 63km south of Benalla, Mansfield is the gateway to the Mount Buller alpine resort. The town is also close to the north arm of Lake Eildon, and to Lake Nillahcootie, so in summer it is a popular spot for water sports. In winter the skiers move into town. This beautiful scenery of area was the setting for the classic "Man From Snowy River" movies. The Visitor Information Centre is at the Railway Station on the Maroondah Highway, *(03) 5775 1464.*

Mount Buller

The ski village is 47km from Mansfield, and is situated at 1600 metres, with the highest lifted point at 1788 metres. The many ski lifts are capable of moving 38,500 people an hour, and there is an equal amount of fun to be had for beginner, intermediate and advanced skiers. Call the Mt Buller Resort Management on *(03) 5777 6077.*

Violet Town

Situated 13km west of Benalla, Violet Town is on Honeysuckle Creek and at the foothills of the Strathbogie Ranges. Surveyed in 1883, it is the oldest inland town in Victoria.

Euroa

Euroa is 45km west of Benalla. Seven Creeks winds through the town with parkland on both banks. International shearing competitions are conducted in Euroa, and Wool Week has become an event known throughout Australia. The surrounding district, which includes Forlonge Memorial and Strathbogie Ranges, appeals to fisherman and bush-walkers.

Mansfield countryside

Seymour

Situated at the northern foothills of the Great Dividing Range on the Goulburn River, Seymour is 84km south of Shepparton. Trawool Valley has been classified by the National Trust for its scenic beauty. Avenel is a small township on Hughes Creek, some 20km from Seymour.

Nagambie

The gateway to the Goulburn Valley, Nagambie is 28km north of Seymour. The eastern shore of Lake Nagambie abuts the main street, with grassy picnic areas on its banks. Buckley Park at the town's southern entrance has picnic and swimming areas and a boat launching ramp. The Visitor Information Centre is at 145 High Street, *1800 444 647.*

Kyabram

Situated only 31km south-west of Echuca, Kyabram is becoming well known as an Arts and Crafts centre.

Rochester

The town of Rochester is 24km south of Echuca on the Northern Highway. It is the Hub of the North, and has palms, peppercorns, quaint shops and sleepy streets. The huge facility in the middle of town is the Devondale complex owned by the Murray Goulburn Co-operative Company.

VIC
Western District Region

The Western District of Victoria covers the whole western region of the state, and stretches from the agriculturally rich city of Mildura in the northern end down to the major exporting city of Portland in the south.

Mildura Population: 28,062. Climate: The average summer temperature in Mildura is 32°C with most days around 29°C.

Situated 560km from Melbourne on the Murray River, Mildura can boast that it enjoys 400 more hours of sunshine every year than Surfers Paradise in Queensland. The city is referred to as the "Oasis in the Desert", and for good reason. Just beyond the border of Mildura is the Great Outback, a wide brown expanse that stretches as far as the eye can see. Mildura on the other hand is a rich agricultural area, with mile upon mile of lush, productive vineyards and orchards. The area is noted for supplying a massive 80% of the nation's dried fruit, 15% of its citrus fruit, as well as 85% of the wine grapes produced in Victoria. Mildura is also a popular riverside resort that attracts hundreds of thousands of visitors every year, a welcome relief from the endless dry brown terrain and wheat fields that lie beyond the town.

Charles Sturt is assumed to be the first European to enter the area, and it is possible he may have passed along the townsite during his exploration of the Murray in 1830. While Frank Jenkins was the first to establish a station in the area, his failure to obtain a license meant that the Jamieson brothers were able to mosey on in with 6000 sheep and snatch the property away from him. Foreshadowing the rich agricultural region the area was to become, the Jamieson brothers also

Tending the Grapevines, near Mildura

Sheep Grazing

planted some grape vines. The property was officially given the name "Mildura" in 1858, an indigenous reference to the "red earth" which would prove to be so agriculturally productive.

The origin of the town as it is today can be traced back to 1885. It was that year that Alfred Deakin, the then Premier of Victoria, travelled to the United States to meet brothers George and William Chaffey. Interested in the model irrigation settlements they had established in the Californian desert, Deakin convinced the brothers to sell up and head to Australia. Pumps were installed to lift water from the Murray, and the Mildura streets were meticulously planned and laid out in an American style grid system. While some initial problems were found with salt pollution, the produce grown in the area was evidence of the irrigation's success, and Mildura's legacy as one of the nation's greatest fruit growing areas continues to this day.

The opportunity to sail down the Murray River on an old riverboat-era barge is one that many tourists take up every year. The *PS Melbourne* is an original steam driven Paddle-steamer that was built 1912, call *(03) 5023 2200* for bookings. For further details on other available cruises check out the notice-boards at Mildura Wharf, or visitors can hire boats or canoes to go on their own little adventure. Mildura also has a thriving arts and culture scene, and the Mildura Arts Centre on the riverbank is evidence of this. Contained within the centre is a sculpture park, museum and theatre. There is also an art gallery which holds a $12 million collection, including a Degas pastel and contemporary works by Australian artists. The Mildura-Wentworth Arts Festival

is also held in the city every March, and is visited by noted authors, poets and musicians from all across Australia and overseas.

Visitor Information:

The Mildura Visitor Information and Booking Centre is located at 180-190 Deakin Avenue, call *(03) 5018 8380* or *1800 039 043* for information. Email them at *tourism@mildura.vic.gov.au* or visit *www.visitmildura.com.au*.

Points of Interest:

The Mildura Arts Centre is responsible for preserving much of Mildura's history, and includes Rio Vista, the stately home of W.B. Chaffey in Cureton Avenue . There is also the Mildura Arts Centre, one of the best provincial galleries in Australia, *(03) 5018 8330*.

Woodsie's Gem Shop is Australia's largest jewellery manufacturing complex, and one of Mildura's top attractions. It includes a workshop open to visitors, a spectacular showroom where finished items are for sale, and an Aladdin's Cave full of glowing rocks and glittering crystals. The complex is on the corner of Morpung and Cureton Avenues, Nichols Point, 6km from Mildura, *(03) 5024 5797*.

The Langtree Hall Museum was Mildura's first public hall when it was built in 1889, and it houses a museum of local history and display of international dolls. Phone them at *(03) 5021 3090* for information.

Orange World is a fully operational citrus property that includes several tours. Services available for visitors include the Citrus Tour, as well as trips on the Tractor Train. Orange World can be found 7km from Mildura on the Silver City Highway, call *(03) 5023 5197*.

Portland Population: 10,000

Situated on the Victorian coast at Cape Sir William Grant, Portland it is the only deepwater port that exists between Geelong and Adelaide. For this reason the city is a major exporting centre for goods produced in both Victoria and South Australia, with some of the goods shipped out of Portland including wool, grains and and manufactured

goods. With the giant Portland Aluminium Smelter situated in the city, the prosperous fishing industry centres upon

Pink Lakes, Hattah Kulkyne National Park

deep-sea trawling, lobsters and crayfish.

As Portland was the first permanent settlement in Victoria, it is filled with historic buildings from the 1840s. There are around 100 historically-important buildings in the city, many classified by the National Trust, and they all offer Portland an old world charm. History House can be found in the old Town Hall, and includes a collection of historical items, photographs and records of Portland's early history. Call *(03) 5522 2226* for details.

The 250km Great South West Walk provides an excellent introduction to the fascinating variety of scenery and wildlife to be found in this region of Victoria. The walk begins and ends at the Visitor Centre and traverses forest, woodland, the Lower Glenelg National Park, the magnificent beaches at Discovery Bay, and the high limestone headlands at Cape Bridgewater and Cape Nelson. Cape Bridgewater is the home of the Petrified Forest, a tangle of weird tree forms fashioned by wind and water from the old root systems of the native scrub. The enormity of the rugged coastline can be experienced from cliff walks, with the powerful ocean pounding the rocks below and occasionally shooting up through blowholes.

Visitor Information:
The Portland Maritime Discovery and Visitor Information Centre is in Lee Breakwater Road, *(03) 5523 2671*.

Outlying Towns in the Western District

Red Cliffs
15km south of Mildura lies the town of Red Cliffs, which is currently enjoying a surge in development. The town gets its name from the nearby striking red cliffs which dominate the Murray River. Today the area is an important part of the citrus and dried fruits industries. Using Red Cliffs as a base, the visitor has a great variety of attractions to see. In the heart of the town, in Barclay Square, is Big Lizzie, the largest traction engine ever built in Australia, which took two years to make the journey from Melbourne.

Hattah-Hulkyne National Park Murray-Kulkyne National Park
This vast Mallee park is about 70km south of Mildura and provides striking contrasts teeming with birdlife, kangaroos, emus and colourful wildflowers. The park information centre can be reached from the Calder Highway turn-off at Hattah - also enter through Nangiloc/Colignan, call *13 19 63*.

Mungo National Park
The Park contains the unique Walls of China, a range of dunes up to 46 metre high shaped by erosion into a barrier 27km long, leaving a foreground likened to a lunar landscape, or part of the Sahara Desert. Many geological and archaeological discoveries have been made in the area, and Aboriginal ovens

can be seen which date back some 50,000 years. The site is about 110km north-east of Mildura, on a dry weather road. Phone *(03) 5021 8900* for more information.

Wentworth

The historic town of Wentworth NSW is situated where the Darling River joins the Murray, and is a 20 minute drive from Mildura. One site that you must not miss is the Old Wentworth Gaol, 1879-1927, in Beverley Street. It was designed to serve a vast outback region, and now stands as a vivid reminder of those harsh and uncompromising days when Wentworth stood on the edge of the lonely Australian inland. The Gaol can be contacted on *(03) 5027 3337*. A walk through town will take you past quaint and notable buildings, some of whch are heritage listed. The Wentworth Visitor Information Centre can be found on 66 Darling Street, *(03) 5027 3624*.

Heywood

Situated 25km north of Portland, Heywood is a rural centre with hosts of apple orchards. The main attractions in the town are the Bower Bird Museum, *(03) 5527 1660*, the Cave Hill Gardens, and Lake Condah Aboriginal Mission.

Hamilton

Known as the Wool Capital of the World, Hamilton is 58km north of Heywood in the heart of fine wool grazing country. The Hamilton Visitor Information Centre is on Lonsdale Street, *1800 807 056*, and they have information on the town's attractions, which include Lake Hamilton and the nearby Nigretta and Wannon Falls.

Macarthur

34km south of Hamilton, and 11km south of Byaduk Caves, Macarthur is also within easy reach of Mt Napier and its volcanic surrounds. Only a few kilometres south-west of the town is the Mt Eccles National Park, in which is found Lake Surprise. There are two first class walks around the crater of Mt Eccles, and camping and picnic facilities are available.

Nelson

Nelson is 70km west of Portland, and is a picturesque fishing hamlet at the mouth of the Glenelg River. It is a popular resort and has numerous bushwalks. A regular boat service takes visitors to the Margaret Rose Caves.

The Murray River

VIC

Great Ocean Road Region

The Great Ocean Road wends its way along the south eastern coastline of Victoria giving access to splendid views and wonderful natural formations such as the Twelve Apostles.

Warrnambool & The Great Ocean Road

Population: 30,000. Climate: Average temperatures: January max 23C - min 13C; July max 14C - min 6C. Wettest six months May-October.

Situated 263km south-west of Melbourne where the Princess Highway meets the Great Ocean Road, Warrnambool is a vibrant little coastal town. It is bounded on both sides by two rivers that reach to the ocean, with the Merri River to the west and the Hopkins River to the east. Attracting international attention as a prime whale watching location, Warrnambool has become known as "Victoria's Southern Right Whale Nursery." While it is not the only area in the world where whales have been known to breed, what makes Warrnambool special is that Southern Right Whales, which are amongst the largest and rarest mammals on the planet, often swim within a hundred metres of the shore at Logan's Beach. They can be viewed either from a specially constructed platform in the sand dunes or from the beach itself. The females arrive to give birth to their calves in June every year and often stay for a further 6-8 weeks, before returning to the sub-antarctic waters in late September.

The Twelve Apostles

Warrnambool is located at the west end of the Great Ocean Road, a landmark that has become synonymous with the state of Victoria. The road follows the coastline for most of its 250 kilometre length, and in some parts is the only thing separating the mountains from the surf beaches. With work on the road taking place between 1919 and 1932, it was built by 3000 First World War veterans. Using nothing more than picks and shovels, they built it in dedication to the memory of those who fought in the war. The panoramic views of the road are nothing less than breathtaking, and the landscape changes so dramatically that three different sections have been identified along the stretch: the Otway Ranges, the Surf Coast and the Shipwreck Coast. Some of the scenery to be seen includes long sections of cliff edges, headlands and hilly slopes, coastal stretches of beaches and river estuaries.

While in parts the road is narrow it is fully sealed, and the scenic route makes its way through some of Victoria's most popular resorts. Pretty coastal towns like Lorne, Apollo Bay and Port Campbell swell to capacity in the high season. But it is during the winter, when massive breakers crash into the limestone cliffs, that the challenge which confronted the captains of the small coastal vessels can be understood. In the period up to 1920, some 80 major shipping disasters were recorded between Port Fairy and Cape Otway. Of these the best known are the *Loch Ard* and the *Schomberg*, relics of which can be seen in the Flagstaff Hill Maritime Village at Warrnambool. The road also passes through some of the richest forests in Australia, including the Angahook Forest Park, the Otway National Park and the Lorne Forest Park.

Visitor Information:

The Warrnambool Visitor Information Centre is at Flagstaff Hill on Merri Street, *(03) 5564 7837*. Email *vic@warrnambool.vic.gov.au* or visit is *www.warrnamboolinfo.com.au*.

Points of Interest:

Flagstaff Hill is the vital link between the Great Ocean Road experience and the history of the Shipwreck Coast. The maritime complex nestles on a hill overlooking the infamous Shipwreck Coast, on the Great Ocean Road. The recreated maritime village offers an interactive journey through Victoria's early maritime history. The museum is on Merri

Street, call *(03) 5564 7841* for details.

Warrnambool's Foreshore area features the 20 hectare Lake Pertobe Adventure Playground, with giant slides, flying foxes and a maze. Another feature of this area is the Foreshore Promenade – walk, ride or skate around the 5.7 kilometre track which stretches from the Breakwater along the coastline to the Southern Right Whale Nursery at Logans Beach.

The Tower Hill State Game Reserve is 14km from Warrnambool, and are the remains of a volcano whose crater walls collapsed inward during its dying stages 6000 years ago. They blocked the 3km wide crater, which later filled with water. There is a sealed road leading to the main island, and there is also a Natural History Centre which conducts tours and bushwalks. Call Parks Victoria on *13 1963*.

The Hopkins Falls are 13km from Warrnambool, near Wangoom. In early summer, thousands of tiny eels (elvers) make their way up the falls to the quiet waters beyond, to grow to maturity before returning to the sea to breed.

Lorne Population: 1,200

Situated on the Erskine River and 140 km south-west of Melbourne, Lorne was the first place declared an area of Special Significance and Natural Beauty by the Victorian Government. Surrounded on three sides by forest ranges and with the Southern Ocean to the south, some of Lorne's attractions including the Erskine Falls, the Pennyroyal Valley and the Angahook-Lorne State Park.

Though the population of Lorne rests at around only 1,200, it can become quite busy during the summer season. The sidewalk cafes, eating houses and boutiques of Mountjoy Parade, along with the ocean setting, lend the town something of a Mediterranean air. The fine old buildings of the town and the beautiful natural surroundings have meant that Lorne has retained a quiet charm about it.

Visitor Information:

The Lorne Visitor Information Centre is at 144 Mountjoy Parade, *(03) 5289 1152*. Email *lornevic@primus.com.au*, or visit *www.visitsurfcoast.com*.

Sunset on the Great Ocean Road

Outlying Towns in the Great Ocean Road Region

Apollo Bay

Apollo Bay was first visited in 1840 by the Henty Brothers, founders of Portland and Mount Gambier. They established a small whaling station on what is now the golf course. One of the three major centres along the Great Ocean Road, it has all the necessary facilities - accommodation, holiday flats, caravan parks and restaurants. Apollo Bay is also an ideal touring centre for the Otway Ranges Forest Park, Otway National Park, and Melba Gully State Park. The Visitor Information Centre is on the Great Ocean Road, *(03) 5237 6529.*

Princetown

Situated on the La Trobe Creek near Gellibrand River, the surrounding limestone cliffs contain interesting fossils and formations. Gemstones can sometimes be found along the coastline, and the area is rich in flora and fauna. Given its location between the western boundary of the Otway National Park and the eastern boundary of the Port Campbell National Park, Princetown is ideal as a base for touring both.

Port Campbell

At the heart of one of Australia's most famed and photographed natural attractions, Port Campbell is a very popular resort. In 1964, 700 hectares around Port Campbell was set aside as a National Park, and in 1981 the park was extended from Princetown through to Peterborough. Port Campbell is roughly at the centre of the park, and has a crayfishing port near the mouth of the river with a safe, sandy beach. Fresh local crayfish is the town's take-away specialty.

Port Campbell National Park

Recognised as one of Australia's most scenic sections of coastline, the 1750 hectares Port Campbell National Park stretches 32km along the Great Ocean Road. The best known features are the Twelve Apostles, Loch Ard Gorge and London Bridge. Gorges, arches, islands, blowholes and stark outcrops create a dramatic foreground to the stormy Southern Ocean which stretches to the Antarctic. Here and there a sandy beach glistens in sharp contrast to the sheer cliffs and deep

The beach at Lorne, Great Ocean Road

VIC

Bellarine Peninsula Region

The Bellarine Peninsula begins with the Bass Strait to the south, and stretches as far east as The Rip at Port Phillip Heads, to Swan Bay and Port Phillip Bay in the north, and the Barwon River to the west. Geelong is the major city of the area.

Geelong Population: 200,000. Climate: Average temperatures: June max 25°C - min 13°C; July max 14°C - min 5°C.

Situated south-west of Melbourne on the shores of Corio Bay, Geelong is the largest regional city in Victoria. With a reputation as an industrial city, Geelong is the commercial centre for the pastoral and agricultural areas located nearby. In 1993, the sprawling areas of Geelong, Geelong West, Corio, Bellarine, Newtown and South Barwon were all amalgamated into the City of Greater Geelong. A major port since early settlement, the heavy industry of the city can be found next to Corio Bay on the flat areas just outside the CBD. Extensive renovations have been made to the waterfront in the last five years, and Geelong is becoming increasionly recognised as a tourist destination in itself, not just as a drive through destination to the Great Ocean Road.

It was explorers Hume and Hovell who recorded the aboriginal word "jillong" when they came to Corio Bay in 1824, and the name was given to the area in the 1830's by Governor Bourke. John Batman moved to claim the land in 1835, following instructions from the Port Phillip Association to look for new pastures to compliment those of Van Dieman's Land. Signing an agreement with 8 Aboriginal elders, the western boundary of Batman's treaty land included the furure site of Geelong. Within two years John Cowie and David Stead had travelled from Tasmania to graze sheep, and before long a wool store had been opened on the townsite. Geelong was proclaimed a town in 1838.

Industry began to grown in the town over the next 15 years, and a rivalry began to develop with the nearby Melbourne as to whom should be named as the state's capital. Geelong could rightfully claim to be the commercial centre of the state, as their exports were exceeding those of Melbourne by the end of the 1840's. But while the prosperity of the town began to decline, Geelong received a big burst of industrial development in the first half of the twentieth century, with many of those industries still remaining there today. The City of Geelong was proclaimed in 1910.

While Geelong may have a reputation as an industrial city, the Victorian architecture of many of the old buildings means that it is not without its charm. There are several

The Geelong Lifesaver Statues on the Promenade
The promenade has been redeveloped with exhibition space, cafes, a five star hotel, Cunningham Pier and gardens making an attractive setting.

---

historic buildings within walking distance of the city centre, and the Information Centre has details of a Heritage Walk that begins at the Post Office. The floral gardens of the city also make it attractive, as does the presence of the Corio Bay and the promenade on Eastern Beach. Cunningham Pier stretches out into the bay, and the foreshore has been extensively revamped to include restaurants and shopping.

Visitor Information:
The Geelong and Great Ocean Road Visitor Information Centre is in Stead Park on the Princes Highway, *(03) 5275 5797*. More information can be found at a Geelong Visitor Information Centre at the National Wool Museum at 26 Moorabool Street, *1800 620 888*. The website to visit is *www.greatoceanroad.org*.

Points of Interest:
The Geelong Heritage Centre was originally established in 1979, and is the largest regional archive and resource centre in Victoria. The centre can be found on 51 Little Malop Street, above the Geelong City Library.

The National Wool Museum is housed in a bluestone wool store and traces the story of wool from the sheep's back to the finished garment, and is the only comprehensive museum of wool in Australia. The museum can be found on the corner of Moorabool & Brougham Street, call *(03) 5227 0701*.

Geelong Gallery has some fine examples of early Australian painters and a good contemporary collection. The gallery can be found on Little Mallop Street, *(03) 5229 3645*.

The Geelong Maritime Museum has displays depicting 150 years of shipping in Corio and Port Phillip Bays, so visit the Osbourne House on Swinburne Street, *(03) 5277 3808*.

The Ford Discovery Centre features the history of car design and engineering, and offers insights into the impact of global influences and environmental change on automobiles in the future. The centre can be found on the corner of Gheringap & Brougham Streets, *(03) 5227 8700*.

Beaches
Apart from the still-water beaches in Corio Bay, Eastern Beach and St Helen's, there are the nearby still-water beaches of Port Phillip Bay. These include Portarlington, Indented Head, St Leonards, Queenscliffe and Barwon Heads. Then you come to the ocean beaches of Point Londsdale, Ocean Grove, Torquay, Jan Juc, Anglesea, Point Addis, Airey's Inlet, Fairhaven, Lorne, and the surfing mecca, Bell's Beach.

Queenscliff Population: 3,263
A township at the entrance to Port Phillip Bay, Queenscliff was named after Queen Victoria in 1853. Connected by an isthmus of the Bellarine Peninsula, the town overlooks The Rip at the entrance to the Bay. With Queenscliff having access to both Port Phillip Bay and Bass Strait, a fishing industry was established relatively early on in the town's development. Queenscliff has recently grown in popularity as a holiday destination, and is a seaside resort that has managed to retain its nineteenth century charm.

The Queenscliffe Historical Centre and Museum can be found on the corner of Hesse and Hobson Street, next to the 1889 built post office. It has around 10,000 different historical artifacts, call *(03) 5258 2511*. Another interesting monument is the impressive Fort Queensland building at the top of Gellibrand Street. Built with a strategic view of the Melbourne and Geelong shipping lanes, the first cannons were stationed during the Crimean War of the 1850's.

Visitor Information:
The Queenscliff Tourist Information Centre is located at 55 Hesse Street, and can be called on *(03) 5258 4843*.

Goldfields Region

The discovery of gold in the centre of Victoria has left a lasting impression on the state's Goldfields region. The legacy of the discovery of gold is most obvious in the cities of Ballarat and Bendigo. The influence of the Victorian-era is evident in the grand hotels and public buildings along the main streets.

Ballarat

A view of Sturt Street with buildings reflecting a style of another era

Ballarat
Population: 84,500. Climate: Ballarat experiences a temperate climate for four seasons. Average daily maximum temperature for January is 24.9°C, while for July it is 10°C. Average annual rainfall is 705 mm.

Located 113km from Melbourne and 985km from Sydney, Ballarat is the largest inland city in Victoria. Situated in the heart of the Goldfields region, Ballarat is a monument to the pioneering adventurers who left their distant homelands in search of prosperity during the gold rush of the 1850's. Also referred to as the "Garden City" and the "City of Statues", Ballarat is all these and more. Steeped in history and one of the best preserved cities in Australia, the appearance of Ballarat gives visitors an appreciation of the grandeur of past centuries. Many of the buildings display Victorian and Edwardian architecture, and there are a wide array of parks, gardens and famous statues. A monument in the city commemorates the discovery of gold in 1851, and notes some of the biggest yields made in the region. While Ballarat has traditionally been a city that prospered from its mineral and agricultural resources, the economy is now driven primarily by tourism, retail, manufacturing and community services.

In 1837, a harsh drought forced a number of Scottish settlers to leave the Geelong area in search of better pastures. William Cross Yuille established the "Ballaarat" station in the following year, and the first gold was discovered in 1851. From that point the rush was on. While much of the surface gold had been depleted by the end of the year, arrivals from England decided they would dig a little deeper. Discovering a huge amount of gold just below the Ordovician bedrock, the rush began again and drew people from all over the world. The Government was more than happy to reap the revenue from the diggings and imposed a licenseing fee, but the miners were less than happy with this arrangement. Organising a meeting to oppose the tax, a confrontation had already occurred by the end of 1851, foreshadowing the famous Eureka Stockade Rebellion which was to occur in 1854. Over 20,000 prospectors were searching for gold by the end of 1853, with close to 10,000 kg of gold shipped out of the town in that year alone. Another 77,700 kg was shipped out over the next several years.

Before long a volatile situation had developed on the goldfields. Fines and jail terms were imposed upon those who failed to pay their license fees, and when Charles Hotham became Lieutenant Governor of Victoria in June 1854 he increased the frequency of inspections and collections. Many of the miners believed the licensing fee to be financially crippling, and this was only further exacerbated by a denial of land rights and political representation. It was the murder of a digger named James Scobie in late 1854 that proved to be the catalyst for conflict. Unsatisfied with how his death had been handled by the legal system, around 5,000 diggers held a meeting outside the hotel were the murder had occurred. While the meeting began in an orderly fashion, it soon degenerated and the hotel was burned to the ground. The incensed diggers formed the Ballarat Reform League with Peter Lalor as their leader, and hostilities between miners and the authority continued. Burning their licenses in opposition to authority, around 120 men formed a crude stockade of wagons, logs and slabs on the evening of December 2, 1854. The bloody Eureka Stockade which made Ballarat famous was to ensue, and in the dawn of the 3rd the troopers attacked. Though the battle lasted only 25 minutes, around 22 diggers and 6 soldiers were killed, and 114 prisoners were taken. The battle was lost, but the miners' rights improved as a consequence.

Ballarat is one of the premier tourist destinations in Victoria, with visitors attracted to the city's architectural and goldfield heritage, as well as the parks, gardens, art and culture. The Tourist Information Centre has put together a self-guided Heritage Walk which takes in many of the city's old buildings. Some of the sites to be seen include Her Majesty's Theatre which was built in 1875, and Craig's Hotel in Lydiard Street

South which was built during the height of the goldrush in 1853. The Eureka Trail also provides a good way to take in the history of the goldfields.

Visitor Information:

Ballarat Tourist Information Centre is at 39 Sturt Street, on the corner of Albert Street, *(03) 5320 5741* or *1800 446 633*. They can be emailed at *tourism@ballarat.vic.gov.au* or visit *www.visitballarat.com.au*. Another website, for the wider region, is *www.visitgoldfields.com*

Points of Interest:

The Eureka Centre opened in March 1998 and cost $4 million to build. It involves a modern, interactive re-retelling of the story of the miner's brief but bloody uprising in 1854. The exhibition is well-done, and should be your first port of call to understand the city's past. The centre can be found on the corner of Rodier and Eureka Streets, call *(03) 5333 1854*. Opposite the exhibition is the Eureka Memorial and Park, near the site where the events actually occurred.

The Eureka Centre
Using the Eurkea Stockade rebellion as a theme the centre provides an excellent description of the area's colonial past.

The Ballarat Fine Art Gallery is the home of the original Eureka Flag, displayed in its own gallery alongside a changing display of related work. The flag was given to James Oddie, the Gallery's founder and president, in 1895, by the widow of John King, a trooper who had taken part in the attack on the Stockade. The Gallery was the first provincial art gallery to be established in Australia, and can be found on 40 Lydiard Street North, call *(03) 5331 5622*.

The Australian Ex-Prisoners of War Memorial is one of the newest tourist attractions in Ballarat, honouring more than 35,000 Australians who were held prisoner during the Boer War, the First World War, the Second World War and the Korean War. Set on the edge of the Ballarat Botanical Gardens, the focal point of the monument is a 130 metre long black granite wall, engraved with the names of all Australian Ex-Prisoners of War. The Memorial can be found on the corner of Wendouree Parade and Carlton Street.

Sovereign Hill offers a trip back in time to the period of Ballarat's gold rush days. It is a re-created gold mining town complete with Main Street, busy with people in period dress and horse-drawn vehicles. You can pan for gold, take a tour of the underground mine, play bowls at the Empire Bowling Saloon, or be photographed in period costume. Sovereign Hill can be found on Bradshaw Street, *(03) 5331 1944*.

Bendigo Population: 93,073

Located in the centre of Victoria and 151km from Melbourne, Bendigo is another town with a rich history of gold mining. The city has preserved many relics of the period, the most tangible of which is the Central Deborah Mine, a complete mine in working condition found in the town. A guided tour allows visitors to don miner's gear and descending 61 metres below the surface, call *(03) 5443 8322* for details. Architecturally, Bendigo has been described as one of the most interesting and integrated provincial cities in Australia. Solidly built with the wealth derived from gold diggings, the city has some of the best preserved Victorian-era buildings and streetscapes to be found anywhere.

One of the most striking monuments is the Alexandra Fountain at the head of Bendigo's Pall Mall. Erected in 1881, the statue is made from 20 tonnes of granite and features seahorses and nymphs. There are too many grand heritage buildings to mention, but many can be found on Bendigo's

The shores of Lake Wendoure in Autumn.

main Pall Mall boulevard. These include the Italianate post office (1887) and law courts (1896), the Shamrock Hotel (1897), the Beehive Store (1872), National Bank (1887). The classic Bendigo Town Hall can also be found nearby, and the Sacred Heart Cathedral dominates the way to the city, like a typical French town.

The Bendigo Trust operate a collection of 34 vintage trams, which are one of Bendigo's most popular tourist attractions. Running through the city centre, the trams leave from Central Deborah Mine, phone *(03) 5443 8322* for details. The Chinese Joss House is an original Chinese temple built of handmade bricks and timber during the 1860's, and can be found on Finn Street in Emu Point, *(03) 5442 1685*. The Golden Dragon Museum and Chinese Gardens are also interesting, allowing visitors to trace the history of the Chinese influence in Bendigo back to the gold rush days. The museum is at 5-13 Bridge Street, *(03) 5441 5044*.

Visitor Information:

The Bendigo Visitor Information & Interpretive Centre is located at the Historic Post Office, 51-67 Pall Mall, call *1800 813 153*. You can send emails to the address *tourism@bendigo.vic.gov.au* or visit the website *www.bendigotourism.com*.

Ararat Population: 10,100

Situated 203km north-west of Melbourne near the Hopkins River, Ararat is the gateway to the Grampians. The commercial centre for the surrounding agricultural districts, Ararat is encompassed by the natural beauty of the Grampians National Park, the Mount Cole State Forest and the Langi

Ghiran State Park. A town that also has a strong history in the goldfields, the precious commodity was discovered in the area in 1854 and evidence of mining still exists for all to see. The area has some of the best agricultural and wine growing land in the state. Fine Merino wool is produced here.

The Ararat district was founded and settled around 1840, and gold was discovered not long after that. The town was named by the first settler, Horatio Spencer Wills, who arrived in 1840 after 11 months of travel. Only one day from his destination, Wills rested on a large mountain which he christened Mount Ararat. The city has many historical buildings classified by the National Trust, and the Tourist Information Centre has details of a City Area Walk which takes in the splendid architecture of the city. Ararat has eight district wineries that are open for cellar sales and tastings, and the Seppelts guided tour is a highlight, *(03) 5361 2239.*

Many visitors to the region use Ararat as a base to explore the magnificent natural resources of the Grampians National Park. The Grampians is Victoria's largest National Park and are only 25km from Ararat. The Park consists of 167,000 hectares and has a rich variety of native flora, wildlife, and Aboriginal rock art sites. The red gum woodland of Victoria Valley's tall eucalypt forest is a special feature. Overall, the Park supports over 860 native plant species. Kangaroos, koalas, echidna, possums and gliders are common, and over 200 bird species have been recorded.

Visitor Information:
Ararat and Grampians Visitor Information Centre, 91 High Street, *1800 657 158.* Email *tourinfo@ararat.vic.gov.au or visit www.ararat.asn.au.*

Outlying Towns in the Region

Clunes
Situated 40km north of Ballarat, Clunes was the first place where gold was discovered in Victoria. Mining ceased in the 1890s and a tree planting programme began, creating one of the prettiest small towns in Victoria. For local information, contact the Clunes Museum on *(03) 5345 3592.*

Hepburn Springs
When the gold ran out in Hepburn Springs, the quality of the waters was found to equal that of Europe's famous health resorts, and soon attracted growing numbers to drink and bathe in the springs. The Hepburn Spa Resort, in the Mineral Springs Reserve, has hot mineral water, herbal, mud, bubble and sinusoidal electric baths. Call *(03) 5348 2034.*

Daylesford
You will find the Daylesford Regional Visitor Information Centre in Vincent Street, *(03) 5348 1339.*

The town of Daylesford

Maryborough
Situated 88km from Daylesford, Maryborough's main street was a thriving thoroughfare by 1856, serving some 50,000 diggers. By 1918, the gold had petered out, and secondary industry took over, making it one of the most highly industrialised towns in Australia. A town tour will give an insight into the town and its historical attractions. The Central Goldfields Shire Office is at 2 Neill Street, Maryborough, *(03) 5461 0610.*

Avoca
This is another former mining town in the foothills of the Pyrenees Range at the junction of the Sunraysia and Pyrenees Highways, on the banks of the Avoca River. Its quiet hills teem with wildlife. The Pyrenees Tourist Association is at 122 High Street, *(03) 5465 3767.*

The Maryborough Railway Station

Castlemaine

Nestling in a dip of the Great Dividing Range 38km south of Bendigo, Castlemaine is another gold mining town. The Castlemaine Visitor Information & Interpretive Centre is in Market Building, Mostyn Street, call *1800 171 888*.

Mount Cole Forest

The Forest straddles the Great Dividing Range about 20km east of Ararat. Mount Cole and Mount Lonarch Forests are excellent examples of forests resulting from multi-use management, and in area total about 12,150 hectares. They produce a steady supply of high quality milling timbers to local sawmills, while providing wildlife habitat and recreational opportunities. Mount Cole Forest has become one of the most popular spots in Australia for Hang Gliding enthusiasts, as well as those interested in nature.

Great Western

Midway between Ararat and Stawell is the little township of Great Western, which gives its name to fine wines, including the champagne-style Great Western Special Reserve, which matures in the cellars beneath the Seppelts vineyards. There are many wineries in the town, for information contact the Tourist Information Centre in Stawell.

Stawell

A former gold mining town 30km west of Ararat, Stawell is probably better known now for the Stawell Gift, the world's richest professional foot running race. It is held for 3 days over the Easter break, and is a handicap race over 120 metres. The Stawell & Grampians Visitor Information Centre is at 54 Western Highway, call *(03) 5358 2314*.

Halls Gap

Halls Gaps is the heart of the Grampians National Park in the picturesque Fyans Valley. The sandstone ranges surround Halls Gap, providing views of rugged escarpments and a tranquil atmosphere. The ridges and valleys are filled with Australian fauna, wildflowers, treefern gullies, strange rock formations, Aboriginal rock art, crystal clear rock pools, and the McKenzie Falls. The National Park visitor centre can be called on *(03) 5356 4381*.

TASMANIA

The Ross Bridge

Australia's only island state, a tour through the many World Heritage Areas of Tasmania will reveal rugged mountains, national parks, rolling green hills and raging rivers. Hobart and Launceston are the two largest cities in the state, while history buffs will enjoy the relics of Australia's convict past that can be seen at heritage locations like Port Arthur and Richmond.

TAS

Hobart and South Tasmania Region

With the state capital of Hobart lying at the centre of the region, Southern Tasmania is characterised by classic colonial buildings, majestic mountains, placid rivers, as well as forests and national parks. The main Tourist centres are Hobart, Richmond and Port Arthur.

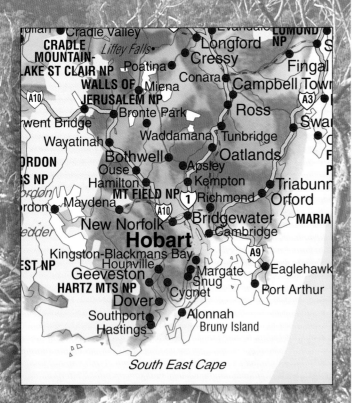

South East Cape

Hobart   Population: 190,000. Climate: Hobart has a mild maritime climate. In January, the maximum temperature is 22ºC and minimum is 12ºC. In July, the maximum is 11ºC and the minimum is 4ºC. Since the average rainfall in Hobart is only 635 mm it ranks as the driest capital city in Australia, apart from Adelaide.

Situated between the broad Derwent River and the dolomite cliffs of Mount Wellington, Hobart is both the capital of Tasmania and the second oldest settlement in Australia. The natural surrounds make Hobart a spectacular location to visit, and it has been recognised as one of the most beautiful cities in Australia. The deep waters of the Derwent River flow out to the Pacific Ocean, and have made Hobart a maritime centre. Fishing boats and cruise ships are anchored in Sullivans Cove only a few hundred metres from the city, while the hundreds of yachts that belong to the King of the Derwent Squadron can be seen just down the river near the Wrest Point Casino. The dolomite corrugations of Mount Wellington have been universally accepted as the symbol of Hobart, and the towering silhouette of the dark, craggy heights will be the first thing seen upon arrival. More than other capital city in Australia, Hobart has preserved its colonial heritage. The Victorian era public buildings and sandstone Georgian warehouses of Salamanca Place all shape Hobart with their history, and fragments of old walls and foundations have been incorporated into modern buildings throughout the city. Though it is the capital of Tasmania, Hobart has managed to retain the feel of a provincial city: small enough to make it a personable place to live, but large enough to have all the amenities of a thriving capital.

The Mouheneer Aboriginal people inhabited the area around Hobart before European settlement, but decided to slip into the hills as the colonisation of their land proceeded. Interestingly, Tasmania was originally settled only as a means to ensure that the French would be kept out of Australia, and a party of 49 soldiers and convicts under the command of Lieutenant John Bowen were dispatched from Sydney in 1803. While the initial settlement was situated at Risdon Cove, the arrival of Lieutenant David Collins in 1804 saw the struggling colony relocate to Sullivans Cove. By 1827 Hobart had developed into a thriving port with a population of 5,000, and was the centre of trade for both Tasmania and the whaling operations in the southern oceans. The Old Wharf in Hunter Street was replaced with the New

Hobart from the water

Near this part of the city at Constitution Dock the Sydney to Hobart yacht race particpants moor after the amazing classic which starts every year on Boxing Day.

Wharf at Salamanca Place during the 1850's, and it was at this spot over three years that around 67,000 convicts stepped ashore in Hobart after a three month voyage from Britain. Following the granting of self–government in 1856, Tasmanian civic pride was expressed through the building of splendid buildings like the Town Hall and Old Government House. Hobart became the port for a prosperous agrarian economy, with their wool, meat, crops and timber being shipped to world markets.

The turn of the twentieth century saw a rise in use of hydro-electric facilities, resulting from a dream of the state to utilise their abundant water resources to produce cheap and plentiful electricity. While many major industries were attracted to Hobart and the surrounding areas during the decades following WWII, industrial manufacturing began a decline in the 70's and cost many Tasmanians their jobs. While a number of companies were able to buck this trend, it has been predicted that growth the economy in Tasmania will instead be derived from service industries like tourism, information technology and innovations in primary industry. While a lack of prolonged economic development has meant that Hobart lags a little behind other capitals in the country, many would argue that this constitues the city's charm.

Franklin Square is situated in the heart of Hobart, and is both a popular meeting place as well as the location of a bus depot. Throughout the day people can be found playing chess at an immense board or simply lounging around the park. A visit to the Royal Tasmanian Botanical Gardens is also essential, and is considered one of Hobart's major highlights. Situated close to Government House on the banks of the Derwent River, the 13.5 hectare gardens feature the widest collection of temperate climate plants found anywhere in Australia. A stroll around Battery Point is another of Hobart's most pleasant excursions. The suburb was named after a battery of guns established in 1818 on the promontory of land lying between Sullivans Cove in the east and Sandy Bay Creek in the west, and the area has changed very little in the last 150 years. Houses and cottages are packed into a jumble of narrow streets and lanes, which gives the area a charming maritime atmosphere. The oldest building in Battery Point is the 1818 Signal Station which was used to relay messages from another station on Mount Nelson. The station allowed news of a convict escape to be relayed from Port Arthur within a few minutes.

Hobart's main shopping area centres on Elizabeth Mall, which stretches between the stately GPO and Liverpool Street. There are a number of specialty shops as well as large department stores where you can buy basic necessities. An even better option for shoppers however would be the Salamanca Markets that take place every Saturday. Stretching along the avenue from Davey Street to the end of Salamanca Place are scores of craftsmen, dealers in second–hand goods, vendors of clothing, paintings, pottery, wood turning, books, just about everything a shopper could hope for. Musicians strum their guitars or hum their didgeridoos, while families with market–garden vegetables rub shoulders with hawkers of New Age crystals. The backdrop to the Salamanca Place Markets is a picturesque row of Georgian sandstone warehouses that were built between 1835 and 1860. The so–called New Wharf that used to lie in front of the warehouses was built of stone taken from a large quarry, and can still be seen in its unused state. The warehouses themselves were built on the levelled land, and have since been converted into restaurants, art galleries and offices. A terrific place for browsing or a cappuccino, the Georgian dockside warehouses are considered the best of their kind remaining in Australia.

Reflecting the strong link the city has with it's past, more than 90 buildings in Hobart are classified by the National Trust. 63 of these can be seen in Macquarie and Davey Streets which run parallel to each other. Hobart's city centre is very close to the wharves on the Derwent, and from certain vantage points it can appear that boats are moored in the streets. The waterfront from Hunter Street is popular with tourists and locals alike as a picturesque place to have a stroll or a relaxing meal. The annual blue water classic, the Sydney to Hobart Yacht Race, begins on Boxing Day and finishes at Constitution Dock right in the heart of the city. The National Trust of Australia organises walking tours of Battery Point on Saturdays, call *(03) 6223 7570* for bookings. Another two–hour walking tour of historical Hobart starts at the Tasmanian Travel & Information Centre, 20 Davey Street, call *(03) 6230 8233* for more information.

Beautiful natural surroundings can be found within an hour's drive from Hobart. Some of the settings to be enjoyed include isolated bushland, rainforests, paddocks full of grazing livestock, sandy beaches and historic settlements where time seems to have stopped. To the tourist's amazement, trucks

Battery Point
A typical view of a street in Battery Point with Mt Wellington as a backdrop.

laden with immense logs often rumble down Macquarie Street, a constant reminder of the untamed bush which lies only a few miles away. Throughout the city are shops that sell camping and trekking equipment, preparing visitors for some of the world's best wilderness areas.

Visitor Information:

The Tasmanian Travel & Information Centre can be found on the corner of Elizabeth and Davey Streets, *(03) 6230 8233*. The Wilderness Society Shop is at 33 Salamanca Place, *(03) 6234 9370*, and has information on backpacking and trekking. Service Tasmania is at 134 Macquarie Street, *(03) 6233 8011*, and has maps of all descriptions.

Points of Interest:

The Tasmanian Parliament House can be found on the other side of Murray Street, opposite the wharves and fronted by spacious lawns and gardens. The famous government architect John Lee Archer originally designed it as the local customs house. The stone for the building came from what is now a lake in the grounds of Government House. The cellars, once the bonded store, still display broad arrows on the brickwork and much of the work was done by convicts. The customs staff opened for business in 1840, and it wasn't until 1904 that they were moved to new offices in Davey Street. Alterations allowed the House of Assembly to conduct its business there from 1856 with the advent of self–government. Visitors are encouraged to visit Parliament House whenever the House or the Council is sitting, with around 25,000 people visiting the building each year.

St David's Park is the original burial ground of Hobart Town, and is now a charming piece of urban greenery. The cemetery was closed in 1872 and when the area was turned into a park in 1926, many of its headstones were incorporated into the walls, gateways and the rotunda. The first to be buried there appears to be a child who died in 1804, and there are many other important Tasmanian memorials to be found. The park can be found nearby to Salamanca Place.

St George's Anglican Church was another building designed by John Lee Archer, and was built between 1836 and 1847. Found on Mona Street, it has Australia's oldest classical revival spire. At night, illuminated by spotlights, it is one of the city's most prominent landmarks. The Tasmanian poet James McAuley wrote a well–known poem about the romance of an escaped convict and the church organist.

The Tasmanian Museum and Art Gallery has an emphasis on Tasmanian Aborigines and early colonial activities, including the penal system. The museum contains exhibits which describe the colonial penal system, as well as an outstanding collection of whaling implements and ship models. For the youngsters there are exhibits of the strange animals of Tasmania and Australia and a few dinosaur skeletons. The Art Gallery on the other hand has a fine collection of colonial paintings. It includes a number of intriguing paintings by John Glover and the tragic tableau by artist Benjamin Duterrau of Protector of Aborigines George Augustus Robinson surrounded by native Tasmanians in 'The Reconciliation'. The collection of modern art is not large but some of Australia's best–known artists are represented, including Emanuel Phillips, Russell Drysdale and Edith Holmes. The museum is housed at 40 Macquarie Street and can be called on *(03) 6211 4177*.

St David's Anglican Church, on the corner of Macquarie Street and Murray Street, is one of the treasures of Australian church architecture. It was designed by George Frederick Bodley of London, a leading nineteenth century authority on Gothic architecture. The timber work is exquisite, with a floor made of Tasmanian blackwood and stringy bark and laid on a base of Huon Pine. The rood screen of English oak is one of Australia's most impressive pieces. The stained glass work is also very impressive. Its solid silver altar vessels were presented by King George III in 1803.

Parliament House

Hobart Harbour

The Treasury Buliding
The building still in use exudes an ambience of the past colonial era.

The **Allport Museum and Library of Fine Arts** features fine furniture, porcelain, glassware and silver dating from the eighteenth century, and rare and fine books. The Tasmanian Library in the same building has an extensive collection of printed material ranging from accounts of the early explorers to current publications. The W.C. Crowther Library includes an interesting collection of whaling artefacts and old medical instruments. The museum can be found in the **State Library** on Murray Street, call *(03) 6233 7484* for details.

The **Anglesea Barracks**, a 10 minute walk up Davey Street, is the nation's oldest military establishment still occupied by the Army. Some of the buildings in the large complex date back to the early 1800s and the guns outside the gate were cast before 1774. The barracks can be called on *(03) 6237 7160*.

The **Wrest Point Casino** is now considered a Hobart landmark, and was Australia's first legal casino when it was built in 1973. The Casino can be called on *(03) 6225 0112*.

Lower Sandy Bay is a family beach that is one of the best

places to go for a swim in the Derwent. For history buffs, there is a granite monolith in a small park there which commemorates Canadians who were exiled in 1840 after a failed rebellion.

The **Mount Nelson Signal Station** provides magnificent panoramic views of Hobart and the Derwent after a very winding trip up the flanks of Mount Nelson. It was originally established in 1811 to spot vessels entering Storm Bay and D'Entrecasteaux Channel. The signal mast, which is still standing, became a link in a chain of semaphore stations from Hobart to Port Arthur. The views are spectacular. The restaurant offers very pleasant Tasmanian fare for lunch and morning and afternoon tea, call *(03) 6223 3407*.

The **Tudor Court Model Village** is a scale replica of a medieval English village. Created and built by John Palotta, who was crippled by polio when he was nine, it is an incredible feat of skill and loving patience. The village can be found at 2273 Huon Highway in Huonville, *(03) 6264 1844*.

Mount Wellington is an essential place to visit when you are in Hobart. The drive to the summit will take you about a half–hour. Drive up Davey Street, bear right onto the Huon Road towards Fern Tree and follow the signs. Half–way up there is a viewing station over the Huon Valley and Bruny Island. Further on, the road winds past 'the Springs', the ruins of a hotel which was burnt down by bush fires. Then below are the Organ Pipes, the immense dolomite cliffs which give the mountain its rugged character. If you clamber to the

Salamanca Markets
Every Saturday without fail, rain, hail or shine the Salamanca Markets just happen. One can purchase anything there - from fudge to a raincoat.

The Antartic Base
Situated in Hobart it is a stones's throw from Salamanca Place..

The township of Richmond

The historic bridge of Richmond overlooked by St John's Catholic Church, the oldest Catholic Church in Australia. It was built in 1836.

top of the rocks surmounted by a trig station, you will be standing on 1270m of rock. At the top is the viewing station, which offers a superb view of Hobart and beyond for up to 100 km away. In winter the mountain is often dusted with snow and sometimes the road is closed. There are many tracks up Mount Wellington if you are interested in doing a walk.

Richmond Population: 754

Situated on the Coal River only 27 km north of Hobart, Richmond is the oldest historic location in Tasmania. The classic sandstone buildings, cottages and manors of the 1800's can still be seen in the town, though its status as one of Tasmania's premier tourist destinations has meant that many of them have been converted into cafes, galleries and boutiques. During the 1820's Richmond was an important military post and convict station, linking Hobart with Port Arthur. The charming Richmond Bridge that spans the Coal River was built by convicts in 1823, and enabled easy movement of military, police and convicts between the two locations. The traffic ceased moving through Richmond after the opening of the Sorell Causeway in 1872. Today the town remains largely unchanged from those days.

Probably the best way to spend a visit to Richmond is a walk up and down the main street. Scattered along it are restored sandstone cottages, many of them now selling craft and antiques. The Richmond Gaol was built in 1825 – five years before Port Arthur – to house people working locally and for prisoners in transit. It is probably the oldest surviving convict gaol in Australia, and is much the same at it was at the height

of development in 1840. The men's solitary cells, each about two metres by one metre, and the flogging yard, with its thick high walls, are terrifying places for anyone with a vivid imagination. Also on display are interesting artefacts from colonial times, call *(03) 6260 2127* for more information. Another of the most popular attractions is Old Hobart Town, a remarkable scale model that depicts Hobart as it was during the 1820's. Highly detailed and historically accurate, the town was created using many of the original plans, prints and drawings. Call *(03) 6260 2502* for information.

Port Arthur Population: 400

Located on the Tasman Peninsula around from Hobart, the town of Port Arthur tells a detailed story of Tasmania's colonial past. Considered as the premier tourist attraction of the state, Port Arthur offers an enticing combination of convict history, scenic surrounds and beautiful waterways. Today Port Arthur is a beautiful picnic spot, with the vast lawns and sandstone ruins of the town sprawling over 40 hectares. But from 1830 to 1877, it was a prison that housed around 12,500 convicts from across the British Empire. Despite the rugged beauty of the dense forests, surf beaches and precipitous sea cliffs, the Tasman Peninsula most likely made for a chilly and forbidding place of exile. Escape was rare, and it was the fate of many to be buried in the mass graves that populate the Isle of the Dead. A series of bushfires ravaged many of the buildings after the settlement was closed as a prison, but in recent years they have been restored so that Australians can fully appreciate their convict past.

Port Arthur was originally established in the area because of an abundance of good timber, coupled with the safe nature of the port. The settlement operated from 1830 to 1877 as a timber–producing 'sawing station', and also as an industrial prison. Many of the convicts were multiple offenders, but some were famous political prisoners. Though early conditions were harsh, they compared favourably with other institutions in the British Empire, representing in many ways a step towards the modern prison system. Its popular image as a cesspit of cruelty and depravity was not really deserved, as brutal punishments like flogging were eased during the 1840's.

Administrative control passed to the colonial government after the end of transportation in the 1860's, and the paupers and lunatics who descended upon Port Arthur eventually outnumbered the convicts. Port Arthur was closed as a prison in 1887 and became a popular tourist destination, with many of the buildings auctioned off and converted into guest houses or hotels. An unfortunate scar on the history of Tasmania is the massacre that took place in Port Arthur in 1996, and a memorial now exists near the Information Centre to commemorate the incident.

The Port Arthur Historic Site is located on the Main Road, and can be called on either *(03) 6251 2310* or *1800 659 101*. Guided tours leave all day on the half hour. The nightly Historic Ghost Tour is one of the most popular features of Port Arthur, and departs from the Visitors Centre. An old boys' prison known as Point Puer is across the bay, and was a place where lads between the ages of eight and eighteen served after being convicted of crimes in Ireland or England. Still left are ruins of the bakers' ovens and the old school.

Visitor Information:

Port Arthur Historic Site can be called on *(03) 6251 2371*. The website for information is *www.portarthur.org.au*.

Points of Interest:

The Lunatic Asylum is housed in a brick building with an impressive clock tower. Built in 1867 designed to accommodate about 100 patients, it was divided into 20 separate rooms with a large amusement and recreation area. The insane or senile were not treated badly, but neither with skill or great kindness either. As the Hobart Mercury noted in 1877, "if an inmate behaves himself well he is tolerated; if he is noisy he is controlled; and if he dies there is an end of him". The museum displays are impressive, including records of the transportees sent to Tasmania with their crimes and punishments, as well as real leg irons and flogging whips that give an idea of the suffering of the prisoners. The museum is next to the Asylum and can be called on *(03) 6251 2315*.

The Model Prison provides evidence of what was the fashionable punishment for difficult cases during the 1840s, a 'separate system' of prison discipline. While prisoners had all the necessary facilities and were treated humanely by the wardens, they were deprived, as far as possible, of all human contact. Whenever leaving their cells for exercise, they had to wear a mask to conceal their identity and were not allowed to

The Penitentiary, Port Arthur Historic Site.

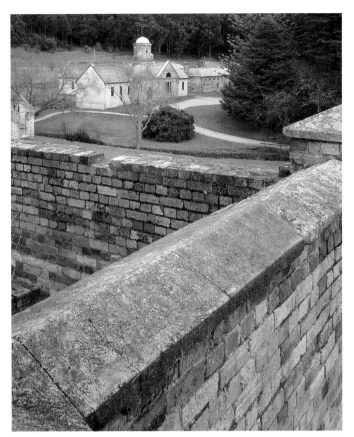

Port Arthur Historic Site with the old lunatic asylum in the background

communicate with other prisoners. The restored Chapel gives you some idea of this ghastly, spirit–breaking way of dealing with hardened prisoners, with the separate compartments designed to allow the convicts to gaze straight ahead and only at the preacher. The Model Prison's silent cells are windowless with walls nearly a metre thick, and are entered through an outer door and three inner doors.

The Official Church of the Gaol has become a symbol of Tasmania itself, a beautiful structure designed with simple grandeur. The foundation stone was laid in 1836. At services, there would have been up to 1000 convicts sitting in the western wing and 200 officials and their families in cushioned, curtained–off pews along the eastern wall on either side of the pulpit. Today you can walk through the sandstone ruins and climb the restored tower, and imagine convicts worshipping below every Sunday under the stern scrutiny of their warders.

The Isle of the Dead is a spot that lies a few hundred metres offshore. It is the last resting place of 180 military and civilian personnel, as well as 1769 convicts and paupers. A boat regularly leaves the jetty for a 40 minute guided tour

of the island. Free settlers were buried on a little knoll, their graves marked by massive headstones with inscriptions cut by convict masons. The convicts were interred in lower ground, six or seven in an unmarked grave. The most famous person resting here is Henry Savery, notorious forger and Australia's first published novelist. A memorial stone was erected in 1992 by the Tasmanian literary community. To make a booking to visit the isle, call *1800 659 101*.

O'Brien's Cottage is evidence that not all the prisoners at Port Arthur were criminals whose lives have been forgotten by history. William Smith O'Brien was a political prisoner so prominent that he was treated to his own cottage. O'Brien was a member of the British Parliament for 17 years and a leader of the Young Ireland Movement, and in 1848 he sought to rally a rebellion against British rule. It was quickly crushed and O'Brien received a death sentence, which was commuted to transportation for life. At Port Arthur he was confined in his movements, but corresponded widely with people in the Colonies and Britain. He finally accepted a ticket–of–leave in 1850 and left Van Diemen's Land in 1854.

The Medical Officer's House has been restored to the way it looked in convict days and is now an award–winning museum. Built in 1847, it served this purpose until the early 1870s when it became successively a private residence, a guest house and hotel. Call *(03) 6251 2352*.

Outlying Areas
South of Hobart

Bruny Island and the D'Entrecasteaux Channel
Kingston–Blackmans Bay

The Southern Outlet from Hobart leaves you at a turn–off for Kingston and Blackmans Bay within 20 minutes – an area which is one of Hobart's fastest growing outer suburbs. Blackmans Bay has a small blowhole, and lookouts at Doughty Point and Piersons Point that offer superb views of Bruny Island and Storm Bay. Kingston is also home to the headquarters of Australia's National Antarctic Program, with a display giving visitors a greater understanding of Australia's involvement in Antarctica and the Southern Ocean.

Margate

About 20 km from Hobart, Margate has a motor museum

and an unusual market, with headquarters in Tasmania's last passenger train. The converted carriages house toy–makers, glass blowers, woodworkers, artists and other craft makers. From the main street on a clear day, you can take a lovely photo of Mount Wellington from a quite unfamiliar angle.

Snug

A few kilometres further south on the Channel Highway, Snug is a small village which was terribly damaged in the 1967 bushfires. The Channel Historical and Folk Museum is worth visiting, while a walk to Snug Falls makes for a good family excursion.

Bruny Island

A little further down the road is the fishing town of Kettering and the terminal for the Bruny Island vehicular ferry. What Tasmania is to the Mainland, Bruny Island is to Tasmania. It is a popular holiday spot for Hobartians and once there, you are well and truly away from it all. With an area of 362 km2, Bruny is Tasmania's fourth largest island. A narrow sand spit links North Bruny, with its open paddocks and drier climate, with South Bruny, with its steep hills and rain forest. South Bruny has a wonderful combination of spectacular cliff views, sandy beaches, rain forest bushwalks, wildlife and historical visits. It takes only 15 minutes from Kettering to reach North Bruny on the Mirambeena, a modern vehicular ferry with a carrying capacity of 70 cars, Call *(03) 6272 3277*. Bruny was the birthplace of Truganini, the last of the Aboriginal Tasmanians. She was the daughter of Mangana, chief of the Nuenonne tribe. Most of the members of her family died at the hands of white men, but she joined George Robinson in his mission as a conciliator and twice saved his life. The last of her five husbands was William Lanny, the last Tasmanian Aboriginal male. She died in 1876 and her skeleton was displayed for many years in the Hobart Museum, but in 1975 her remains were cremated and the ashes scattered in the channel off Bruny. The Aborigines called their island Lunawannaalonna and the name lives on in the townships of Lunawanna and Alonnah.

The Huon Valley

The Huon Highway (A6) follows the Huon River until Surges Bay, where it crosses overland to Dover. It is a lovely drive, with rolling hills and steep green paddocks, and stands of tall gums and pines. The section between Glendevie and Dover is especially picturesque. As you drive along, you can see the striking silhouette of Hartz Peak.

Grove

The principal attraction in Grove is the Huon Valley Apple and Heritage Museum. It has displays of the technology of the apple industry and of 500 different types of apples.

Huonville

South and inland from Snug and Bruny Island is Huonville, the commercial centre of the Channel. It is a pretty area which has pleasant rural and seascape scenery. The Huon Valley was a large apple exporter before Britain joined the EEC. The population is a little over 1300 people.

Franklin

A small town along the river, with an 1853 pub and several arts and crafts shops, which still has the aura of a nineteenth century river port. A good place to browse for antiques.

Geeveston

This timber town is 31 km further south of Hounville and is a base for visits to the Hartz Mountains National Park and the rugged valleys of the Huon and Picton Rivers. The main attraction is the 597m long Tahune Forest Air Walk, which reaches 38m above the Huon River and offers a magnificent

Bruny Island

The Neck joining the northern and southern parts of the island is featured here.

Adamson's Peak, Dover

view of the surrounds. The Tahune Forest Reserve is about 25 km along the Arve Road from Geeveston. The attached Visitor Centre sells local produce, and during summer it also offers a smorgasbord barbecue.

Dover

From Geeveston the Huon Highway leads south to Dover, a further 21 km. It is the last petrol stop for motorists heading into the lonely and rugged country towards South–East Cape. The Dover Hotel claims to be 'Australia's southernmost hotel–motel'. There are two fish processing factories and it is an important base for the aquaculture industry, with fish farms producing gourmet Atlantic salmon and ocean trout.

Southport

Another 21 km south of Dover is the small fishing town and resort of Southport, whose 'Southport Settlement' claims to be 'Australia's most southern watering hole' with a pub, restaurant and coffee shop. It is the oldest town in the Huon area. Turn left as you enter, away from the beach–front houses and follow the unsealed road to a camping area and white sandy beaches. Nearby is the Hastings Thermal Pool, which is 28ºC all year round. Rain water enters the dolomite area near the caves, descends 600m and rises under pressure as a warm spring. Newdegate Cave is about 15 minutes drive away and has crystalline formations, built up over aeons by calcium saturated water. Its highlight is Titania's Palace, a chamber with a flowstone floor which is rich in straws and stalactites. There are daily tours of the caves (45 minutes). Lune River is a popular place where you can find fossilised fern, wood agate and crystal. A tramway still operates taking tourists for a 6 km trip through bushland from the township to The Deep Hole across the bay from Southport.

The Derwent Valley

New Norfolk

New Norfolk is a town of about 10,000 people, about half an hour from Hobart on the banks of the upper Derwent. It is a mixture of quaint old buildings with stately oaks, poplars and pines and ramshackle cottages from the Fifties and Sixties when the Boyer Paper Mill was in its heyday. The immense weatherboard Oast House, one of the most impressive buildings in the town, is the only hop museum in the southern hemisphere. St Matthew's Church of England is the oldest church in Tasmania and one of the most beautiful parish churches in Australia. The Bush Inn was built in 1815 and licensed in 1825, making it the oldest continuously licensed hotel in Australia. The Jet Boat departs from the Esplanade at New Norfolk and takes passengers through shallow, fast–flowing rapids of the Derwent, past the hop fields along the willow–lined river on a 30 minute ride.

Salmon Ponds

About 11 km upriver at Plenty are the famous Salmon Ponds, the oldest trout hatchery in the southern hemisphere. The first trout came here in 1864. This is a great place for a picnic, with its towering exotic cypresses planted more than 100 years ago. For 20¢ you can buy a handful of fish food to throw to schools of huge, fat and hungry tiger trout, rainbow trout, brown trout, brook trout, albino trout and Atlantic Salmon.

Bushy Park

On the way to Mount Field, you pass through the picturesque town of Bushy Park. During the summer months there are rows upon rows of hops protected from the wind by rows of poplars fencing the paddocks. In the autumn, the poplars

A home in Bothwell

turn yellow, their leaves drift across the road and it looks as if telegraph poles are growing in the hops paddocks.

Mount Field National Park

Only about one and a half hours from Hobart, through lovely undulating paddocks, Mount Field is the favourite national park for Hobartians. Along with Freycinet, it is the oldest national park in Tasmania. It has a great variety of scenic features and wildlife in its 16,265 hectares and offers a great range of facilities for day visitors. Around the park entrance are picnic facilities and Russell Falls. These cascade in a veil of mist down a cliff face and are surrounded by rain forest. A bit further afield, the 30 minute Tall Trees Walk over duckboards will take you through a forest that features the world's tallest flowering plant, 85m swamp gums. For those in a more adventurous mood, drive up the winding unsealed road towards the top of the mountain. The one hour Pandani Grove Walk skirts the edges of Lake Dobson and passes through groves of ancient pencil pine and tall pandani. There are some wonderful day walks to other tarns in the area gouged out by ancient glaciers. The combination of the stark beauty of the lichened rock, exotic plants like pencil pine and fagus, and the mountain ridge towering overhead, make hiking here a very special experience. Snowfalls can occur in the high country at any time of the year.

Ouse

This little town has a very attractive convict–built Anglican Church dedicated to St John the Baptist (1843), with five stained glass windows and skilful wood carving.

Hamilton

Located 74 km northwest of Hobart on the Lyell Highway, the town of Hamilton is one that has changed significantly since settlement in the 1800's. In 1844 Hamilton was a bustling town, but following this prosperity, the population of Hamilton steadily declined in the latter part of the nineteenth century. Today it is a quiet hamlet full of charming historic sandstone buildings. The Emma's, Victoria's and George's cottages were all built of local sandstone by convicts. **The Anglican Church of St. Peters** is one of Australia's oldest. Built in 1834, makes it even older than the foundation of Melbourne. It has only one door, a detail attributed to a desire to keep convicts from absconding during services. The Old Schoolhouse is the other significant attraction in Hamilton. A huge two storey structure erected by convicts in 1858, the school has been converted into b&b accomodation. Tasmanian Travel Centre can handle any inquiries on *1300 655 145*.

Bothwell

Located only 74 km north of Hobart off the Midland Highway, the town of Bothwell is another location in Tasmania's south that offers a reflection on the state's colonial past. Most buildings were built using convict labour, and have explanatory plaques that can be examined on a leisurely walk. Bothwell's attractions include the War Memorial Sundial. The Anglican Church of St Michael and All Angels (1891) is an imposing place of worship with the circular staircase leading to the belfry, carved lecterns, an Italian mosaic of the Risen Christ, and a high sandstone altar. The plainer Presbyterian Church of St. Luke, designed by John Lee Archer and built in 1831, stands like a sentinel at the top of Alexander Street. Archer' s original design called for rounded windows, but Lieutenant–Governor Arthur directed him to change them. He considered the design 'unchristian'. Some of the best trout fishing takes place not far from Bothwell. The Information Centre is at the Australasian Golf Museum, call *(03) 6259 4033*.

Waddamana

Less than an hour from Bothwell, towards the northwest, is Waddamana, a retired power station that has become a popular tourist attraction. This was the first major hydro–electric development in Tasmania. There are exhibits.

The local hotel, Hamilton

TAS

The North East, Launceston & Roads North from Hobart

The North Eastern Tasmania region is an area that stretches from the city of Launceston in the north, along to the Freycinet National Park in the south east. The region is the area responsible for producing Tasmania's acclaimed fine wine and foods.

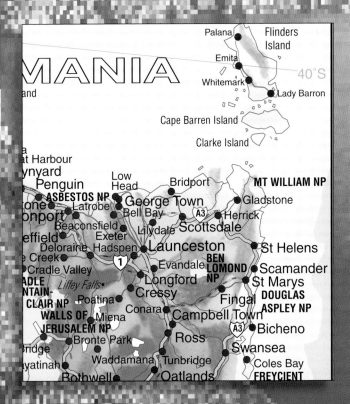

Launceston Population: 96,000. Climate: In the summer the temperature ranges between 21°C and 13°C and in the winter between 13°C and 5°C. The average rainfall is approximately 750mm.

Located at the head of the Tamar River in the central north of Tasmania, Launceston is both the second largest city in the state and the largest inland port in Australia. Known as Tasmania's "Garden City" due to the many parks and reserves, Launceston is showcased by the 13 hectare City Park amid the striking Cataract Gorge Reserve. Wood–frame houses sprawl over the steep hills, overlooking the highway and the businesses of the commercial district. The city contains many quaint malls and shopping centres such as

Cataract Gorge , Launceston

Tamar River, Launceston

the Quadrant Mall and Yorktown Square. The hinterland is home to rich agricultural country, with wineries, orchards and farms producing Tasmania's famed wools, foods and wines. The fortunes of Launceston have declined somewhat since the city's heyday in the late nineteenth century. It was once considered a very progressive city – the first place in the Southern Hemisphere to use anaesthetic in 1847, and the first city in the country to use electric lighting in 1895. Today it still gives the impression of modest prosperity: an attractive city with many well established beautiful public parks and private gardens.

The Tamar River upon which Launceston lies was discovered by Bass and Flinders in 1798, during their navigation around Van Diemen's Land. Shortly after Colonel William Paterson's group had been sent to secure Tasmania from any potential incursions from the French, an expedition heading southwards came across the present site of Launceston. So impressed were they with this area that Paterson himself decided to relocate there. The town's natural port allowed the economy to develop, and by 1824 the northern military command had established their headquarters in the area. In 1852 Launceston was declared a municipality and was the second largest service centre in the state.

Justifying its reputation as a progressive city, Launceston has been known throughout its history as a city of "firsts". The occasions when Launceston was first past the post are too numerous to mention, but a few memorable instances include: the Launceston Hotel was the first licensed establishment of its kind in 1814, the Launceston Horticultural Society was the first in the nation to be established in 1836, the nation's first underground sewerage system was built in Launceston in 1860, and the city was the first place that sound was recorded on wax cylinders in 1890. Of note to outsiders is the intense rivalry that exists between Hobart and Launceston, not unlike the rivalry between Sydney and Melbourne.

The City Park at the centre of Launceston was established in the 1820's, the spacious and well laid-out gardens set amid old elm and oak trees. It contains a small zoo, and houses the John Hart Conservatory. The Cataract Gorge is another spectacular asset for the city, and is only a few minutes by bus from the centre. A 1.5km walk along the face of the cliff ends in the Cataract Cliff Grounds Reserve, from which a chairlift with the longest single span in the world crosses the gorge. The lift's total length is 457 metres and its central span is 308 metres. Manicured gardens, complete with strutting peacocks, merge with native flora on the upper bank, while on the city side, gardens surrounding a swimming pool extend to the lake over which you pass in the chairlift.

Launceston is home to the Penny Royal Gunpowder Mill. The replica features 14 barges which take visitors underground to see how gunpowder was made during the 19th century. The sloop-of-war *Sandpiper* sails around the central lake and passengers can fire her canons – but fire will be returned in a mock battle. Over a set drawbridge is an island housing an armoury, gaol and gunners' quarters. Gourlay's Famous Sweets has been a Launceston institution since 1897, and at Penny Royal, visitors can see the sweets being made to the same old recipes. Electric trams were introduced to Launceston in 1911 and the last working specimen travels through the gardens of the Penny Royal complex.

Visitor Information:

The Launceston Travel and Information Centre is at the corner of St John and Paterson Streets, call *(03) 6336 3133*.

Points of Interest:

The Queen Victoria Museum and Art Gallery is a fascinating place to visit. It has a collection of Tasmanian fauna and Aboriginal artefacts, one of Australia's finest collections of colonial paintings, and a reconstructed joss–house which gives an insight into Australia's Chinese heritage. Launceston Planetarium is also part of the Museum and is one of four planetariums in Australia. The Museum and Art Gallery is on Wellington Street, and can be called on *(03) 6323 3777*.

Ben Lomond National Park in winter.

The Old Umbrella Shop is built entirely of Tasmanian Blackwood, and is preserved by the National Trust as the last genuine period shop in Tasmania. There is a collection of umbrellas used during the last 100 years, and the gift shop has a wide variety of Tasmanian and National Trust goods. The shop can be found at 60 George Street.

Franklin House is a Georgian style home that was built in 1838. It has been restored and furnished by the National Trust, and is named after Sir John Franklin, Governor of Van Diemen's Land. Built by Mr Britton Jones, then in 1842 it became a Boys' School, one of the leading educational institutions in Tasmania. The house can be found 8 km south of Launceston at 413 Hobart Road, *(03) 6344 7824*.

Outlying Towns

Travelling South from Launceston

Longford

About 10 km off the Midlands Highway is Longford. First settled in 1813, it still retains the charm of a bygone era. Two of the best–known attractions are the well preserved colonial homes, Woolmers Estate and Brickendon Historic Farm.

Evandale

Best known nowadays for the National Penny Farthing Championships, Evandale is an historic town with beautifully preserved colonial buildings only 15 minutes away from Launceston. Every Sunday Evandale is the site of Tasmania's biggest country market.

Ben Lomond

Evandale is also the gateway to Ben Lomond National Park. With its steep cliffs, Ben Lomond is visible over much of the northern midlands. In the winter it has the best ski fields in the State with excellent facilities. In the summer, its craggy heights offer plenty of opportunities for bushwalking, abseiling and rock climbing. The plateau is roughly 14km in length, 6 km in width and more than 1300m high. Legges Tor on the plateau is the second highest point in Tasmania at a height of 1572 metres. It is an excellent place to observe the vegetation of the exposed mountain tops, as well as the dolerite columns and scree slopes will interest geologists.

Detail of the Meander Falls Track.

Liffey Falls

Around 60 km south–west via Carrick and Bracknell, are the Liffey Falls. They are a popular destination for bushwalkers. The falls are in a reserve and drop into a beautiful rainforest.

Travelling North from Launceston

Exeter

Situated 24 km to the north–west along the Tamar River, Exeter is the centre of a fruit growing area, and even the local school has its own farm. At the mouth of the Supply River are the remains of Tasmania's first water–driven flour mill.

Batman Bridge

The bridge spans the Tamar River another 30 km downstream at Whirlpool Reach. It was one of the world's first cable–stayed bridges. Dominated by a 100 m high steel A–frame inclined 20º from the vertical, it leans out 30m across the river and carries almost the entire weight of the 206m main span. The bridge was opened in 1968.

Bell Bay

Further north downstream and very close to the coast, Bell Bay has become an important inland port mainly nourished by Comalco's aluminium smelter and Tempco's manganese steel furnaces. The Hydro–Electric Commission runs a thermal generating plant here.

George Town

The town is the residential and commercial centre for Bell Bay, but offers little in the way of accommodation. One of the earliest settlements in Australia, it has a beautiful Georgian mansion, The Grove, which has been restored and is open for inspection. The house is at 25 Cimitiere Street, their phone number *(03) 6382 1336.*

Low Head

Just 5 km north of George Town is Australia's oldest continuously running pilot station, the Low Head Pilot Station. The building itself was erected in 1835 and now houses the Maritime Museum. Low Head is also a popular holiday resort and picnic area.

Beaconsfield

Now a quiet country town, Beaconsfield became a thriving mining centre when gold was discovered there in 1869. The mine was closed in 1914 because of water seepage. The Grub Shaft Gold Mine and Heritage Museum displays a fascinating collection of local memorabilia.

Asbestos Range National Park

Established in 1976, this park is teeming with wildlife and is an important grazing ground for the endangered Forester Kangaroo. You can also find sandy beaches, flowering heath and splendid views to the Western Tiers. Asbestos was once mined at the park's southern end near Beaconsfield.

Lilydale

Situated north–east of Launceston, Lilydale was first settled in the 1850's, and officially known as Upper Piper and colloquially as German Town because of the number of German families in the district. It was then well–known for dairy farming, apple growing and its timber industry, but today it is a prime wine–growing area of the state. Attractions include a Wine Route, Lilydale Falls, Walker Rhododendron Reserve and Hollybark Forest Reserve.

Travelling West from Launceston

Trevallyn State Recreation Area

5 km from the centre of Launceston is Lake Trevallyn, which was formed by the damming of the South Esk waters for hydro–electric power in 1955. This dam replaced the Duck Reach Power Station further downstream which was

The main street of Kempton

Tasmania's first hydro–electric power station, built in 1895.

Hadspen

Entally House, 18 km south–west of Launceston, is the most historic of the National Trust houses. It is thought to have been built in 1819 by Thomas Haydock Reibey, the eldest son of Mary and Thomas Reibey of Sydney. Entally was opened to the public in 1950, and it has a very good collection of Regency furniture and silverware. It is set in beautiful grounds, and has a green house, chapel, coach house and stables. Worth a visit.

Westbury

Settled in the 1820's, Westbury still has the atmosphere of the nineteenth century, with a famous village green that is used for fetes and other celebrations.

Travelling North from Hobart

The Midlands

A rich farming and grazing area, the Midlands was one of the first regions settled in Tasmania. Many of the little towns off the Heritage Highway from Hobart to Launceston are of great historic interest. Time has passed most of them by and they now have a quaint period character. You will find what is probably the largest collection of Georgian architecture and colonial buildings in Australia.

Bridgewater

This town is close enough to be counted as an outer suburb of Hobart. It is the location of the main north–south crossing of the Derwent River. The Causeway across the river was constructed in the early 1830s by 200 convicts in chains who wheelbarrowed in two million tons of stone and clay. The first bridge was opened in 1849. Today's bridge dates from 1946.

Brighton and Pontville

Just beyond Bridgewater are the adjoining towns of Brighton and Pontville. Since 1826, Brighton has been the home of Brighton Army Camp, which was the main military post in Tasmania. More recently it was used to house refugees from the war in Kosovo. Pontville dates from 1830.

Kempton

First settled in the 1820s, Kempton had Tasmania's first market–place for stock and produce. Other industries of the day included a flour mill and a brewery. Numerous hotels and lodging houses catered for weary travellers along the highway. Many of the buildings can be seen today.

Oatlands

Once mooted as the State capital, Oatlands has about 140 original Georgian sandstone buildings – the largest collection in a village in Australia – and it still retains the atmosphere of a nineteenth century country town. It was established as a military garrison in 1827 to guard settlers from marauding Aborigines. The Loal Church was built as a small medieval village church according to a design by Augustus Pugin, the English architect who created the decorative detail in the Houses of Parliament in London. He took a great interest in Tasmania and had a hand in several Catholic churches here.

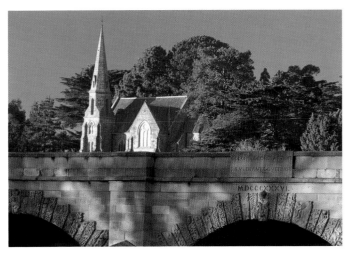

Ross Bridge and Church

Ross

The town of Ross lies exactly on the 42nd parallel and is probably the most picturesque of the towns along the Midland Highway, with charming colonial building and the leafy elms lining its streets. Peering into the back yard of the local homes you can see sandstone sheds and you feel as if you have been transported back 120 years. The best–known feature in Ross is the 1836 sandstone bridge. The arches contain 184 stones depicting Celtic symbols interspersed with images of notable personalities and carvings of animals.

With many other buildings from the colonial era, Ross has been classified by the National Trust. In the heart of the town is an intersection with buildings on each of the four corners which the locals are said to call 'Temptation', the Man O'Ross Hotel; 'Salvation', the Catholic church; 'Recreation', the town hall; and 'Damnation', the former gaol. The tourist information centre is located in the tearooms, which were originally St John's Anglican Church. There are many other interesting buildings in the village.

Travelling North-east from Hobart

The north–east region forms an enormous triangle north from Hobart to Launceston and east to St Helens, a landmark for anyone flying from the mainland to Hobart. The principal tourist attractions are along the winding roads of the coast, although there are some fascinating old mining towns and excellent bush–walking inland. The Sun Coast, Tasmania's favourite holiday spot, has sheltered beaches, rocky coastline, terrific surf and great fishing.

Buckland

After leaving Hobart, drive past Hobart airport, to Sorell, then follow the A3 highway to Buckland and Orford. Buckland is a small country town sprawling on either side of the highway whose main attraction is a handsome stone Anglican parish church dedicated to St John the Baptist, built in 1846. It looks as if a bit of England had been transported to this distant pocket of Van Diemen's Land. The beautiful east window was done in a style known as 'white grisaille', and apparently dates to between 1350 and 1400.

Orford

Once an important port, Orford is now a popular holiday resort and fishing village. There are many interesting walks in the area. About 6 km south of Orford is the Thumbs Lookout, 550 m above sea level with spectacular views of the Mercury Passage and Maria Island. If you are using Orford as a base for an exploration of the area, you might take in the Sandspit Forest Reserve, which has a 20 hectare stand of relict rainforest. It is a survivor from an era thousands of years ago when the climate on the East Coast was much wetter and favoured rainforest. A 20 minute, duck–boarded walk has been constructed to show off the rainforest.

Triabunna

Triabunna, the destination of many of the log trucks that thunder along the highway, is a commercial port that houses the APPM woodchip mill. The Pioneer and Working Horse Museum is a popular attraction, with shearing, blacksmithing and Clydesdales.

Maria Island National Park

This popular park lies 15 km off the coast and 88 km north-east of Hobart. It can be reached by a ferry that leaves from

Cliffs on Maria Island

Derwent River, New Norfolk

near the Triabunna Visitor Information Centre, corner of Esplanade & Charles Street, *(03) 6257 4772*. The island possesses spectacular scenery and a fascinating history, and was the first penal colony established in Tasmania in 1825. It is well–known for its abundant animal life, the only national park in Tasmania where all 11 of the state's endemic bird species can be observed. There are a number of walks, and the local limestone is studded with fossils. Facilities on Maria Island are basic, with no shops and limited accommodation.

Swansea

Situated 137 km from Hobart and 51 km north of Triabunna, Swansea has abundant accommodation and is ideally suited for a beach holiday or as a base for exploring Maria Island. Take a stroll around the town. The All Saints Anglican Church on Noyes Street is a lovely example of late Victorian stonework.

Freycinet Peninsula & Coles Bay

The Freycinet Peninsula (pronounced fray–sin–nay) is a place of captivating pink granite cliffs, dazzling blue seas and long white sandy beaches. It is now the most popular national park in Tasmania, with much of the park covered in coastal heathland with brilliant wildflowers in the spring. Moulting Bay Lagoon is a wetland of international importance with many black swans, while the lookout over Wineglass Bay is one of WA's most photographed spots, with an unspoilt white beach stretching in a perfect curve along the clear blue water. A three-hour walk to the top of Mt Amos gives some spectacular views. The adventurous should try Schouten Island, a seldom–visited section of the national park just off the tip of the peninsula.

Bicheno

The town of Bicheno is 43 km north of Swansea, and is an artist's and photographer's paradise. The beaches are covered in an incredibly soft silver sand that is unique to the area. Off the main beach is Diamond Island, home to the fairy penguin, which it is possible to walk out to at low tide. Bicheno entered history as a whaling station, and is now a popular fishing and boating spot. The surfing off Cape Lodt is usually very good.

Douglas Apsley National Park

North of Bicheno are the forested hills and river gorges

Coles Bay

of the Douglas–Apsley region. Its hallmark, the dramatic dolerite spire of Nichols Cap, is visible from the Tasman Highway. It takes in Tasmania's largest remaining area of dry sclerophyll forest, as well as waterfalls, gorges, lookouts and two rivers. A website that includes information is *www.tasmaniasouth.com/freycinet/douglas.html.*

Fingal

Inland from St Marys is the Fingal district, and many of the small townships in the area flourished and faded with the rise and decline of coal mining. North of Fingal, off B43, are some interesting forest reserves. Forestry is now one of the main sources of employment in the area after local mines ceased operation. The Mathinna Falls is a four-tier waterfall which drops over 80m. To the east of Mathinna is the Evercreech Forest Reserve which contains the 'White Knights', the tallest white gums in the world – 300 years old and 89m high.

Scamander

Situated at the mouth of the Scamander River, this town has spectacular ocean beaches. Mainly a resort town, it has some first–class accommodation and a large resort.

St Helens

This resort town is on Georges Bay, a further 37 km north. It is a popular holiday and commercial fishing centre, and the most northern town on the east coast. From here the road swings westward towards Scottsdale through some beautiful mountain country. The permanent population of St Helens is 1000 but this swells during the summer. For those interested in bushwalking while holidaying at St Helens, the Blue Tier is a must, an all–timber village classified by the National Trust. A mountain plateau which was once the site of a hectic tin mining industry, there are many ruins of mines and houses. Around St Helens are Humbug Point State Recreation Area, St Helens Point State Recreation Area and the Bay of Fires Coastal Reserve. Here you can take a number of scenic walks along some of the State's most beautiful beaches.

Mount William National Park

This national park was proclaimed in 1973 for the conservation of the Forester Kangaroo, now restricted to several small areas of the state. They can be seen throughout the park. From Mount William there are breathtaking views all the way to the Furneaux group of islands in Bass Strait.

Weldborough

For history buffs, the Chinese burial plot in the little town of Weldborough is worth visiting. Chinese first arrived in Tasmania from Canton in about 1870 to work in the tin mines. They once outnumbered Europeans in the area, but the last of the once–flourishing community died in 1994. The town once had its own joss house and Chinese casino and in the surrounding bush are many Chinese artefacts.

Derby

More history can be found in Derby in the Derby Tin Mine Centre, with a museum display of machinery, photographs and gemstones that chronicles the rise and fall of the area as a centre for alluvial tin mining. A mining shanty town has been recreated in the gardens surrounding the museum.

Scottsdale

Scottsdale, with a population around 5000, is 70 km north–east of Launceston, and is the centre of a large market garden area. Oil poppies are grown in the area, and when they bloom in January and February the countryside is a blaze of colour. Lavender is grown around Nabowla, 13 km west of Scottsdale. It blooms in late December through January and the air is filled with its perfume. One local landmark is the Sideling, a 577m hill which gives a magnificent panoramic view as far as the northern coastline and the Bass Strait.

Bridport

Bridport Wildflower Reserve in Richard Street, has a large collection of Tasmanian wildflowers, and offers coastal and mountain views. The Granite Point Conservation Area, *(03) 6356 1173*, is within easy walking distance of the town and also has loads of wildflowers in the spring.

Freycinet Lodge

TAS

North West Tasmania Region

The North West Tasmania region is a vast area that takes in the towns of Devonport, Burnie, Strahan and Queenstown. It is a land of spectacular capes and coastal scenery, rich paddocks over rolling hills, almost untouched wilderness areas and historic mining towns.

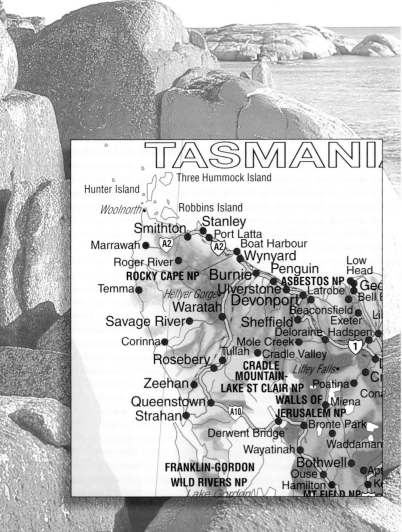

Devonport Population: 25,000.

Situated on the north coast of Tasmania where the Mersey River enters Bass Strait, the city of Devonport is the most important port on the north coast of Tasmania. Known as the "Gateway to Tasmania" for the car and passenger ferries that travel from the mainland, it is the point of arrival for the *Spirit of Tasmania I*, *II* and *III*. It is the city's close proximity to the mainland that is responsible for its importance as a port. Devonport had its beginnings as the centre of a rich agricultural area, and today the Mersey Valley remains one of Tasmania's main orchard districts. Referred to as "Australia's Market Garden", it is responsible for producing 40% of Tasmania's vegetable crop. Because of its link to the mainland, Devonport can boast the best range of accomodation in Tasmania outside of Hobart and Launceston.

The Mersey River was first explored in the first half of the 1820's, though early reports claimed the area was unfit for habitation, failing to predict the rich source of agriculture that it would become. In 1826 the Van Diemen's Land Company explored and surveyed the district, and settlers arrived later that year. Like so many other settlements the Europeans were met with opposition from the local indigenous population, which in the case of the Mersey River district resulted in the death of the district's first settler, Captain Bartholomew Boyle Thomas. The port facilities were already beginning to be used by the 1850's, predominantly by the timber and boat manufacturing industries. The town of Devonport was created in 1893 when the two towns on opposite sides of the Mersey River, Formby and Torquay, decided to amalgamate.

The ferry *Torquay* makes the crossing between East Devonport and West Devonport every half hour. The Victoria Bridge also connects East Devonport to West Devonport, and it is 2 km downstream from the ferry terminal. To get to the bridge follow Formby Road along the river bank. Walking and bicycle tracks circle the city and are found along the eastern shore, and the Visitors Centre can advise on where bicicyles can be hired. Victoria Parade is a scenic garden walk that follows the river and sea to Mersey Bluff, which is one of only thirteen major sites where rock carvings by the Tasmanian Aboriginals can be viewed.

Devonport

Visitor Information:
The Devonport Visitor Centre is located at 92 Formby Road, and can be called on *(03) 6424 4466*.

Points of Interest:
The Tiagarra Tasmanian Aboriginal Culture Centre and Museum features dramatic dioramas which show the lifestyle of the Tasmanian Aborigines, with "Tiagarra" meaning "keep" in the indigenous language. Found at the Bluff headland, the centre can be called on *(03) 6424 8250*.

The Devonport Gallery and Arts Centre's emphasis is on works by Tasmanians. The Gallery is at 45-47 Stewart Steet *(03) 6424 8926*.

Home Hill was the family home of Tasmania's only Prime Minister Joseph Lyons, as well as Dame Enid Lyons, Australia's first woman member of the House of Representatives. The house was built in 1916 and they lived there for the rest of their lives. Dame Enid passed away in 1981, and the home is now operated by the City Council in conjunction with the National Trust. Home Hill is as Dame Enid left it, containing many interesting and historic mementoes, and can be found at 77 Middle Road, *(03) 6424 8055*.

The Don River Railway is is an operating railway museum that is open daily throughout the year, with steam trains running hourly every Sunday and public holiday afternoons. The museum has the largest collection of steam locomotives in Tasmania, dating from 1879 to 1951, and the largest collection of passenger carriages dating from 1869 to 1961. The railway museum can be found off Bass Highway on the road to Ulverstone, phone *(03) 6424 6335*.

Outlying Areas from Devonport

Deloraine
Set amidst rolling hills midway between Launceston and Devonport is this charming colonial town, which has been classified by the National Trust. Many of the buildings date back to the 1830's. Among the many attractions in the district are the King Solomon and Marakoopa Caves near Mole Creek. Marakoopa Cave is part of the Wilderness World Heritage Area, a wet cave with two small rivers flowing through it and illuminated glow-worms. King Solomon is

smaller, but dry, with impressive pillars, cathedral chambers and light-reflecting crystals. There are good walking tracks at the Great Western Tiers, dolerite cliffs which rise sharply from the coastal plains. The Liffey Forest Reserve has several places for picnics and short walks, while the Meander Forest Reserve has a number of waterfalls and spectacular views.

Latrobe

Known as the platypus capital of the world, Latrobe was one of the first towns established on the north–west coast. The Mersey River with its willow-lined banks flows through the town. In recent years Latrobe has been classified as an historic town, and has developed a small but sophisticated restaurant and specialty boutique trade.

Port Sorell

The port is 19 km east of Devonport on the Rubicon River estuary. It is a popular holiday resort with prolific native flora and fauna. Good swimming and boating are available at nearby Hawley Beach. Nearby attractions include the Bass Strait beaches and the Asbestos Range National Park.

Sheffield

Standing guard over Sheffield and dominating the skyline is the 1231m high Mount Roland which seems to rise straight out of the rolling countryside. It is a spectacular backdrop for this town of around 5000 people with a surprisingly vigorous artistic life. The lake is part of the Mersey Forth hydro-electric development, with seven power stations and seven man–made lakes..

Ulverstone

About 20 km west of Devonport is the prosperous seaside town of Ulverstone. It is the business centre of rich agricultural country reaching south from the sea to the mountains. Safe and extensive beaches and river, woodlands, and mountain resorts provide ideal conditions for people to stay a while. The town is the woodchopping centre of Australia. A round trip to Gunns Plains, which is the site of a new hop industry, also traverses magnificent rural, mountain and river scenery. The spectacular Leven Canyon, about 40 km from Ulverstone via Netta must be visited. A short walk leads to to a lookout over a breathtaking 250m sheer drop down to the Leven River.

Penguin

The town of Penguin, 12 km further west, was named after the fairy penguin colonies along the coastline. It is situated on three bays which provide safe beaches for bathing and picnicking. It is best to take the Scenic Drive (old Bass Highway) between Penguin and Ulverstone for the superb views of rugged coastal scenery, including the off–shore islets which are bird sanctuaries.

Burnie Population: 20,000

Located 152 km northwest of Launceston on the Bass Highway, the city of Burnie is an important industrial centre and deep water port which handles more than 2 million tons of cargo every year. Built on the banks of Emu Bay and trading directly with more than 40 overseas ports, it

Mt Roland

Burnie.

is also surrounded by a wide forest belt that runs parallel with the coastline, about 50 km inland. About 22 million super feet of quality timber is produced each year from this area. Aesthetically, Burnie is remembered for the charming wooden houses attached to the hills which overlook the bay. The Tasmanian Travel & Information Centre is located at Civic Square Precinct off Little Alexander Street, their phone number *(03) 6434 6111*.

Wynyard

About 16 km from Burnie with a population of around 4500 people, Wynyard is a pretty town with an English ambience. The town is located on the Inglis River, and the airport for Burnie is found here. It is a major gateway to the north–west coast and offers panoramic views, while Fossil Buff (just beyond the Wynyard Golf Course) is a unique area rich in ancient fossils, including Australia's oldest marsupials.

Table Cape

Table Cape is a flat topped promontory with a sheer drop to the sea that juts out 7 km into Bass Strait. The whole of the plateau was purchased by Martin Alexander in 1870 and the lighhouse was built in 1885. The farm was sold in the early 1900s and named the Table Cape Farm.

Inland sights

Hellyer Gorge

The gorge is about 50 km from Burnie on the Waratah Highway, which links the north–west with the west coast. It is a mountainous scenic reserve with thick myrtle forest.

Waratah

About 80 km from Burnie (via Hellyer gorge) is the historic mining town of Waratah. It was here in 1871 that James 'Philosopher' Smith discovered the Mount Bischoff tin ore body. The scarred slopes are a reminder that it was once the richest tin mine in the world. The mine closed in 1946 and today it is a rugged outcrop of colourful rocks honey–combed with tunnels and shafts.

Savage River

Low-grade iron-ore was found in this region in 1877, but it was nearly 100 years before extraction became economical. Savage River is a company town, 125 km from Wynyard,

Table Cape.

which was built to accommodate about 1500 people working in the Savage River open cut iron mine. The ore is crushed, concentrated and pumped in a slurry over an 85 km pipeline to the Port Latta plant near Stanley on the North-west coast. It is possible to book tours of the mine, *(03) 6446 3235*.

Corinna

Once a tough gold rush town with 2500 people, Corinna sprawls over both sides of the Pieman River. It lies about 150 km from Burnie (via Hellyer Gorge), and is now almost a ghost town with a few facilities for tourists.

Along the Coast

Boat Harbour

This attractive town about 16 km from Wynyard is a popular resort. The view from the road that leads down the hill from the farming hinterland is one of blue-green seas and fine white sands. The crystal-clear water is ideal for underwater photography.

Rocky Cape National Park

About 30 km east from Wynyard is Rocky Cape National Park, the smallest of Tasmania's National Parks. Some of its geological formations are 700 million years old, and it also contains some of the richest Aboriginal sites in Tasmania. Two of the most impressive Aboriginal shelters are just a short walk from the car park. There are also some interesting caves, and several bushwalks in the park. The walk from Sisters Beach to Rocky Cape is noted for its spring displays of wildflowers. No camping is allowed in the park.

Stanley

The dominant feature of Stanley is The Nut, Tasmania's answer to Ayers Rock, a 150m rocky outcrop with a 35

Seal watching, Stanley.

hectare summit that dominates the coastal scenery for many kilometres around. The Nut is connected to the mainland by an isthmus about 7 km long, and if one wishes to climb it, there is an easy walking track which begins opposite the post office and ends at the summit cairn.

Smithton

The administration of the Circular Head Municipality of the far north–west is based at Smithton. It has a large modern butter factory as well as a bacon factory, a large piggery and several saw mills. The district has an ideal climate for growing peas, and the town boasts of a pea freezing factory. Air services connect Smithton with King Island, and aerial tours of the many shore islands may be booked at the airport. Driving directly south, the Allendale Gardens at Edith Creek can be visited (a botanical gardens in miniature), Balfour Track Reserve, Julius River Reserve, Lake Chisholm, West Beckett Reserve and Milkshake Hill Forest Reserve.

Woolnorth

In the north–western most corner of Tasmania is Woolnorth,

The Nut, Stanley.

a sprawling pastoral property with 34 km of ocean frontage. It is the remaining holding of the Van Diemen's Land Company which was founded in 1825 by Royal Charter of King George IV. The countryside is pretty, but rugged. The last four Tasmanian Tigers in captivity were caught in 1908 in the backblocks of Woolnorth. Woolnorth provides day tours for groups of tourists. They have a multitude of displays, activities and walks, and refreshments are available.

Marrawah

Situated at the western end of the Bass Highway, 48 km from Smithton, is the settlement of Marrawah, the westernmost town in Tasmania. It is well worth a visit as wildflowers and native fauna are plentiful.

The West Coast

The rugged wilderness of the West Coast draws tourists from all over the world. The rainforest, the wild hills, the tea–coloured rivers, the immense trees, and the wind-swept beaches makes one feel as though civilisation has been left behind for ever. The few people who live here are clustered in a few small settlements based on mining or fishing.

Nelson Falls

Queenstown Population: 4000

Situated on the rugged west coast of Tasmania, Queenstown is known for its rainy temperament. During the year it rains 320 days out of 365, and the annual rainfall is over three metres (3000mm). The locals are tough – the football ground has a gravel surface, the only one in Australia, as the cold wet winters make turf unsuitable. With the mine at Mt. Lyell having sustained the town since the late 1800's when gold, silver and copper were discovered, Queenstown is firstly and lastly a mining town. After seeing so many trees along the way, the first glimpse of Queenstown may come as a shock to many as the hills around the town are so denuded of greenery. This has been caused by a combination of tree felling, sulphur fumes, fire and heavy rain. As the Lyell Highway descends steeply into Queenstown via the Linda Valley, there is a panoramic view of the naked hills strewn with multi-coloured boulders that reflect the sun's rays. In the evening, the setting sun causes the mountains to change from shades of brilliant gold to hues of deep pink – an unforgettable sight. With the recent decline of mining, Queenstown has taken up tourism as a replacement. Its stripped and desolate landscape is now described as having 'outstanding heritage value' and being 'a visual and psychological icon' or 'one of the great cultural landscapes of Tassie'.

The history of Queenstown is fascinating. In 1883, two prospectors discovered a strange iron outcrop which rose about 10m above the surface. This was the famous Iron Blow, where mining of the riches of Mt Lyell began. The Blow was worked as a gold mine for ten years, with everybody ignoring the millions of pounds of copper within it. The Mt Lyell Mining and Railway Company was formed in 1893, one of the oldest mining companies in Australia. Failing to raise enough money for an extensive development program, mining at the Blow nearly came to a stop. Then an incredibly rich silver seam with an average of over a thousand ounces of silver to the ton was discovered, the lucky discovery helping the young company out of its financial difficulties.

In 1895, a metallurgist from the United States by the name of Robert Carl Sticht was given a free hand by the company to design the first Mt Lyell smelters. His pyritic smelting process, which represented an important advance in the technology of copper smelting, became famous and was copied in many countries. By 1891, the little shanty town of Penghana had sprung up around the smelters, but in 1896 was wiped out by fire. The refugees set up home in a newly planned town on the banks of the Queen River, and called it, appropriately enough, Queenstown. Mount Lyell had a long history, with a succession of owners opening, closing and re–opening it. But while the longterm future of the mine may be in question, in 1995 it was decided that excavation would continue into the next century, relieving some of the economic pressures on the town. Nowadays however, industries relating to tourism have increasingly become an option for those living in Queenstown, with thousands of tourists visiting every year.

An historic tour walk has been mapped out around the town, and information plaques have been erected at places of interest. No stay in Queenstown would be complete without a visit to the Mt Lyell Mine, and guided tours depart from the Western Arts & Crafts Centre, call Doug Hayden on *0407 049612* for more information. The original gold mine in Queenstown, Iron Blow, has also been developed as an area of historic and scenic interest, and offers excellent panoramic views over the mountains and Linda Valley. The Miners Siding Park in Driffield Street is a Queenstown Centenary Park Development, and incorporates the Miners Sunday Sculpture by Stephen Walker. The sculpture is made of bronze and Huon Pine, and depicts an early miner and his family on the day of rest. Also in the park is a restored Abt Locomotive, which was the only transport link between Queenstown and the outside world until 1932.

Visitor Information:
The Visitor Information Centre is located within the Eric Thomas Gallery Museum, *(03) 6471 1483*.

Points of Interest:
The Eric Thomas Galley Museum features displays of old photographs dealing with the West Coast, as well as items of household equipment and personal effects in use during the early days. The main feature of the museum is the photographic collection which dates from the 1890's, as well as the extensive display on the Mount Lyell diaster which claimed 42 lives. The museum can be found on the corner of Driffield and Sticht Streets, call *(03) 6471 1483*.

TThe West Coast Wilderness Railway is expected to become the state's premier tourist attraction. It is a restored 1896 rack and pinion railway that travels through one of the world's last pristine wilderness areas, crossing 40 bridges over wild rivers. The trains depart from both Queenstown and Strahan several times a day, and the journey takes about three and a quarter hours, including stops at Lower Landing, Dubbil Barril or Lynchford. The Queenstown Station can be found in Driffield Street, call *(03) 6471 1700*.

The Crotty and South West Access Road turns off the Lyell Highway 10 km north of the town, and was once the railway line for the North Lyell Copper Company. It provides access to the Darwin Meteorite Crater, the Franklin River, Fincham

Gordon River

Ocean Beach near Queenstown

Park, Kelly Basin, the King Power Development and Crotty Camp. Information on the area is available from the Visitor Information Centre in Queenstown.

Lake Margaret was one of Tasmania's first hydro–electric schemes, and was built and owned by the Mt Lyell Company in 1914. The station and village remain as they were in the 1900's, with the original machines still working. A 2134m wooden stave pipeline still delivers water from the lake to the Penstock, and a walk up the hill provides great views of the rugged west coast. The lake is just north of Queenstown.

The Balancing Rock can be seen on the Zeehan Highway only 14 km from Queenstown, and gives an insight into the unique geology of the area. The parking area here offers views over the glacial valleys of the Henty and Yolande Rivers. There are information plaques, and a sign–post to the rock.

Rosebery

About 10 minutes outside the town are the 104m high Montezuma Falls, the highest in the State – well worth the short hike to see them.

Tullah

The tiny town of Tullah is about 110 km from Burnie and 50 km from Queenstown. The Hydro–Electric Commission once used it as a base for its power developments; now it is an ideal spot to use as a base for exploring the wilderness areas of the West Coast. The Wee Georgie Wood is the only operational steam locomotive on the West Coast and offers a real thrill for the kids as they travel along the 1.6 km track.

Zeehan

About 33 km north of Queenstown is the town of Zeehan. Over the years its fortunes have fluctuated wildly as prices rose and fell and technologies developed. A number of buildings have survived from the glory days, including the Gaiety Theatre, St Luke's Church and the Post Office. The excellent West Coast Pioneers' Memorial Museum is housed in the old School of Mines, and contains number of exhibits. Places to visit around Zeehan include Trial Harbour (20 km), Heemskirk Falls (19 km), Granville Harbour (40 km) and the Lower Pieman Dam (50 km). Both harbours are popular with fishermen seeking crayfish and abalone.

Strahan

Once a sleepy fishing and mining town, Strahan is a prosperous and sophisticated village of about 550 people. The gateway to the State's fabulous rainforests, it was named Tasmania's premier tourist town in 1995. There are only two safe anchorages on the West Coast, Strahan on Macquarie Harbour and Port Davey further south. Macquarie Harbour is larger than Sydney Harbour, but Hell's Gate, the entrance, is only 200m wide. The sea becomes a frothing torrent as it rushes through the heads. The Ocean Beach is the longest beach in Tasmania, stretching for over 30 km from Macquarie Heads in the south to Trial Harbour in the north. The Henty Dunes are a series of 30 metre high dunes about 14 km out of town which are well worth exploring. The innovative Strahan Visitors Centre is a museum displaying the history of the region.

TAS

World Heritage Areas

In 1982, the three largest national parks in Tasmania were placed on the World Heritage list in recognition of their outstanding international significance. Additions in 1989 to what is known as the 'World Heritage Area' now means that almost 1,400,000 hectares, more than one–fifth of the State, are protected under an international convention.

Hartz Mountains National Park

Only 90 minutes from Hobart, this is the perfect place to experience Tasmania's alpine country and see the effects of ancient glaciers. Sculpted by the movement of glaciers and extremes of weather, the 7200 hectares of the park offer spectacular landscapes with both wet eucalypt forest and alpine heath. Because of its easy access from the Huon Valley and relatively short walking distances, this park is one of the best areas in the state for a day visitor. The park can be reached by driving through Geeveston on the Huon Highway, with the last 15 km a gravel track. For information about weather conditions, ring the regional office on *(03) 6264 8460.*

Spikey Ridge National Park

Southwest National Park

With an area of 608,000 hectares, this is the largest of Tasmania's national parks. Rugged peaks and thickly-forested valleys are interspersed with extensive buttongrass plains. Most of the park remains completely untouched and bushwalking off well-marked tracks is only for the experienced. It can be approached from south of Hobart, past Dover, or from west of Hobart, past New Norfolk and Mt Field.

Lake Pedder and Strathgordon

From the north, you enter the park from the Lyell Highway. Past Mount Field, the last real town is Maydeena. The first attraction is the Junee Cave State Reserve, ten minutes north of Maydeena, off a right–hand turn as indicated by a sign. There is a platform from which you can see a river spewing from an underground cave system. At Frodshams Pass a left fork heads south on gravel towards the shores of Lake Pedder.

Southwest National Park, Port Davey

The road eventually reaches the Huon Campground near Scotts Peak Dam. At the lakes there is boating and fishing, with picnic areas and camping grounds. It is hard to describe the wilderness here, wild and vast, with impassable rainforest, open moors and low scudding cloud. The knife-edge quartzite hills slicing the sky have names like The Needles, the Sawback Range and Mount Wedge. The dam has created Australia's largest water storage, with about 27 times the volume of water in Sydney Harbour, and at 140m is the highest concrete arch structure in the South Hemisphere.

Cockle Creek

From the south, the attraction for tourists who want day walks is the four–hour return walk from Cockle Creek to South Cape Bay. Once a nightmarish track through knee–deep mud, the walk is now almost entirely on raised duckboards and allows visitors access to the windswept beaches and headlands of this large bay. After crossing Blowhole Valley and some shady patches of forest, one arrives at an immense cliff ledge looking down on South Cape Bay and the Southern Ocean. Then one can descend a long staircase to a long white beach and admire Lion Rock, a beautiful offshore feature. For information about weather conditions, ring the ranger station on *(03) 6298 3137.*

The Overland Track

The Cradle Mountain Lake St Clair National Park is world–renowned for its dramatic scenery, trackless forests and unspoilt lakes and waterfalls. It is a high country park that takes in Tasmania's tallest mountain, Mount Ossa at 1617m, and many other smaller but equally spectacular mountains. Cradle Mountain is 1545m high. The most famous track in Tasmania lies between Cradle Mountain and Lake St Clair in the south. The track is 80 km long.

Cradle Mountain

Cradle Mountain is one of the best–known features of the Tasmanian wilderness, a great rocky plug rising from level country. Not long ago, a London newspaper ranked it with Italy's Lake Como, Scotland's Loch Lomond and Canada's Niagara Falls. For information about weather conditions, ring the regional office on *(03) 6492 1133.*

Lake St Clair

At the southern end is Lake St Clair, Australia's deepest lake (200m) and the source of the River Derwent that traverses Hobart. From Cynthia Bay there are at least two top walks that anyone can do. For information about weather conditions, ring the regional office on *(03) 6289 1115.*

Walls of Jerusalem

Steep mountains create a natural amphitheatre in a scenic subalpine wilderness. This park covers 51,800 hectares of wilderness and lakes, and is best known for the massive cliffs rising from a landscape dotted with tiny tarns. It is not as easy to get to the Walls as to the main features of other parks in Tasmania. For information about weather conditions, ring the regional office on *(03) 6471 7122.*

Franklin-Gordon Wild Rivers

This 440,000 hectare park forms the central portion of the World Heritage Area. The Franklin River attracts wilderness adventurers from around the world and is considered to be one of the most challenging rafting rivers in Australia. Most people think of this park as the most remote and inaccessible part of the State, but in fact many spectacular views are readily accessible by car. The Lyell Highway passes right through the park from Derwent Bridge to Queenstown.

TAS

Tasmanian Islands

King Island   Population: 4000

Located 80km from Tasmania and around 90 km southeast of Cape Otway on the Victorian coast, King Island is a name that has become associated with quality produce. Reknowned for the high standard of their dairy products. All of the company's products are made exclusively at their factory on King Island, and all of the milk used for production is sourced from local dairy farmers. The island is a low plateau that is 70 km long and 28 km wide. The two main towns are Currie on the west coast and Grassy in the south-east. The appearance of the terrain ranges from sandy beaches to rain forests with enormous tree ferns and paddocks, much like Ireland. King

Cape Wickham Lighthouse, King Island

Island also has almost 150km of coastline, close to 60 offshore shipwrecks, and a wide variety of wildlife and seabirds. For those visiting the island, Currie is the administrative centre and contains almost all available accommodation.

During the nineteenth century there were some appalling shipwrecks and remarkable survivals, especially on the island's west coast. Australia's worst marine disaster occurred in 1845 when the *Cataraqui*, a ship full of immigrants, ran ashore and 399 people were lost. The King Island Lighthouse, a massive granite building, was built at Cape Wickham on the island's northern tip. Ten years, later a lighthouse was built at Currie on the east coast. The best way to reach the island is via a cargo vessel that passes through on the way from Stanley to

Melbourne. The establishment of the Reid Rocks Nature Reserve has led to a proliferation of native fauna, and King Island abounds with wallaby, pheasant, quail, wild turkey and peacocks. For nature lovers, penguins and seals can sometimes be sighted on the island.

Visitor Information:

The King Island Tourism Incorporated is on George Street in Currie, and can be called on *1800 645 014* and *(03) 6462 1355*. Their email address is *tourism@kingisland.net.au*.

Points of Interest:

The Currie Lighthouse is a cast iron construction that was built in England in 1880, before being subsequently dismantled and shipped to the Island in 312 pieces. The lighthouse is now a National Trust building, and is open every weekend for viewing. Next to the iron lighthouse is the lighthouse keeper's brick cottage, an elegant 1879 building that is now a historical museum.

The Cape Wickham Lighthouse is the tallest structure of its type in Australia, at a towering 52 metres high. The beam from the lighthouse can be seen from 54 km away. Nearby are a number of graves of men and women drowned off the coast. It is not open to the public.

The Calcified Forest is composed of tree trunks that were covered by sand 7000 years ago, and now look like an eerie lunar landscape. Access is off the south road along a sandy track. Cars can be driven to within a few hundred metres of the forest, but the final stage must be done on foot.

Currie Harbour, King Island

Macquarie Island

From Macquarie Island to the Antarctic is only about three days sailing if the weather is right. This isolated chunk of rock is a small part of Tasmania, 1466 km south–east of Hobart. The island is home to about 20 scientists, 100,000 seals and four million penguins. It is the best preserved fragment of deep ocean crust known above sea level, and in 1997 it was declared a World Heritage site. The island is 34 km long and up to 5 km wide. It is mainly a long plateau ranging from 100 to 350 m above sea level, bounded on all sides by steep slopes or cliffs. There are several larger lakes and many smaller lakes and tarns. The weather is awful: cold, wet, windy and foggy. It is regarded as one of the richest wildlife sanctuaries in the world. As the only land in millions of square kilometres of ocean, it is a breeding ground for millions of birds, including albatrosses, petrels, skuas and four species of penguins. The island can only be reached by sea, and is the most remote, difficult and expensive place in Tasmania to visit.

Flinders Island

Flinders Island is the largest of a collection of the 70 islands in the Furneaux group, a scattered chain of islands in the Bass Strait between Victoria's Wilson's Promontory and Tasmania's Cape Portland. About 1100 people live on the island. Flinders Island has many deserted beaches and secluded coves with good fishing, mountains and nature reserves. Commercial facilities are generally only available in the townships of Whitemark and Lady Barron, at the southern end of the island.

In the late eighteenth century the seal–hunting colony established on Cape Barren Island. The sealers kidnapped Aboriginal women and the descendants of these unions are numbered amongst today's Tasmanian Aborigines.

LIA

South Australia is responsible for producing seventy per cent of Australian wines, and is famous for the vineyards of the Barossa and Clare Valleys. Those wishing to explore the rest of South Australia will be taken from the mining town of Coober Peddy in the outback, the iconic vastness of the Flinfers Ranges, across to the vibrant city of the state's capital, Adelaide.

The Flinders Ranges

SA

Adelaide Region

Located beside the River Torrens between the Adelaide Hills and the Gulf St Vincent, Adelaide is the capital city of South Australia. With the city designed in 1836 by Colonel William Light, the centre of Adelaide is laid out on a square mile grid of wide streets and over 900 hectares of parklands.

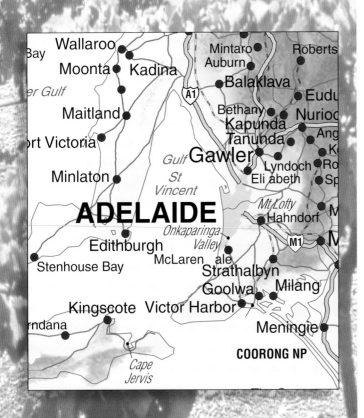

Adelaide Population: 1,072,585. Climate: Adelaide has a Mediterranean type climate with warm dry summers and cool winters. Average temperatures: January max 30°C - min 16°C; July max 15°C - min 7°C. Average annual rainfall is 530mm.

Situated beside the Torrens River and nestled between the Adelaide Hills and Gulf of St Vincent, Adelaide is the capital city of South Australia. With the streets surrounded by 930 hectares of parklands and laid out in a series of neat, easy to follow grids, Adelaide gives off a distinct impression of regularity. If any visitor to the city were to assume the layout of the streets was planned from the outset, they would be correct: Adelaide was designed by Colonel William Light in 1836. While a gracious city with a relaxed lifestyle, Adelaide has still managed to retain the feel of a large country town.

Edward Gibbon Wakefield was among the first Europeans to get the ball rolling in South Australia. Proposing in 1829 a scheme for careful and systematic colonisation, he planned it easy for visitors to find their way around the streets of Adelaide. At the centre of the city is Victoria Square, with the main street (King William) running directly through it. For a diverse insight into the history and culture of the South Australian capital, a walk can be taken down the North Terrace Boulevard. A large number of interesting attractions can be found here, including the South Australian Art Gallery, the South Australian Museum, the State Library and Parliament House. Other attractions found here include the SkyCity Adelaide Casino, the Adelaide Festival Centre, the Adelaide Convention Centre and the University of South Australia.

To get a taste of consumer culture while in Adelaide, you can't go past Rundle Mall. The main shopping centre of the city, it features most of the big name department stores as well as some quality restaurants and boutique shopping at the east end. The Adelaide Festival of the Arts is an important event on the city's calendar. Taking place every second year during Febuary and March, the two-week event features international performances, art exhibitions, poetry readings, live drama, dance and musical events. The Adelaide Fringe Festival offers a more offbeat and left-of-centre look at art, while Womadelaide is a famous outdoor festival with a focus on world music.

Adelaide City

to drive growth by selling a large amount of Crown Land and using the funds to pay for the immigration of labourers. But it wasn't until 1834 that his plan came to fruition, with the formation of the South Australian Association. Later in 1836, a fleet of English ships captained by John Hindmarsh arrived at the future site of Glenelg.

Colonel William Light, the man responsible for Adelaide's genesis, was sent out to choose a suitable site for the future settlement. Though his decision received heavy criticism, the city was built away from the sea on an inland muddy plain, which was dusty in summer and mud soaked in winter. Colonel Light's plans moved ahead, the city was designed along a clearly defined grid pattern, with the two major centres of Adelaide Central and North Adelaide to be surrounded by parklands. Not unlike the similarly planned capital city of Canberra, the careful planning is still evident today in the neatly geometric streets.

With the Central Business District following a grid pattern,

Visitor Information:

The South Australian Visitor & Travel Centre can be found at 18 King William Street in Adelaide, and you can phone them phone on *1300 655 276*. Email them at *informationandb ookings@southaustralia.com*, and the website to explore is *www.southaustralia.com*.

The Glenelg Visitor Information Centre is found on the Foreshore at Glenelg, *(08) 8294 5833*.

The Port Adelaide Visitor Information Centre is at 66 Commercial Road in Port Adelaide, *(08) 8405 6560*.

The Rundle Mall Visitor Information Centre is located in Rundle Mall in Adelaide, *(08) 8203 7611*.

Points of Interest:

The Adelaide Festival Centre is the home of the biennial Adelaide Festival, and is comprised of a multi-purpose concert hall and lyric theatre, a drama theatre, experimental theatre and an open air amphitheatre. An interesting feature is the 1.2 hectares of open plaza and terrace surrounding the complex, and the bistro overlooking the river. The centre can

Sunset over Adelaide

be found on King William Street, *(08) 8216 8600.*

Adelaide Zoo has an extensive collection of birds from right around the world, including endangered species and an extensive collection of Australian birds. Some of the most popular attractions in the zoo include the Australian Wetlands Exhibit, a walk-through Australian Rainforest Exhibit and a recreation of Seal Bay on Kangaroo Island. The Adelaide Zoo can be found at Frome Road, and you can phone them on *(08) 8267 3255.*

The Adelaide Botanic Gardens, along with the State Herbarium and the Conservatory, have numerous heritage buildings and subtropical and Mediterranean plant displays. Established in 1855, the Botanical Gardens cover 16 hectares and includes many landscaped gardens, tranquil lakes and shady trees. The Adelaide Botanic Gardens can be found at North Terrace, and can be phoned on *(08) 8222 9311.*

The Skycity Adelaide Casino is elegantly housed in the converted Old Adelaide Railway Station, in the middle of the CBD. The casino has around 80 gaming tables, 700 gaming machines, two restaurants, a cafe and live entertainment. Skycity Adelaide Casino can be called on *(08) 8212 2811.*

The Art Gallery of South Australia is located in North Terrace, and has a fine collection of Australian, Indigenous, European, Asian and Colonial art. Admission is free, and they can be called on *(08) 8207 7000.*

The South Australian Museum is literally a treasure-trove of objects, with collections including the Ngurunder, an Aboriginal Dreaming, and the Egyptian Room. The museum can be found at North Terrace, *(08) 8207 7500.*

Adelaide Hills

If there is one feature that characterises Adelaide's landscape, it is the rim of hills along the city's eastern country. Within a half an hour of the city centre is another world – a world of tranquility and greenery. In the summer it is a refuge from the heat; in winter, a touch of Europe.

Adelaide Hills is also the oldest wine region in South Australia, with a cool climate that produces many varieties such as Pinot Noir, Sauvignon Blanc, Chardonnay, and new varieties with over 40 labels.

Hahndorf

Hahndorf is 28km from Adelaide, and the people who settled Hahndorf were emigrating from the eastern provinces of Prussia. Founders Day is held on the Sunday of the Australia Day Long Weekend holiday in January.

The Adelaide Hills Information Centre is at 41 Main Street, and their freecall number is *1800 353 323.* Some of the town's main attractions include: the Pioneer Memorial Gardens in Main Street, opened in January 1939 to mark the centenary of the town, and the Hahndorf Oval in Pine Avenue, which was established in 1936 to mark the State Centenary.

Torrens Gorge

The North East Road from Adelaide leads to the semi rural setting of St Agnes, and a few minutes further on at Tea Tree Gully is the 100 year old Angoves Winery. A further 2km on, turn left into Range Road North to Upper Hermitage, on the Ansteys Hill to Gawler Scenic Tourist Drive there are panoramic views of the city, northern suburbs and Adelaide

Plains and across the Gulf of St Vincent to Yorke Peninsula. The next town is Inglewood, about 30 minutes from the city, with the Historic Inglewood Inn, one of only three Historic Inns in South Australia. Other towns in the Gorge include Birdwood, Mt Pleasant, Keyneton, Springton, Mt Torrens, Charleston, Tungkillo and Lobethal.

East Torrens

The East Torrens area is a nature wonderland with its many parks sheltering the native wildlife and birds. The winding roads, breathtaking views, cool waterfalls, bubbling creeks, pear, apple, cherry and plum orchards, make a trip here a memorable experience. The parks in the area are Black Hill Conservation Park, Morialta Conservation Park, Horsnell Gully Conservation Park, Ferguson Conservation Park, Waterfully Gully, Cleland Conservation Park and Montecute Conservation Park.

The waterfalls of Morialta are its best known feature, but there are also walking trails and picnic areas in this park. The dark wooded contours of Black Hill are easily seen behind Adelaide's north-eastern suburbs. Towns in East Torrens include Norton Summit, Ashton, Basket Range and Summertown.

Onkaparinga Valley

The Heart of the Hills is a beautiful valley, and the small river which gives this valley its name meanders through orchards, rich pasture and meadow land, flanked by the Mount Lofty ranges. Verdun is the beginning of the Onkaparinga Valley, and other towns that are in the valley include Balhannah, Oakbank, Woodside, Lenswood and Forest Range.

Mt Lofty Area

Conservation and Recreation Parks in the Mt Lofty area include Mt Lofty Summit Lookout, Mt Lofty Botanic Gardens, Mt George Conservation Park, Beechwood Gardens, Loftia Park, Sturt George Recreation Park, Scott Creek Conservation Park, Brownhill Creek Recreation Park, Belair Recreation Park, Mt Bold Reservoir and Cleland Conservation Park. The Mount Lofty Summit Visitor Centre & Gift Shop is on Mt Lofty Summit Road at Crafers, and can be called on *(08) 8370 1054*.

Blackwood Hills District

The Wittunga Botanic Gardens, Shepherd Hills Road, Blackwood, have two lakes and a sand-plain garden. There are

The Harndorf Hotel

Government House, Adelaide.

dazzling displays of Australian and South African plants, and they can be phoned on *(08) 8370 8370*. The Coromandel Valley is located between Blackwood and Clarendon, and has stands of large trees, streams and gullies.

Mt Barker Area

Mt Barker is the largest town in this area of the Adelaide Hills, and is a service centre for the surrounding rural district. One of the town's best known landmarks is the historic steam flour mill. It has been restored and is now The Flour Mill Tea and Coffee Shop and gallery. Other towns in the area are Clarendon, Meadows, Macclesfield, Wistow and Nairne.

Outlying Towns in the Adelaide Region

Port Elliot

Situated on Horseshoe Bay, Port Elliott is a popular tourist town, Boomer Beach on the western edge of the town being a gathering point for the surfing fraternity.

Cape Jervis

The cape, 109km from Adelaide, is mostly known as a jumping off place for Kangaroo Island. A car ferry takes passengers to Kangaroo Island from its moorings nearby, *(08) 8553 1233*. The Heysen Walking Trail begins at Cape Jervis and goes all the way to the northern Flinders, and allows people to explore the rugged coastline near Cape Jervis.

Murray Bridge

Situated about 80km east of Adelaide, Murray Bridge is popular with water skiers, particularly the river between White Sands and Willow Banks. As with many South Australian towns, Murray Bridge has great parks, and the town is also the base for trips down the Murray River.

The structures that give Murray Bridge its name.

SA

Fleurieu Peninsula & Kangaroo Island

The Fleurieu Peninsula encompasses the famous wine district of the McLaren Vale, the gulf beaches south of Adelaide, around Cape Jervis to the coastline, then to the western side of the Coorong wetlands.
Only 16 kilometres from the tip of the Fleurieu Peninsula, Kangaroo Island possesses an incredible 480 kilometres of coastline.

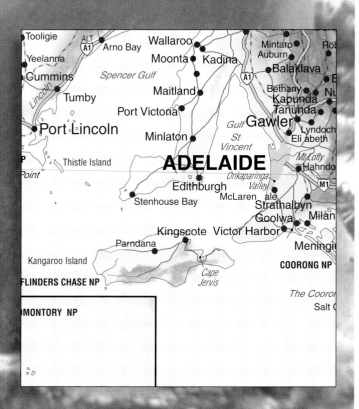

Christie's Beach

McLaren Vale

Population: 2,500. Climate: The McLaren Vale is described as having a chatacteristically Mediterranean climate: warm dry summers and cool wet winters, with low humidity and high evaporation.

Situated 39 km south of Adelaide, the McLaren Vale is an appealing little township at the centre of the wine coast. With over 87 wineries doing business in the area, the McLaren Vale is surrounded on all sides by endless fields of grape vines. There are friendly signposts on every corner urging visitors to come and taste the locally produced wines, and the township has an overwhelmingly inviting feel. With a moderate maritime climate and a long ripening period between summer and autumn, the McLaren Vale is recognised as one of Australia's premium wine growing regions.

From the early stages of settlement in the McLaren Vale, grape growing has been what has defined the area. The classic Hardy and Seaview wineries were operating their business from as early as 1850, and Thomas Hardy's purchase of the Tintara vineyard in 1853 is considered as the symbolic event that led to the town's genesis. The role played by the vineyards and wineries remains of optimum importance to this day.

Visitor Information:

The McLaren Vale Visitor Information Centre can be found on the Main Road in McLaren Vale, *(08) 8323 9944*. Their email address is *information@mclarenvale.info.*

Points of Interest:

The **Chapel Hill Winery** was established in 1979, and specialises in dry red and white table wines, as well as dessert ports. The winery can be found on the Chapel Hill Road north of McLaren Vale, *(08) 8323 8429.*

The **Coriole Vineyards** was established in 1969, and specialises in dry red and white table wines. They can be found on the Chaffeys Road north of McLaren Vale, and their phone number is *(08) 8323 8305.*

The **Rosemount Winery** has a long and prosperous history, and was originally established in 1850. The winery specialises in red and white table wines and sparkling wines, and they can be called on *(08) 8323 8250.*

The **Tatachilla Winery** is another Mclaren Vale institution with a long history, having been established in 1901. They specialise in red and white table wines and sparkling wines, and can be called on *(08) 8323 8656.*

Victor Harbour Population: 12,000

Located 83 km south of Adelaide, Victor Harbour is the largest of the towns on Horseshoe Bay. While once the most important port in South Australia, it now has more of a reputation as a popular holiday destination. The town's most popular tourist attraction is the horsedrawn tram service that travels along the causeway to Granite Island. With the service first used in 1896, it is today the only horse drawn tram in the whole of Australia. The tram service is considered a living tribute to the Clydesdale "Heavy Horse", who were responsible for pulling hundreds of kilograms throughout the day in years gone by.

One of the best known landmarks on the south coast is Rosetta Head, also knowns as the Bluff. A natural rock formation which dominates the skyline just west of the town, a magnificent view can be seen from the top if you can face the climb.

Visitor Information:

The Victor Harbour Visitor Information Centre can be found at the causeway on the Esplanade, *(08) 8552 5738.*

Goolwa Population: 4,500

Located only 83 km from Adelaide, Goolwa is an attractive

Victor Harbour

holiday town that was once a main port on the Murray River. Heritage is still very much alive in Goolwa: the boats now carry tourists, the historic buildings have been restored as art galleries and cafes, and on Sundays the steam trains continue to roll in and out of the grand old wharf area.

Visitor Information:

The Goolwa Signal Point Visitor Information Centre can be found at The Wharf, and can be called on *(08) 8555 3488*.

Kangaroo Island

Located 110 km south-west of Adelaide and easy to reachvia ferry, Kangaroo island is considered one of the most beautiful places in Australia to visit. The third largest inland island in Australia, Kangaroo Island stretches for approximately 155km and contains nearly 1600km of roads. The island is unique in that more than one third is dedicated to national and wildlife parks, with its removal from the mainland meaning that the impact of settlers has been minimal. The sheltered beaches are complimented by rugged and windswept coastlines, while the clean air and lack of water pollution has made Kangaroo Island popular with visitors.

While archaeological evidence suggests Aboriginals were present in Kangaroo Island around 10,000 years ago, the area was uninhabited when Mathew Flinders discovered it in 1802. Flinders named the island after the plentiful supply of food he found there: upon arrival he slaughtered 31 kangaroos, and he and his crew feasted on "as much steaks given... as they could consume by day and by night." In gratitude for this huge supply of food, Flinders named it Kangaroo Island.

American sealers and whalers established an operation on the island in the following year, and dominated the coasts for the next several centuries. Seperated from the European settlers and devoid of any form of law and order, the actions of the sealers were far from civilised. They forced Aboriginal women to help them hunt and capture seals, and explorer Captain Sutherland described them in 1819 as savages who "dress in kangaroo skins with linen, and wear sandals made of seal skins." While various attempts have been made to colonise the island since then, the low rainfall and the poor quality vegetation meant that it remained uninhabited for most of that time. However, the twentieth century saw tourism develop as Kangaroo Island's most important industry.

To fully explore all that it has to offer takes a minimum of five days. The main towns on the island are American River, Kingscote and Penneshaw, and they all have hotels, motels, licensed restaurants, coffee shops and delicatessens. The island is home to many Fairy Penguins, who come ashore at night to roost or feed their young, and can be seen on the foreshore at Penneshaw and Kingscote.

Visitor Information: The Kangaroo Island Gateway Visitor Information Centre is in Howard Drive, Penneshaw, and can be called on *(08) 8553 1185* or emailed at *tourki@kin.on.net*. There is also a National Parks and Wildlife Service office in Dauncey Street, *(08) 8553 2381*.

Remarkable Rocks, Kangaroo Island

SA
The Limestone Coast Region

Stretching south from the Coorong National Park along the coast to the Victorian border, the Limestone Coast was named after the ancient bedrock that inhabits the area. The area also includes the Coonawarra Wine region and other inland pastoral districts.

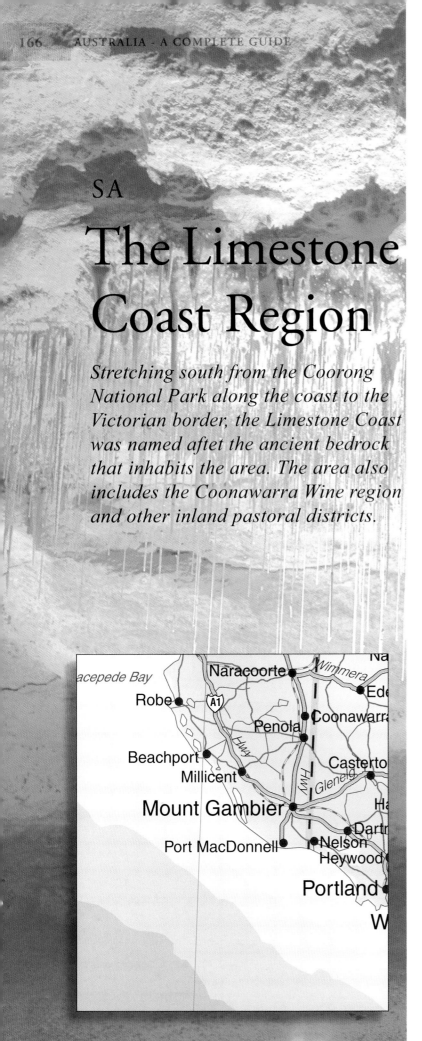

Blue Lakes

Mount Gambier   Population: 23,175. Climate: Average temperatures: January max 25°C - min 11°C; July max 13°C - min 5C. Average annual rainfall: 708mm.

Located 451km south-east of Adelaide on the slopes of an extinct volcano, Mount Gambier is one of the most attractive cities in the state's south-east. A number of agricultural industries are sustained by the healthy surrounds of the area, and vegetable farmers toil off the rich soil while the timber industry surviving off the plantations of radiata pine. One of Mount Gambier's most remembered features is the magnificent Blue Lake in the centre of the city. Both an object of natural beauty and the source of the town's water supply, Mount Gambier has become known as the "Blue Lake City". Situated in an extinct volcanic crater, what makes the lake so notable is that it changes color with the seasons. Every winter it transforms to an icy grey, before changing back to an intense blue every November. While many theories have been put forward to explain the occurence, what is truthfully responsible for the colour change remains a mystery.

It was the crew of the HMS Lady Nelson who first discovered Mount Gambier in 1800, with Lieutenant James Grant spotting what would later be called the Gambier Mountain. While the area remained empty of Europeans over the next several decades, the Henty Brothers sidled into the area in 1839 to exploit the little knowledge or control the South Australian Association had over this isolated section of the state. While the Brothers had to contend with very little interference (financial or otherwise) from the government, they ran into other problems with the indigenous population. While the Buandig tribe were less than thrilled with the arrival of European settlers on their traditional lands, neither were the Henty Brothers impressed when the Aboriginals developed an appetite for the sheep they were grazing.

The self-imposed isolation of the Henty Brothers did not last long however, and they were ordered back to the capital by the South Australian Association in 1844. Following this the government moved to take advantage of the area's rich resources, and the town of Mount Gambier was officially proclaimed by 1854. It was eventually named as a city in 1954, coincidentally exactly a century after the area had been proclaimed a town.

Along with the famous Blue Lake, Mount Gambier is also known as the "City Around A Cave", due to the cave that is found nearby. Set in an attractive garden full of roses, the open cave was the original source of water syupply for early settlers. The Cave Gardens can be appreciated from a number of viewing areas, with a suspended viewing platform offering an awesome view into the spot where storm water run-off from the city streets is directed down under the city.

Visitor Information:
The Lady Nelson Visitor & Discovery Centre can be found at Jubilee Highway East in Mout Gambier, and called on either *(08) 8724 9750* or *1800 087 187*. You can contact them via email at *theladynelson@mountgambiertourism.com.au*, or check out *www.mountgambiertourism.com.au*.

Alternatively, Limestone Coast Tourism is 3 Allan Drive in Mount Gambier, and can be called on *(08) 8723 1644*.

Points of Interest:
The Blue Lake is the premier tourist attraction in the area, and is 197m deep. An obelisk marks the spot where the poet Adam Lindsay Gordon made a famous leap on horseback over a fence on to a narrow ledge overlooking the lake.

The Cave in the centre of town is the tourist location of next importance, and its sunken gardens are worth a visit. Facing the Cave Gardens is the modern Civic Centre, which houses the offices of the City of Mount Gambier, Council Chambers, City Library and the Sir Robert Helpmann Theatre – a 528 seat venue which is host to local and visiting artists.

Narracoorte Caves

The Lady Nelson Visitor & Discovery Centre is of major historical and social interest, and commemorates the sighting and naming of Mount Gambier in 1800 by Lt James Grant from the deck of The Lady Nelson. The major feature of the complex is the full scale replica of the brig, which forms part of the structure of the building. Call *1800 087 187*.

The Centenary Tower is 190 metres above sea level, and offers spectacular views of the lakes, the city and the surrounding countryside.

The Umpherston Sinkhole is sometimes referred to as "the sunken garden," and is another popular tourist attraction. The beauty of the landscaped gardens can be enjoyed during the day while the floodlit gardens are turn into a natural noctarium at night, with possums descending to feed.

Port MacDonnell Population: 740
Situated 28km south of Mount Gambier, the town of Port MacDonnell is the most southerly port in Australia. Originally busy with freight sent by early settlers between Adelaide and Melbourne, it is now a base for the largest lobster fleet in South Australia which fishes the Southern Ocean between October and May. Surrounded by attractive parklands and coastline, Port MacDonnell has since settlement retained the atmosphere of a small fishing village.

Port MacDonnell was once the home of well-known poet and horseman Adam Lindsay Gordon, and the National Trust have transformed his 1860's cottage into a historic museum.

The Historic Royal Oak Hotel, Penola

The Port MacDonnell Maritime Museum offers a reflection on the town's history as a port, while the lighthouse at Cape Northumberland is South Australia's most southerly light.

North of Port MacDonnell is Mt Schank volcano, which was sighted and named by Lt Grant as he sailed by on the Lady Nelson in 1800. From the top of the mount there are spectacular views of the surrounding countryside, and walking tracks have been built on both the inside and the outside of the crater. The Little Blue Lake is 3km from Mt Schank, and like its larger counterpart at Mount Gambier the lake changes colour with the seasons.

Visitor Information:
The District Council of Grant can be found at 5 Charles Street. The office can be called on *(08) 8738 2380.*

Penola Population: 1,200

Located 51km from Mt Gambier, the town of Penola is the oldest found in the state's south east. With the Coonawarra area lying just north of the town, Penola also finds itself at the centre of one of the most prolific wine growing districts in South Australia. There are a total of around 25 wineries on the 7km stretch between Coonawarra and Penola, and the area's famous red terra-rosa soils of the area have been producing excellent red wines for over 100 years.

The early lifestyles of the settlers can still be seen in the many remaining slab and hewn cottages erected in the 1850's.

Many famous names have been tied to Penola – poets Adam Lindsay Gordon, John Shaw Neilson and Will Ogilvie all spent time there. Penola was also the home of Australia's first saint Mother Mary MacKillop, and the Mary MacKillop Interpretive Centre in Portland Street tells the history of both Mary's life and the district.

Visitor Information:
The Tourist Information Centre is at 27 Arthur Street, *(08) 8737 2855,* and has details of all the attractions.

Outlying Towns in the Region

Coonawarra

The Coonawarra grape growing and wine producing area now occupies a significant position in the Australian Wine Industry, and has over 20 wineries open for visitors. Call the Tourist Information Centre in Penola, *(08) 8737 2855.*

Naracoorte

Situated 39km north of Coonawarra, Naracoorte is one of the region's larger commercial centres. The town's main claim to fame is the Naracoorte Caves Conservation Park that is 12km south-east of the town, *(08) 8762 3412.*

Millicent

Millicent is 40km west of Mount Gambier, in the centre of the South-East. The Tantanoola Caves are 19km east of Millicent, in the Tantanoola Caves Conservation Park, *(08) 8734 4153.* The Millicent Visitor Information Centre is in 1 Mount Gambier Road, *(08) 8733 3205.*

Beachport

35km west of Millicent is Beachport, a quiet seaside town involved in the lobster and fishing industries.

Robe

Robe is 50km from Beachport, and the road there passes Lakes George, St Clair and Eliza. The Visitor Centre is located in the Library on Mundy Terrace, *(08) 8768 2465.*

Kingston

The entrance to the town of Kingston is guarded by a 17m lobster named Larry, letting everyone know that this is lobster country. Tourist information is found in the Big Lobster Complex on the Princes Highway, *(08) 8767 2555.*

SA

The Riverland Region

Continuing along a 300km stretch of the Murray River and a two hour drive northeast of Adelaide, the Riverland region extends from Blanchetown to the Victorian border. The consistent good weather and sunshine has allowed for a thriving fruit industry to exist, and over 90 per cent of the citrus, stone fruit and nuts consumed in South Australia are produced in the region.

The Big Orange, Berri

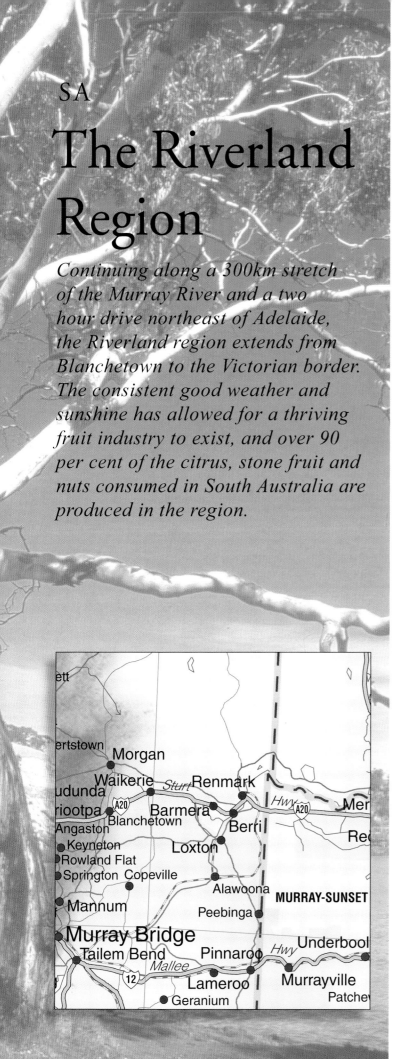

Renmark

Population: 10,000. Climate: Average temperatures: January max 31°C - min 15°C; July max 15°C - min 5°C. Average annual rainfall: 312mm.

Situated on the Murray River in the centre of the Riverland, Renmark has been recognised as the River Holiday Centre of Australia. Visitors to the town can enjoy a wide range of river holiday experiences, from the relative simplicity of self-drive houseboats and daily river cruises, to dining aboard the cruising Renmark River Cruises restaurant. The Paddle Steamer Industry is moored adjacent to the Visitor Centre and available for tourists to look at, and steams on the first Sunday of each month. There are a number of other ways the river setings of Renmark can be enjoyed, such as relaxing in riverside caravan parks, and recreational pursuits such as skiing, boating, canoeing or fishing. Renmark is also at the centre of a prosperous orchard area, and a wide variety of fruit and vegetables are grown in addition to the wine grapes. On an aesthetic level, Renmark is characterised by wide streets and an extensive collection of park areas.

It was the great explorer Charles Sturt who discovered Renmark in 1830. In stark contrast to most other European colonies of the time, those settling in Renmark actually had

Murray River Cliffs near Walker Flat

a healthy and cooperative relationship with the Aboriginal population. The Europeans were even taught how to properly exploit the food source provided by the river and surrounding environment, and they lived off a plentiful diet of fish, kangaroos, turtles, emus, ducks and lizards.

However, Renmark remained largely underpopulated until the South Australian government decided at the end of the century to establish an irrigation scheme. While the scheme had some teething problems, Renmark eventually became the fruitful agricultural area that it is today. Of interest to history buffs, Henry "Breaker" Morant worked in the local area at the Paringa Station. Later he was to join the Bushveld Carbineers and serve in the Boer War, before being subsequently executed by the British military. Renmark was proclaimed as a town in 1904, and is today one of the major service centres for all of the towns on the Murray River.

Visitor Information:
The Renmark Paringa Visitor Information Centre is located at 84 Murray Avenue, and can be called on *(08) 8586 6704*. Their email address is *tourist@renmarkparinga.sa.gov.au*.

Points of Interest:
The Renmark Rose Festival is held every October.

River Cruises - 1.5 hour day cruises, luncheon, dinner and sunset cruises are available from several companies, and the Visitor Centre has all the necessary information.

The Bredl Reptile Park & Zoo is located 5km from town on the Sturt Highway, has over 400 species of reptiles, birds and animals. It includes deadly taipans, cobras, death adders, tiger snakes, pythons, boa constrictors, crocodiles and monitor lizards. The park can be called on *(08) 8595 1431*.

Chaffey House was the original home of the Chaffey brothers, who played a large part in the town's early settlement. It is a site that is listed by the National Trust of South Australia, and includes a museum. It can be found on the corner of Renmark Avenue and Twentyfirst Street, and can be called on *(08) 8586 5745*.

David Ruston's Rose Garden is a 6 hectare reserve with over 30,000 rose bushes, a large collection of flowering trees and shrubs, and many varieties of iris and day lilies. A viewing tower gives a chance for some great photographs, and the gardens can be called on *(08) 8586 6191*.

The PS Industry was built in Goolwa, SA, and commissioned in January 1911 as a workboat for the South Australian Engineering and Water Supply Department. It played a major part in keeping the river open for traffic by removing snags. It is located on Murray Avenue, and can still be seen chugging down the river.

Harding's Folklore Gallery has a large ceiling mural depicting colonial Australian bushrangers, and a good collection of Australian art and weapons of the colonial days. The gallery

On the Murray River at Berri

is at Murtho Street and can be viewed on appointment, call *(08) 8586 6972*.

Morgan Population: 5,320

Situated on the Murray River and 166km from Adelaide, the township of Morgan has been known by a variety of other names including the North West Bend, the Great Bend and the Great Elbow. The site of the town was passed by Charles Sturt on his voyage down the Murray and back in 1830, and later became a point for overlanders on their way to Adelaide with stock. In 1878 the town was proclaimed, and the Kapunda to Morgan railway officially opened.

Shortly after the town was proclaimed, Morgan became the second busiest port in the state after Port Adelaide. At the peak of its importance, there were six trains a day leaving for Adelaide and steamers queueing up and down the banks for loading and reloading. Changing times saw the river trade fall off, and the railway service was forced to close in 1869. Relics of this era remain however with the original Station, Station Master's Residence, Turntable and Rest Rooms, which are all all in excellent condition.

Visitor Information:

Morgan Visitor Information Centre is at 14-18 Fourth Street, and can be called on *(08) 8540 2354*.

Outlying Towns in the Region

Berri

Situated on the Murray River, 18km from Renmark and 238km from Adelaide, Berri was originally settled as a pastoral area. When irrigation commenced in 1908 it became a major fruit growing area, specialising in grapes for wine and drying, and stone fruits and citrus. Large industries grew to process these fruits, examples being Berri Estates Winery, Berri Company Co-operative Ltd, and Berrivale Orchards Juice Plant and Food Processing Plant. Now Berri has a population of 7000, and is a pretty town with many parks and gardens along the town riverfront. The Berri Visitor Information Centre is on Riverview Drive *(08) 8582 5511*.

Loxton

256km from Adelaide, and about 30km from Berri by river, Loxton was settled in 1895 as a farming community. The Loxton Visitor Information and Arts Centre is in Bookpurnong Terrace, *(08) 8584 7919*. On Wednesday night the *Murray Princess* pulls into Loxton on her cruise down the Murray, and includes true riverboat celebrations.

Barmera

Barmera is situated on the shores of Lake Bonney, a freshwater lake whose source is the Murray River through Chambers Creek. Along with other Riverland towns, Barmera has been developed along community and co-operative lines. The ideal climate, combined with the water based activiities the lake provides, makes Barmera an ideal place to visit. The Tourist Information Centre is in Barwell Avenue, *(08) 8588 2289*.

Waikerie

Situated on the Murray River, Waikerie was settled in 1894, and is a well-planned, pretty town with award winning gardens. Street names bear evidence of a strong German heritage. The town is acclaimed as a glider's paradise, and also has the largest citrus packing house in Australia, the Waikerie Co-op Producers Ltd. Tourist Information is available at The Orange Tree on the Sturt Highway, *(08) 8541 2332*.

Blanchetown

Blanchetown is your first port of call in the Riverland if you are travelling the 134km from Adelaide, or the last if you are travelling from the eastern States. It is the start of the River Murray lock and weir system for water quantity control, which was completed in 1922 and is an impressive sight from the lookout at the Blanchetown Bridge. The town is a popular holiday resort with many holiday homes lining the river banks, and good fishing and skiing areas nearby.

Murray River Cliffs near Walker Flat

SA

Barossa Region

The Barossa region, comprised of the Barossa and Eden Valleys, is known as one of the world's greatest wine producing areas. Twenty kilometres wide and around thirty kilometres long, the area is rich with European heritage and is full of English-style villages, churches and chateaux.

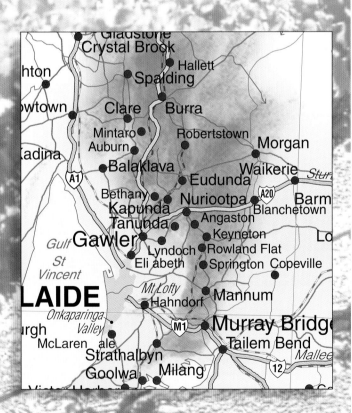

The Barossa Valley   Population: 19,700.

Climate: Average temperatures: January max 29C - min 14°C; July max 13°C - min 3°C. Average annual rainfall: 633mm.

The Barossa Valley is the heart of the Australian wine industry, and a name known around the world. The Valley is the vineyard of the nation, producing nearly 60% of Australia's wine and exporting more than 6 million litres of the fine drop every year. Those visiting the Barossa Valley will find premium wines, fine restaurants, magnificent old churches, and a fine selection of wineries and cottages. All this is set in a peaceful rural setting that accentuates the beauty of the undulating hills and surrounding vineyards. Some of the most reknown Chardonnay, Shiraz, and Grenache are produced in the region, with some of the most popular locations including Peter Lehmans, Jacobs Creek, Richmond Grove and Yalumba.

Following the state's proclamation in 1836, the South Australian Company sent German mineralogist Johann Menge out to inspect the ranges north of Adelaide. Menge returned from his survey with positive news: "I am quite certain that we shall see... vineyards and orchards and immense fields of corn throughout all," he said. With Menge encouraging the company to select land that encompassed

Chateau Yaldara, Barossa Valley

valleys, hills and open range land, two hundred Lutherans settled in the region in 1842.

The region was named Barrossa, after the site of a victory by the English over the French in the Peninsula war, though the consistent misspelling eventually gave it the unique Australian name of Barossa. More German-speaking immigrants soon arrived and settled in Langmeil and Light Pass, and the Lutheran churches dotted throughout the region testify to their influence. British settlers were also attracted to the area, but they tended to settle in Angaston and the Barossa Ranges. The two cultures blended over the years, creating the uniquely Barossan heritage of today.

The sheer number of big names who are located in the Barossa Valley is the biggest testament to the importance of the wine industry in the region. Some of these include Penfolds, Wolf Blass, Orlando, Seppelts, Peter Lehmann, Yalumba, and Krondorf, as well as a number of important boutique producers like Greenock Creek, Charles Melton, St Hallett, Rockfords, Henschke and Dowie Doole. It would be an understatement to claim that the Barossa Valley is the focal starting point for those discovering wine in Australia.

Visitor Information:

The Barossa Wine & Visitor Information Centre is at 66-68 Murray Street in Tanunda, call *(08) 8563 0600*. Email *info@barossa-region.org*, or visit *www.barossa-region.org*.

The Gawler Visitor Information Centre is at 2 Lyndoch Road at Gawler, call them on *(08) 8522 6814*.

Points of Interest:

The Barossa Wine Centre was opened in 1996 as Australia's first wine interpretative centre. It offers visitors the opportunity to view the history of wine making in the Barossa Valley, and information is available on the more than 50 cellar doors that exist in the area. The centre is contained within the Visitor information Centre at 66-68 Murray Street in Tanunda, *(08) 8563 0600*.

The Barossa Goldfields that are found within Para Wirra Recreation Park offer visitors the opportunity to check out the brief history of goldmining in the Barossa region. The discovery of gold in the late 1800's drew almost 10,000 frenetic fortune hunters to the area, though almost all of them were cleared out within a decade. The remanants of

their activities can be seen within the barossa Goldfields, and the mining history can be viewed on one of two interesting walking trail loops (1.2km or 5km). The Gawler and Barossa Visitor Information Centres can provide information.

Luhr's Cottage offers a unique experience of 'Barossa' German culture, and serves as a reminder of how tough life was for the German pioneers in the area. Hidden away in the tiny town of Light Pass, German settlers took up land in this area in 1845 and Johann Heinrich Luhr built the cottage the following year. The cottage was restored in 1984 and furnished with articles from the days when the Luhr family lived here, and it can be found on the main road in Light Pass, phone number *(08) 8562 1296*.

The Jacob's Creek Visitor Centre Gallery is built on the banks of historic Jacob's Creek. Beyond the Cellar Door Sales which are available, the gallery houses a number of displays which cover viticulture, winemaking and the history of the wine brand. The Jacob's Creek Visitor Centre Gallery is at Rowland Flat in Barossa Valley Way, *(08) 8521 3000*.

Seppelt's Mausoleum is styled like a Greek Doric temple, and dominates the hillside on which it is placed. The climb to the top has the reward of great views across the valley and ranges, and a pathway of palms leads to the settlement of Seppeltsfield, home of Seppelts Winery. The family's history

Elderton Winery, Nuriootpa, Barossa Valley

Vinyard, Barossa Valley

in Australia dates back to 1849 when Silesian chemist Joseph Ernst Seppelt migrated to the Barossa Valley.

Outlying Towns in the Barossa Region

Gawler

Gawler was the second country town to be created in South Australia, and its official birthday is January 31, 1839. Many of the buildings reflect the architectural design and influence of the late 19th and early 20th centuries, with beautiful stonework. From Gawler, the main road to the Whispering Wall Reservoir turns off to the right in Sandy Creek, passing the village of Cockatoo Valley. Near here are the remains of the old Barossa Goldfields along Goldfields Road.

Further on is the Barossa Reservoir, built in 1898 and the largest in South Australia. Rosedale is on the western side of the Barossa Valley Highway, driving from Sandy Creek north to Lyndoch, and in the district there are many beautiful old buildings. The Gawler Visitor Centre is at 2 Lyndoch Road, *(08) 8522 6814*. You can email them at *visitor.centre@gawler.sa.gov.au*, or visit the website *www.gawler.sa.gov.au*.

Lyndoch

In Lyndoch today there are ten wineries in the immediate area, all family owned, ranging in size from very small to one of the largest in the Barossa. Tourist Information is available at Kies Family Wines, Barossa Highway, *(08) 8524 4110*, and they can provide a map pinpointing the location of the various wineries, and a pamphlet outlining a walking tour.

Rowland Flat

Rowland Flat is well known today for the large winery complex. Driving towards Tanunda there are four wineries along Krondorf Road, running from Hallett Valley, on the western side, to the foothills of Kaiser Stuhl on the east. There are many typical valley buildings, many of which have been restored and offer farm-style accommodation. A nearby road gives access to the Heysen Trail, and the high country of the Barossa Ranges.

Bethany

Situated near Tanunda, Bethany has many lovely old stone houses, farms and cottage gardens, and many of the old buildings have been tastefully restored. Some of the old buildings are still used as houses. Also of interest in the town are the Pioneer Cemetery and the Lutheran Church.

Tanunda

A drive through the back streets of Tanunda, on the western side of the main street, takes you through Goat Square and Langmeil Road where many of the early stone buildings can still be seen. Goat Square was the site of early town markets, and many of the bordering cottages have now been classified by the National Trust. Restored buildings in the tree-lined main street include the hotel, the museum and the old institute. The Barossa Wine and Visitor Information Centre, *(08) 8563 0600*, can advise on attractions in the town.

Barossa Valley Way

It only takes about five minutes to drive between Tanunda and Nuriootpa, through the vineyards that stretch across the valley to the Barossa Ranges. Enjoy the history of Dorrien contained in murals at the old Seppelt winery building, which is on the corner of Seppeltsfield Road. The village of Siegersdorf was also in this area, and the name was one of those changed during World War I (to Bultawilta) and restored in 1975. Just past the Dorrien corner on the Seppeltsfield Road there is an old cemetery, and from the corner the road takes you to Angaston.

Marananga

Marananga, which is Aboriginal for 'my hands', was settled in the mid-1840s and originally named Gnadenfrei, meaning 'Freed by the Grace of God', by the pioneers who had gained freedom from religious persecution in Silesia. The original Gnadenfrei Church was begun in 1857, and there are many other interesting old buildings including the old school house.

Seppeltsfield

The town was established in 1851 when Joseph Seppelt arrived with his family and workmen and began to experiment with winemaking. Soon Seppelts became the largest winery in the colony, and the cellars and stores were described in the London Gazette 1892 as 'the most modern in the world'. They have been maintained in their original condition. The winery to visit here is Seppelt's, and they have tastings of their award winning wines daily, *(08) 8568 6200*.
Southcorp Winery, Nuriootpa, Barossa Valley

Krondorf Winery, Barossa Valley

Greenock

Situated on the western edge of the Valley en route to the mid-north, Greenock is a pretty place to visit. The town is home to one of the Barossa's famous bakeries, and the local hotel dates back to the 1870's.

Nuriootpa

The North Para River winds through the town of Nuriootpa, at the northern end of the Barossa Valley. The town is the commercial and service centre of the region, with a number of government agencies' regional offices. The Barossa Wine and Visitor Information Centre in Tanunda have information on a walking tour of the town, which visits about 20 sites.

Stockwell

Situated at the northern approach to the Valley, the peaceful village of Stockwell is dominated by the Lutheran Church and the old flour mill group of buildings, both of which played an important role in the town's history. The hotel and the winery offer a change to experience the days gone by.

Angaston

The town is named after George Fife Angas, a prominent figure in South Australia's history, who took up large land holdings in the Barossa Ranges and Valley in the 1830s. Angas himself settled Lindsay Park, near the present town, in 1851. Angaston is the centre of a rich pastoral district, with viticulture and fruit growing playing an important part in the local economy. Visitor Information is available at Timeless Books, 48 Murray Street, *(08) 85642635.*

The Eden Valley

Part of the Mount Lofty Range and situated south of Keyneton, the Eden Valley is an area of rugged beauty. The rocky countryside conceals the fantastic wines produced in the area, and the valley is home to classic regional wines. The novelty of an old Melbourne tram is available as a location to taste the valley's wines, and there are also a number of picnic spots, barbecue areas and nature walks. The Eden Valley shares its border with the Barossa Valley, and wine lovers would be well advised to make a stop off. Although it is primarily a vineyard area, there are still a good amount of cellar doors which can be visited.

Keyneton

Keyneton is a small village 10km south-east of Angaston in the Barossa Ranges. In the early 1900's, there were five wineries, all with large vineyards, located in the Keyneton area. The one remaining today, Henschke, is noted for the quality of its wines and old stone buildings. Henschke is owned by the fifth generation of winemakers and was established in 1868, call *(08) 8564 8223.*

Springton

At Springton is the historic Herbig Gum Tree, where pioneers Caroline and Friedrich Herbig began their married life and had two of their sixteen children! The original old stone blacksmith shop is now a small winery and cafe, and the old store and post office has been restored and is now an art and craft gallery.

SA

Clare Valley Region

The Clare Valley lies one and a half hours drive north east of Adelaide, and along with the Barossa Valley, is one of Australia's most famous wine producing regions. First inhabited by settlers from England, Ireland and Poland in the 1800's, the Clare Valley has a rich heritage reflected in the architecture of its villages.

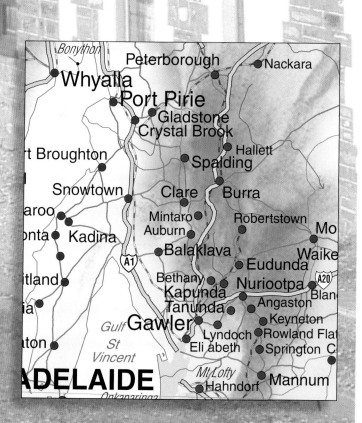

Old Colonial Houses, Burra

Clare Population: 4,500.

Situated around 135km north of Adelaide and 43km south-west of Burra, Clare is a thriving agricultural district. Located among the tree filled hills of the northern Mt Lofty Ranges, the historic beginnings of Clare are now an important part of the premium wine growing that is constantly underway in the region. Many of the 42 wineries in the district offer cellar door tastings and sales, and Knappstein Wines, Jim Barry Wines and the Emerald Estate are merely a sample of the famous wineries that can be visited.

Clare also features a large number of interesting places for those interested in the town's extensive history. The many historical sites include the Old Clareville Museum and Wolta Wolta, the home of early European settler John Hope. The Gourmet Weekend in May and the Spring in the Clare Valley festival that runs from September to November are among the region's most special events.

Visitor Information:

The Clare Valley Tourist Information Centre can be found at 229 Main North Road in Clare, and can be phoned on either *(08) 8842 2131* or *1800 242 131.*

Vinyard, Clare Valley

Points of Interest:

The Riesling Trail is a 27-kilometre path which links Clare with Auburn along the route of a disused railway line. It has been covered with a gravel that makes it easy to walk on and contains links to many cellar doors.

The Old Clareville Museum was once a historic cooperative winery in the area and has since been converted into a museum of wine making. Located in Lennon Street, the museum can be called on *(08) 8842 2576*.

Knappstein Wines is open throughout the week for tastings and purchases, and is one of the most recognisable producers of wine in the Clare Valley. Knappstein Wines can be found at 2 Pioneer Avenue, *(08) 8842 2600*.

Jim Barry Wines was first established in 1959, with Jim Barry having first entered the industry in 1947. They are located on Main North Road, call *(08) 8842 2261*.

Outlying Towns in the Region

Burra

Located 157km north of Adelaide, the town of Burra is widely known as a "Historic Copper Town". The mining days of the town have been well preserved, and the most essential place to visit is the The Burra Mine Open Air Museum. It conserves the history and remains of the Burra Mine that operated between 1845 and 1877. The Burra Visitor Centre is at 2 Market Street, call *(08) 8892 2154*.

Mintaro

Mintaro is a historically important town that has had its heritage preserved. The fact that the town is removed from the Main North Road has meant it has remained oblivious to the various changes taking place nearby.

Auburn

The southern gateway to the Clare Valley, Auburn is also the birthplace of CJ Dennis, who wrote The Sentimental Bloke.

SA

The Yorke Peninsula Region

The Yorke Peninsula is only a 60 minute drive from Adelaide, and is situated between Port Broughton and the Gulf of St Vincent. The secluded peninsula becomes more rugged and isolated at the southern end towards Innes National Park.

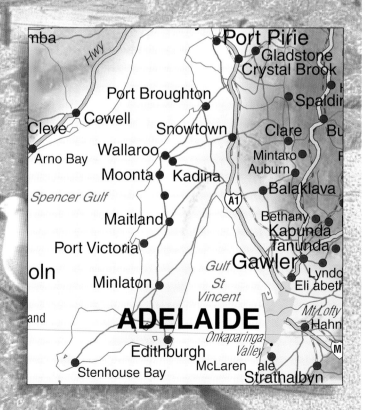

The Yorke Peninsula Region

Population: 24,000. Climate: The average rainfall along the central spine is about 50 centimetres falling off to about 35 centimetres towards the coast.

Located west of Adelaide across the Gulf of St Vincent, the Yorke Peninsula offers a delightful mix of rural and coastal living. While the 600 kilometres of coastline offer a

Foreshore at Ardrossan

lot of surf, sand and rugged cliffs to enjoy, the agricultural industries are driven by some of the richest wheat and barley crops in Australia. Fishing is one of the best recreational activities that can be enjoyed, particularly on the Copper Coast where some of the most popular specimens include salmon, King George Whiting and summer crabs. There are a plentitude of jetties and beaches where visitors can try their hand at reeling in a catch, and aspirational fisherman flock to the area. The biggest town in the Yorke Peninsula is Kadina, followed by Moonta, Wallaroo and Edithburgh.

Aboriginal tribes lived in the Yorke Peninsula for thousands upon thousands of years prior to European settlement, with artefacts found in coastal sand dunes dating right back to

Lime Kiln, Edithburgh

40,000 BC. Matthew Flinders was the first European to discover the Yorke Peninsula in 1802, but it wasn't until 1846 that Charles Parrington established the region's first sheep station in Oyster Bay. Copper reserves were discovered in both Kadina and Moonta during the early 1860's, and the trainlink that was constructed between the two towns in 1866 pushed ahead the economy of the region.

The Yorke Peninsula is renowned for its safe and beautiful swimming beaches, making them one of the main attractions that draws tourists to the area. Locations in the south-west corner of the Yorke Peninsula like West Cape, Pondalowie Bay, Daly Head and Chinamans offer some great attractions for experienced surfers. Fishing and snorkeling are also among the popular recreational pursuits, with the abscence of pollution, clear waters and abundant marine life making it an irresistable attraction of those who love to dive. There are more than 85 known shipwrecks scattered along the coastline, and the maritime Heritage Trail features over 25 wrecks. The state branch of the Department of Environment & Heritage can be phoned for further information, *(08) 8204 1910.*

Visitor Information:

The Yorke Peninsula Regional Visitor Information Centre can be found at 50 Moonta Road in Kadina, and can be called on either *(08) 8821 2333* or *1800 654 991.*

Points of Interest:

The Innes National Park represents perhaps the best area in the Yorke Peninsula to view untouched nature, situated on over 9000 hectares of natural coast mallee. Located in the south-west section of the Peninsula, the park ranger can be called on *(08) 8854 3200* .

The National Dry-Land Farm Museum and Tourism Centre at Kadina is one of the biggest sources of history in the Yorke Peninsula, with the various displays depicting the region's agricultural, mining, social and personal history. Particularly useful if you want to gain an insight into the lives of the early settlers, it can be found in the Visitor Information Centre, call *(08) 8821 2333.*

The Bublacowie Military Museum and Memorial was built in the grounds of the local school, and was established to honour the memories of those who have fought in war. The museum is surrounded by two acres of bush, and features a large collection of photographs and personal items from those who served in our country's major conflicts. The museum is located at Bublacowie on the Southern Yorke Peninsula, call *(08) 8853 4379.*

The Moonta State Heritage Area includes a museum, an old sweet shop, an 1860's methodist church, a narrow gauge tourist train, a miners cottage and mine ruins.

The Wheal Hughes Copper Mine is an underground tourist mine at Moonta, and allows an experience of the underground workings of the tunnels. Call *(08) 8825 1892.*

The Captain Harry Butler Memorial "Red Devil" is a tribute to one of the area's most famous historical icons, with the tiny historic warplane that he flew in WWI on display. The memorial is on the Main Street in Minlaton.

SA

Eyre Peninsula Region

Covering a vast portion of the state, the Eyre Peninsula encompasses the large regional town of Whyalla in the east, the imposing Gawler Ranges in the north, and the beautiful town of Port Lincoln in the South. A solid mix of stunning coastlines, arid desert and sandy bays, the Eyre Peninsula stretches all the way to the Western Australian border.

Point Labatt near Streamy Bay

Whyalla

Population: 22,00. Climate: Average maximum temperature is 29°C; minimum is 7C in winter and 19°C in summer. There are 301 days of sunshine every year, and the average annual rainfall is 268mm.

Situated 394km north-west of Adelaide on the western side of Spencer Gulf, Whyalla is the second largest regional city in South Australia. Referred to as the place "Where the outback meets the sea", Whyalla is also the nation's third largest steel producer. The BHP iron and steel works (now known as OneSteel) have ensured Whyalla's reputation as an industrial city, and the town has been dependent on the company's decisions for most of its lifetime. However, the mediteranean climate and and sunny weather of Whyalla has meant it is visited by tens of thousands of tourists every year.

While Mathew Flinders first discovered Whyalla in 1802, it wasn't until the 1860's that European settlement began in the area. It became obvious before the end of the nineteenth century that Whyalla was to become a major source of natural resources, and in 1886 BHP seized the opportunity with a plan to transport iron ore to Broken Hill. BHP continued to dominate the town's development throughout the twentieth century, and Whyalla was effectively under the company's control until as late as 1945. Even after Whyalla achieved the status of a "city commission", the local members continued to share control with BHP representatives, until 1970.

Red Banks, Spencer Gulf, Port Augusta

Whyalla was transformed into a major production centre, and at one point they became the largest shipbuilding port in Australia. Over sixty-three ships were built by 1978, with the *Clutha Capricorn* being the largest ever ship built in Australia. The first ship to be constructed in the shipyard was the 650 tonne *HMAS Whyalla*, and to this day it still remains on display overlooking the Lincoln Highway. There are a number of sites that visitors to Whyalla can see to gain a sense of the city's rich history in the Australian steel industry, including the Maritime Museum and the local steelworks.

Visitor Information:
Whyalla Visitor Centre is on the Lincoln Highway, *(08) 8645 7900* or *1800 088 589*, and can be emailed at *visitor.centre@whyalla.sa.gov.au*. Visit the website *www.whyalla.com* for further information.

Points of Interest:
The Maritime Museum was first established in 1988, and consists of the former HMAS Whyalla, the museum building and the Australian native plants garden. Some of the most interesting things to see in the museum include the naval history of several WWII corvettes constructed in Whyalla, and the material on the extensive history of BHP in the city. The Maritime Museum is located on the Lincoln Highway and can be contacted on *(08) 8645 8900*.

The Whyalla Conservation Park covers an area of 1,011 hectares and contains many good examples of the native flora and fauna of the Eyre Peninsula. Notable for its importance to Aboriginal groups and inclusion in Dreamtime stories, the Whyalla Conservation Park is located off the Lincoln Highway just 10km from the city.

The Whyalla Leisure Centre has been described as the best such facility existing in South Australia outside of the metropolitan areas. The centre includes a heated indoor swimming pool, diverse gym facilities, a number of different sports courts as well as other essential services. The Leisure Centre is located on Nicholas Avenue, *(08) 8645 5488*.

Port Bonython & Point Lowly are located twenty kilometres east of Whyalla. The area is home to a lighthouse as well as a frequent population of dolphins and coastal bird life, and the rocky shoreline is popular with tourists and locals alike

Boston Bay, Port Lincoln

for swimming, fishing and picnicing. The Point Lowly Lighthouse is the oldest building in South Australia having been built in 1883, and remains in operation.

Port Lincoln Population: 14,00
Located 656 km west of Adelaide on the easterly side of the Eyre Peninsula, Port Lincoln has become informally known as the region's capital. With the city located on Boston Bay (which is almost four times the size of Sydney Harbour), the grain and fishing industries are of great importance to Port Lincoln. Boston Bay is also ideal for sailing, swimming, water skiing, fishing and diving.

Highlights of the town and surrounds include the Mayne and Arteyrea galleries, Mill Cottage Museum and Alex Stenross Maritime Museum. From Winter's Hill lookout, 5km from the town, there is a very good view of York Peninsula, and short trips can be made to Sleaford Bay, Lincoln National Park, Whaler's Way and Flinder's Well.

Visitor Information:
The Port Lincoln Visitor Information Centre can be found at 3 Adelaide Place, *(08) 8683 3544*. Their email address is *info@visitportlincoln.net*.

Ceduna Population: 3,500
Located 1964 km from Perth and 781 km northwest of Adelaide, Ceduna is the last area of any importance before the vast emptyness of the Nullabor Plains. The port at the edge of the Great Australian Bite, Ceduna is a popular overnight stop for the east-west traveller, and is gaining a reputation as a holiday destination in its own right.

Ceduna provides access to the scenic drives of Decres Bay, Laura Bay, the Davenport Creek wilderness area and Denial Bay. The town has a reputation for its fabulous fishing and quality seafood, and a visit to Denial Bay Oyster Farm is essential for seafood lovers. Further along the coast, near Penong, is Cactus Beach, regarded as having one of the best surf breaks in the world.

Visitor Information:

The Ceduna Visitor Information Centre is located at 58 Poynton Street, and can be called on *(08) 8625 2780.*

Port Augusta Population:

Lying on the saltbush plains between the Spencer Gulf and the Flinders Ranges, Port Augusta has become known as both the "Crossroads of Australia" and the "Gateway to the Outback". The spot was surveyed in 1852, and has a number of historical places of interest. It is an ideal base for access to the attractions of the Flinders Ranges, Eyre Peninsula and the Outback of South Australia.

Visitor Information:

The Port Augusta Tourist Information Centre is in the Wadlata Outback Centre complex at 41 Flinders Terrace, *(08) 8641 0793.* Email at *wadlata@portaugusta.sa.gov.au.*

Goverment Jetty, Carpenter's Landing, Port Augusta

Outlying Towns from Whyalla

Port Bonython

The Port is home to the Santos Fractionation Plant, and although tours do not operate over the plant, it can clearly be seen from the roadside and shoreline vantage points. Liquid hydrocarbons, oil condensate and LPG are mixed at Moomba, and pumped through a 659km underground pipeline to Port Bonython, where the liquids are split into their various components by a distillation process. Port Bonython has been operating since 1984.

Iron Knob

The township of Iron Knob is 52km north west of Whyalla, on the Eyre Highway which links Port Augusta with Western Australia. Flora of the area is mainly low, stunted growth of mallee scrub and saltbush. Sheep grazing is the major local primary industry. Mining began in 1899, the ore being used as a flux in the smelters of Port Pirie.

Cowell

Situated on the sheltered Franklin Harbour, which is more like a large lagoon, is the sleepy village of Cowell. It is a safe fishing and boating resort, with night crabbing in the shallows a special attraction. Jade is mined at nearby Mt Geraghty, and is brought to the factory in Cowell where it is cut and polished.

Old Railway Station & Historic Buildings

Elliston

The drive to Elliston, about 140km up the coast, passes Sheringa Beach, salt lakes, the Old Hamilton Eating House, and you can detour to Locks Wells, a favourite with fishermen and photographers. The little fishing village of Elliston is nestled between some small hills and Waterloo Bay, and there are spectacular stretches of rugged cliffs rimming the coast. Flinders Island is 35km off the Elliston coast. Visitor information is available from the Elliston Community Information Centre in Memorial Drive, *(08) 8697 9200.*

Outlying spots from Port Augusta

Port Pirie

Port Pirie is 95km south from Port Augusta. Today it has the largest lead smelter in the world, and produces lead, zinc, gold, cadmium, antimony and copper by-products, and sulphuric acid. Lead is South Australia's biggest single-produced export income earner. Port Pirie has all the facilities you would expect for a city of its population. The Tourist Information Office is at 3 Mary Elie Street, *(08) 8633 0439.*

Peterborough

Situated 162km south east of Port Augusta, Peterborough is one of only two known towns in the world where three different rail gauges meet. It is the gateway to the Flinders Ranges for travellers from NSW, or from Adelaide via the historic mining town of Burra. The Visitor Information Centre is located in a restored 1917 Railway Car on Main Street, *(08) 8651 2545.*

SA

Flinders Ranges & Outback Region

The Flinders Ranges & Outback region extends from Southern Flinders near Melrose to Innamincka, which lies 1,100 km north of Adelaide. The outback covers around 75 per cent of South Australia, and borders on Queensland, Western Australia, New South Wales and the Northern Territory.

Donkeys & Ruins in the Flinders Ranges

Flinders Ranges Climate: Semi-arid climate which leads to dry-country vegetation, including saltbush and light timber. Summer is very hot with temperatures ranging from 30-40°C, while winter can get very cold.

Beginning at the northern end of St Vincent's Gulf and stretching approximately 800km into the dry outback region, the Flinders Ranges are notorious for the stunning sights they offer. Any artist or photographer will be delighted by the vast and uncompromising landscapes that make up Ranges, and they have become truly synonymous with images of the Australian outback. The area is composed of granite mountain ranges with towering peaks, razor backed quartzite ridges slashed by precipitous gorges, and creeks with cool, deep waterholes framed by stately gums.

Matthew Flinders was the first to look upon the Flinders Ranges in 1802, and it was his name that was chosen to describe the low lying range of hills. The areas around the Flinders Ranges contain some of earth's most ancient landscapes, estimated to be around 1.8 billion years old.

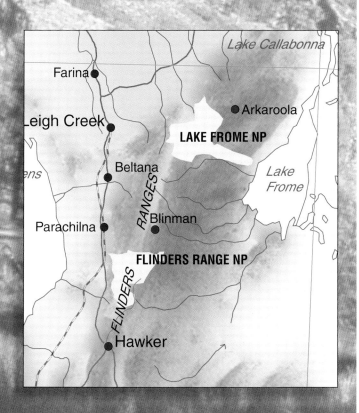

Lake Callabonna

Farina

Leigh Creek

Arkaroola

LAKE FROME NP

Beltana

Lake Frome

RANGES

Blinman

Parachilna

FLINDERS RANGE NP

FLINDERS

Hawker

Opal Mining, Coober Pedy

Remains of dinosaurs and early life forms can be found as fossils in many places, along with rare specimens of wildlife, plants and rock formations. Much of this is preserved by the several National Parks in the area, which are all worth visiting. The main towns in the region include Quorn, Hawker and Wilpena Pound.

Visitor Information:

The Flinders Ranges Visitor Information Centre is at 3 Seventh Street in Quorn, and can be called on *(08) 8648 6419*. Their email address is *vic@flindersranges.com*.

The Wilpena Pound Visitor Centre is located at the Wilpena Pound Resort, *(08) 8648 0048*. Useful information can also be found at *www.flindersoutback.com*.

Points of Interest:

The Pichi Richi Railway is a working railway museum which features restored steam trains, diesel rail-cars and carriages from the original Ghan railway. The train operates a three hour return journey through the Pichi Richi Pass between March and November, and can be called on *(08) 8648 6598*.

The Mt. Painter Sanctuary and Historic Reserve is a unique experience, with its rugged outback beauty and wildlife. Steeped in history and dotted with geological monuments, the reserve offers a variety of experiences to visitors including hot springs, picturesque gorges, waterholes and rare wildlife.

The Yourambulla Caves are only a few kilometres south of Hawker, and contain some excellent examples of Aboriginal rock paintings. The caves are also worth checking out for the panoramic view of the surrounding ranges.

Coober Pedy Population: 3,500

Situated around 846 km north of Adelaide, Coober Peddy is one of Australia's most fascinating and unique locations for opal mining. Placed right bang in the middle of some of the nation's most difficult and unforgiving environments, Coober Peddy is notable in that close to 80% of the town's population live undergroud. This is to help them escape the harsh temperatures of the outback, as the temperature in Coober Peddy has been known to rise as far as 60°C. Much larger than other opal areas like White Cliffs or Lightning Ridge, Coober Peddy is one of the largest sources of opals in the world.

Opal was originally located in Coober Peddy in 1913, the discovery made by 14-year-old Willie Hutchison who has since had the main street named after him. It was said to be soldiers who had fought in the first World War who started the town's fascination with living underground. Having become accustomed to living and fighting in the trenches of Europe, they knew of the possible advantages that a hole in the ground could provide. The Progress and Mining Association officially named the town in 1922, and the story behind the name is nothing if not amusing. Taken from aboriginal language, the word "coober" means white man, with "pedy" referring to a

Hucks Lookout, Flinders Ranges

hole. So the name Coober Peddy actually refers to what the local Aboriginal population viewed as baffling and bizzare behaviour – "white men down holes."

The third Mad Max film "Beyond Thunderdome" was filmed largely around Coober Peddy, and the film gives a good idea of what the desolate and dust-swept landscape looks like. Visitors can stay in an underground hotel and backpacker lodge, dine underground, shop underground, and even pray underground at the local church. Annual events include the Easter Opal Festival and the Coober Pedy Races each October.

Visitor Information:
The Coober Pedy Information Centre can be called on *1800 637 076.*

Outlying Towns of the Flinders Ranges & Outback Region

Quorn

Situated 334km from Adelaide, the old railway town of Quorn is an ideal holiday base. The town has many historic buildings that reflect its former importance as a railway junction. Nowadays, the only railway sounds are when the old steam trains (Afghan Express, Pichi Richi Explorer and Barwell Bull) run through Pichi Richi Pass to Woolshed Flat and Stirling North.

Only a short distance from town are the Wankerie Falls, Warren, Buckaringa and Middle Gorges. About 14km south of the town is Mt Brown, and at 900m it is the highest point in the area. Nearer town are Devil's Peak and Dutchman's Stern, both of which are richly coloured and have walking trails to the summit. The Quorn Tourist Information Centre can be called on *(08) 8648 6419.*

Hawker

A typical outback town, Hawker is the hub of the Flinders Ranges, being the junction of roads from Port Augusta, Orroroo, Leigh Creek, Marree and Wilpena/Blinman. It is 374km from Adelaide, and was a thriving railway town before the line was relocated in 1956. Hawker is an important tourist centre in the Flinders, and a Town Heritage Walk has been developed to take you through the town's pioneering history.

A walking trail and scenic lookout have been established at Jarvis Hill, 5km south-west of Hawker. The lookout provides a spectacular panorama of the surrounding countryside. Easy day trips from Hawker include to Quorn and Pichi Richi Pass, Wilpena, Brachina and Parachilna Gorges, Leigh Creek coalfield and Aroona Dam. The Tourist Information Centre is at Hawker Motors, corner of Wilpena & Cradock Roads, *(08) 8648 4014.*

Wilpena Pound

Situated 54km north of Hawker, the Pound is probably the best known feature of the Flinders Ranges. It is an oval bowl 16km long and 10km wide, surrounded by high quartzite cliffs. Enough rain falls on the higher walls of the range to keep the inner gorges and valleys green for at least part of the year, making it an oasis in the dry heart of Central Australia. Handsome red rivergums line the watercourses.

Blinman

Situated 60km from Wilpena, and 485km from Adelaide, Blinman was once a bustling copper mining town, and some of the old mine machinery can still be seen. East of Blinman, the road winds through the scenic Eregunda Valley to Chambers Gorge, a rugged area with sparkling rock pools and Aboriginal carvings. North of Chambers Gorge is Big Morot Gorge with numerous rock pools and cliffs, while to the south, on the Wilpena road is the extensive and prominent rocky outcrop called the Great Wall of China.

Western Australia is the nation's largest state, covering a third of the continent and larger than the whole of Western Europe. While the eastern border is made up of hot red desert, the western border is hundreds of kilometres of beautiful coastline. The state's capital Perth is the sunniest of all the the Australian cities, and visitors exploring the rest of Western Australia will encounter bountiful National Parks, quaint gold towns and an impressive outback.

WA

Perth & The South West Area

With over 1 million tourists visiting the South-West Region of Western Australia, in addition to the 1.4 million that populate the state's capital Perth, the south-west area is the most popular destination of the state. Those who yearn for bright lights and tall buildings can visit the skyscrapers and riverside parks of Perth, while the rest of the surrounding region contains a wide range of natural delights: beaches, forests, state parks, wineries, rolling hills and endless pastures.

Perth Population: 1,400,000. Climate: Perth is the sunniest of all Australian cities, averaging eight hours of sunshine a day. It boasts an average summer day temperature of 30C, and an average night temperature of 17C. The average winter day temperature is a mild 18C, and the night is 9C. The annual rainfall averages 974mm.

Situated on the banks of the Swan River in the south-west corner of the country, Perth is the capital city of Western Australia. The kilometre-wide expanse of the Swan River that stretches alongside the city has the appearance of a lake or harbour, and is edged by expensive suburbs and white sandy beaches. It was known as the city of millionaires before the 1987 Stock Market crash, and still is a place of energetic growth and vigorous youth. It is a well planned city with an efficient freeway system, yet within walking distance of the city centre is Kings Park. A native bushland with gum trees and wildflowers, the park offers magnificent views of both the city and the Swan River. While the tall buildings of the Central Business District dominate the skyline, this is contrasted by the parks and gardens that run along the banks of the Swan River.

Perth was actually sighted long before the arrival of Captain James Cook in the late eighteenth century, with Dutch sailor Willem de Vlamingh noting what he described as an arid region when he sailed along the coast in 1697. While it was explored during the first decade of the nineteenth century, it

South side of Hay Street.

The Old Goverment Printing Office.

wasn't until 1827 that botanist Charles Fraser and Captain James Stirling began to see potential in the area. With the British growing concerned that the French would start to seize coastal areas along the nation, Captain Stirling was given the go-ahead to establish a settlement along the Swan River. And for the first time in Australian history, the colony was to consist of free settlers. The colony struggled during its first few years and was characterised by frequent clashes with the indigenous population, and Perth's growth fell well behind that of other major Australian cities. By the 1890's the population was still sitting at less than 10,000, but a building boom in the city was finally precipitated by the discovery of gold in Western Australia. The eventual arrival of a railway and the prosperity of the surrounding areas meant that Perth had finally developed into a competitive city, and the influx of immigration that followed WWII meant the population had risen to almost a million by the 1980's.

Interestingly enough, Perth has always been a city recognised for its entrepreneurs, and for the frequent speculation that takes place. This perhaps stems from Perth's origin as a colony consisting entirely of free settlers – the city was founded by wealth seeking individuals who had to contend with little government inteference. This persisted throughout the twentieth century, mostly due to the vast amounts of mineral resources that were discovered in the state.

The history of Perth can be seen in many of the city's heritage buildings, with many of the finest examples built using convict labor. The Town Hall, on the corner of Hay and Barrack Streets, was built by convict labour between 1867

The Royal Mint, Perth

and 1870, in the style of an English Jacobean market hall. A tablet set into the footpath in the nearby in Barrack Street commemorates the founding of Perth in 1829. A large number of these historic buildings remain today along Murray Street, and though built in the late nineteenth and early twentieth centuries, are classified by the National Trust of WA. Among these include the Government Printing Office which was built in 1870, the Government Stores Building which was completed in 1911, the Health Department building which was built the following year, as well as the Young Australia League Building foundation stone that was laid by William Morris Hughes, the Prime Minister of Australia, in 1922.

While twenty years ago Perth was considered to be lacking when it came to options for top-class entertainment, this has changed drastically in recent years. The Perth Concert Hall and the Perth Entertainment Centre have both recently been constructed. While the Concert Hall is home to the WA Symphony Orchestra, the Entertainment Centre is an 8000 capacity venue frequented by circuses, rock bands and musical productions. The famous His Majesty's Theatre has also received refurbishment, and is home to the WA Opera Company, the WA Ballet Company and the WA Arts

Swan Bells on the Swan River, Perth

Orchestra. The prominance of taverns, restaurants, cinemas and nightclubs has also grown in Perth, with Northbridge emerging as a centre of the city's nightlife. And of course, there is the Burswood Casino. Overlooking the Swan River and a prominent landmark on the city skyline, the Burswood Casino connects with the get-rich-quick image that has become associated with Perth. Situated in 100 hectares of rolling parklands that takes in an 18-hole golf course, the glamorous casino itself can boast 111 gaming tables, 1,145 video gaming machines and a 240 seat Keno lounge. The resort also includes a 5-star hotel, a theatre and a 20,000 seat indoor stadium called the Dome. The Burswood Casino can be called on *(08) 9362 7777*.

The get-rich-quick aspect of Perth also carries across to the many opportunities for shopping in the city. Hay Street has always been regarded as the very heart of Perth shopping: while prior to the 1970's it was likely the most congested section of roadway in WA, all that changed when it was converted into a pedestrian mall. The Murray Street Mall is also linked to the Hay Street Mall by numerous arcades, and the whole effect has created a pleasant, roomy and traffic-free shopping precinct. The two major department stores in the city include Aherns between Murray and Hay Streets, as well as a store of the nationwide Myers chain between Wellington and Murray Streets. The new Myer building is architecturally impressive, with overhead walkways linking it to several of Perth's arcades and to the modern Perth Train Station, which is in turn linked to the city's cultural centre. The London Court near Barrack Street is also of interest, an authentic piece of Olde England which was built in Tudor style. It contains carved woodwork, wrought ironwork, hanging signs, paved roadway and medieval towers at each end.

Visitor Information:

The Western Australian Tourism Commission operates the Western Australia Visitor Centre, located in Albert Facey House on the corner of Forrest Place and Wellington Street, *1300 361 351*. The website to visit is *www.westernaustralia.com*, or email at *travel@westernaustralia.com*.

Points of Interest:

The Old Court House was erected between 1836 and 1837, and is one of the earliest surviving buildings in the city. During the 19th century it served as church, school, immigration depot, supreme court house and store. The Old

The Western Australia Museum

Court House can be found in the middle of Supreme Court Gardens.

The Government House is another of Perth's most classic buildings, the official residence of the Governor of Western Australia and built between 1859 and 1864. It is constructed in the romantic style with Gothic arches and turrets reminiscent of the Tower of London, and can be found at St George's Terrace opposite Pier Street.

The Swan Bell Tower is one of Perth's main tourist attraction. Situated on the Barrack Street Jetty, the tower overlooks the Swan River and the entire city skyline. Construction began on the Swan Bell Tower in November 1999 and work was completed in 2001. Towering at a height of over 82.5 metres, it contains twelve bells of St. Martin-in-the-Fields from the 14th Century which were recast in the 16th Century by Queen Elizabeth I.

The Art Gallery of Western Australia displays traditional and contemporary paintings, prints, drawings, sculpture and bark paintings. The gallery can be found in the Perth Cultural Centre in James Street Mall, *(08) 9492 6600.*

The Aboriginal Art and Craft Gallery is a gallery specialising in the art of Western Australia's Indigenous people. The gallery can be found on Fraser Avenue in King's Park, *(08) 9481 7082.*

The Old Gaol is perhaps one of the best examples of colonial architecture in the State. Built in 1856, it served as Perth's original prison until 1888. Many public executions took place in the grounds. Today it has been extensively restored, and in rooms which once housed prisoners, there is an old fashioned dental surgery and pharmacy and many mementoes of Perth's early days. The Old Gaol can be found in the museum complex in Francis Street.

The Western Australian Museum features a number of different displays, including an Aboriginal Gallery, the skeleton of Albert the Dinosaur, and the 11-tonne Mundrabilla meteorite, as well as various displays on Western Australian history. The entrace to the museum can be found at James Street, call *(08) 9427 2700.*

The Perth Train Station was originally built between 1893 and 1894, replacing an earlier station built when the railway was opened in 1881. The front of the station has been

Perth City

London Court off Hay Street Mall

Fremantle Hotel

renovated, and the structure behind extensively remodelled, with walkways connecting it to Myers and the Perth Cultural Centre. The station can be found in Wellington Street.

The Perth Mint is a world leader in the manufacture and marketing of precious metal coins, medallions and collectables. Housed in one of Australia's most elegant late-19th century heritage buildings, it is the nation's oldest operating mint and one of the oldest mints in the world still producing coins from its original premises.
Call *(08) 9421 7277*.

Outlying Towns from Perth

Fremantle

Located 19km from Perth at the mouth of the Swan River, Fremantle is Western Australia's chief port. It was founded in 1829 by Captain Charles Howe Fremantle, in a ceremony claiming the entire west coast of New Holland in the name of King George IV. Many of the original buildings still standing were built with convict labour, and parts of the city retain a 19th century atmosphere. Fremantle can be reached from Perth by bus, train, ferry and taxi. A tram tour makes for one of the best ways to get acquainted with Fremantle, call *(08) 9339 8719* for more information.

The Town Hall in St John's Square is an elegant and gracious building, officially opened in 1887 as part of Queen Victoria's Jubilee Celebrations. Found on the corner of Adelaide and William Street, the Fremantle Visitor Information Office is also here, (08) 9431 7878. The Western Australian Maritime Museum has displays dating from the 1600s to the time of British Settlement, including a partial reconstruction of the 1629 Dutch wreck *Batavia*. The museum is on Cliff Street and can be called on *(08) 9431 8444*.

Rottnest Island

The name means Rats' Nest, and was given to the island by Dutch mariner, William Vlamingh in 1696, as he thought the small rock wallaby (quokka) inhabitants were rats. Rottnest Island is approximately 11km x 5km, and is 19km west of Fremantle. Contrary to most people's thinking, Rottnest is not a deserted island. There is a wide variety of accommodation and other facilities, and the Rottnest Island Visitor Information Centre can be called on *(08) 9372 9752*. The most popular pastime is swimming in the clear water, without having to worry about sharks or rips.

Rockingham

Situated 47km south of Perth on Cockburn Sound, Rockingham is one of the safest stretches of water in Australia. The two main islands in the area are Garden Island and Penguin Island, and a flat-bottomed ferry operates between the mainland. Captain Stirling and the first settlers of the Swan River colony used Garden Island as a temporary base, and it is now the site of the naval base, HMAS Stirling. Visitors are not allowed access by the 4km causeway, but they may visit the island by boat provided they stay outside the fenced naval area. Penguin Island is a part-time home for a colony of dainty fairy penguins, one of only two such colonies in Australia. The Rockingham Visitor Centre can be found at 43 Kent Street, *(08) 9592 3464*, and they have information on both the Rockingham Heritage Trail and the Rockingham-Jarrahdale Heritage Trail.

Swan Valley

The rich, alluvial soil of the valley has attracted many farmers, who have turned their attention to grapes, and the area is now noted for its range of high quality wines. The vignerons welcome visitors to their cellars to sample the wines, and details should be obtained from the Tourist Office in Perth before setting out. Midland is the hub of the Shire of Swan, and for over 100 years it has been a busy railway centre, with all trains inland and to the Eastern States passing through

Developments on the waterways of Mandurah

the town. Guildford, at the junction of the Swan and Helena Rivers, has many historic buildings that offer excellent examples of early Australian town life. Some are small townhouses not open to the public, while others are open for inspection. They include: Guildford Court House; Rose and Crown Inn; Guildford Gaol; St Matthew's Church; Wesley Chapel and Manse; All Saints Church; Convict Depot Commissariat; Brockman's House; and Kinsella's Hotel.

Armadale

The town of Armadale is about 30km south-east of Perth on the Albany Highway. Attractions include: Araluen Park; Canning Dam; Churchman's Brook Dam; Wungong Dam; History House; Elizabethan Village, an authentic period reconstruction with many fine antiques; and Signal Box Arts and Crafts (which houses the Bert Tyler Vintage Machinery Museum). The Armadale Visitor Information Centre can be found in Jull Street, *(08) 9497 3543.*

Mundaring

On the Great Eastern Highway, 34km east of Perth, Mundaring is the Gateway to the Foothills. The Mundaring Visitor Information Centre is in the Old School, 7225 Great Eastern Highway, and they will advise on the area's attractions, which include: Mundaring Weir Gallery Arts and Crafts; the Hills Forest Discovery Centre; Mundaring Weir; the Bibbulmun Track; and the C.Y. O'Connor Museum.

Kalamunda

Located in the hills area, Kalamunda is 26km east of Perth. Places to see are: Kalamunda History Village Museum, Railway Road; Hills Art Gallery, Railway Road; Stirk Park and Cottage, Kalamunda Road; and Lesmurdie Falls, Falls

Road, Lesmurdie, in the Lesmurdie National Park. Drop into the Visitor Information Centre at 55 Railway Road, *(08) 9293 0299.*

Mandurah Population: 51,000.

Located 74km south of Perth around the calm protected waters of the Peel Inlet and the Harvey Estuary, Mandurah is situated on one of the largest inland waterways in Australia. There are 40km of sandy Indian Ocean beaches within the vicinity, so the area is popular with those who enjoy boating, fishing, surfing and windsurfing. While Mandurah used to be known as little more than a seaside resort for retirees, in recent times it has changed into a certifiable commuter town. Many of Mandurah's residents make a daily trip to and from the Central Business District of the Perth, or alternatively to the factories in Kwinana and the aluminium refinery in Pinjarra. With this renewed focus on attracting commuters, Mandurah has grown to become the largest and fastest growing regional city in Western Australia.

Wild dolphins can be found in the waters of Mandurah, with visitors not only allowed the opportunity to see and watch them, but also to swim with them at certain parts of the year. The dolphins are of the bottle nose variety, medium grey in colour with an average length of around 3 metres. The remains of a nineteenth century shipwreck that can be seen at the town's beach is another coastal area of interest. The tragic wreck that occurred on the coast in 1878 left many dead who are buried at the churchyard, and the only relic of the wreck is the James Service Anchor which now lies at the beach. The Barragup Botanical Garden in Caponi Road, *(08) 9581 2738*, is not too far from Mandurah. Wander through WA's largest rare cacti and succulent gardens and nursery and see all the flowers in bloom.

Visitor Information:

The Mandurah Visitor Centre can be found at 75 Mandurah Terrace, *(08) 9550 3999.* You can contact them at *visitor@mandurah.wa.gov.au* or visit their site at *www.peeltour.net.au.*

Bunbury Population: 30,000.

Located at the western end of Leschenault Inlet and 185km south of Perth, Bunbury has a thriving industry base that stems from the city's port. As well as being the largest centre in Western Australia outside the metropolitan areas, Bunbury is also the major seaport and administrative centre for the region. While the port in Bunbury was once the location where the wheat from the surrounding hinterland was shipped, alumina and woodchip now make up the majority of what is shifted through. The city continues to expand due to its wealth of natural and man-made resources in the area, and is surrounded by much of WA's best agricultural land. Bunbury, however, is primarily a holiday centre: thousands of vacationers flock to the city evey year, and the city is also used as a base to visit many the beauty spots of the South-West.

French explorer Nicolas Baudin was the first to sight the Leschenault Inlet in 1803, and he named it after botanist Jean Batiste Leschenault. In 1836, seven years after the founding of the Swan River settlement, Governor Sir James Stirling accompanied an expedition to explore the Port Leschenault and Busselton regions. Lieutenant Henry William Bunbury made the overland trek to meet Stirling in December 1836, and was rewarded for his efforts by having the port named in his honour. John Scott and his family arrived as the first settlers in Bunbury in 1838, and by 1841 over 400 Europeans had moved to the town. The town's port was increasingly used to export the wood being extracted from the hinterland,

and it continued to play a key role in Bunbury's development throughout the twentieth century. It was in the 1950's that the area's rich mineral deposits were discovered, and Bunbury was declared a city in 1979.

To experience panoramic views of Bunbury that take in many of the sights, the Boulter's Heights lookout makes for a great place to visit. From here you get a great view of the city, the port, the north shore and the Leschenault Estuary, and nearby there is a man-made waterfall that cascades down the eastern face of the heights. Boulter's Heights can be found on Withers Crescent, and can also be reached on foot from the base of the waterfall at the junction of Stirling and Wittenoom streets. The Dolphin Discovery Centre should also be visited, and Bunbury is famous for the group of wild dolphins that live off the coast of Koombana Bay. The centre allows a close up view of the magnificent mammals behaving naturally, and displays of marine environments are also contained within the marine interpretive centre. The centre can be found off Koombana Drive, call *(08) 9791 3088.*

Visitor Information: The Bunbury Visitors Centre can be

Bunbury's old school, now an arts and crafts centre.

found in Carmody Place, *(08) 9721 7922*. Go online at *www.justsouth.com.au* or email *welcome@bunbury.wa.gov.au*. Alternatively, Australia South West is located at 61 Victoria Street, *(08) 9791 9197*.

Points of Interest:

The War Memorial in Bunbury is a fine memorial to the armed forces who served in World War I. The memorial can be found in Anzac Park, on the corner of Stirling and Parkfield Streets. Alongside is another memorial, to John and Helen Scott, the first farmers in the Bunbury District.

The Bunbury Regional Art Galleries are located in the old Convent of Mercy building, which was opened and blessed in December,1897. The convent complex was purchased by the City Council in 1981, as it was no longer being used to house the Sisters of Mercy and their pupils. The Galleries contain the City of Bunbury Art Collection, which numbers 300 works, and has grown from an initial gift of 20 paintings by Claude Hotchin in 1949. The galleries is on Wittenoom Street, and can be called on *(03) 9721 8616*.

The Sir John Forrest Monument was erected is in honour of Western Australia's greatest son, Sir John Forrest. John Forest was born near Bunbury in 1847, and he spent 18 years in State politics, all in executive office, then 18 years in Federal politics, almost half as Cabinet Minister. First MLA for Bunbury, the first Premier of WA, five times Federal Treasurer, and for a time Forrest was Acting Prime Minister. In 1918 he received the title of Baron Forrest of Bunbury, the first Australian to be raised to the British peerage. He died that year at sea, aged 71, and is buried in Karrakatta Cemetery. Mark Le Buse was commissioned in 1979 to sculpt Forrest's head, and it can be seen in St Paul's Place on the corner of Victoria and Stephen Street.

The Centenary Gardens were built in 1936 to commemorate the town's 100 year anniversary, and have a shade pavilion dedicated to Lt Bunbury, and a wishing well built by the Apex Club in 1952. The gardens can be found of the corner of Wittenoom and Princep Street.

The Bunbury Tower is an unmistakable landmark, and can be found off Victoria and Wittenoom Street. With 11 storeys, the building design is meant to look similar to the bow of a ship, and accommodates some 400 government officers.

Bunbury Regional Art Galleries

The Bunbury Lighthouse is a striking landmark and one of a fine collection of lighthouses that are part of the state's heritage, and can be found at Ocean Drive, on the ocean side of Casuarina Point.

The Bunbury Basaltic Rock is formed from a volcanic lava-flow believed to have occurred 150 million years ago in the cretaceous period. Volcanic activity was quite extensive over the South-West corner for a short period of time. A considerable amount of basalt can still be found west of a line from Bunbury to Windy Harbour, buried beneath sedimentary layers of sand and clay. The basalt rock formation can only be seen in Bunbury at the northern end of Ocean Beach, and Black Point, south-east of Augusta.

The King Cottage Museum is a small, well kept cottage that dates from 1880, and was opened as a local history museum in 1968. It houses a valuable collection of pioneer material of the area. One of Bunbury's oldest buildings, the cottage was the home of Henry King. Aided by four sons and using home-made bricks, Henry King erected the family dwelling of unique Flemish bond brick design. The cottage can be found at 77 Forrest Avenue, *(08) 9721 7546*.

Busselton Population: 6,500

Located 228km south of Perth just off the highway, Busselton is an attractive beachside holiday town on the shores of Geographe Bay. One of the most visited locations in rural Western Australia, Busselton was awarded WA's Top Tourism Town status in both 1995 and 1996. Boasting a well developed town centre with a good assortment of accommodation options, there are also plenty of green parks, historic buildings, and 30km of sandy beaches.

The Busselton Beachfront is the main attraction in the town, and is where you will find the Busselton Jetty, the longest wooden jetty in the Southern Hemisphere. Construction began in 1865 and it took over 95 years to build, with the jetty stretching an incredible 2km into the ocean. A small train runs the entire length of the jetty. The Underwater Observatory is situated at the end of the 2km jetty, and allows visitors to dive to the bottom of the ocean and observe the colourful coral and marine life, staying dry throughout the whole experience.

Visitor Information:

The Busselton Tourist Bureau is located at 38 Peel Terrace, *(08) 9752 1288*, and they have details of available accommodation and of the numerous scenic drives.

Dunsborough Population: 4,000

Located 258km from Perth at the western end of Geographe Bay, Dunsborough is a small tourist spot famous for having retained its natural appeal. Situated at the beginning of the Leeuwin Naturaliste National Park, the surroundings of the town are an aesthetically soothing blend of sandy beaches, placid coves, national park and nature reserves. Dunsborough has only been a recent discovery, as less than several years ago it only had a population of several hundred. Since then Dunsborough has gone on to be voted the Top Tourism Town in WA in 1999, and becomes surprisingly busy at certain times of the year. The area has remained largely untouched by over development, and there are plenty of cottages outside of the town centre which can be rented by those wishing to find alternative accomodation options.

Visitors to Dunsborough can enjoy the surrounding national parks, as well as the beautiful coastline stretches that have remained untouched. The area around Sugarloaf Rock is a great example of the area's striking coastal scenery, and the calm, tranquil bays that surround the rocky outcrop. It is popular with snorkellers, swimmers and fishermen. The Cape Naturaliste Lighthouse and Maritime Museum are only 13km from the town, and give excellent views of the bay as well as a reflection on the town's maritime history. The *H.M.A.S Swan* is the largest accessible dive wreck in the Southern Hemisphere, a 120 metre long decommissioned naval destroyer that was blown up in Geographe Bay and deliberately sunk off Meelup Beach in 1997. Diving Tours are available to the wreck. Other attractions include the Old Dunsborugh Winery on Cape Naturaliste Road, the Newberry Gallery at the Newberry Manor, as well as the Dunsborough Gallery at Naturaliste Terrace.

Visitor Information:

The Dunsborough Visitor Centre is located at Shop 14, Dunsborough Park Shopping Centre, Seymour Boulevard, *(08) 9755 3299*. Email *info@dboro.downsouth.com.au*.

Margaret River Population: 4,500

The south-west coastal town of Margaret River is 52km south of Busselton on the Bussell Highway. The annual concert at Leeuwin Estate lures the cultural set, while the pounding surf in Prevelly Park challenges competitors in the annual amateur and professional surf competitions.

The dainty Margaret River funnels through to the ocean waters passing through rich vegetations of flora. The surrounding ferns, palms and jarrah trees encapsulate an image of an enchanted forest that wreaths the quiet town. The **Mammoth Cave** which was discovered in the early

Busselton Wharf

The beach just north of Prevelly

1850s lies south of Margaret River, with fossils dating back as far as 35,000 years. The cave is named after it's enormous size and is now a high tech, self discovery tourist attraction.

Visitor Information:

The Margaret River Visitor Centre is on Bussell Highway in town, *(08) 9757 2911*. The town's website can be visited at *www.margaretriver.com*, while their email address is *welcome@margaretriver.com*.

Augusta Population: 1,600

Situated 95km south of Busselton on the Bussell Highway, Augusta is renowned as having some of WA's most picturesque scenery. In addition to being the town at Australia's most southern-west tip, Augusta is also the third oldest settlement in the whole of Australia. With stunning forests found only a short drive from the town, Augusta also has some of the most pristine and perfect beaches found anywhere in the state. Ideal for swimming, surfing, diving and boating, the waters have also encouraged a vibrant fishing community, with both professionals and casual fishermen scouring the seas for all kinds of marine life. Hamelin Bay is one of the most beautiful attractions to be found in Augusta: with stunning limestone formations surrounding the spot, the area is comprised of a sweeping bay and sheltered pools for swimming. The stingrays that inhabit the bay are friendly towards humans, and it also includes a shipwreck trail.

The Cape Leeuwin Lighthouse is Augusta's single biggest tourist attraction, and is visited by thousands every year. Opened by Sir John Forest in 1896, the lighthouse is built on limestone foundations which reach over 6 metres below the surface and can be spotted over 25 nautical miles out to sea. The Jewel Cave is another beautiful natural attraction, with the limestone cave containing an antechamber as well as two main caves. The main cave is 100 metres high and 90 metres long. A fossil of an extinct Tasmanian Tiger has been discovered inside. Naturaliste Charters Whale Cruises (*08 9755 2276*) offer whale watching tours, while the Augusta Historical Museum can be found at Blackwood Avenue.

Visitor Information:

The Augusta Visitor Centre, corner of Blackwood Ave and Ellis Street, *(08) 9758 0166*. Email *augusta@margaretriver.com* for advice on accommodation.

Outlying towns from Augusta

Manjimup

Manjimup is 307km south of Perth at the junction of South West and Muirs Highways, right in the heart of the Karri and Jarrah forest. The town has over 5000 residents, and the Manjimup Visitor Centre is off Giblett Street, *(08) 9771 1831*. The town has modern shopping facilities and most sports are well catered for, including golf and lawn bowls.

Collie

Situated 57km inland from Bunbury, and 203km south of Perth, Collie is important as a coal mining town, and has in fact been WA's only source of coal since the 1890s. Muja Power Station supplies the State electricity grid. The Collie Visitor Centre is situated at 156 Throssell Street, *(08) 9734 2051*. You can contact them by email at *colshire@collie.wa. gov.au* or check out the website at *www.collie.wa.gov.au*.

Albany Population: 31,000

Situated 409km south of Perth, Albany lies at the heart of the Great Southern area of Western Australia. Though not proclaimed a city until 1998, Albany is a constantly expanding regional centre and now has a population of over 30,000. The town is nestled next to the gorgeous and tranquil waters of the Princess Royal Harbour, known as one of the largest natural harbours in the world in terms of size and depth. Albany is also situated in an area that remains relatively unspoiled, and an assortment of National Parks, forests, rugged coastline, mountains, rivers and walking trails are all within easy reach. The first European settlement to be established in Western Australia, there are many memories and heritage buildings to be seen within Albany.

On the foreshore of the city of Albany lies a full-scale replica of the Brig *Amity*, the sailing ship which brought the first settlers to Princess Royal Harbour in 1826. The replica was first displayed in 1975 and is situated only 200 metres from where the original ship landed. The nearby Torndirrup National Park also provides an efficient way to view the beautiful natural surrounds of Albany. Panoramic views of the area can be viewed from the Stoney Hill Heritage Trail, and some of the other notable features of the National Park include the Gap, the Natural Bridge, the Blowholes, the Gorge, Newles Inlet and Peak Head. The park is also home to Whale World: the last mainland whaling station to exist in Australia before closure in 1978, the museum now plays a part in the preservation of the mammals. The museum can be called on *(08) 9844 4021*.

Visitor Information:

Albany Visitor Centre can be found in Old Railway Station on Proudlove Parade, *(08) 9841 1088* or free call *1800 644 088*. Visit the website at *www.albanytourist.com.au* or email them at *avc@albanytourist.com.au*.

Outlying towns from Albany

Denmark

Situated 55km west of Albany on the South Coast Highway, Denmark has a population of around 4000. The Denmark River flows through this charming little town, and the local industries are salmon fishing (February to April) and farming - beef cattle, dairying, sheep, pigs and potato growing. The Denmark Visitor Centre is in Strickland Street, *(08) 9848 2055*, and they will be able to advise on local attractions.

Kataning

Katanning is in the Heart of the Great Southern region, call *(08) 9821 2634* for information. You can visit them at *www.katanningwa.com* and *www.katanning.wa.gov.au*, or e-mail *kghevo@bigpond.com.au*.

Patrick Taylor Cottage, Albany

Cape Leeuwin

WA

Goldfields Region

Bordered to the north and east by the Great Victoria and Gibson Deserts, the Goldfields region has a rich history of gold strikes. While they were some of the last areas in Australia where gold was discovered, the precious resources continue to be extracted to this day. The climate of the region is harsh and a lack of water supply plagued early settlers, yet a pipeline from Perth now supplies water to the area.

See Map p.326 for the rest of the region

Kalgoorlie-Boulder   Population: 29,000.
Climate: Average temperatures: January max 34°C - min 18°C; July max 17°C - min 6°C. Average annual rainfall: 263mm.

Located 597 km east of Perth at the terminus of the Great Eastern Highway, Kalgoorlie-Boulder is one of the greatest gold mining towns in Australia. Situated in an area named for gold and riddled with reminders of its presence, it is Kalgoorlie-Boulder's association with the precious metal that distinguishes it. The community was built on the discovery of gold over 100 years ago, and to this day it is what continues to drive the econorny. Although over a century of mining has seen a billion dollars worth of gold removed, there is plenty left to be excavated. It is a city full of rich heritage and echoes of its boisterous past can still be seen, particularly in the nineteenth and early twentieth-century buildings which line both Hannan and Burt Street.

Though gold was being excavated from plenty of other places in Australia during the nineteenth century, these places had been exhausted by the 1890's and the government was

York Hotel, Kalgoorlie

note contained detailed instructions on how to finish the pipeline. It was completed the following year and eventually recognised as a resounding success.. Gold production reached a peak in 1903, and then declined until the Depression of the 1930's, when world prices increased dramatically.

Some of the original locomotives that chuffed along the Golden Mile are still in operation today. During the late 1890s the Golden Mile Loop Line was the busiest and best paying in the colony. Over 60 passenger and goods trains passed through Boulder City Station on weekdays, 33 on Saturdays and 27 on Sundays. The locomotives used in those days were N class, and were worked extremely hard. Visitors are able to relive some of the past events of the area while they 'Ride the Rattler', travelling over some of the Golden Mile in a Wickham Track Inspection vehicle or Z1153, a jetty shunting locomotive. A full recorded commentary is played so that every feature is explained as you pass.

The Mining Hall of Fame is one of Australia's most unusual tourist attractions, and provides a unique chance for the whole family to go underground in a real gold mine in safety. Located on the Goldfields Highway, the Hall of Fame can be called on *(08) 9026 2700*. The Mining Hall of Fame also contains the original statue erected to honour the memory of Paddy Hannan, one of the Irishmen to discover gold in the area. It was completed in 1929 and constructed out of soldered copper. An exact replica of the original statue can also be seen on the corner of Wilson Street and Hannon Street. And for an insight into life in a goldtown at the turn of the century, the Western Australian Museum can be found at 17 Hannan Street, *(08) 9021 8533*.

Visitor Information:

The Kalgoorlie/Boulder Tourist Centre is at 250 Hannan Street, Kalgoorlie, *(08) 9021 1966* or *1800 001 880*. If you have online access, visit *www.kalgoorlie.com* for a preliminary peek or drop them a message at *visitor@kalgoorlie.com*.

Points of Interest:

Mt Charlotte Reservoir holds Kalgoorlie's permanent fresh water supply, which comes by pipeline from the weir at Mundaring in the Darling Range. In January 1903, Sir John Forrest, explorer and Premier of WA, turned on the water at the Mt Charlotte reservoir, and the town went wild. At the official banquet that night, Sir George Reid said that he had

offering rewards for new discoveries. In June 1893, several Irishmen discovered gold near Mt Charlotte. They registered their claim in June that same year, and within several days over 300 men had already flooded the area. Two other prospectors discovered further deposits three miles to the south, what became known as the world famous "Golden Mile". The goldrush sparked by these discoveries was staggering in size and speed. Men came in thousands from all over the world, ready to live in the improvised shacks they knocked up in arid conditions. Hundreds of mining companies were floated to cash in on the gold rush, many of which were fraudulent.

A railway and five civic buildings were constructed before long, and by the early 1900's there were nearly 100 hotels, 10 breweries and a population of over 30,000 people. While the lack of water appeared to be an insurmountable problem, a solution was found in the Goldfields Water Scheme devised by C.Y. O'Connor. A 563km pipeline was built from a reservoir near Perth, but received large amounts of criticism during the construction process. Subjected to a hard hitting press campaign, O'Connor committed suicide in 1902. Though he never saw his dream realised, his suicide

Town Hall, Kalgoorlie

never heard so much talk about water, and seen so little of it consumed. From the lookout at the Reservoir there is a good view of the town.

The Kalgoorlie Town Hall was built in 1908, and has a fine stamped metal ceiling and Victorian style cast seats on the balcony. On the first floor is the Art Collection.

The Golden Mile Art Exhibition is in the upstairs gallery at the Boulder Town Hall. It is a permanent exhibition with works by local artists. The exhibition is open for viewing on Wednesday, and enquiries should be directed to the Kalgoorlie/Boulder Tourist Centre, *(08) 9021 1966.*

The Cornwall Hotel, probably the most picturesque in the area, was built in 1898 and is in vintage condition. It photographs well, and can be called on *(08) 9093 2510.*
The Eastern Goldfields Historical Society Museum is in the Boulder City Railway Station, *(08) 9093 3360,* while the Goldfields War Museum can be found in Burt Street in Boulder.

Esperance Population: 14,000

Situated 369km south of Kalgoorlie and 720km south-east of Perth, Esperance is known as 'The Bay of Isles'. Small yet beautiful, the scenic coastlines, rounded granite cliffs and white sandy beaches are considered some of the most impressive in Western Australia. The sands on the beaches are so impossibly white they could be mistaken for snow, and the winds along the coast of Esperance can lift the sand dunes to a height of almost 50-60 metres. There are around 100 small islands in and around Esperance Bay, and some of the marine life that inhabits the waters includes dolphins, Cape Barren Geese, New Zealand Seals and Australian Sea Lions.

The town's history began in 1627 when Pieter Nuyts, in command of the Dutch East India Company vessel *Gulde Zeepard*, charted the coast and the Recherche Archipelago. The first to set foot in the area were men attached to a French scientific mission under the command of Admiral D'Entrecasteaux, whose ships sought shelter from a gale. The first ship to enter the bay was L'Esperance, hence the name of the bay. The next 50 years saw visits by explorers Flinders and Eyre, and in 1863 the Dempster brothers took up the first landholding in the area. Other farmer settlers soon followed, and the discovery of gold at Coolgardie caused Esperance to become the port for the Goldfields overnight.

Diving is a popular activity around the islands of Esperance Bay, and some of the shipwrecks that experienced divers can visit include the Lapwing Wreck and the Sanko Harvest Wreck. Several National Parks are also in close proximity, all of them offering good opportunities for bushwalking and camping. They include the Cape le Grand National Park (*08 9075 9022*) and the Cape Arid National Park (*08 9075 0055*) to the east of Esperance, the Peak Charles National Park (08 9071 3733) to the north, and the Stokes National Park (*08 9076 8541*) to the west. Other attractions in Esperance include the Pink Lake, which actually turns pink at certain times of the year, as well as the Municipal Museum between Dempster Street and the Esplanade.

Visitor Information:

The Esperance Visitor Centre is in Dempster Street, *(08) 9071 2330,* at the Museum Village. They have information on the accommodation available, where to fish, the best place to swim, or where to play golf, or any other sport.

Outlying Towns in the Goldfields Region

Coolgardie

The town was built to accommodate 15,000 people, and the present population is 1100, so Coolgardie can be regarded as the best-cared-for ghost town in Australia. It is situated 45km west of Kalgoorlie, on the site of a reef of rich gold, found by Arthur Bayley in 1892, and called 'Bayley's Reward'. Gold continued to be extracted until 1963, but the town's boom time was really over by 1914 when World War I saw the prospectors volunteer for service.

The Coolgardie Tourist Bureau and Goldfields Exhibition is at 62 Bayley Street, *(08) 9026 6090*. There are a series of historical markers around the township, documenting the history of Coolgardie, with photographs of what each site looked like in times gone by. It is fascinating to compare the photos with what is now found in the town. The Goldfields Exhibition in the same building as the Tourist Bureau.

Menzies

Named after L.R. Menzies, one of the men who discovered gold in the vicinity in 1894, Menzies is another town that has declined. Within months of gold being found the population was 10,000, within thirteen years it had dropped

Menzies

to 1000, now it is home to 110. The town is 132km north of Kalgoorlie, and many buildings from its heyday remain, including the town hall and the railway station. The Menzies State Battery for processing gold is the most modern in Australia, and visitors are welcome.

Leonora

Situated 237km north of Kalgoorlie, Leonora is a railhead for nearby copper and nickel mines, and the meeting point of the roads radiating north, south and east. It is the administrative town of the North Eastern Goldfields, and the centre of a wool growing area. Mt Leonora was first named by the explorer John Forrest in 1869, and rises 100m above the town, so is the best place to get an overall view.

The Sons of Gwalia Goldmine ran continuously for 67 years, and was the largest underground mine outside the Golden Mile. It closed in 1963, and the town of Gwalia died as a result. However, recent technological advances have resulted in lower production costs, and the mine has re-opened, as have some others in the area. A visit is worthwhile, and it is best to allow about half an hour to explore. The ghost town of Gwalia is also worth a visit. The town was never officially gazetted, due to its tendency to flood, so it just grew like Topsy, with buildings mostly of galvanised iron. It is hard to imagine now, but the town was once so prosperous that it had the State's first electric tram service.

Situated 69km south-east of Leonora is the township of Kookynie which had a population of 1500 in 1905, and now has 10, many of whom work at the local hotel, which in itself is worth a visit. Niagara is about 10km from Kookynie, and is another ghost town, with not much to see except for the Niagara Dam, built in 1897. The cement for the 250m long wall was carried from Coolgardie by camels!

Laverton

Laverton is 361km north-east of Kalgoorlie, and prospectors from Coolgardie found gold near the present town site in 1896. The town died when the surface gold ran out, but was revitalised by the Windarra Nickel Project, and is the support base for the recently reopened Lancefield Mine. Attractions include the Billy Goat Hill, which gives panoramic views, and Mt Windarra, from where there is a good view of the Windarra Nickel Mine. Ghost towns in the area include BurTVille, Gladiator, Heffernans and Just in Time.

Leinster

This town was established in 1977 to service the nickel-mining industry, and is the terminus of a sealed highway north from Kalgoorlie on the way to Wiluna. It is 378km north-west of Kalgoorlie. The Leinster Lodge in Mansbridge Street, *(08) 9037 9556*, can answer all your sightseeing and accommodation enquiries. Attractions include the old towns of Agnew, Lawlers and Poison Creek.

Kambalda

Situated 57km south of Kalgoorlie, Kambalda is a nickel town constructed by the Western Mining Corporation in the 1960s and 1970s. Originally, of course, it was a gold town, the precious metal having been found in 1887 by Percy

Larkin, but gold mining ceased around 1907. The town has approximately 6000 people, and the Kambalda Visitor Information is at the corner of Emu Rocks and Marianthus Road, Kambalda West, *(08) 9027 0192*.

Norseman

Known as Western Australia's 'Eastern Gateway', Norseman is 187km south of Coolgardie, 724km south-east of Perth, and 724km west of the Western Australia/South Australia border. Beacon Hill Lookout, from where there is a good view of the old mines, the chain of salt lakes, the gypsum hills and the Jimberlana Dyke, is reputed to be in one of the oldest geological areas in the world. The Norseman Tourist Centre is in Welcome Park, Robert Street, *(08) 9039 1071*.

Salt Lake near Kambalda

WA
The Mid-West Region

The Mid West Region extends from Kalbarri in the north, east to Yuna and south to Dongara. The regional centre is the city of Geraldton, which has a major port for mineral sands, stock and grain from the agricultural areas.

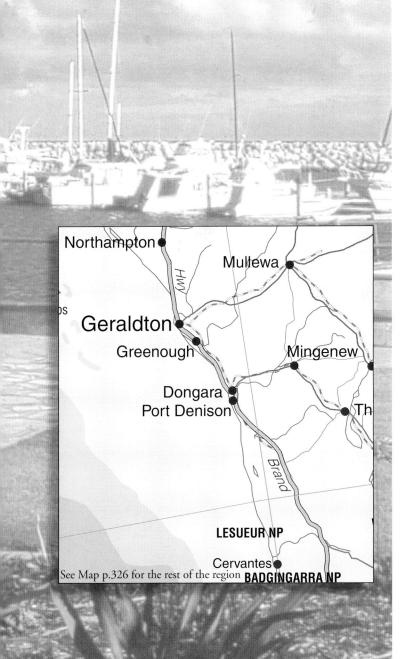

Northampton
Mullewa
Geraldton
Greenough
Mingenew
Dongara
Port Denison
Th
LESUEUR NP
Cervantes
BADGINGARRA NP

See Map p.326 for the rest of the region

Geraldton
Population: 33,000. Climate: Average temperatures: January max 32°C - min 19°C; July max 19°C - min 9°C. Average annual rainfall: 475mm

Located 424km north of Perth on the Brand Highway, the city of Geraldton is the largest in WA's Mid-West region. The surrounding area is referred to as the Batavia Coast, named after one of the many ships that was wrecked on the shore. The hub for all the activities taking place in the nearby hinterland, the port city is also the centre for the fishing, manufacturing, construction, agriculture and tourism industries of the surrounding areas. Well known as the "Sun City" because of the sunshine it enjoys throughout the year, many tourists are drawn to Geraldton for the variety of outdoor activities available. The city can boast a boundary of safe beaches, a year long surf scene, great windsurfing conditions, and is also very popular with fishermen. The pristine waters of the Batavia Coast are also renowned for the quality rock lobster fishing that takes place there, and the city has the largest lobster fleet on WA's coastal stretch.

While George Grey was the first European to enter the area in 1839, it was the expeditions of A. C. Gregory a decade later that lead to the town's colonisation. Geraldton was gazetted in 1850, and farmers realised within a few years that the

HMAS Sydney Memorial, Geraldton

hinterland was an effective place to settle, graze and grow crops. While it was briefly a convict settlement, the next major development in Geraldton's history was when it became the biggest port north of Fremantle, officially proclaimed a town in 1871. While the local indigenous population was estimated at around 1000 before settlement occurred, a sad consequence of the town's establishment was that they were nearly all removed. Close to 300 Aborigines perished in 1853 as a result of an outbreak of measles, while massacres by the European settlers was another cause of their demise. The town was helped along by the building of a railway line in 1879, and the discovery of gold in the Murchison during the 1890's precipitated a major period of growth. Geraldton had become the service centre for the surrounding agricultural areas by the nineteenth century, a position it still maintains to this day.

With the beaches in Geraldton considered some of the windiest in Australia, windsurfers and kite surfers flock there from all over the world. Even better are the Abrolhos Houtman Islands just off the coast of Geraldton, with the big ocean swells and windy conditions complimented by the beautiful coral reefs. For a good overall view of Geraldton, the Wishing Well Lookout in Brede Street looks down upon the city and the Norfolk pines that line the beach front. For a look at some of Australia's oldest shipwrecks that were smashed along the Batavia Coast, Geraldton's Western Australian Museum also makes for an interesting visit. Three Dutch ships, the Batavia (1629), Zuytdorp (1712) and

St Francis Xavier Cathedral, Geraldton

Zeewijk (1727) were wrecked on route to Holland's wealthy trading empire, and a variety of relics have been recovered. Other displays depict the region's intriguing variety of plants, animals and minerals, interwoven with the absorbing story of settlement in Geraldton.

Visitor Information:
The Geraldton Visitor Centre is situated on the corner of Chapman Road and Bayly Street at the Bill Sewell Community Recreation Complex, *(08) 9921 3999.*

Points of Interest:
The St Francis Xavier Cathedral, on the corner Cathedral Avenue and Maitland Street, was built in stages from 1914 until the opening in 1938. The Byzantine style architecture is one of Monsignor John Hawes' masterpieces.

Bill Sewell Community Complex can be found on the corner of Chapman Road and Bayly Street. Originally this building was the Victoria District Hospital, dating from 1887 to 1966, then it was used as a Regional Prison until 1984. The building had major restoration work done, and was re-opened in 1988. The Geraldton Visitor Centre is situated in this beautiful building and the Old Gaol Craft Centre is adjacent, call *(08) 9921 3999.*

The Lighthouse Keepers Cottage, on the corner of Chapman Road and Grenville Drive, was built in 1870 and was the original lighthouse keeper's residence for the Port of Geraldton. The Historical Society is based here.

Geraldton Regional Art Gallery is located in the city's original Town Hall in Chapman Road. The Town Hall was opened in 1907 and renovated in 1984. Admission to the Gallery is free, and they can be called on *(08) 9964 7176.*

The Point Moore Lighthouse is rather difficult to overlook, due to its broad red and white stripes. It was built in 1879, is 35m high, and its light is visible for up to 26km .

Outlying Towns from Geraldton.

Greenough
Situated 25km south of Geraldton on the Brand Highway, Greenough features many examples of early pioneering history dating from the 1850's. The Greenough Village

Murchison River

complex looks very much as it did in its heyday and is maintained by the National Trust (WA). It features Pioneer Tea Rooms and an Art Gallery, where works by significant Mid-West artists are displayed and sold. Guided tours through the buildings are highly recommended.

Dongara/Port Denison

The Shire of Irwin has three townships: Dongara, Port Denison and Irwin. For years Dongara and the adjacent townsite of Port Denison have been popular retirement destinations for farmers of the surrounding rural areas. Now tourists and holiday makers are discovering the delights of this historic region. The Dongara Denison Visitor Information Centre is in the Old Post Office Building, 9 Waldeck Street, Dongara, *(08) 9927 1404.*

Northampton

Northampton, 52 km north of Geraldton, has one of the richest histories in Western Australia and was awarded "Historic Town" status by the National Trust in 1993. Northampton is situated 52km north of Geraldton. The hills of the town, drained by creeks with permanent pools, attracted game and proved a haven for Australian Aborigines. The annual big event in Northampton is the Airing of the Quilts held on the last Saturday of the WA September/October school holidays. Over 300 locally made patchwork quilts are hung from the historic buildings and shops along Hampton Rd. Lots of other locally made arts & crafts also

displayed along with the Art Prize Exhibition at Chiverton House Museum. The Northampton Visitor Centre is on Hampton Road, in the Old Police Station, opposite the Shire Offices, *(08) 9934 1488.*

Kalbarri

Kalbarri is one of the fastest growing holiday resorts in WA, and is 591km north of Perth, 167km north of Geraldton. The climate is suitable for all year round swimming and fishing, and the scenery is unique. The town is on the mouth of the Murchison River and it is the river gorges that provide much of the unique scenery in the area, not to mention spectacular coastal scenery south of the town. Fishing from the beach or from boats is first class, and the town's main activity, along with tourism, is the rock lobster industry. Abundant and beautiful flora is just another attraction. The Kalbarri Visitor Centre can be found in Grey Street, *(08) 9937 1104.*

New Norcia Population: 30

Situated just 132 km north of Perth in the middle of WA's wheatbelt, New Norcia is a heritage town founded by Dom Rosendo Salvado in 1846. Originally a monastery for Benedictine Monks, who did much good work among the local aboriginals for a centry or more. The settlement is an amazing testament to hard work and culture. The place has a strong Spanish and South American flavour in its art and architecture, surrounded by a setting of natural bush and

New Norcia Monastery Gate

wheatfields. For the religiously inclined, the monastery in this quiet country location is a suitable background for a period of silent prayer and reflection.

Considered to have some of the most beautiful architecture in Western Australia, the town of New Norcia is a combination of a monastery, two schools, a church, and several other tourist attractions. Visitors can attend a Mass with the Monks at the Holy Trinity Abbey Church at special times during the week, while other prayer times at the Monastery Chapel can be organised. The Museum in New Norcia contains one of the finest collections of movable heritage in the country, donated to the monks by Queen Isabella of Spain. Paintings by Spanish masters are on display as well as a fascinating array of artefacts, and the Gift Shop allows you to purchase local produce such as bread, nutcakes, biscottis, olive oil, honey, religious items and more. A Heritage Trail can be taken to explore some of the other sites of New Norcia.

Visitor Information:

The New Norcia Visitor Centre can be contacted at *(08) 9654 8056*. It is located within the Museum and Art Gallery grounds. The site is *www.newnorcia.wa.edu.au*.

Outlying Towns from New Norcia.

Moora

Moora is located on the Midlands Road, 190km north of Perth via New Norcia, or 175km via Mogumber. The town is recognised as the heart of the wheat district of the Midlands, and is on the banks of the Moore River. It stretches across the clay flats deposited by an ancient waterway, and the area in its virgin state was a large salmon gum forest. Visitor Information is in the Moora Shire Office, 34 Padbury Street, *(08) 9651 1401*.

Morawa

100km south west of Geraldton, is the centre of a well established district. It was settled about 1905 and declared a townsite in 1912. It has a population of around 1350, and the area is based on wheat and wool growing. Prater Airport which accommodated Dove and DC3 aircraft, is now a regular port of call for light aircraft. A fully illuminated strip allows for night landing for the Flying Doctor and courier planes. Visitor Information is available from the Morawa Shire Council, *(08) 9971 1204*.

Mullewa

Situated 96km east of Geraldton, Mullewa is the gateway to the Murchison pastoral and old goldfield area. The Mullewa Tourist Information Centre is open during the tourism season (July - October) and information can also be obtained from the Mullewa Shire Council at 5 Thomas Street, *(08) 9961 1007*. The major attractions include Our Lady of Mt Carmel Catholic Church and Priest House built by Monsignor John Hawes, and the many wildflowers, particularly the wreath flower, which blossom each winter/spring.

Cervantes

Cervantes is a crayfishing centre, and appeals to anglers because of the wide range of fish that can be caught from the shore, or from a small boat in the local waters. The town is about 245km north of Perth and was established in 1963 as a support town for the lobster fishing industry. Nearby is the Nambung National Park, whose main attraction is the Pinnacles, an area of sand of varying colours, where there are thousands of limestone pinnacles that range in size from ankle high and pencil thickness to 5m high and 2m thick at the base. The Pinnacles Visitor Centre can be found on Cadiz Street, *(08) 9652 7700*. Other main attractions are Lake Thetis (living Stromatolites), Lesueur National Park (incredible diversity of flora), Stockyard Tunnel Cave and kilometres of pristine white beaches.

On the road to Moora

WA

Gascoyne Region

The Gascoyne region of Western Australia extends along the coastline north from Kalbarra National Park, through to Denham, Carnarvon, Coral Bay, and then north to Exmouth on the North West Cape with neighbouring Ningaloo Marine Park.

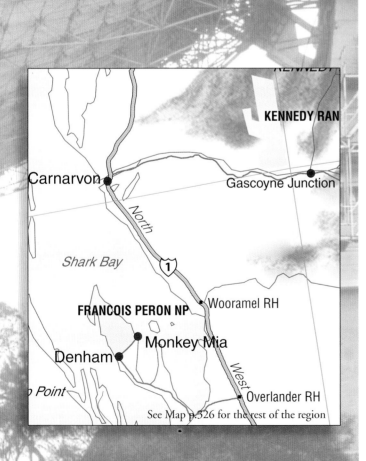

Carnarvon Population: 7,000. Climate: Average temperatures: January max 32°C - min 22°C; July max 22°C - min 11°C. Average annual rainfall: 225mm.

Situated 902km north of Perth at the mouth of the Gascoyne River, the city of Carnarvon is the commercial centre of the surrounding district. Often described as 'the sun's winter home', Carnarvon is a friendly town with a tropical, relaxed atmosphere, and an abundance of fish and fruit. Plantations extend along both banks of the River for about 15km, some of which welcome visitors to buy their mangoes, pawpaws, bananas, oranges and grapefruit. While the Gascoyne River is nothing more than a dusty river bed during the dry season, the irrigation channels are responsible for pumping the water to the plantations along the river flats. Occasionally the river can be seen after heavy rains upstream, and levee banks have been built to protect low-lying areas during floods.

The coastal area around Carnarvon was known to Dutch sailors during the seventeenth century, yet none showed any interest in attempting settlement due to the harsh desert settings and lack of any proper water supplies. The first European to charter the site was Lieutenant George Grey on his failed expedition to the North West Cape in 1839,

See Map p.326 for the rest of the region

The Blowholes

who named the river after a naval officer Captain Gascoyne. Though the harsh conditions led many to believe the area was inhospitable, settlers finally began to arrive by the end of the 1870's. C.S. Brockman, Aubrey Brown and John Monger established the district with the arrival of 4000 sheep, and by the time it was gazetted in 1883 there was a huge wool producing industry. While over a million sheep grazied in Carnarvon by the 1930's, the planting of banana crops is what eventually became the town's economic focus.

One of the most famous events in Carnarvon history occurred with the establishment of the NASA tracking station in 1964. Referred to as the 'Big Dish', the 26.5m diameter reflector was of major importance to global communications. This stemmed from the fact that it sent commands for the Trans Lunar Insertion, which sent Apollo missions to the moon. When Neil Armstrong stepped out of Apollo 11 in July 1969, his moon walking was transmitted to the world via the tracking station at Carnarvon. While the station was closed down in 1987 when the technology became outdated, the site remains open for visitors as an tourist attraction. The site also provides a magnificent view of Carnarvon and the plantations.

Visitor Information:

The Carnarvon Visitor Centre is in the Civic Centre, Robinson Street, *(08) 9941 1146.* Send emails to *cvontourist@wn.com.au*

Points of Interest:

Jubilee Hall in Francis Street, was opened in 1887 and for years served as Council Chambers and Shire Offices. The first 50 pounds received for the construction of the hall was donated by Queen Victoria!

St George's Church of England, in Francis Street opposite the Shire Offices, was erected in 1907. The first Bishop of North-West Australia was enthroned here on July 4, 1910. It is the most westerly parish in Australia, and part of the largest Anglican diocese in the world.

Chinaman's Pool is a great picnic area and swimming spot in the Gascoyne River, between Marmion and Saw Streets. It was originally a watering hole for the township, and now attracts many varieties of birdlife, especially in the early morning or evening.

One Mile Jetty, on Babbage Island, actually stretches 1,493 metres out into the bay. It was built in 1904, and widened in 1912, and was used by ships until 1966. The jetty end was burnt by vandals in 1985, but the locals raised the funds to have it rebuilt. To get there take the main street to Babbage Island Road and turn right at the lighthouse. In the lighthouse keeper's cottage there is a museum restored to the times of the pioneers who looked after the structure. If you turn right just before you get to the One Mile Jetty you'll come to Dwyer's Leap, an area that is usually sheltered from the wind.

The Blowholes near the town are spectacular, as the trapped water is forced out through a hole to a height of 20m. Nearby is a good beach where people go for oysters, fish and crayfish. Enjoy snorkelling in the coral lagoon.

Cape Cuvier - 30km north of the Blowhole is a deep port where ships load salt for Japan. It is fascinating if you are there when they are loading, although not if you are too close. The port is situated beneath a 60m cliff and they simply bulldoze the salt over the cliff onto a conveyor below.

The HMAS Sydney Memorial Cairn was erected near High Rock, Quobba Station, to commemorate the tragic battle between the *Sydney* and the German raider *Kormoran* off Carnarvon on November 19, 1941. To get there, follow the signs from the Blowholes and the memorial is 7km to the north.

The Fascine is the bay formed by the South Arm of the Gascoyne River. The name is derived from the Latin word meaning 'bundle of sticks', because in the old days bundles of sticks were placed on the foreshore to help prevent erosion during the major river flows. Now the waterway is lined with stately palms. The area is a favourite spot for a picnic, or an evening stroll. Free gas barbecues are located at the end of the main street on the Fascine.

Pelican Point is a popular swimming and fishing spot about 5km out of town. To get there turn left at the end of causeway on Babbage Island Road.

Bibbawarra Bore is 16km north of Carnarvon, and the best way to get there is via the Bibbawarra Road Crossing (when the river is dry). The Bore was originally worked for coal in 1905 to a depth of 914m, and now produces a continuous flow of hot water around 65°C. Be very careful with children and pets. The adjacent stock trough is 175 metres long which allows the water to cool.

Bush Bay and New Beach are both excellent for swimming and fishing. They are reached from the Geraldton Road. The turn-off to Bush Bay is about 20km from town, that to New Beach, about 40km.

Outlying Towns in the Gascoyne Region

Shark Bay

The only town in Shark Bay is Denham, the westernmost town in Australia. It has a permanent population of around 400, and has excellent recreational facilities. The Shark Bay Tourist Bureau, 71 Knight Street in Denham, *(08) 9948 1253*, has accommodation and sightseeing details. It also has information on the Shark Bay Heritage Trail, a 130km self-guiding drive that features sites of historical interest and the unique natural environment.

Shark Bay

Kennedy Ranges

Denham

Denham is both the westernmost town in Australia (at the 113°32" East meridian of longitude) and the gateway to Monkey Mia with its friendly dolphins. Located on the western coast of the Peron Peninsula, Denham is 23 km south-west of the dolphins and 831 km north of Perth. It has an almost Mediterranean feel about it with a small and beautiful beach and a jetty from which fishing and boating are popular activities. The Nanga Station can be found 48 km south of Denham. It is a huge sheep station which has embraced the growing tourism in the region by providing plenty of places to stay and shops to visit.

Monkey Mia

Some 260km south of Carnarvon and about 25km from Denham across the peninsula, is Monkey Mia, where friendly bottlenose dolphins visit, apparently just to interact with people. The local Dolphin Information Centre has loads of information on these creatures *(08) 9948 1366*. Monkey Mia is also an excellent spot for fishing, boating, or lazing on the clean white beaches.

Taking the road to Hamelin you'll reach Hamelin Pool, a place where the peculiarities of Shark Bay have created hypersalination – twice the salination of normal seawater – and where strange domed stromatolites have been formed on the water's edge. These unusual formations are created by single celled organisms known as cyanbacteria and they grow at a rate of less than 1 mm per year. They are known as 'living fossils' because these cyanbacteria formations are probably as old as any form of life on earth.

Gascoyne Junction

About 13km north of Carnarvon is the turn-off for Gascoyne Junction, which lies a further 164km to the east, at the junction of the Gascoyne and Lyons Rivers. It is the only town in the Shire of Upper Gascoyne, which covers an area of 57,146 square kilometres. There are huge sheep stations in the area which produce an annual wool clip of over 1.5 million kilograms. Further along is Minnie Creek and the Kennedy Ranges, which have Aboriginal caves and rock paintings. The Ranges are known for the semi precious gemstones to be found there, so you might like to take some time out for fossicking.

Kennedy Ranges

Mount Augustus

Situated 289km north-west from Gascoyne Junction, Mount Augustus is a rock. In fact it is the largest rock (monocline) in the world. It is not as famous as that other one in Central Australia, but by its geological formation it should be, and it is well worth the trip through the rugged bush country. The Mount was of significance to the Aborigines, so there are plenty of rock paintings.

Coral Bay

Located 250km north of Carnarvon, and 150km south of Exmouth, Coral Bay is situated in a lagoon formed between the Ningaloo Coral Reef and the coastline. The Reef is the longest continuous and most accessible reef complex in Western Australia, extending from north of Point Murat, round North West Cape, to Amherst Point in the south, a distance of about 260km. Coral Bay is a blue-water paradise that has yet to be commercialised. There is only one small hotel and several caravan parks, and the beach and bay area provide a perfect place for beachcombing, fishing, swimming and exploring.

Exmouth

Located 155km north of Coral Bay, and 400km north of Carnarvon, Exmouth is one of the newest towns in Australia.

It was founded in 1967 as a support town for the US Naval Communications Station, and now has a population of around 3000. Exmouth is the home of the big fish, and draws many people eager to experience the feel of a taut line. To date, 13 world and Australian game fish records have been landed at Exmouth, as well as the largest sailfish ever caught. The town has six large charter vessels, an offshore rescue group, and a variety of accommodation and caravan parks. The Exmouth Visitor Centre can be found on the corner of Murat Road and Truscott Crescent, *(08) 9949 1176.*

The town is situated on a peninsula surrounded by Ningaloo Marine Park, and the reef is accessible by small boat. Surrounding Exmouth is some of Australia's best bush country with its wildlife and flora. On a scenic drive through Cape Range National Park and Ningaloo Marine Park's perimeter, there are many rugged gorges and canyons for you to explore. For details of the many wonders of the Cape Range National Park, visit the Milyering Visitor Centre, about 52km from Exmouth in the heart of the Cape Range National Park.

Mount Augustus

WA

The Pilbara

Stretching from the Indian Ocean all the way to the Northern Territory border, the Pilbara covers more than 500,000 square kilometers. The region is comprised of four major areas - the Shires of Ashburton, East Pilbara and Roebourne, and the town of Port Hedland.

Port Hedland

Population: 15,000. Climate: Average temperatures: January max 36°C - min 25°C; July 26°C - min 12°C. Average annual rainfall: 304mm.

Located 1763km north of Perth on the shores of the Indian Ocean, the city of Port Hedland is one of Australia's most substantial iron ore ports. Almost everything in the town revolves around mining and iron ore, and some of the biggest ships in the world visit the wharves of Port Hedland to collect the precious commodities. With over 70 million tonnes of product to the value of $3 billion shipped out every year, the port is one of the world's largest in terms of tonnage. A combination of light and service industry premises are contained in the Wedgefield Industrial Area, while the heavy industries such as Boodarie Iron, operated by BHP Billiton, are contained within the Boodarie Strategic Industrial Area. The main landmarks Port Hedland is remembered for include the giant iron ore crushing mill at Nelson Point, the trains that carry resources back and forth between the mines at Mount Newman, and of course the gigantic port.

The first Europeans to explore the coast of Port Hedland were Dutch vessels during the seventeenth century, with Dirk Hartog passing through the area in 1616. It was Captain Peter Hedland who later discovered the bay of the the future townsite, sailing his craft through a narrow entrance to a channel in 1863 and uncovering what appeared to be an inland lake. The first station in the Pilbara was started on the nearby De Gray River in 1864. During the 1870's pearls were found along the coast, and Port Hedland became the home base for the pearling luggers. Gold was discovered inland, which also attracted new settlers. The town declined when the gold ran out, and in 1946 the population was lying at 150. The 1950's saw some investment return, but it was during the 1960's that the embargo on iron ore was lifted and the modern industry was born.

Those who wish to get a taste of the town's highly industrialised nature will not be short of things to do when visiting Port Headland. Tours are held every morning of BHP Billiton's iron ore crushing works at Nelson Point, and bookings can be made with the Tourist Information Centre. The Port Hedland-Newman Railway line is the longest private railway in Australia, and the long trains shipping iron ore can be seen at any time of the day along the North West Coastal Highway. A stroll along the port will   reveal

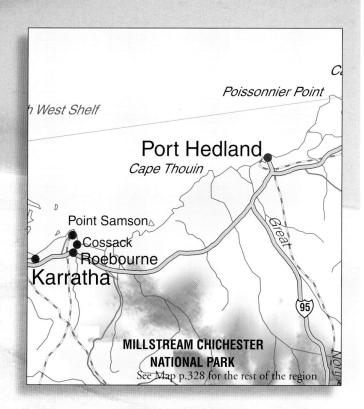

Poissonnier Point

h West Shelf

Port Hedland
Cape Thouin

Point Samson△

●Cossack
●Roebourne

Karratha

Great

95

MILLSTREAM CHICHESTER NATIONAL PARK
See Map p.328 for the rest of the region

Rocky Outcrop near Port Headland

the huge ships which carry the resources out of the town, while the salt that is produced from the extensive evaporation ponds can be seen in huge pyramids not far from there. The Port Hedland Cultural and Heritage Trail is a 2.25km walk retracing the development of the early port township, taking in the historical buildings and sites.

Visitor Information:

Port Hedland Visitor Centre is at 13 Wedge Street, Port Hedland, *(08) 9173 1711*.

Points of Interest:

The Don Rhodes Mining Museum is an open air establishment that contains displays on the pastoral, railway, manganese and iron ore industries which have shaped Port Hedland. Three restored locomotives from the BHP Iron Ore railway provide the centrepiece of the museum, and there are also relics of the early mining days. The museum can be found in Wilson Street.

Cemetery Beach is a great fishing spot at high tides, and nearby is a children's playground. Pretty Pool is also good for fishing and picnics. Due to the dangers of stonefish, blue-ringed octopus, sea snakes and sharks, it is not recommended that you swim in the ocean or the creeks, but there is an olympic pool, with a wading and diving pool in the town, and in South Hedland there is a big aquatic centre. The tides in the area range up to 8m, and create good fishing spots and chances to collect shells.

Lion's Park, in Anderson Street, is a good picnic area with lots of shade and lawn.

Outlying Towns in the Pilbara Region

Roebourne

Situated 201km west of Port Hedland, Roebourne was the first capital of the North-West, and has many old stone buildings. The town is about 14km from the coast on the Harding River, and was established in 1864, making it the oldest town on the north-west coast of WA. From the top of Mount Welcome, behind the town, there is a panoramic view of the coastal plains and rugged hills which surround Roebourne. You can see the railroad from Cape Lambert weaving its way through the hills to Pannawonica in the south, and the pipeline carrying water from Millstream to Wickham and Cape Lambert. The Visitor Centre is in the 'Old Jail' on Queen Street, *(08) 9182 1060*.

Cossack

Nearby is the first place settled on the north-west coast (1863). Cossack was a bustling seaport with a colourful multi-racial population in its heyday, though the wharf facilities were removed and it became a ghost town when the pearling industry relocated to Broome. The old graveyard and the Courthouse are the only man-made attractions, but the ocean and river scenery make a visit worthwhile.

Karratha

In the same area is Karratha, meaning 'good country', so named because of the area's natural supply of food sources enjoyed by the local Aborigines. Today, the inhabitants enjoy the same resources along with the modern shopping centres and facilities. Karratha is about 230km west of Port Hedland on the North West Coast Highway, and the Karratha Visitor Centre is located in Karratha Road, *(08) 9144 4600*.

Around the town there is much evidence of early Aboriginal life, and on the 3.5km Jaburara Heritage Trail you can see Aboriginal carvings, shellfish middens, grinding stones, artefacts and spiritual taboo sites. On the nearby Burrup Peninsula area there are over 40,000 identified petroglyphs (Aboriginal etchings) some dating back thousands of years. One of the etchings is of a man in uniform, who some say is William Dampier, the English buccaneer, explorer and naturalist, who visited the coast aboard the *Cygnet* in 1688.

Dampier

Dampier is really a small satellite town of Karratha, about 17km to the west. It is a well-kept town, and the bay and sound area is almost picture-like with the vivid blue and earthy colourings. The town overlooks Hampton Harbour, and was built in the 1960's by Hamersley Iron to export the iron ore from the mines at Tom Price and Paraburdoo. Dampier Salt also uses the shipping facilities to export salt from the nearby pans. The Dampier Archipelago incorporates the only coral reefs found in a tropical arid setting within Australia, and they are home to more than 200 species of living coral.

Onslow

Situated on Beadon Bay, Onslow is said to have more

potential as a tourist retreat than any other coastal spot in the north of WA. The laid-back atmosphere of the town encourages just lazing around, or you can visit the site of the old township, about 45km out of town, which was abandoned in 1925-26. Everything that was transportable was moved to the new site, but there are still the stone and cement buildings to explore. The Onslow Visitor Centre is on Second Avenue, *(08) 9184 6644.*

Tom Price - Paraburdoo

The two mining towns of Tom Price and Paraburdoo, in the heart of the rocky Pilbara country and on the edge of the Hamersley Range gorge area, were built to service the iron ore industry. Paraburdoo is 394km south-east of Onslow, and Tom Price is 79km north-east of Paraburdoo.

Hamersley Range National Park

The Park is one of WA's largest, and within its borders are some of the most ancient parts of this planet. The slow process of erosion has carved an intriguing landscape in a complex ecology. Within the ranges there are many gorges, and in most are permanent pools of clear fresh water, some of which are pleasant places to swim. Dales Gorge has sunken gardens, deep pools, ferns and waterfalls. Joffre, Red, Hancock, Weano and Knox Gorges are for those who like rock climbing. Kalamina Gorge is easily accessible and has a clear shaded pool, ferns, tropical paperbarks and river gums. Yampire Gorge has magnificent rock formations, and the ruins of an old asbestos mine.

Wittenoom

The small town of Wittenoom is in the heart of the Pilbara, and information on the town and the Range can be obtained from Auski Tourist Village Roadhouse, Great Northern Highway, *(08) 9176 6988.* If you are travelling through Wittenoom, you are advised to keep in mind that there was an asbestos mine nearby, which still poses a health problem. It is considered that, while the risk of cancer from inhaling asbestos fibres to short term visitors and tourists is minimal, the following precautions should be taken:
• Keep to main roads in the town and gorge areas.
• Camp only in areas set aside for that purpose. Camping is not allowed in the Wittenoom Gorge.

Newman

Newman is often described as an 'oasis in the wilderness' and was built in recent times for workers at the world's largest open cut mine, Mt Whaleback. It is 416km south of Port Hedland and 238km south-east of Wittenoom. Tours are conducted of the world's largest open cut mining operation. For more information call *(08) 9175 3502.* The Newman Visitor Infomation Centre and Museum Gallery can be found in Fortescue Avenue *(08) 9175 2888.*

Marble Bar

Marble Bar has the reputation of being Australia's hottest spot, earned in 1923-24 when the town experienced 160 consecutive days of temperatures over 38°C. In those days it was said that a beer at the town's hotel, The Iron Clad, was worth more than its weight in gold, as there was more gold in the town than beer. The town gets its name from the bar of jasper marble across the Coongan River, and all visitors are directed to the spot. Other places to visit are Chinaman's Pool, Miles House and the State Government Offices, which were completed in 1895.

Doolena Gorge

WA
The Kimberley Region

Located in the north-west corner of Australia, the Kimberley Region in Western Australia is one of the last great wilderness areas anywhere on earth. The region covers an area of 421,000 square kilometres, and has fewer people per square kilometre than almost anywhere else on earth. The major towns are Broome, Kununurra, Derby, Wyndham, Halls Creek and Fitzroy Crossing.

Broome   Population: 13,000. Climate: Due to its coastal location, Broome's climate is more moderate than the rest of the Kimberley. During the dry winter, it has warm, sunny days averaging about 28°C with cool nights. The summer months average about 33°C during the day, with beautiful balmy nights and coastal breezes.

Located at the Southern gateway to the Kimberley on the North West coast of the state, Broome is known as the pearl capital of the world. Lying next to what is one of the last great unexplored wilderness areas on earth, up until the mid 1980's the town could only be accessed by a dirt road. Broome has a history that is defined by its isolation from the rest of Australia, and by the initiative of those able to overcome these difficulties. "Broome Time" is an expression that has come to be associated with the laidback atmosphere which permeates the town. Broome's development grew out of the

James Price Point

Map

Archipelago · Collier Bay
Cape Leveque
Lombadina
King Sound
Baskerville
Derby
· RAAF Base
DAMPIER LAND   Hwy
Roebuck RH
① 1
Broome
Roebuck Bay

See Map p.328 for the rest of the region

CANNING BASIN

discovery of pearls in the area, and the rich cultural mix of the people who immigrated there can be seen in the contrasting Colonial and Asian architecture that fills the streets. Broome has in recent times become an increasingly popular visiting place for tourists wanting to soak in the beautiful natural locations of the town, as well as the vast outback lying just beyond its border.

It was on the 27th of November 1883 that the Governor of Western Australia, Sir Frederick Napier Broome, formally announced that a townsite on the North Western point of Roebuck Bay would be established. Funnily enough, although the town was named after him, the WA Governor wanted nothing to do with the settlement. This was most likely related to the fact that the town had very little to offer at the time, populated by a mere few pearlers and their equipment. Yet the "Fat Years" between 1889 and 1891 brought significant changes to the town: the price of mother of pearl shell rose to new heights and established Broome as a port. Often referred to as the 'Queen City of the North', by 1898 Broome was the principal cargo port for north Western Australia, and second only to Fremantle by the time of the First World War. While the men who ran the early pearling industry were predominantly from the UK, the town's population grew into a cosmopolitan mix of Malaysians, Chinese, Japanese, Filipinos, Europeans and Aborigines.

Broome is not short of natural attractions, and an essential activity is a visit to Gantheaume Point to see the dinosaur's footprint, estimated to be 130 million years old. Cable Beach can boast 24km of clean, white sand, and is 6km from Broome. Opposite the beach is the Cable Beach Club, a multi-million dollar development. To gain a sense of the history surrounding the pearl industry in Broome, the Willie Creek Pearl Farm can be visited. Just 38 km north of Broome, the farm is the only of its kind offering tours to the public and is one of the area's biggest tourist attractions. Visitors are able to learn first hand about the pearling industry in Western Australia, and find out how pearls are grown.

Visitor Information:

The Broome Visitor Centre is on the corner of Bagot Road and Broome Road, and can be called on *(08) 9192 2222*. On the web go to *www.broomevisitorcentre.com.au* or email the Bureau at *tourism@broome.wt.com.au*.

Broome Jetty

Cable Beach, Broome

Points of Interest:

The Broome Crocodile Farm has some of the largest crocodiles in captivity, allowing visitors to witness their true nature during their feeding time. The farm can be found on Cable Beach Road, *(08) 9192 1489.*

Gantheaume Point has an ancient dinosaurs footprint, estimated to be 130 million years old, visible only during low tides. Red sandstones that seeps from land to sea also abound this area.

The Historical Society Museum holds the secrets of Broomes history, and can be called on *(08) 9192 2075.*

The Japanese Cemetery provides further on the history of pearling in the town, and is the final resting place of more than 900 pearl divers that came here to seek their fortune.

The Minyirr Park has a number of self guided trails and great bushwalking.

The Budha's Santuary is a great place to relax, reflect and meditate, with ornamental gardens to enjoy, a pavillion and a crystal Buddha that's close to 4 metres tall. Located just behind the Cable Beach Club Resort.

Derby Population: 5,000

Situated 2354km north of Perth at the southern end of King Sound, the town of Derby is the Gateway to the Kimberley Gorges and the magnificent coastline of the Buccaneer Archipelago. Surrounded like so many of WA's other locations by a vast and unending outback, Derby is a town that sprawls in all directions and has no clearly defined main street. The first town to be settled in the Kimberley, many of the attractions are based on its historical heritage and close proximity to some of the region's best countryside and coastlines. Half of the town's population are Aboriginal, and five different indigenous languages are spoken.

An interesting legend in the history of Broome is that of Pigeon, the leader of the Aboriginal population and a strong guerilla fighter. His story is indicative of the conflicts between Europeans and the indigenous population during early settlement. Convinced in 1894 that a stand needed to be taken against the white invaders, Pigeon shot and killed Police Constable Richardson before staging a successful

Boab Prison Tree

attack on stockmen at Windjana Gorge. He taunted police over the next few years, his superb bushman skills allowing him to evade capture until he was finally killed in 1897. In the meantime, the local authorities carried out a policy of indiscriminantly punishing the indigenous population, killing hundreds of Aborigines of whom most had no connection with Pigeon. A full account of Pigeon's operations around Derby can be seen on the Pigeon Heritage Trail, contact the Derby Visitor Centre for more information.

Derby characterised by the tidal marsh which surrounds it and the boab trees which line the main street. Boabs are unusually shaped trees which resemble a bottle, and one around 7km south of the town is hollow with a girth of 14m. Nearby is Myalls Bore with one of the largest cattle troughs in the southern hemisphere, 120m long by 1.2m wide. More of the town's history can be absorbed by visiting the heritage listed Wharfinger House Museum and the Old Derby Goal. Call in at the Visitor Centre for a walking guide. The Cultural Centre in Derby houses a regional museum, library and art gallery, built of Kimberley colourstone from Mt Jowlaenga, south-west of Derby.

Visitor Information:

The Derby Visitor Centre is located at 2 Clarendon Street, Derby, *(08) 9191 1426* or *1800 621 426.* They have a website at *www.derbytourism.com* and can be emailed at *derbytb@comswest.net.au.*

Outlying Towns in the Kimberley Region

Halls Creek

Situated on the Great Northern Highway, 555km east of Derby, is the old town of Halls Creek, the site of Western Australia's first gold rush. Today it is a cattle centre, but remnants of the old town remain. Near here an almost vertical quartz vein projects above the surrounding rocks to form a startling white stone wall, which is known as the Great Wall of China. A major attraction in the area is 133km north near Carranya Station, the Wolf Creek Meteorite Crater, which is 835m wide and 50m deep. The Purnululu National Park is within Halls Creek Shire and scenic flights can be taken from Halls Creek to view this incredible sight from the air.

Kununurra

A rich green oasis amid the rugged land of the Kimberleys, Kununurra is in the centre of the Ord River Irrigation Scheme, about 1057km north east of Broome. As a result of the Ord River Scheme, a wide variety of crops are now grown. Lake Argyle, which was formed as a result of damming the Ord River in the Carr Boyd Ranges, has many tranquil bays, inlets and islands, and the irrigation canals are a fascinating feature of the district. A panoramic view of the Ord Valley can be obtained from Kelly's Knob, 2.5km from town.

Hidden Valley or Mirima National Park, 3km from town, has some interesting rock formations, birdlife and Aboriginal rock paintings. South of Kununurra is the huge Argyle Diamond Mine with a visitors' centre at the site. Other attractions: Ivanhoe Crossing, Ord and Diversion Dam, Valentine's Springs, Middle Springs, Black Rock Falls, Hoochery, Melon Farm, and Barra Bananas. There are also a number of art galleries around. The Kununurra Visitor Centre is in Coolibah Drive, *(08) 9168 1177.*

Wyndham

In the old days, crocodiles were attracted to Wyndham because of the meatworks, which were kept busy by the thousands of cattle on the vast Kimberley stations. Now that a Crocodile Lookout has been built, crocodile-sighting is not such a blood-curdling exercise. Wyndham, a port established originally to land hopeful prospectors heading for the goldfields of Halls Creek, is now used for exporting produce from irrigated areas around Kununurra. The town stands on Cambridge Gulf, with its fast running tides, and the best views of both the town and the Gulf beyond are to be had from the Bastion, which is higher than Uluru. The Grotto, near Wyndham, is a pleasant pool surrounded by rocks and boulders, with plenty of trees providing shade. The Wyndham Visitor Information Centre is at Kimberley Motors, Great Northern Highway, *(08) 9161 1281.*

Hidden Valley, Kununurra

RITORY

The Northern Territory covers one-sixth of Australia, and is renowned for its stunning outback beauty. The Territory stretches from the inland city of Alice Springs in the centre of Australia, right up north to the city of Darwin in the Top End region. The Territory is also home to some of Australia's most iconic locations, the monolithic Uluru (Ayers Rock) and the 36 domes of Kata Tjuta (The Olgas).

NT

Darwin & The Top End

The Top End of the Northern Territory encompasses the tropical north of the state, and includes the city of Darwin, as well as World Heritage Areas like the Kakadu National Park, Litchfield National Park and the Katherine Gorge.

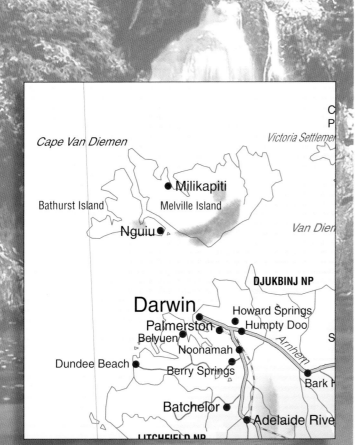

Darwin   Population: 80,000. Climate: Average temperatures: January max 32C - min 25C; July max 30C - min 19C. The average annual rainfall is 1525mm.

Situated on the tropical north coast alongside the Arafura Sea, Darwin is the capital city of the Northern Territory. It is also Australia's most northerly city, and is actually closer to South East Asia than to some of the nation's other capitals. Settled on a rocky peninsula that stretches out into one of the most attractive harbours on the Australian north coast, Darwin rises above the cliffs and is surrounded by water at several angles. The city is reknowned for its tropical weather conditions, and during the famed "wet season" between November and April the area experiences over 90 days of thunderstorms and close to 1500mm of warm, humid rain. Comprised of an eclectic mix of different cultures, more than 60 different ethnic groups from all across the globe call Darwin their home. An indicator of the city's contrasting cultural aspects is the Chinese Temple that lies less than 5 minutes away from the busy town centre. Over the decades Darwin has gained a reputation as a booze heavy capital, a frontier of prawn trawlers, buffalo-catchers, croc shooters and wild waterfront bars. But while the city's status as an isolated outpost has associated it with a rough and resilient lifestyle, Darwin has nonetheless developed into a modern city that boasts a wide assortment of restaurants, pubs, galleries and the glitz of the MGM Grand Casino.

Records show that the first Europeans to explorer Darwin were the Dutch aboard the *Arnhem* in 1623, though an attempt at settlement did not occur until much later in the nineteenth century. Frustrated by the overwhelming failure of their attempts to establish settlements on the north coast, the South Australian Government was determined to ensure the success of the settlement at Port Darwin. A plan had been drawn up for the town by 1869, and while during the early days Darwin appeared to be heading in the same direction as other north coast developments, it was saved by the construction of the Overland Telegraph. The next several decades saw a large number of settlers moving to the town, including a heavy Asian contingent who would come to play an integral role in Darwin's culture.

While the economy in the area was far from prosperous, Darwin was finally linked up with the rest of the country during World War II when it became a strategic base for

Darwin

Allied actions against the Japanese in the Pacific. Amazingly, Darwin is a city that has been destroyed several times over during its existence. While the cyclone of 1893 was the first to ravage the town, Darwin's status as a military base meant that it was the only place in Australia to suffer prolonged attack during the World War II, the city suffering from over 60 attacks and almost 250 deaths. But the most significant event in the town's history occurred on Christmas Eve 1974, when the area was hit by the full force of Cyclone Tracy. One of the greatest natural disasters in Australian history, the cyclone was responsible for killing 65 people and left standing only around 500 of the city's 8000 homes.

A stroll around the city will allow visitors to view some of Darwin's most important historical sites. The Tree of Knowledge, behind the Civic Centre on Harry Chan Avenue, has been a famous local landmark throughout the city's history. It is a banyan tree, a species revered by Buddhists worldwide as the tree under which Buddha gained enlightenment. Darwin has all the shops and facilities expected of a modern city, and many of the Northern Territory's most characteristic items can be found for sale.

These include handcrafted leather goods, local fashion items and a wide selection of Aboriginal arts and crafts. The Smith Street Mall is Darwin's main shopping area, and there are also shopping centres at Casuarina and Palmerston. And for a relatively small city, Darwin has a large selection of galleries and shops that cater for collectors of arts and crafts. The Museum & Art Gallery of the Northern Territory is one such location, and is full of art, artifacts, maps and photos – including the legendary Sweetheart, a huge crocodile who used to terrorise trolling fishermen. The Art Gallery contains works by Lloyd Rees, Sidney Nolan, Clifton Pugh, Russell Drysdale, Donald Friend and Arthur Streeton, and can be found at Conacher Street in Fannie Bay, *(08) 8999 8201*.

The city of Darwin makes an effective base for those visiting the surrounding World Heritage spots, and the Kakadu National Park is only 200km away. Declared a World Heritage area for its natural and cultural importance, the Park covers an area of almost 20,000 square kilometres. More than a third of the Top End's plant life and a huge assortment of animal life is contained within. Characterised by a uniquely rugged form of outback beauty, the diverse landscape takes in flat savanna woodlands, flood plains, billabongs, cascading

Gagudju Crocodile Hotel

waterfalls and rock plateus. The area has been inhabited by Aboriginals for an estimated 25,000 years before European settlement, and many examples of indigenous art and culture remain preserved within the park.

Visitor Information:

The Northern Territory Visitors Centre can be found at 38 Mitchell Street, call *1300 138 886* or *(08) 8936 2499*. They can be emailed *info@tourismtopend.com*.

The Northern Territory Tourist Commission has its head office in Darwin at 43 Mitchell Street, *(08) 8999 3900*.

Points of Interest:

Brown's Mart was intended as a mining exchange when it was built in 1882. It has served many purposes through the years, despite the roof being blown off by two cyclones. In recent years it has been restored and converted to a community theatre. It can be found on the corner of Harry Chan Avenue & Smith Street, *(08) 8981 5522*.

The Old Town Hall is in Smith Street, and when it was erected in 1883 during a mining boom it created a streetscape of stone. In World War II it was used for naval administration, and after that was an art gallery. Now, the ruined walls make a dramatic backdrop for outdoor theatre.

The Old Courthouse and Police Station was built in 1884 for the South Australian government, in early South Australian style. The navy used these buildings from World War II until Cyclone Tracy. The interior was then reconstructed, and the building now houses the offices of the Administrator of the Northern Territory. They are located on the corner of Smith Street and The Esplanade.

The Hotel Darwin in The Esplanade is one of Darwin's oldest hotel sites. The original pub, The Palmerston, was proud of its 'accommodation suitable for ladies' when it opened in 1883. It was severely damaged by Cyclone Tracy, but a convention and function centre was added to the rebuilt hotel in 1983. It is now the Holiday Inn, *(08) 8980 0800*.

Lyons Cottage was built in 1924-25 to house the manager of the British Australia Telegraph Company (BAT). The Georgian Revival-style bungalow was later occupied by one-time Darwin mayor John Lyons. The house is now the BAT Museum, and can be found at the corner of Knuckey Street & The Esplanade, *(08) 8981 1750*.

The National Trust headquarters are housed in Myilly Point Heritage Precinct, at 2 Khalin Avenue on the outskirts of the city centre. It is composed of four pre-World War II houses, built originally for government employees. The Trust has an information centre and can be called on *(08) 8981 2848*.

The Botanic Gardens were first planted by Dr Maurice Holtze more than a century ago. They have the Southern Hemisphere's largest array of tropical palms, an orchid farm, nursery, rainforest, waterfall and wetlands flora, as well as an amphitheatre where there are often live concerts. To view the gardens, head to Gardens Road off Gilruth Avenue.

Aquascene is among Darwin's most popular attractions. Every day at high tide, hundreds of fish come in from the sea to be fed, and visitors can be there to serve them. Aquascene is at Doctors Gully Road on The Esplanade, *(08) 8981 7837*.

The Australian Aviation Heritage Centre has the major exhibit of a B52 bomber on permanent loan from the US Air Force, one of only two displayed outside the USA. Also of interest is the wreckage of a Zero Fighter shot down in 1942, during the first air raid on Darwin. There are many other exhibits from World War II, as well as displays documenting the history of aviation in the Northern Territory. The centre is on the Stuart Highway, Winnellie, call *(08) 8947 2145*.

The Fannie Bay Gaol Museum closed in 1979 after 84 years of service, and opened as a museum in 1983. The gaol was emptied in 1942, after Japan bombed Darwin, and again in 1974, after Cyclone Tracy damaged the complex. Fourteen men were hanged in the gaol, the last two in 1952. The Gaol can be found on East Point Road, *(08) 8999 8290*.

Crocodylus Park is one of Darwin's more recent attraction. It feaures crocodiles, of course, as well as other interesting wildlife, including lions and tigers. The park can be found on McMillans Road, Berrimah, *(08) 8922 4500*.

Outlying Areas from Darwin

South of Darwin

Palmerston

Palmerston is a new town, 20km south of Darwin, which was designed to become a self-sufficient city. The present population is around 8000 and four suburbs have been developed, but it is envisaged that it will grow very quickly. The town has many tourist attractions, and foremost among them is Marlow Lagoon, noted for its year-round swimming, playground, barbecue and other facilities.

Howard Springs

Situated 34km south of Darwin, on and around the Stuart Highway, Howard Springs is the centre for the Howard Springs Nature Park. The Park has the closest and most attractive public fresh water swimming pool to Darwin. Next to the Park is the Territory's only duck and goose hunting reserve, for a shooters permit enquire at a police station or the Parks & Wildlife Commission, *(08) 8983 1001*.

Mindil Beach, Darwin

Cullen Bay, Darwin

Noonamah

The town of Noonamah is 40km south of Darwin on the Stuart Highway, and its main attraction, the Crocodile Farm, is 2km before the town itself. The Farm is the first and largest in Australia and the reptiles are bred here for their skin and meat. The Farm can be called on *(08) 8988 1450*.

Berry Springs

Territory Wildlife Park is 10km west of the Stuart Highway turnoff, which is 48 km south of Darwin. The park is a world-class wildlife sanctuary set in more than 400 hectares of bushland, and exhibits native and feral animals of the North Territory. The park can be called on *(08) 8988 7200*. Next door to the wildlife park is the Berry Springs Nature Park. The springs create natural swimming pools fringed with rainforest, call *(08) 8988 6310*.

Batchelor

Batchelor is 13km west of the Stuart Highway, from the turnoff 87km south of Darwin. It was established as a town for miners working the Rum Jungle Uranium Mine in 1954. While both the mine and treatment plant had been closed by the 1970's, its main function now is as the gateway to Litchfield Park, one of the Territory's newest parks.

Litchfield National Park

The 65,700 hectare park features permanent water and changing terrain that makes it one of the better bush walking areas in the Top End. There are monsoonal rainforests, hot springs, the Tabletop range escarpment with its imposing sandstone outcrops, spring fed creeks, huge groves of cycads and historic tin mines. For the more adventurous there is the Lost City, a limestone rock formation that appears to be a huge petrified city of castles, statues, people and animals. Call Road Report, *1800 246 199*, for info on road conditions. Call the Parks & WIldlife Commission on *(08) 8976 0282*.

Adelaide River

The town of Adelaide River is 110km south of Darwin on the Stuart Highway. It is situated on a river of the same name, and was a major military centre during World War II. Attractions include the War Cemetery, Snake Creek Arsenal and Robin Falls. The pub is worth a visit, and the owners also offer some good value tours of the local region, *(08) 8976 7047*.

Adelaide River War Cemetery

East of Darwin

Humpty Doo

Humpty Doo is situated on the Arnhem Highway, 11km east of the Stuart Highway, and 45km from Darwin. A very large crocodile on the roadside, complete with boxing gloves, tells passers by that they are entering 'croc country', which is a good thing to keep in mind. The town is mainly a service centre for the rural belt, and has basic facilities and services. A great attraction in the town is the *Adelaide River Queen*, a flat-bottomed river boat that departs Adelaide River Bridge for cruises along the river. It cruises along a stretch of river which is home to about 60 crocs, call *(08) 8988 8144*.

Kakadu National Park

The Kakadu National Park is a natural wonderland - 20,000 square km of magnificent sights, sounds and experiences. It has a World Heritage listing, and is owned by the Aborigines under the Gagudju Association. Kakadu begins about 250km east of Darwin on the Arnhem Highway, and is made up of three regions: the almost inaccessible Arnhem plateau; the rolling lowlands; and the flood plains. There are 120 known rock galleries of Aboriginal art along the escarpment, with

Stokes Hill Wharf

those at Obiri Rock and Nourlangi Rock being the most easily accessible. Although almost one-third of Kakadu is bare rock, the rest is lush lowlands which support 960 identified species of plants and an incredible variety of animal life.

A cruise on the Yellow Waters Billabong or South Alligator River offers one of the best opportunities to see the water flowers and wildlife. There are excellent bushwalks throughout the park, and drives into the bush lead to spectacular sights such as Twin Falls and Jim Jim Falls. Visit the Bowali Visitor Information Centre near Jabiru for information, *(08) 8938 1120*. There is also a Tourist Centre at Tasman Plaza in Jabiru, *(08) 8979 2548*.

Arnhem Land
Arnhem Land is the area east of Kakadu National Park, and is traditionally inhabited by the Aborigines. A restricted number of tours take visitors through tropical bush abundant with wildlife and on to the coastal dunes from which the seascapes are truly magnificent. Entry permits can be obtained from the Tiwi Lands Council, Lot 2162 Armidale Street, *(08) 8981 4898*. The rock galleries of Aboriginal Art in Arnhem Land are regarded as even more impressive than those in Kakadu.

Typical vegetation in the National Park

North of Darwin

Bathurst and Melville Islands
The islands are 80km off the coast of Darwin, and are owned by the Tiwi Aborigines. Until recently, the islands had received almost no visitors from the mainland for thousands of years, but there are now day and half-day tours to Bathurst Island, or visitors can stay overnight at Putjimirra camp on Melville Island. Tiwi Tours can be called on *(08) 8924 1115*.

Cobourg Peninsula/Victoria Settlement
The peninsula north-east of Darwin is in Arnhem Land, and was where a brave but futile attempt was made to first settle the area. The ruins of the Victoria Settlement at Port Essington can still be seen, but a permit is required.

NT
Katherine
Region

Covering an area of approximately 408,500 square kilometres, the Katherine region takes in the Daly River area, northeast to Kakadu, south to Dunmarra, west to the Keep River National Park and east to Borroloola and the Gulf of Carpentaria.

Katherine Town
Population: 11,000. Climate: Weather is sub-tropical with distinct wet and dry seasons, average annual rainfall is 1040mm. Average temperatures range from 25°C to 35°C from November to December.

Situated on the Stuart Highway 317km south of Darwin, the remote township of Katherine is considered the true heart of the outback. Settled on the banks of the Katherine River, it is one of the few populated places that will be encountered on the route between Alice Springs and Darwin. While the town's distance from the coast means that it is not as excessively tropical as Darwin, neither is it completely dominated by the endless stretches of desert that lie nearby. A thriving regional centre provides services to communities stretching from the WA border to the Gulf of the NT, Katherine Town is also a major regional base for Commonwealth and Territory Government Departments. An increasing number of visitors have been attracted to Katherine in recent years, and tourism has gradually become the town's biggest industry. Attractions include places of historic interest, caves and gorges, Aboriginal lore and art, and for the adventurous, magnificent waterfalls, canyons and billabongs that remain unspoilt.

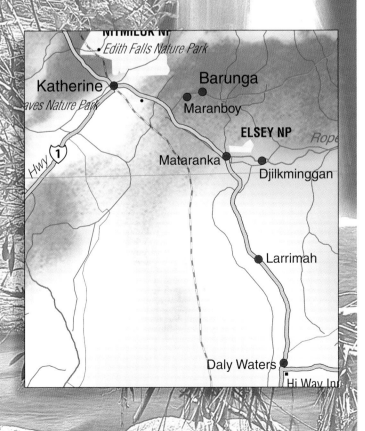

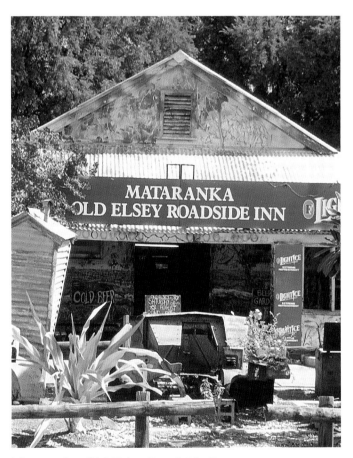

Mataranka Old Esley Roadside Inn

For the indigenous population, Katherine was the spot where the traditional lands of the Dagaman, the Jawoyan, the Walpiri and the Wardiman coincided, and for that reason the river and the gorge was traditionally a place of meeting. In the second half of the nineteenth century, a South Australian pastoralist by the name of James Chambers became interested in the idea of establishing a communications link with Europe. The expeditions of John McDouall Stuart were sponsored as part of this research, and it was on his sixth expedition across the country in 1862 that he encountered what would later be called the Katherine River. A decade later the Overland Telegraph was responsible for the birth of Katherine Town. The agricultural industry saw Katherine gradually develop over the next several decades, and by 1926 a bridge over the river had been built and a rail link completed.

The town's main street has plenty of shops, restaurants and other facilities, yet it is the isolated landscape of the outback for which Katherine is most remembered. The attractive Hot Springs along the Victoria Highway are only a short drive away, while the swimming hole by the weir on the Katherine River also makes for a good place to visit during the dry season. The Katherine Low Level Nature Park is only 5km from the town, and the river here flows over the weir into a series of shallow rapids. The Nitmiluk (Katherine) Gorge National Park that is 30km from the town attracts over 200,000 visitors every year. Consisting of 13 separate gorges which are separated by rocky areas during the dry season, the park covers an area of over 180,000 hectares and offers plenty of opportunities for bushwalking and swimming.

Visitor Information:
The Katherine Visitor Information Centre can be found on the Stuart Highway on the corner of Lindsay Street, *(08) 8972 2650*. Email them at *information@krta.com.au*.

Points of Interest:
The **Katherine Outback Heritage Museum** has many exhibits of Katherine's colourful past, including the Gypsy Moth flown by Dr Clyde Fenton in 1934. The museum is on Gorge Road opposite Katherine Hospital, *(08) 8972 3945*.

The **Railway Station Museum** is the National Trust headquarters, and can be found at Railway Terrace. The township was provided with the essential railway link it needed after the railbridge was built in 1926. The museum

has interesting displays of railway memorabilia, information on historic sites of Katherine, and items of interest for sale.

Knott's Crossing is 5km from Katherine, and was the original river crossing for the young settlement of Katherine.

Katherine School of the Air has guided tours on business days, and can be found on Gorge Road, *(08) 8972 1833*.

Outlying Areas in the Region

Nitmiluk Katherine Gorge Park
The main entrance is 32km from Katherine, and the 180,000 hectare National Park was created to preserve one of the Northern Territory's greatest natural wonders. Over millions of years, torrential summer rains in Arnhem Land during the west season have caused the waters of the Katherine River to cut thirteen spectacular serpentine gorges. Cut into ancient rock, the canyon walls climb steeply above cool blue water. The Park is owned by the Jawoyn Aboriginal people.

Cutta Cutta Caves Nature Park
Situated 27km south of Katherine on the Stuart Highway, the caves were formed millions of years ago. They are about 15m below the earth's surface, and spread for almost a kilometre. Ranger guided tours are available, call *(08) 8972 1940*.

Edith Falls Nature Park
Edith Falls is a series of waterfalls on the edge of the Arnhem Land escarpment. The main waterfall runs all year into a huge natural billabong surrounded by pandanus palms.

Mataranka
Mataranka is 110km south of Katherine on the Stuart Highway, in the heart of Never-Never country. The Mataranka Pool Nature Park has been dedicated as a reserve, the pool a constant 34C and flowing at an amazing 22.5 million litres each day. The surrounding rainforest survives from an earlier age, feeding from the thermal spring's deep source. Mataranka Homestead was established in 1916 and has become a major tourist resort, call *(08) 8975 4544*.

Larrimah
Gateway to the tropics, Larrimah is 72km south of Mataranka. The Larrimah Green Tourist Complex is on the Stuart Highway, call *(08) 8975 9937*.

Daly Waters

The small township of Daly Waters is 72km south of Larrimah on the Stuart Highway, and is home to the oldest pub in the Territory - the Daly Waters Pub, *(08) 8975 9927*. The pub is virtually an institution, and you really can't say you have seen the Territory if you haven't spent some time in the bar.

Victoria River

On the Victoria Highway, 190km west of Katherine, is the township of Victoria River. In town is a motel and camping ground that services the nearby Gregory National Park.

Timber Creek

Continuing along the Victoria Highway, 290km west of Katherine, is Timber Creek, with a population of around 100. The town lies on the Victoria River and gained its name when Augustus Charles Gregory used timber from the banks of the creek to repair a hole in his vessel.

Pine Creek

Pine Creek is situated 92km north of Katherine on the Stuart Highway. Mining activities have recently been restarted and there are numerous historical buildings still standing. Private operators conduct tours of the surrounding area, contact the Pine Creek Hotel on *(08) 8976 1288*.

Umbrawarra Gorge Nature Park

The Park is 122km from Katherine, and 22km south-west of Pine Creek. The gorge is very rugged, and there is a camping ground, picnic facilities, wood barbecues and toilets.

Daly Waters Pub

The Escarpment

NT
Tennant Creek Region

With the heart of the region situated around the junction of the Stuart Highway and the Barkly Highway, the area stretches from the Newcastle Waters in the north, to the old Telegraph Station at Barrow Creek in the south, and right to the Queensland border in the east.

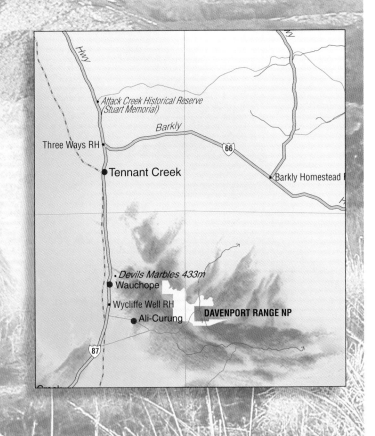

Tennant Creek

Population: 3,500. Climate: Average temperatures: Dry Season max 35°C - min 10°C; Wet Season max 43°C - min 26°C.

Located on the Stuart Highway and 675km south of Katherine, Tennant Creek is the fourth largest settlement in the Northern Territory. From hard beginnings the town has steadily developed, and the townsfolk have worked hard to acquire facilities that people 'down south' took for granted. While Tennant Creek was born in the rough and unrefined gold mining era, it now has all the facilites of a modern town and a rich and present heritage which complements the outback surroundings. The rugged charm of the early days is still present in Tennant Creek, with some of the highlights including underground mines, an operational gold processing plant, as well as gold fossicking and campfires at night. People from all over the world have settled at Tennant Creek in the last 50 years, and today it is a harmonious multi-cultural township. Growing from their beginnings as a small and dusty outback settlement, Tennant Creek has become a busy community that is a vital part of the Northern Territory.

Tennant Creek derives its name from the nearby watercourse, which was named by explorer John McDouall Stuart in 1860 in recognition of the help given to him by South Australian pastoralist John Tennant. A connection to the famous Overland Telegraph line was established near the watercourse in 1872, though the outpost remained relatively isolated until the discovery of gold in the 1930's. Known as the last great gold rush in Australian history, hundreds of men chose to ignore the Federal Government's warnings of limted facilities and flocked to the district. In 1934 the amount of people living there had reached such a large number that the government was prompted to establish a new township, referred to as Tennant Creek.

For a site that takes in good views over the town, the lookout at One Tank Hill along Peko Road should be visited. The site includes plaques set into a semi-circular wall that provide direction markers for 11 significant sites. For an insight into the history of the isolated town, there are two interesting graves to the west of the Telegraph Station, which is 11.4km north of the Tennant Creek. The northernmost one is that of Tom Nugent, the owner of the Banka Banka Station who died in 1911. Nugent had apparently in his younger days been a member of the Ragged Thirteen, a gang of cattle

Telegraph Station Historical Reserve

duffers (rustlers) who roamed the Territory at the turn of the century. Another member of the Ragged Thirteen was Harry Redwood, who built Brunette Downs, and was immortalised in Boldrewood's novel Robbery Under Arms as Captain Starlight. The other grave is not his, though, it belongs to Archibald Cameron, an OTS linesman who died around 1918.

The Pebbles are an interesting granite rock formation scattered over a large area. To see them drive 11km north of Tennant Creek on the Stuart Highway, then turn left on a dirt road for a further 6km. The best time to visit is at sunset when the rocks seem to come alive as they are stuck by the sun's rays. For an even more stunning natural attraction, head to the Devils Marbles Conservation Park, which is approximately 104km south of Tennant Creek. Scattered across a shallow valley in the Davenport Ranges, the Devils Marbles are a collection of gieand red, spherical granite boulders that are balanced on top of one another. The "marbles" were created an estimated 1,700 million years ago when magma deep below the earth's surface was fractured to create blocks, which have since eroded and been gradually exposed by the weather. At the south end of the park there is a camping area with toilet facilities and a fireplace.

Visitor Information:

Tennant Creek Visitor Information Centre is located at Battery Hill on Peko Road, call *(08) 8962 3388*. They can be emailed at *info@tennantcreektourism.com.au*, and the website is *www.tennantcreektourism.com.au*.

Points of Interest:

Nobles Nob was the richest gold mine in Australia – $64,975,256 worth of ore was discovered there between its opening in 1933 and its closure in 1985. Situated on Peko Road 16km east of the town, unfortunately the site can no longer be visited: in March 2002 a collapse of the pit wall moved the edge 15 metres, and is no longer accessible.

The National Trust Museum building was constructed by the army in 1942, then used as the Outpatients Clinic until it was taken over by the National Trust in 1978. Items of interest include: the old gaolhouse; reconstruction of a miner's camp; archive collection; and early photographs. The Museum is located in Schmidt Street.

The Old Australian Inland Mission was built in 1934, and is the oldest building constructed here. It is a good example of the early corrugated iron buildings, most of which have not stood the test of time. The Mission is in Paterson Street.

The Aboriginal Mural in Paterson Street was a community project, and it encompasses Aboriginal mythology and contemporary life. Many local Aboriginal artists participated in its planning and painting.

The Government Stamp Battery is further along Peko Road, Number 3 Battery is the last of the Government batteries still operating in the Territory. It is used to crush and treat free milling or easily freed gold ores. Interesting things to see include an operating 10 head 575.6kg stamper, displays of historic artifacts, and the former battery site and buildings. Contact the Visitor Information Centre for details.

The Old Telegraph Station is 10km north of town. It was completed in 1876 as part of a network stretching from Adelaide to Darwin. Only 4 of the original 11 buildings still remain, and they are the oldest in the Territory. They now forms part of a conservation area and are being restored as a museum. The old buildings in their pastoral setting provide an insight into the lives of early pioneers.

Outlying Areas in the Region

South of Tennant Creek

Devils Marbles

Located 108km south of Tennant Creek on the Stuart Highway, the Marbles are huge rounded boulders, incredibly balanced on each other. Some of the boulders seem to have been cleanly sliced in half, but in fact, their shape comes from millions of years of erosion. Sizes of the boulders vary from half a metre to six metres, and some weight thousands of tons. Aboriginal people say that these formations are the eggs of the Rainbow Serpent, and for this reason the site is sacred to them. Devils Marbles Tours operate out of Tennant Creek, and can be contacted on *0418 891 171*.

Wauchope

Wauchope (which incidentally is pronounced 'walk up') is 113km south of Tennant Creek on the Stuart Highway. The settlement is actually a pub, and is a good base for exploring the Chinese diggings in the Murchison Ranges. Call the Central Lands Council in Tennant Creek on *(08) 8962 2343* for rules on accessing the Ranges.

Wycliffe Well

Wycliffe Well is 136km south of Tennant Creek, and is a holiday park with excellent facilities, including a caravan park, a lake, a store and a recently modernised pre-war roadhouse. Tourist information can also be found here.

Barrow Creek

The tiny township of Barrow Creek is 224km south of Tennant Creek. It consists of the historic Barrow Creek Telegraph Station, as well as 'The Barrow', the ultimate in outback pubs. It is exactly like those portrayed in movies of the outback, with real outback characters as patrons. The pub offers accommodation and facilities, call *(08) 8956 9753.*

North of Tennant Crrek

Three Ways

Situated at the junction of the Stuart and Barkly Highways, 25km north of Tennant Creek, Three Ways is the major intersection in the heart of scrub country. There is a roadhouse, a motel, tourist information and facilities. The roadtrains pull in here, and hitchhikers wait here for a lift in one of the three possible directions.

Attack Creek Historical Reserve

The reserve is 70km north of Tennant Creek, and there is a monument to John McDouall Stuart, whose first attempt at crossing the continent from the south ended here in 1894 when the party was attacked by Aborigines. Churchill's Head is 10km further north. Camping in the area is allowed, and there are picnic tables and wood barbecues.

Renner Springs

Renner Springs, 94km north of Tennant Creek, is a wayside inn that is completely surrounded by the Helen Springs Cattle Station. The roadhouse offers accommodation, and good homestyle food, *(08) 8964 4505.*

Elliott

The town of Elliot is 187km north of Tennant Creek, and approximately half way between Alice Springs and Darwin. It has a population of around 600, and is the second largest settlement in the Barkly. The hotel can be contacted on *(08) 8969 2069*. North of Elliot is the old droving township of Newcastle Waters. It features historic buildings, and a Drovers' Memorial Park.

Signpost at Tennant Creek

NT

Central Northern Territory Region

The Central Region of the Northern Territory is a large area that takes in the Tanami Desert in the south-west and the Barkly Tableland in the north-east. While the Tanami Desert is sparsely populated, the Barkly Tableland is the opposite and is characterised by large beef cattle stations. The major town in the region is Alice Springs.

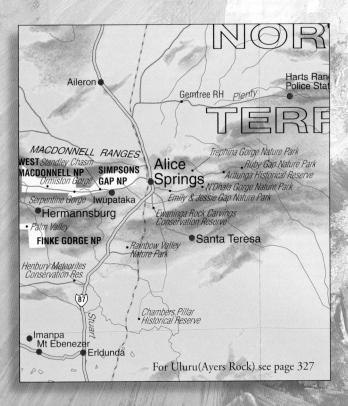

For Uluru(Ayers Rock) see page 327

Alice Springs
Population: 28,100. Climate: Average temperatures: January max 36°C - min 21°C; July max 20°C - min 4°C. In summer the temperatures can reach up to 42°C, but the humidity is always low.

Situated in the geographical heart of the continent at the foot of the MacDonnell Ranges, the town of Alice Springs is recognised as the "Centre of Australia". The most famous town in the Northern Territory, "The Alice" is both a great place to visit in its own right as well as a good base from which to explore the wonders of The Centre. A modern town which has all the facilities of a larger city, the booming tourist industry has been facilitated by the incredible natural attractions of the region. The spectacular MacDonnell Ranges stretch for 150km to the east and west of Alice Springs, and contain many beautiful chasms and gorges. Outside of Alice Springs is the iconic Ayers Rock in Uluru, as well as the Olgas (Kata Tjuta) which lie to the south-west. Like many other locations in the NT, Alice Springs is a diverse community made up of people from all over the world, with indigenous Australians making up 20% of the population.

For over 40,000 years, the area now known as Alice Springs

Telegraph Historical Reserve

had been a traditional 'meeting place' for the Arrernte people John McDouall Stuart was again the first European to explore the Centre, leading an expedition through the area in 1862. The construction of the Overland Telegraph link to Darwin made it feasible for settlers to begin taking up leases in the Centre, but it was the Afghan Cameleers who also played a major part in the beginnings of Alice Springs, driving their camel trains across 600 km of desert to deliver essential provisions to the population. The town was surveyed in 1887 and the discovery of gold at the nearby Arltunga led to a growth in population, but it wasn't until the arrival of the Central Australian Railway in 1929 that Alice Springs was allowed to transcend its "lonely outpost" status.

Your first stop when visiting Alice Springs should be Anzac Hill, which offers a good view of the town and the surrounding ranges. To get there by car turn off the Stuart Highway at Hungry Jacks, or travel via the Lions walk opposite the Catholic Church on Wills Terrace. And for an introduction to the landscape of the Australian desert, visit the Alice Springs Desert Park ten minutes drive from the town. The park features a striking landscape of red sand dunes, dry creeks and salt lakes. The Telegraph Station was the

device that led to the birth of Alice Springs, and the original communication post can be seen 3km north on the Stuart Highway. The Alice Springs Memorial Cemetery is the final resting place of many pioneers and famous personalities.

Visitor Information:

The Central Australian Tourism Industry Association is in Gregory Terrace, call *(08) 8952 5800* or *1800 645 199*.

The Northern Territory Tourist Commission is at 67 North Stuart Highway, call *(08) 8951 8555*.

The Parks and Wildlife Commission of the Northern Territory offer Ranger guided tours, call *(08) 8951 8788*.

Points of Interest:

Museum of Central Australia has a focus on local natural history. Some of the displays include exhibits of fossils, flora, fauna, meteorite pieces, minerals, as well as Aboriginal arts and artifacts. The museum can be found in the Alice Springs Cultural Precinct on Larapinta Drive, *(08) 8951 1121*.

The Adelaide House Museum was built by the Australian Inland Mission between 1920 and 1926 as the first Alice Springs Hospital, and was designed by Rev John Flynn. The Museum can be found in Todd Mall, *(08) 8952 1856*.

The Old Court House, was built originally as the Administrator's Council Rooms and as the Mining Wardens Court. The National Pioneer Womens Hall of Fame is housed within, and it can be found on the corner of Parsons & Hartley Streets, *(08) 8952 9006*.

The Old Stuart Town Gaol is the oldest building remaining in the Alice Springs town area, in use between 1909 and 1938. The Gaol is on Parsons Street, *(08) 8952 4516*.

Frontier Camel Tours is a camel museum that offers camel rides. One of the most popular attractions in Alice, it is located on the Ross Highway, *(08) 8953 0444*.

Uluru

Located 465km south-west of Alice Springs, the Uluru National Park is not only the greatest tourist attraction in the NT, but also home to one of Australia's most recognisable icons. The park takes up an area of 1325sq km, measuring 72km to the east-west and 16.5km to the north-south. The park is internationally famous for being home to Ayers Rock, the greatest rock monolith in the world, as well as the 36 rock domes and deep gorges which are known as The Olgas (Kata Juta). Ayers Rock is without a doubt the Territory's premier attraction, and takes its place alongside the Sydney Harbour Bridge and the Opera House as one of Australia's most iconic locations. The whole of the area around Uluru is sacred to the country's indigenous population, and it was in 1987 that the park was named a World Heritage Site and finally handed back to the Aboriginal population for ownership.

Towering above the plains at a height of 348 metres and stretching for 3.6km by 2.4km, Ayers Rock is a single piece of sandstone that extends 5 km below the desert surface. Positively a joy for photographers, the rock undergoes amazing colour changes depending upon the weather, varying from bright red, dark grey or black. Ayers Rock is considered a site of marked cultural significance for a number of Aboriginal tribes, and evidence suggests they have lived there for well over 20,000 years. While many wish to climb the gigantic rock, it should be noted that it should only

undertaken by those with a high level of fitness. However, the local aboriginal people prefer you do not. For those who do attempt the climb there is a hand chain to aid in the trek, while others may simply choose to take advantage of the guided walks on ground level that are offered by the Australian National Parks and Wildlife Service, *(08) 8956 2299.*

Located 42km west of Ayers Rock, the Olgas (Kata Juta) are comprised of a series of 36 large domes with an impressive colouring and shape. While Ayers Rock is unquestionably the most famous landmark in the NT, many believe the Olgas to be even more spectacular. Spreading across an area of 3,500 hectares with a circumference of around 22 km, the tallest of the domes rises to a height of 546 metres. There two major walking trails which can be enjoyed by visitors include the Mount Olga Gorge and the Valley of the Winds. The Ranger Station at Uluru should be consulted for details. Facilities at the Olgas include walking trails, parking areas and toilets.

Uluru (Ayers Rock)

In 1965 it was decided some form of accomodation was needed in Uluru, but establishing any form of settlement in such an isolated area had proved extremely difficult. The temperatures were extreme and there was no electricity, water or sewerage. While various studies were carried out to determine how it could be achieved, construction on the Yulara Resort was finally finished in 1984 after the highway to Alice Springs had been completed. Now with a population of around 3000, the town is responsible for providing services to the 400,000 tourists that visit Ayers Rock every year.

Visitor Information: Visitors Centre is in Yulara Drive in Yulara, and can be called on *(08) 8957 7377.*

Outlying Areas in the Region

West of Alice

John Flynn's Grave Historical Reserve

7km west of Alice Springs on Larapinta Drive, there is a stone cairn which contains the ashes of Reverend John Flynn. He was the founder of the Australian Inland Mission, The Royal Flying Doctor Service, the first inland medical centre and an outback padre patrol system. The reserve has no facilities.

Simpsons Gap National Park

The Park is located in the West MacDonnell Ranges, with the turn off 18km west of Alice Springs on Larapinta Drive. Two kilometres from the turn off is the Visitor Information Centre and Ranger's Office, and Simpsons Gap is a further 6km drive. Facilities and Visitor Information are available.

Standley Chasm

The Chasm is a steep cleft in the MacDonnell Ranges, and is about 50km west of Alice. The reserve has a kiosk, barbecues and toilets, and the Chasm is a photographer's delight when the sun is overhead and lights up the red walls.

Ellery Creek Big Hole Nature Park

93km west of Alice Springs on Namitjira Drive is another gorge with high red cliffs and a large waterhole with shady River Red Gums. There are picnic facilities and toilets.

Serpentine Gorge Nature Park

This gorge is 104km to the west, and is narrow and winding with waterholes and bush scenery. The entry road is a bit rough and a 4WD is recommended, and there are facilities.

Ormiston Gorge National Park

The Ormiston Gorge National Park is the largest park in the Western MacDonnell Ranges. Its most popular feature is the Ormiston Gorge of the title, the catchment area of the Finke River, thought to be the oldest river in the world. The Visitor Information Centre can advise on all the bush walks and facilities available, or call Road Reports on *1800 246 199.*

Glen Helen Gorge Nature Park

Glen Helen Gorge is 133km from Alice Springs, and has been formed by the Finke River cutting through the MacDonnell Ranges. There is a 30m deep waterhole, which the Aborigines believed was the home of the Giant Watersnake. Next door to the Park is the Glen Helen Homstead, *(08) 8956 7489.*

Redbank Nature Park

Redbank Gorge is 30km west of Glen Helen, and there are several very deep and cold pools along its 800m length. As with the other gorges, the scenery is magnificent.

Hermannsburg

The historic buildings of Hermannsburg are 123km south-west of Alice Springs on Larapinta Drive. It was established as a mission by the Lutheran Church, and is now owned by the Aranda People who are restoring the old buildings with the help of the National Trust. The Kata Anga Tearooms are open daily, and Aboriginal artefacts are available.

Finke Gorge National Park

The Park covers 46,000 hectares, including the famous Palm Valley. The Park is best known for its population of the rare palm *Livistona mariae* or Red Cabbage Palm. The Park is 16km south of Hermannsburg, and 138km from Alice Springs. The road requires 4WD and facilities are available.

South of Alice

Rainbow Valley Nature Park

The Park is 101km south of Alice Springs, turning off the Stuart Highway at 85km. The park's main attraction is seen at its best in later afternoon, when the setting sun shines directly onto a stark range of richly-coloured sandstones. A 4WD is recommended and there are somefacilities.

Chambers Pillar Historical Reserve

Henbury Meteorites Conservation Reserve

Located 145km south-west of Alice Springs, the Reserve contains twelve craters which were formed when a meteor hit the earth's surface and disintegrated 4700 years ago. Facilities are available, but visitors should bring drinking water.

Watarrka National Park

This park is about 310km south-west of Alice Springs and contains the western end of the George Gill Range, which includes the scenic Kings Canyon, attractive rockholes and areas of lush vegetation. The Canyon features a plateau of rock domes, and sandstone walls rising up 100m. Accommodation is at Kings Canyon Resort and Kings Creek Station.

Ewaninga Rock Carvings Conservation Reserve

The Reserve is 39km down the Old South Road from Alice Springs, and the carvings are thought to predate the Aborigines who reside in the area now, as they have no knowledge of their origin or meaning. Facilities are available.

Chambers Pillar Historical Reserve

This impressive sandstone pillar was used as a landmark by early pioneers, and many tales of hardship have been carved in the base. It is 149km south of Alice on the Old South Road, and access is by 4WD only.

East of Alice

Emily and Jessie Gap Nature Park

These are two gaps in the MacDonnell Ranges, 13km and 18km respectively, east of Alice Springs. They are very scenic and have great significance to the Aborigines. There are toilet facilities at both locations, while Jessie Gap also has BBQs.

Corroboree Rock Conservation Reserve

Another scenic pillar of rock which is significant to Aborigines is 48km east of Alice Springs, and has facilities.

Trephina Gorge Nature Park

Situated in the Eastern MacDonnell Ranges and 85km east of Alice Springs, Trephina Gorge Nature Park is noted for its sheer quartzite cliffs and River Red Gum lined watercourses. There are two gorges in the park – Trephina Gorge, with its wide views and sandy creek bed, and John Hayes Rock Hole. Camping areas are located at the Trephina Bluff and Gorge.

N'Dhala Gorge Nature Park

Access to this park is 4WD recommended, and it is 98km east of Alice Springs. The scenery is magnificent, and there are ancient Aboriginal rock carvings. The park has facilities.

Arltunga Historical Reserve

The Reserve is 110km east of Alice Springs, and can be reached and explored in conventional vehicles. There is a small interpretive visitor display and toilet block near the entrance. Call the Park Rangers on *(08) 8956 9661*.

Ruby Gap Nature Park

Access to this park is by 4WD only, and there are no facilities, just beautiful gorges along the Hale River.

ASSAYERS RESIDENCE

Arltunga Historical Reserve

QUEENSLAND

Queensland, as the travel brochures say, is 'beautiful one day, perfect the next'. A true tropical paradise, the state offers beautiful beaches, verdant rainforests, the stunning outback, vibrant cities and a myriad of other attractions. Best of all is the tropical paradise of Australia's Great Barrier Reef, the longest series of coral reefs and islands in the world.

QLD

Brisbane Region

As the capital city of the state of Queensland, Brisbane combines the relaxed atmosphere and beautiful weather synonomous with the state with all of the features of a modern city. Located on the banks of the Brisbane River, the city has plenty of food, entertainment and shopping to offer.

Brisbane Population: 1,700,000. Climate: Average temperatures: January max 30°C - min 19°C; July max 18°C - min 6°C. Average annual rainfall - 1148mm.

Located 32km upstream from Moreton Bay on the banks of the Brisbane River, Brisbane is the capital city of Queensland. Known for its relaxed and easygoing lifestyle, Brisbane provides a gateway to the more tourist focussed regions of the state, which include the heavily developed Gold Coast and Sunshine Coast. Affectionately known by locals as "Bris Vegas" due to the sunny weather and somewhat glitzy lifestyle,

City offices for the University of Queensland, Brisbane

the landscape of Brisbane has been altered significantly in the last several decades. Recent developments have taken place on the city's river, including Southbank and The Riverside Centre (famous for the popular Sunday craft markets). For those wanting to see the sights along the Brisbane River, a sightseeing cruise on the traditional *Kookaburra Queen* paddlewheeler makes for a good way to start. Downtown Brisbane offers a wide variety of shopping options for visitors, and the Queen Street Mall is linked to a number of other popular shopping arcades. For many years considered a "big country town", Brisbane has slowly but aggressively sought to shun this reputation, and in recent times has acquired new roads, office blocks, business locations and cultural facilities.

While much of Australia's history has traditionally focussed on the original settlement in Sydney, what is often forgotten is the effort made by the convicts responsible for getting the Brisbane settlement off the ground. The Sydney colony was already overflowing only a few short decades after it had been established, and it was decided that a new location was needed to house some of the more difficult and uncooperative convicts. So in 1822 the New South Wales Governor Sir Thomas Brisbane was instructed to locate a suitable area for a new penal colony, and he eventually decided on a tropical area some 900 miles to the north. In 1823 explorer John Oxley happened to stumble across several escaped convicts, who directed him to one of the best sources of fresh water in the area. It was named the Brisbane River in honour of the New South Wales Governor, and Brisbane Town was established shortly after.

The Moreton Bay penal colony quickly gained a reputation as one of the harshest in the country, home to the "worst of the worst" prisoners, and in 1826 Captain Patrick Logan was appointed to rule over the settlement with an iron fist. Though he was responsible for locating significant resources in the surrounding areas during his pioneering explorations, Captain Logan was hated by both convicts and soldiers alike for his cruelty. Brisbane's major Queen Street Mall now stands at the place where convicts were publically flogged on a regular basis. 693 convicts were housed in the colony by 1828, but it was only two years later that Logan was involved in a skirmish with the local indigenous population from which he would fail to emerge alive. The Moreton Bay penal settlement lasted for another 9 years without his brutal guidance, before eventually being opened up to free settlers in 1842.

The cultural heart of Brisbane can be found at the Queensland Cultural Centre, which houses the Queensland Museum and Art Gallery, Performing Arts Complex and the Conservatory of Music. Important events on the cultural calendar include the annual Riverfestival in August, where the Brisbane River is showcased with fireworks and jazz

Stamford Plaza, Brisbane River

music, as well as the Brisbane Writers Festival, the Brisbane International Film Festival, and Valley Fiesta – one of Australia's largest free music festivals. The Queen Street Mall is the central location for shopping with over 500 stores and food outlets, while South Bank offers a wide variety of family friendly attractions. Many interesting delights also await at the nearby Subtropical Brisbane: wild dolphins can be fed at the Tangaloom Wild Dolphin Resort, as well as the heritage-listed Brisbane Forest Park.

Visitor Information:

The Brisbane Visitor Information Centre is situated in the Queen Street Mall, *(07) 3006 6290*. Their email address is *enquiries@brisbanemarketing.com.au*, and the website to visit is *www.brisbanemarketing.com.au*.

The Queensland Travel Centre can be found at 30 Makerston Street, *13 8833*. Email *queensland@qttc.com.au* or visited at the website *www.tq.com.au*.

Points of Interest:

Queen Street Mall is a colourful, lavish and modern pedestrian mall. Containing more than 500 specialty shops, it is the premier shopping venue in the city of Brisbane. The mall stretches between George & Edward Streets, and

Story Bridge. with the Brisbane Business District in the background

provides access to the nearby Wintergarden on the Mall, Brisbane Arcade and T & G Arcade. Rowes Arcade and Post Office Square are nearby.

The Queensland Cultural Centre was completed during the 1988 World Expo, and houses a number of cultural facilities. The Art Gallery has an extensive collection of Australian art from colonial times to the present, and can be called on *(07) 3840 7303*. The Museum takes the visitor from the prehistoric age of dinosaurs up to Australia's colonial history, and can be called on *(07) 3840 7555*. The Performing Arts Complex can be called on *(07) 3840 7444*.

Brisbane Bridges – The Story Bridge, the Captain Cook Bridge, the Victoria Bridge, the William Jolly Bridge and the Goodwill Bridge are all close to the city and cross the Brisbane River. All of have a unique architectural style that is worth viewing. The impressive Gateway Bridge can also be seen east of the city at the mouth of the Brisbane River. Opened in 1986, the bridge links the city with the Gold Coast and the Sunshine Coast. Those traveling north from the Gold Coast can bypass Brisbane by using this route.

The City Botanical Gardens are located on the banks of the Brisbane River and cover over 20 hectares of land. The soils of the riverbank and consistently warm climate always makes for a fantastic display of exotic flowers, and the gardens make for a great place to escape the financial district.

The Riverside Centre is situated at the heart of Brisbane's financial district. Set back from the Brisbane River with many up-market restaurants and designer boutiques, Riverside can be found at Eagle Street.

The South Bank Parklands development is just south of the Victoria Bridge, and is a popular destination for the locals. It includes restaurants, cinemas, parklands, markets, subtropical gardens, lagoons, park areas, sightseeing attractions, as well as Australia's only inland city beach. Nearby is the Queensland Maritime Museum which has a number of impressive vessels on display from varying eras, their contact number is *(07) 3844 5361.*

Roma Street Parklands are a recent addition to the city, and have been built on the site of the old railway yards. You can enjoy several self-guided walks past the lake, over bridges, through palm forests and formal gardens.

The Old Windmill Observatory makes for an interesting legacy of early settlement. Located on the hill to the north of the city in Wickham Terrace, it was built as a windmill in 1829 by convict labour. Due to defects it was never operational, and has been used as a treadmill, a signal post and a meteorological station.

Outlying Towns in the Brisbane Region

Moreton Bay and Island

Moreton is the second largest sand island in the world (after Fraser Island), and provides an opportunity for an island holiday without travelling far from Brisbane. Much of it is National Park, and there are unspoiled beaches, abundant birdlife and magnificent sand dunes. Mount Tempest is one of the highest coastal sand dunes in the world. The Wild Dolphin resort at Tangalooma, the site of the old whaling station, offers standard and deluxe motel and cabin accommodation and a restaurant. The Moreton Island Tourist Information Services can provide further details, *(07) 3408 2661*, and are located at The Strand Bulwer.

North Stradbroke Island

North Stradbroke Island is larger and has more varied scenery than Moreton Island. There are mangrove swamps, lakes, bushland and great surfing beaches. Vehicular ferries operate from Cleveland and Redland Bay, and the Stradbroke Island Tourist Information Centre is at the end of Middle Street, Cleveland, *(07) 3821 3821.* Stradbroke Island Tourism is

Western side of the city, Brisbane

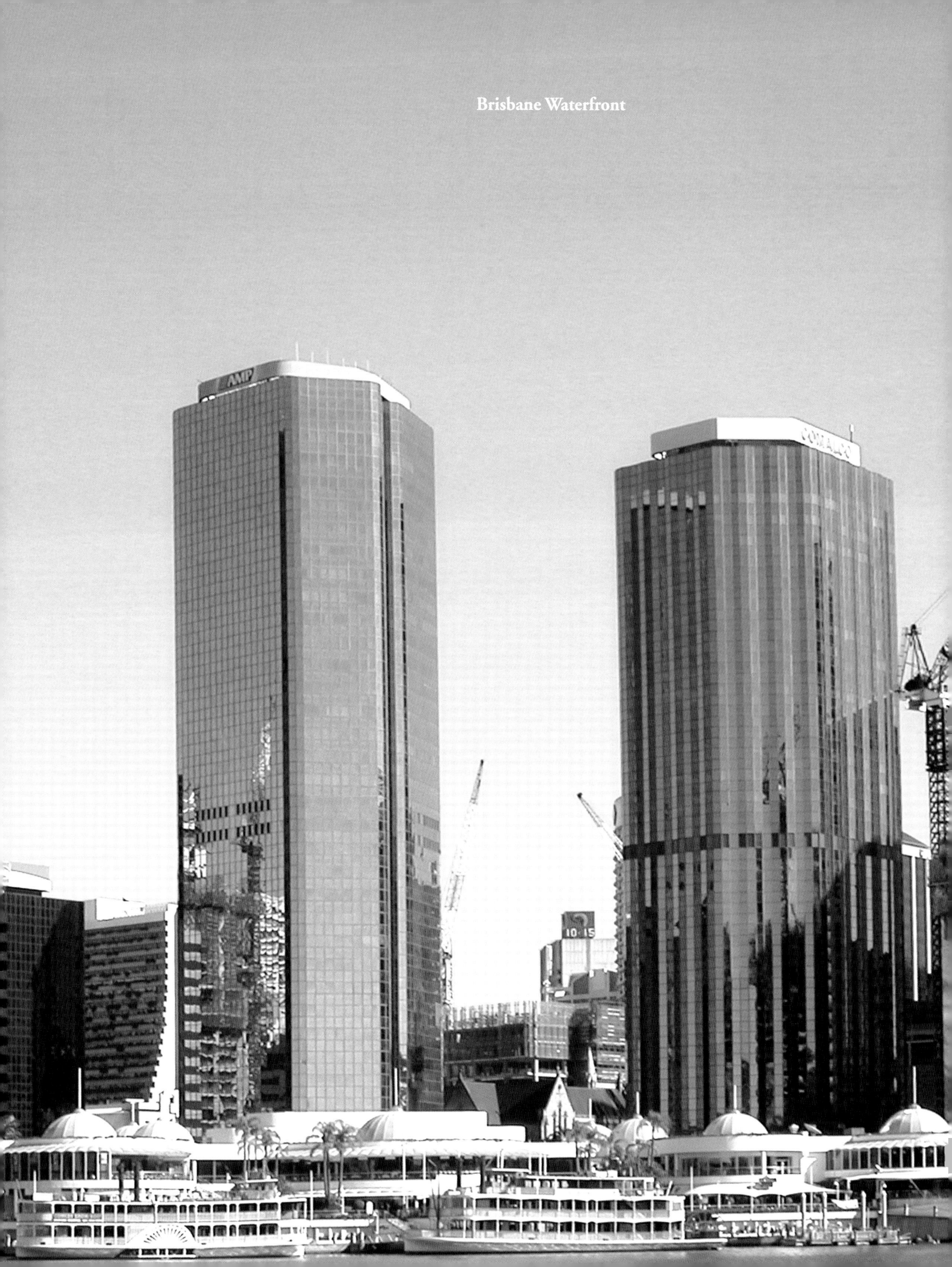

Brisbane Waterfront

QLD

Gold Coast Region

Located on the eastern seaboard of Australia just 80km south of Brisbane, the Gold Coast Region perfectly encapsulates the beach and surfing lifestyle that Queensland is known for. With plenty of natural sites such as beaches, waterways and national parks, as well as manmade attractions - Casinos and theme parks - the Gold Coast is one of Australia's most popular destinations for tourists.

Surfers Paradise
Population of the Gold Coast: 420,000. Climate: Average Temperatures: January max 28°C - min 20°C; July max 21°C - min 9°C. Average annual rainfall: 1724mm.

The Gold Coast is one large urban sprawl. Incorporating Surfers Paradise and other previously independant settlements.

Surfers Paradise is famous for, there are plenty of beautiful beaches and waterways in the area. There are a wide variety of attractions that can be visited by tourists, and there are more themeparks in the area than any other location in the Southern Hemisphere. Some of the other sites holding appeal for both domestic and international visitors include World Heritage listed national parks and reserves, golf courses, convention facilities and shopping venues.

The indigenous population were aware of the Gold Coast's attractions long before the arrival of European settlers, drawn to the area because of the excellent fishing. While the famous coastline was travelled along by Captain Cook

Little Nippers at the beach

in 1770, it wasn't until 1822 that the nearby Broadwater was established by John Bringle. Europeans began to settle in the area during the 1840's, and the establishment of a timber industry was followed by the agriculture, cotton growing and sugar industries over the subsequent decades. It was in 1869 that the district was surveyed, and the nearby Southport was established in 1874.

The development of Surfers Paradise began in 1923 when James Cavill purchased a block of land. Cavill was the one responsible for beginning the town's obsession with high-rise accomodation, building Surfers Paradise Hotel and a bridge across the Nerang River. Many soldiers used his hotel as a base during the first World War, with many of them later returning with their families after being impressed by the sandy beaches and warm climate. The town's growth into a major tourist destination began in the 1950's, with the large amount of people who arrived leading to an endless succession of high-rise apartments up and down the coastal strip. The city was declared in 1959, and residential areas developed over the following decades. The demand for tourism in the area is

never ending, and the coastal strip along Surfers Paradise and the surrounding beaches of the Gold Coast have now been inundated with high-rise development.

The main attractions are, of course, the beaches - and there are plenty of them, all offering clean, golden sand, and sparkling surf. But Surfer's Paradise (and all of the surrounding areas of the Gold Coast) have much more to offer, with more attractions for tourists than could possibly be mentioned. Crammed with a multitude of places to eat, drink and shop, Surfers Paradise has been described as 'a pristine Miami Beach'. For entertainment there are performances by international stars, spectacular revues, cabaret shows, top restaurants, intimate bars, discos, and dinner cruises departing from the Nerang River on the western side of Surfers. There are several different cruises, from a two- hour 'scones and cream' tour, to a tropical luncheon feast, a night shipboard cabaret, a twilight trip, or a raging nightclub.

Visitor Information:

Gold Coast Tourism can be found at the Cavill Mall, *(07) 5538 4419.*

You will also find the head office of the Gold Coast Tourism Bureau in Surfers Paradise on Level 2, Ferny Avenue, *(07) 5592 2699.* They have a web site at www.goldcoast tourism.com.au, and an email address at info@gctb.com.au.

Points of Interest:

Main Beach, just to the north of Surfers Paradise, is one

Surfing on the Gold Coast

of the most popular beaches in the region. Nearby there is also Broadwater, which offers still water swimming as an alternative to the open surf.

Wet'n'Wild Water World is the largest water theme park in Australia, featuring a wide selection of slides, pools, toboggan drops and a giant fresh water wavepool that has one metre surf. Found inland from Southport on the Pacific Highway, Wet'n'Wild Water World can be called on *(07) 5573 2255*.

Dreamworld is the premier themepark on the Gold Coast, with the 100 hectare site having been open since 1981. There are more than 10 different themed areas to visit in the park, with some of the attractions including the Coca-Cola IMAX Theatre, Rocky Hollow Log Ride, Model T Lane, Captain Sturt Paddle Wheeler and the Dreamworld Gold Coast Railway. The recently installed Giant Drop and Tower of Terror are among the fastest and tallest rides in the world. The park can be found at Dreamworld Parkway, and can be called on *(07) 5588 1111*.

Warner Bros Movie World is located near to Dreamworld, and has the theme of trying to recreate a Hollywood set. Lethal Weapon and Batman Adventure are among the leading

attractions at the park, and new rides are being opened up on a regular basis. Movie World also has movie-making facilities which are actually used for film productions, and the park can be called on (07) 5573 8485.

Seaworld is the most famous marine theme park in Australia, and beyond being home to such exotic aquatic creatures as performing dolphins, killer whales and sea lions, it also has the country's first monorail, a Free Fall Water Slide and the Three Loop Corkscrew. They can be called on *(07) 5588 2205*.

The Currumbin Wildlife Sanctuary is home to the world's largest collection of Australian native animals, and is located at the centre of the Gold Coast. With over 27 hectares of landscaped surrounds and bushland catering for over 1400 mammals, birds and reptiles, it offers a unique natural experience. The Currumbin Wildlife Sanctuary is situated beside the main highway and is only minutes away from the beaches of the Gold Coast, *(07) 5534 1266*.

Ripleys Believe It Or Not Museum is a dedication to the bizarre, the freakish, the unusual and the mysterious, and incorporates hundreds of exhibits, illusions and interactive displays. Typical of the stories told there include the tale of Bosco the labrador, a famous dog who outpolled two humans to become mayor of a small Californian community for eight

Polar Bear at Seaworld

Lamington National Park

years. The museum is located in Raptis Plaza on Cavill Avenue, call *(07) 5592 0040*.

Jupiter's Casino is an internationally famous establishment, the perfect place to visit for those with a taste for high rolling. Jupiters is Australia's third largest casino, with about 110 tables (including about 20 Roulette tables) and some 1000 machines, attracting 16,000 visitors per day. It is also the site of a world class hotel known as the Conrad, and a monorail links the casino with the Oasis-On-Broadbeach Shopping Resort and Pan Pacific Hotel. Jupiter's Casino can be found on a small island in the area of Broadbeach off the Gold Coast Highway, call *(07) 5592 8100* or *1800 074 145*.

The Lamington National Park is the largest preserved natural stand of sub-tropical rainforest in Australia. The park has 160km of graded walking tracks leading to many of its highlights, including Mount Merino, Echo Point, Coomera Gorge, Picnic Rock, and the Aboriginal Cooking Caves. In all the park has more than 500 waterfalls, and majestic blackbutt, bloodwood, and giant cedar trees. The Lamington National Park is 45km from the Coast, near the state border.

Mount Tamborine is a plateau on the McPherson Ranges, 35km west of the Gold Coast, and is comprised of seven small National Parks. Reaching a total of 375 hectares of rainforest, in which there are 15,000-year-old Macrozamia palms, it is said to be one of the oldest living things in the world. St Bernard's historic hotel, one of the mountain's oldest establishments, is famous for its smorgasbord lunches and beautiful gardens, and there are many other guest houses and restaurants in the area.

Outlying Centres in the Gold Coast Region

Southport

Situated across the Broadwater from The Spit, the town Southport was the Gold Coast's first settlement when it was established in 1875. It is now the business and commercial centre for the region, along with neighbouring Labrador, Biggera Waters and Runaway Bay. With a mixture of small and large businesses in the district, Southport has over 8,000 registered businesses and several shopping centres. It can also boast an impressive range of established gardens and giant leafy trees.

Broadbeach

The town is internationally famous as the site of Jupiter's Casino, and the Gold Coast's first world-class hotel, the $185 million Hotel Conrad. It also hosts the immense Pacific Fair Shopping Centre.

Burleigh Heads

Burleigh is the half-way point between Coolangatta and Surfers, and hosts one of the greatest week-long surfing events in Australia, held in March each year. The town has a more relaxed atmosphere than Coolangatta or Surfers, and many people choose to stay here and visit the other two when they want to get into the action. If interested in bushwalking, there is a 3km graded track that meanders among the habitat of koalas, bandicoots and other animals in the Burleigh Heads National Park. The Gold Coast Highway then continues past the surfing beaches of Miami, Nobby's and Mermaid to Broadbeach.

The Hinterland

Away from the coastal plain of the Gold Coast, the terrain climbs steadily but steeply up over 1000m into some of Australia's richest highlands, passing through rolling rural landscapes along the way to the peaks. The Hinterland is easily accessible by a number of roads, and offers spectacular views and walking trails into rainforests. One of the most popular lookouts is called 'The Best of All' and is reached from Lyrebird Ridge Road. Good views can be also be obtained from Purlingbrook Falls, which cascade about 190m to the

rocks below. You can walk to the base of the cliff and follow a track that leads behind the falls. In the Numinbah Valley, just within the Queensland border, is the Natural Arch in the Natural Arch National Park. Here there are several walks through rainforest, one of which leads to the stone archway through which a waterfall plummets to a rock pool below. There is also a Glow Worm Cave for walkers to discover.

Coolangatta and Tweed Heads

The twin towns of Coolangatta and Tweed Heads are the southern gateway to the Gold Coast, and occupy opposite headlands of the Tweed River, with Tweed Heads in New South Wales, and Coolangatta in Queensland. Both towns have holiday resort centres, shopping, restaurants and tour facilities, and opportunities for all water sports on the river and the beaches. The Coolangatta Visitor Information Centre is in Shop 14B at Coolangatta Place, on corner of Griffith and Warner Streets, Coolangatta, *(07) 5536 7765*. For more information on Tweed Heads, contact the Visitor Information Centre at 4 Wharf Street, *(07) 5536 4244* or *1800 674 414*.

The Hinterland, Beechmont.

QLD

Golden West Region

The Golden West Region is made up of a vast expanse of rural Queensland, taking in some of the most attractive country towns in the state. The region encompasses the agriculturally rich Darling Downs, and is easily accessible via major highways.

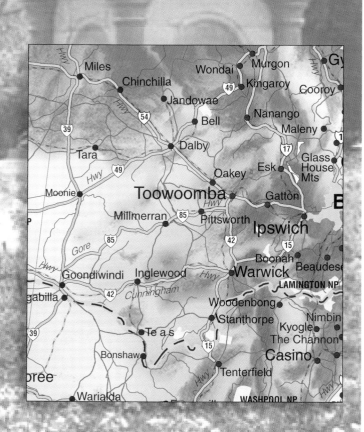

Toowoomba

Population: 93,000. Climate: Toowoomba has a temperate climate and is therefore less humid than on the coast. Average temperatures: January max 27°C – min 17°C; July max 16°C – min 4°C.

Situated on top of the Great Dividing Range and 130km inland from Brisbane, Toowoomba is the commercial centre of the Darling Downs pastoral area. Placed on the edge of a plateau and around 700 metres above sea level, the surroundings of Toowoomba are nothing if not dramatic. Often referred to as "The Garden City", the streets of Toowoomba are lined with trees and there are over 1000 hectares of parkland. This includes the centrally located Queens Park, as well as the Redwood and Jubilee parks that are found on natural bushland escarpment. The extravagant garden beds and immaculately kept laws of the Botanical Gardens are at the heart of Toowoomba, and are only part of the annual Carnival of Flowers display which is held every September. The largest inland town in Queensland and one of the largest in Australia, Toowoomba's population is expected to reach 100,000 within a few years.

Allan Cunningham was the first to explore the areas around Toowoomba, choosing to name the Darling Downs after the New South Wales Governor Sir Ralph Darling. While the area was originally thought to be too swampy, the scarcity of water in other nearby settlements led to a reassessment of this position. Squatter Thomas Alford settled there in 1852, and the name Toowoomba was derived from the rather romantic Aboriginal meaning of "the swamp". It was during the late nineteenth century that the town began to bloom aesthetically into what it is today, with trees being planted and large numbers of Victorian buildings built. Toowoomba was finally declared a city in 1904.

The large number of historic buildings and tree-lined streets make Toowoomba a real treat for the eyes, and the city is reknowned for its gracious nature. Anyone walking along the picturesque main streets will encounter many National Trust preserved sites, including the 1878 Italian-style Post Office, the nearby 1870's Court House which was built in a Classic Revival style, as well as the Strand Theatre across the road. Toowoomba's central business district also has a number of heritage churches. The St Patrick's Roman Catholic Church which was built in the 1880's lies in the town centre, as does the simillarly aged St Luke's and St Stephen's churches.

State Rose Garden, Toowoomba

Visitor Information:

The Toowoomba Visitor Information Centre is located at 86 James Street, *(07) 4639 3797*. The email address is *infocentre@toowoomba.qld.gov.au*, The website is *www.toowoomba.qld.gov.au*. There is also the Toowoomba & Golden West Regional Tourist Association, located at 4 Little Street, *(07) 4632 1988* or email *admin@tgw.com.au*.

Points of Interest:

The Carnival of Flowers is held every September and attracts people from all over the state. It is the best time to view the beautiful tree-lined streets, parks and private gardens. Toowoomba's chosen flower is the violet, with the floral emblem flourishing in the town.

The Darling Downs Delicious is a week-long festival of gourmet indulgence, taking place in Autumn every year. With attendees treated to a superb selection of food and wines, the festival is kicked off on the 15th of May with the "Long Lunch," held at Jimbour House.

The Picnic Point Lookout offers a good way to take in the panoramic views of Toowoomba. On one side is the city, and on the other side, the Lockyer Valley with the Table Top and Sugar Loaf Mountains in the foreground. The range stretches off into the distance to the south. West of the city is the distinctive Gowrie Mountain and the Kings-Thorpe Hills.

The Prince Henry Drive is a breathtakingly scenic experience. Both starting and finishing at the eastern end of Bridge Street, it follows the cliff top around a small spur of the Great Dividing Range. A one-way traffic thoroughfare, it goes through the suburb of Prince Henry Heights, and past Redwood Park Fauna Sanctuary.

The Cobb & Co Museum was opened in 1987, and is home to one of Australia's best collections of horse-drawn vehicles. The museum received an extension in October 2001, with space created for a display on the history of Toowoomba and the Darling Downs. The Cobb & Co Museum can be found at 27 Lindsay Street, and can be called on *(07) 4639 1971*.

The Toowoomba Regional Art Gallery is the oldest public gallery in regional Queensland, and was established in Toowoomba in 1938. It has an interesting collection of paintings and antiques, and can be found adjacent to the City Hall at 531 Ruthven Street, call *(07) 4688 6652*.

The Lionel Lindsay Art Gallery and Library Collection has a collection of works by great Australian artists, authors and poets. It is housed within the Toowoomba Regional Art Gallery, *(07) 4688 6652*.

Roma Population: 8,000

Situated 479 km west of Brisbane, the prosperous community of Roma is famous for its sheep and cattle grazing, and is home to the largest store cattle market in Australia. Crops in the district include wheat, sorghum, oats and sunflowers, and a number of fruit crops are also produced, from stone-fruit to citrus. Festival time in Roma is during Easter, and is celebrated with street parades, goat races, traditional horse races, dancing, open-air concerts and rodeos.

Roma is home to a large icon known as the Big Rig. Standing high on the horizon, the Big Rig is a high-tech interactive complex that has the major attraction of the 42 metre high Emsco Rig. Steam driven, it is a reminder of the oil rush that took place during the 1920's and 30's, when both investors and prospectors flocked to the town's oil fields. Located at the outskirts of the town on an old oil derrick, the Big Rig is part of the Queensland Heritage Trail Network, which links 43 authentic heritage attractions across the state.

Visitor Information:

The Roma Tourist Information Centre is at 2 Riggers Road, *(07) 4622 4355*.

St Patrick's Cathedral, Toowoomba

Outlying Towns

Oakey

Oakey is half an hour's drive north-west of Toowoomba, on the Warrego Highway. The Museum of Australian Army Flying, (07) 4691 7666, has one of the best displays of aviation memorabilia in the world. In several hangars and an outdoors area are the aircraft, which range from a fully restored replica Box Kite, and the first aeroplane in service, as well as Bristols, Cessnas, Bells, Austers and more.

Dalby

Known as the Hub of the Downs, Dalby is 83km from Toowoomba and home to one of Queensland's principle agricultural colleges. An oasis in the middle of town is the Thomas Jack Memorial Park, facing the Warrego Highway. The park consists of more than 3 hectares of lawns, gardens and shrubberies, with a children's playground, shelters, barbecue facilities, a lily pond and a large area suitable for social cricket. The Dalby Information Centre is located in the north-eastern corner of the park, *(07) 4662 1066.*

Miles, Chinchilla & Boongara

Continuing along the Warrego Highway from Dalby to Roma, next is Chinchilla and further on is Miles. Miles is well known for the Miles Historical Village & Museum in Murilla Street, *(07) 4627 1492.* Chinchilla is near one of the largest petrified wood areas in the world, and the wood is from the Jurassic Age around 140-180 million years old. The Chinchilla Tourist Information Centre is on Warrego Highway, *(07) 4668 9564.*

At Boongara, 8km east of Chinchilla, the Cactoblastis Hall is a memorial to a small insect imported from South America in the 1920's to eat out a plant that had become the curse of the west, the prickly pear.

A Toowoomba Street

QLD

Sunshine Coast Region

The Sunshine Coast Region extends from Caloundra to the Glass House Mountains and Blackall Ranges, north to Tin Can Bay, and west through the Mary Valley. The region is home to pristine beaches, ancient mountain landscapes, lush hinterland and sub tropical rainforests. It boasts around 55km of immaculate sandy beaches broken only by an occasional headland or the clear water of a river estuary.

Noosa   Population: 6000. Climate: Average Temperatures: January max 29°C - min 20°C; July max 21°C - min 7°C. Average annual rainfall - 1776mm.

Located only 178 km from Brisbane, Noosa has grown from what was once a quiet and discreet seaside village to become the Sunshine Coast's most popular holiday destination. While Noosa has in recent times taken on the characteristics of a trendy inner-city suburb, strict building controls limit the height of building development to that of the surrounding trees. Developed over the years into an international standard resort, it is the combination of shopping and facilities with a relaxed beachside ambience that has made Noosa such a popular holiday destination with tourists. The stylish Hastings Street in particular, at the heart of Noosa Heads, is overflowing with accommodation, cafes, restaurants and boutique stores.

Escaped convict David Bracefell was the first European to lay eyes upon Noosa in the late 1820's. Fleeing imprisonment at Moreton Bay to live with the indigenous Gubbi Gubbi tribe, Bracefell was captured only to return on four seperate occasions. Finally in 1842 he was allowed to participate in an exploration of the coast, assisting Henry Russell Petrie with a survey of the area. Very little development occurred in Noosa over the next several decades – a timber industry was created in the 1860's, while an estuary was built in Noosa in 1869. Fittingly, it was tourism that began to drive development following the First World War, and both a surf lifesaving club and the Noosa National Park had been established by 1930.

With a northerly facing beach, Noosa Heads is protected from the prevailing south-easterly winds. Although some may not appreciate the proliferation of high-rise buildings in the town, the stylish facilities along Hastings Street have made the spot extremely popular with tourists. The headland is a National Park and there are several walks that meander through it to the various attractions, including Boiling Pot, Hell's Gates and Paradise Cave. Upstream from the Noosa River there are a number of lakes and wetlands which are full of bird life, and the area is known as the Cooloola National Park. Lake Cootharaba has a special area for beginner water-skiers, and many visitors spend their holidays sailing the river system on houseboats.

The beach at Noosa Heads

Visitor Information:

The Noosa Information Centre is located in Hastings Street, and they can be phoned on *(07) 5447 4988.*

Points of Interest:

Hastings Street will surely be the most popular destination for those visiting Noosa, with a number of restaurants situated right on the ocean front. Thomas Street at Noosaville and Gympie Terrace overlooking the Noosa River are also worth noting, as are the restaurants in the busy Noosa Junction.

The Noosa National Park is 477 hectares of native forest, heathland and high cliffs, which opens out onto some spectacular panoramic views. Visitors can indulge in the 10.5km of bush and coastal walking tracks, unspoilt flora and native animals such as koalas, possums, goannas and hundreds of bird species.

Sunshine Beach is only five minutes drive from Main Beach, and the excellent surf is complimented by a surf club with gourmet meals and a great view of the beach. Peregian Beach is also only 10 minutes away, and calm water swimming, fishing and boating can be enjoyed on the Noosa River.

The Big Pineapple is nearby to Noosa and is one of the premier tourist attractions of the area. Along with the famous 16 metre high fibreglass pineapple, which can be entered and climbed by visitors, beautiful views can be enjoyed along with souvenirs, arts and craft. The Big Pineapple is in Woombye and can be reached by taking the Nambour Connection Road exit off the Bruce Highway, and you can call them on *(07) 5442 1333.*

Caloundra Population: 80,000

Located at the southern entrance to the Sunshine Coast and an hour north of Brisbane, the city of Caloundra is an attractive and affordable holiday destination. The population of Caloundra has exploded since the mid 1980's, with the economy driven by manufacturing, clothing and building supplies and tourism. Apart the from 30km of beaches,

Caloundra is also famous for the gentle waters of the Pumicestone Passage, which are popular with those who like to indulge in water sports or more leisurely cruising. Caloundra can also boast two of the safest swimming beaches on the Sunshine Coast in the form of Bulcock Beach and Golden Beach.

Fishing is a popular activity in Caloundra, and every morning people can be seen reeling in catches on the strait between the town and Bribie Island. The beautiful hinterland section of the city is less than half an hour's drive from the coast, and takes in the spectacular Glass House Mountains, volcanic fields which were active around 25 million years ago. They tower imposingly over rich fertile plains, the place were most of Queensland's fresh tropical fruit is produced.

Visitor Information:
The Caloundra Tourist Information Centre can be found at 7 Caloundra Road, call *1800 644 969* or *(07) 5491 9233*.

Maroochydore Population: 17,500

Situated at the mouth of the Maroochy River around 98km from Brisbane, Maroochydore is a thriving tourist and business centre that has grown continuously since the 1950's. Maroochydore has a popular patrolled surfing beach, and is home to one of the first surf life saving clubs established in Queensland during the 1920's. The calm waters of the Maroochy River are ideal for young swimmers, boating, waterskiing and fishing, while the foreshore is perfect for picnics and barbecues. While industries exists in the Hinterland, Bunderim being higher has a pleasent climate.. Travelling north along the coast the townships are Coolum Beach, Peregian Beach, Marcus Beach, Sunshine Beach and Noosa Heads.

Visitor Information:
Maroochy Tourism can be contacted on *(07) 5479 1566*, while the website to visit is *www.maroochytourism.com*.

Outlying Towns

Gympie

Gympie is a large township situated about halfway between Maryborough and Maroochydore on the Bruce Highway. Like many towns in the north of Queensland it was once known for its abundance of gold, springing up during a rush in 1868. Gympie's attractions are mainly historic, including The Gold and Mining Museum, the Woodworks Forestry and Timber Museum and a number of buildings reminiscent of the town's colonial heritage. Contact the Coloola Regional Development Bureau for more information, 224 Mary Street, Gympie, *(07) 5482 5444*.

Blackall Range

The Blackall Range, on the Sunshine Coast, is a world apart, with its art and craft galleries, restaurants and tea rooms, comfortable pubs, green fields, hedgerows, and a feeling of Olde England. From high vantage points between Mapleton and Maleny, the small farms and cane fields of the coastal plain stretch out to join the blue Pacific, and south from Maleny are the dramatic Glass House Mountains.

Throughout the Blackall Ranges are national and forestry parks, offering superb walks through sub tropical rainforest, picnic spots beside waterfalls, and rock pools for swimming. The scenic drive through the Blackall Range is one of the most popular day outings in south-east Queensland. The southern end of the range drive is little more than an hour north of Brisbane, and access is no more than half an hour from most Sunshine Coast resort towns.

Caloundra

QLD

Fraser Coast & South Burnett Region

The Fraser Coast South Burnett region is home to some of the most spectacular natural locations in Southern Queensland, from the historic port of Maryborough, the whale watching in Harvey Bay, to the largest sand island in the world that is Fraser Island.

Bundaberg

GREAT
SANDY
NP

Hervey Bay

Fraser Island

25°

ers

Biggenden

Hervey Bay

Maryborough

Double Island Point

van

Hwy

Gympie

gon

aroy   Cooroy   **Noosa**   **Sunsine Coast**

Nambour

ango

Maryborough
Population: 26,500. Climate: Maryborough has a sub-tropical climate with moderate winters and warm to hot summers. A high percentage of the region's annual 1100mm rainfall falls in the January to March period.

Situated 255km north of Brisbane on the curve of the Mary River, the historic port of Maryborough played an important part in the settlement of the area. Known as the "Heritage City" due to its magnificent homes and public buildings, Maryborough illustrates the real environment of early Australian settlement. Many of the old features can still clearly be seen within the town, with the landing, the inns, the sawpits, the water supply, the industries, and even the burial ground all within walking distance. As well as catering for the hundreds and thousands of tourists who visit every year, the city of Maryborough services all of the timber, sugar, grazing and engineering industries in the surrounding areas.

While Captain James Cook and Matthew Flinders were the first to explore the coast to Maryborough, Andrew Petrie was the one who discovered the Mary River in 1842. The potential for grazing was immediately recognised and sheep farming was quickly attempted, yet the venture had failed within a year due to disease and attacks from the indigenous population. It was decided however that the potential of the area would be pursued. In December 1847 the schooner *Sisters* arrived to load wool from the stations, and Maryborough became a wool port. Within a year over 1000 bales of wool were being moved out of the site, and Maryborough had become a thriving township by the time it was declared a municipality in 1861.

Immigrants from Europe continued to arrive in Maryborough, and by the end of the 1860's their numbers had reached 23,000. The Walker foundry and engineering works was established during the 1860's to provide mining equipment to Gympie and other areas in the colony, and the first locomotive was built in 1873. It was in 1905 that Maryborough was declared a city, and the economy was driven in the first half of the century by the onset of the World Wars. Walkers were responsible for building 6,600 ton ships during the First World War, and production ramped up again at the beginning of World War II. At the height of their production they were employing 1,200 men.

The restoration of some of the old Queenslander houses in the area has enabled Maryborough to retain its heritage. Many of the old public buildings can still be seen in the streets, including the famous 1908-built City Hall in Kent Street. And with a construction history that stretches over 120 years, more railway engines have been built in Maryborough than any other Australian city. The Mary Ann was the first steam locomotive to be built in the city in 1873, and a replica of the train was built as a tourist attraction in 1999. On display on the last Sunday of every month, the reconstructed Mary Ann runs through and around Queens Park and along the Mary River.

Visitor Information:

The Maryborough Tourist Information Centre is on the Bruce Highway at the Matilda Travel Stop, and can be called on *(07) 4121 4111*.

The Fraser Coast - South Burnett Regional Tourism Board Ltd is located at 388-396 Kent Street, *(07) 4122 3444*. The email address is *info@frasercoast.org.au* while the web address is *www.frasercoastholidays.info*.

Points of Interest:

The Pioneer Graves at the northern-most extremity of the original Maryborough township make for an interesting reflection on early settlement. While the harshness and difficulties of frontier life ensured that the early township experienced loss of life, death from natural causes or old age was virtually unknown. The Pioneer Graves can be found at Aldridge Street in Baddow.

Queens Park was established more than a century ago, and many of its huge trees were planted as experiments by the Acclimatization Society. Features of the park include the fernery, waterfall and lily pond, lace-trimmed band rotunda built in 1890, and the 13cm gauge model railway built by the Model Engineers and Live Steamers Association. Queens Park can be found on Sussex Street.

The Ululah Lagoon was the original water supply in the early days of settlement. The lagoon is now a wildlife sanctuary where tame black swans, ducks and waterfowl can be hand fed. The lagoon is surrounded by tree-studded parkland with picnic tables and barbecues, and is in Lions Drive.

Caltex Mountain View Roadhouse has an extensive range of rocks, minerals, gems and fossils, including thundereggs and petrified woods. They can be found on the Bruce Highway in Bauple, and can be called on (07) 4129 2267.

Maryborough

The **Macadamia Plantation** has brought the world of macadamia nuts to the public. Stage one of the complex, the processing and retail plant, is a major tourist attraction. Guided tours of the plantation aboard the Nutty Choo Choo, with running commentary, are very popular. The Macadamia Plantation can be found on the corner of the Bruce Highway & Owanyilla Boundary Road, south of Maryborough.

The **MV Duchess** has hourly cruises on the Mary River on Wednesday, Thursday and Sunday afternoons. Her low profile design enables her to travel un-restricted up river under all the bridges, passing past and present sites of early industry and architecture, an island bat colony and much more. The Maryborough Tourist Information Centre should be contacted for more information.

Fraser Island Population: 300

Located only 11km from Hervey Bay, the World Heritage listed Fraser Island is the largest sand island in the world. One of the last wilderness areas on the planet with plenty of untouched rainforests and freshwater lakes, Fraser Island is composed almost entirely of siliceous sands. The dunes reach a height of 240 metres in some areas, and rocky outcrops can be found at Indian Head, Middle Rock, Waddy Point and Bun Bun Rocks. While the island has hundreds of kilometres of white sand, up to 72 different colours of sand have been recorded on the island, the most famous being the coloured sand cliffs of The Cathedrals on the eastern side.

The history of Fraser Island is interesting to say the least. Captain James Cook was the first to pass along the coast in 1770, and noted that the extraordinary amount of sand would not exactly make for good grazing conditions. But the most interesting aspect of the Island's history occurred when Eliza Fraser and her companions from the *Stirling Castle* ship struck the Great Barrier Reef in 1836. Eliza's husband Captain James Fraser tried to get his 18 passengers to Moreton Bay, but was eventually forced to land on the Island due to lack of water. Before long they were set upon by the local indigenous population, who stripped the survivors naked, drove them into the bush and forced them to work under arduous conditions.

Eliza was seperated from her husband, and she later wrote a book were she told of how the crew were forced to live for seven days and nights without food or water, and were subjected to slavery and torture at the hands of the New Holland savages. While one crew member was burnt alive slowly over a fire, Eliza Fraser herself was tortured and speared, as well as forced to witness the murder of her husband. One of the crew members eventually escaped to Moreton Bay, and a search party was sent out to locate any survivors. A convict named John Graham eventually located Eliza Fraser and escorted her back to the European settlement, and the Island was later named after her.

Most of Fraser Island is either crown land, national park or State forest reserve. There are five main tourist centres at Eurong, Happy Valley, Orchard Beach, Cathedral Beach and Dilli Village. Others may prefer to camp in a secluded spot and explore the island's forest tracks by 4WD. There are over 40 freshwater lakes on the island, including perched dune lakes and window lakes, formed when the shifting sand falls below the level of the island's dome-shaped water table. Remarkable is Lake Wabby, the deepest of the island's lakes, which contains a great variety of fish. The island also has

Sunset on Fraser Island

A maritime wreck on Fraser Island

its own shipwreck in the form of the *Maheno*, which was beached during a cyclone 50 years ago.

Visitors to the island are required to have permits, with the fee used to provide facilities for visitors and to provide effective protection for the island's environment. Permits can be purchased from the Department of Environment & Heritage on Rainbow Beach, *(07) 5486 3160*, or alternatively in Brisbane, *(07) 3227 7111*. Fraser Island can be reached by sea and air, with cruises and vehicular barges operating from Hervey Bay, Mary River Heads and Rainbow Beach.

Visitor Information:
The Hervey Bay-Fraser Island Visitors Centre can be found at The Esplanade in Hervey Bay, Fraser Island, and can be called on *(07) 4124 8741*.

Hervey Bay Population: 36,109

Situated 34km east of Maryborough, the tourist-friendly beaches of Hervey Bay are complimented by one of the best whale watching experiences anywhere in the world. From July to November the town is flooded with whale watchers, while the Humpback Whales make a stop-off on their way south to Antarctica. They frolic freely in the warm waters of the ocean, oblivious to those watching eagerly from the safety of tour boats. With a climate similar to that of Hawaii, the safe and sheltered swimming found in Hervey Bay has made it a popular destination for tourists all year round.

Visitor Information:
The Hervey Bay Tourist & Visitors Centre is located at 401 The Esplanade, and can be called on *(07) 4124 4050*.

Outlying Towns

Burrum Heads, Toogoom, Howard, Torbanlea

Burrum Heads and Toogoom are two small coastal resorts located at the mouth of the Burrum River, both popular for their good fishing and relaxed atmosphere. Burrum Heads is growing rapidly and is well serviced with shops. Toogoom has plenty of picnic spots, and over ninety species of birds have been identified in the area. Both of these resorts have caravan parks and holiday homes. The Burrum River crosses the highway between Howard and Torbanlea. Most houses in these two townships are the cool high-set timber Queenslander homes. Howard has all the facilities of an up-and-coming small town.

QLD

Bundaberg, Coral Coast & Country Region

The gateway to the Southern Great Barrier Reef, the Bundaberg, Coral Coast & Country region is home to 140 kilometres of coastline, 17 prisitine beaches and an abundance of coral bays.

Bundaberg Population: 44,556. Climate: Average temperatures: Jan max 30°C - min 21°C; July max 21°C - min 11°C. Average annual rainfall: 1149mm; heaviest rainfall falls December-March.

Situated on the Burnett River and 360km north of Brisbane, Bundaberg is one of the largest and most prosperous coastal cities in Queensland. In a similar fashion to other towns like Townsville, Rockhampton and Mackay, the influence of the nineteenth century settlers can still be seen in Bundaberg. While historic buildings still remain, they blend in with the tropical parks, gardens and modern architecture of the central business district, offering the regional city a touch of rural charm. One of Australia's most famous spirits is produced in the town, and the Bundaberg Rum Distillery has become a local icon . Bundaberg is also loosely referred to as the "Sugar City", with the district responsible for growing approximately one-fifth of Australia's sugar crop.

The first European to explore the area was Henry Russell in 1842, five years before surveyor James C. Burnett returned to have a look. Burnett was less than impressed with the agricultural potential of the area and he failed to notice the

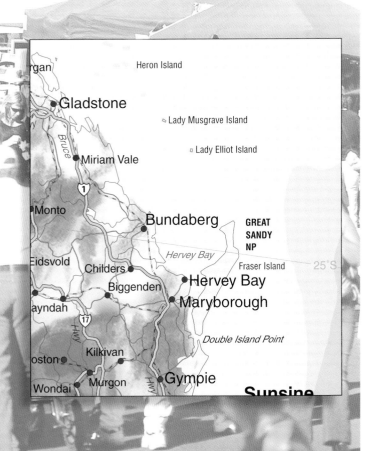

The Bundaberg foreshore

richness of the soil, so it wasn't until 1866 that any settlers returned. The Steuart brothers arrived in the 1870's to take advantage of the timber in the hinterland, and Bundaberg soon became the centre of the state's sugar industry. A brewery began operating in 1883, and the arrival of a railway line meant that the sugar industry continued to boom in the town.

With the Great Barrier Reef right on its doorstep, Bundaberg can boast a wide range of activities that take advantage of its natural surroundings. The most picturesque sections of the southern reef can be found around Lady Elliot and Lady Musgrave Islands, the mainland coastline just 13 km from Bundaberg. The reef can be seen on a sunny day by snorkeling just a metre or two from the shore, and beachfront accommodation is available. Turtle watching season takes place from November until March at the nearby Mon Repos Beach, the largest turtle rookery in mainland Australia, and tiny turtle hatchlings can be seen emerging from their shells.

Visitor Information:
The Bundaberg Region Visitor Information Centre is at the Hinkler Glider Museum, 271 Bourbong Street, next to the Base Hospital, call them on *(07) 4153 8888*. They can be emailed on *info@bundabergregion.org*, and their email address is *www.bundabergregion.info*.

Points of Interest:
The MV Lady Musgrave allows visitors to take a trip to the reef, and takes just over two hours from Bundaberg. The office is located in Shop 1 Moffat Street at the Bundaberg Port Marina, and they can be called on *(07) 4159 4519*.

Herbert John Louis Hinkler was Bundaberg's most famous son. Locally he was known as 'Hustling Hinkler', and in 1928 he was the first aviator to fly solo from England to Australia. The Hinkler House in Mt Perry Road was transported brick by brick from Southampton in England to Bundaberg during 1983. Hinkler had designed the house and lived in it from 1926 to 1933. It is now an aviation museum, and they can be called on *(07) 4152 0222*.

The Bundaberg Rum Distillery, the producers of one of Australia's most famous spirits, conducts tours every weekend that allow a look in at how the rum is processed. The distillery can be found on Whitred Street, *(07) 4131 2900*.

The Mystery Craters just north of Bundaberg are said to be 25 million years old, and their origin remains unexplained. The fascinating area has a garden setting, observation tower, kiosk, rocks, souvenirs, currency display and playground. It can be found at Lines Road in South Kolan, and they can be called on *(07) 4157 7291*.

Bargara Beach is the aquatic playground for the sun and sea aficionados of Bundaberg. Just a 15 minute drive from Bundaberg, it offers safe surfing at Neilson Park. The centre known as 'Bargara Centrepoint' caters for everyone's needs.

Outlying Towns

Eidsvold
Situated on the Burnett Highway 250km west of Bundaberg, via Gayndah, Eidsvold was established as a gold mining town in 1888 and is now a major producer of beef cattle. The Eidsvold Motel & General Store, 51 Moreton Street, can provide you with tourist information, *(07) 4165 1209*.

Munduberra
Mundubbera is situated on the banks of the Burnett River, 35km south-east of Eidsvold on the Burnett Highway. The River passes through the small sub-tropical valley of the Central Burnett. A third of Queensland's citrus is produced here and the area is surrounded by orchards, and has the enormous Ellendale Tourist Centre. Information can be obtained from here in Durong Road, *(07) 4165 4549*.

Gayndah
Found 166km south-west of Bundaberg on the Burnett

Local Festival in Bundaberg

The Bundaberg Town Hall and Cenotaph

Highway, Gayndah is Queensland's oldest town. In the 1840's Gayndah was originally settled as sheep country, and it wasn't until 1892 that William Seeney planted the first orchard, for which Gayndah is now famous. The town's Big Orange complex would be hard to miss, *(07) 4161 1500*.

Biggenden
Craggy, blue mountain ranges are the backdrop for Biggenden, 100km south-west of Bundaberg. Along with agricultural pursuits, the area is rich in minerals. Established in the goldrush of 1889, attractions include the historic Chowey Bridge, the old Mt Shamrock Gold Mine, the operational open-cut magnetite mine, the Coalstoun Lakes, Mt Walsh National Park and Mt Woowoonga Forest Reserve. You will find tourist information at the Biggenden Shire Council, Edward Street, *(07) 4127 1177*.

Childers
Located 50km south of Bundaberg, Childers has rich red soil, and is famous for its avenue of leopard trees, and colonial buildings. Less than half an hour's drive away is Woodgate Beach and Woodgate National Park. The Visitor Information Centre is in the Palace Building at 72 Churchill Street, *(07) 4126 3886*.

QLD

Central Queensland Region

Encompassing the Gladstone and Capricorn areas, the Central Queensland region is most famous for its huge number of beaches, a vast outback, lush rainforests, as well as the stunning natural beauty of the world famous Great Barrier Reef.

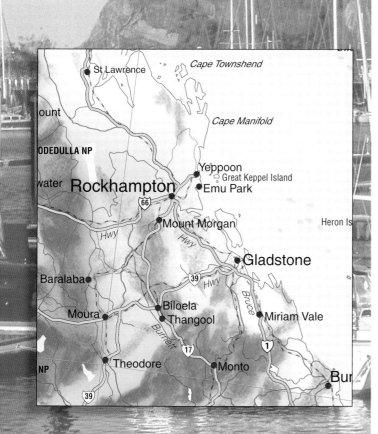

Rockhampton Population: 59,475. Climate: The region's climate supports an outdoor lifestyle all year round. The average maximum temperatures range from 23°C – 32°C, while average minimums range from 9°C – 2°C.

Situated on the Fitzroy River and 660km north of Brisbane, the city of Rockhampton is the gateway to the Capricorn Coast. Known affectionately as by the locals as "Rocky", the city is the unofficial capital of Central Queensland. Rockhampton is also the "Beef Capital of Australia" – the main breeds of cattle include Brahman, Hereford, Braford, Santa Gertrudis, Belmont Red and Droughtmaster. A reminder of the role played by beef in the city's economy are the statues situated at different locations, depicting Santa Gertrudis, Brahman, Braford and Droughtmaster bulls. A giant "big bull" can also be seen on top of a shopping centre at the southern end of town, and the meatworks in Rockhampton is capable of processing in excess of 2000 head of cattle per day.

Charles and William Archer were the first to explore the area around Rockhampton, and in 1853 they named the Fitzroy River after Governor Charles Fitz Roy. Charles Archer returned to establish a station in 1855, and as Queensland had not yet been named as a separate colony, the New South Wales Government were the ones to begin a settlement in the following year. The town's name was derived from "Rock", a reference to the rocks in the river which prevented further navigation of ships upstream, and the English word "Hampton" which means village. A number of stores were built that year and the discovery of gold at nearby Canoona led to an increase in population, with many choosing to remain when the gold rush died down.

The resources which were discovered in the town later in the century contributed further to the creation of wealth in Rockhampton. The Morgan Brothers purchased a gold mining lease on a nearby mountain which would later be named after them, and together in a partnership with several other local businessmen they grew to become incredibly rich. The wealth generated had a flow on effect to the growing settlement of Rockhampton, and many of the famous heritage buildings that were built are still in use in the city. Rockhampton was designated as a city in 1902.

The Fitzroy River is the heart of the city of Rockhampton:

Cattle House, Rockhampton

visitors can stroll the boardwalk, or relax with a picnic or barbeque at the Riverside Park. Nearby is a bronze bust of Rod "The Rocket" Laver, a world champion tennis player who came from Rockhampton. Many historic buildings can still be seen in the city, and the historic Quay Street on the waterfront contains over 20 buildings which have been classified by the National Trust. Queens Wharf is all that remains of the port that originally resided in the town. The St Joseph's and St Paul's Anglican cathedrals were both built from local sandstone, while the Royal Arcade theatre was built in 1889 with a special feature – the roof could be opened on hot nights.

Visitor Information:

Capricorn Tourism, is at 'The Spire' in Gladstone Road, *(07) 4927 2055*, adjacent to the Tropic of Capricorn Spire. Their email address is *infocentre@capricorntourism.com.au*, while their web address is *www.capricorntourism.com.au*.

The Rockhampton Tourist Information Centre can be found in the historic Customs House on Quay Street, *(07) 4922 5339*. They can be emailed at *rtbi@rockhamptoninfo. com*, and their website is *www.rockhamptoninfo.com*.

Points of Interest:

The Botanic Gardens are reputed to be one of the finest tropical gardens in Australia. Spreading over 4 hectares, these gardens contain many native and exotic trees, ferns and shrubs, as well as a large walk-in aviary, orchid and fern house and a Zoo, which includes its own Koala Park. As part of a sister city agreement with Ibusuki City in Japan, separate Japanese Gardens were created in 1982. The gardens can be found in Spencer Street, *(07) 4922 4347*,

Rockhampton Historical Society Museum is located on the north side of the Fitzroy River near the Fitzroy Bridge. The building was originally completed in 1885 to house the North Rockhampton Borough Council, and the museum now contains an interesting collection of memorabilia from the local area. Call *(07) 4927 8431*.

The Pilbeam Theatre, *(07) 4927 4111*, and Art Gallery, *(07) 4936 8248*, in Victoria Parade, form the cultural centre of Rocky. The Art Gallery has an extensive collection of Australian paintings, pottery and sculpture. The Pilbeam

Theatre attracts regular performances by national and international stars.

The Callaghan Park Racecourse, *(07) 4927 1300*, is Queensland's premier provincial racetrack. Thursday night has greyhounds, Saturday evening has harness racing, and on Saturday afternoon and various week days it is the gallopers' turn.

Fitzroy River Ski Gardens, near the Barrage bridge, beside the boat launching facilities, has picnic facilities, a children's playground and electric barbecues.

Old Glenmore Homestead is a 130- year-old complex consisting of a log cabin, slab cottage and an adobe house. Old Glenmore holds Queensland's first Historic Inn Licence, so visitors can sample some of the State's best fermented beverages in this pleasant old world setting. The homestead is just north of the city, *(07) 4936 1033*.

The Capricorn Caverns are privately owned cave systems which are open to the public. Cave coral, fossils and gigantic tree roots can be inspected in these dry, limestone caves. Tours are conducted on the hour, and adventure caving is also available by request. The caverns are approximately 23km north of Rockhampton, *(07) 4934 2883*.

The Dreamtime Cultural Centre is a large Aboriginal and Torres Strait Islander Cultural Centre, and is on the Bruce Highway opposite the turn-off to Yeppoon. Aiming to introduce visitors to the culture of the local indigenous population, they can be called on *(07) 4936 1655*,

Rockhampton Heritage Village village displays life as lived in Rockhampton from white settlement in 1854 through the first 100 years. Tours are held daily, and the village can be found on Boundary Road in Parkhurst, *(07) 4936 1026*.

Gladstone Population: 28,000

Located 107km south of Rockhampton, Gladstone is one of the busiest and largest port centres in the country. From modest beginnings in 1847, the wider Gladstone region has grown to become home to more than 45,000 people. Just off the coast of Gladstone are the outlying Curtis and Quoin Islands. The Gladstone Art Gallery and Museum can be found in Goondoon Street, and is a unique mix of architectural designs which compliment the collection of Australian art and local memorabilia contained within.

Visitor Information:

The Gladstone Tourist Information Centre can be found at the Ferry Terminal on Bryan Jordan Drive, *(07) 4972 9000*.

The Capricorn Coast / Yeppoon
Population: 20,000

The Capricorn Coast is approximately 40km away from Rockhampton, and is one of the largest and fastest growing coastal communities in Queensland with access to more than 40km of safe beaches. The area stretches some 48km from Yeppoon and the Byfield area in the north to Keppel Sands in the south. The main area of the Capricorn Coast begins at the town of Joskeleigh in the south, and reaches north to the

Art Gallery and Museum, Gladstone

Horse riding at Yeppoon

Wreck Beach, Great Keppel Island

forests and national parks of Byfield. The primary town on the coast is Yeppoon.

Yeppoon is situated on the shores of Keppel Bay, with palms and pines lining the main street and continuing all the way to Rockhampton. Cooberrie Park, 15km north of Yeppoon on Woodbury Road, is a bird and animal sanctuary with barbecue and picnic facilities. Wreck Point provides a spectacular view that overlooks the Keppel group of islands, and it can be found at Cooee Bay on the southern outskirts of Yeppoon.

Visitor Information:
The Capricorn Coast Tourist Organisation is located in Yeppoon at the Ross Creek Roundabout, *(07) 4939 4888.*

Outlying Towns in the Central Queensland Region

Great Keppel Island
Great Keppel Island is fringed by 17km of white, sandy beaches and offshore coral reefs, and provides an ideal setting for holiday makers and day trippers alike. The Keppel Island group of 30 islands is situated 55km from Rockhampton, and 15km east of Rosslyn Bay on the Capricorn Coast.

Great Keppel is the only island in the group to have been developed, and this is because of its permanent water supply as well as its size (14 square kilometres). There are ample opportunities for fishing, cruising, boom netting, windsurfing and bushwalking.

Some islands in the group are national parks – North Keppel, Miall, Middle, Halfway, Humpy and Peak. Although not situated on the Reef, Great Keppel is the gateway to the Outer Reef and North West Island, the largest coral cay in the Great Barrier Reef. It is a major breeding ground for Green Turtles, White Capped Noddy Terns, Wedge Tailed Shearwaters and Olive Head Sea Snakes. A glance at a map will show that the Great Barrier Reef is a long way from the mainland at this point, but there is some good diving closer to Great Keppel Island. Bald Rock and Man & Wife Rocks are popular diving venues, and there is some good coral between the southern end of Halfway Island and Middle Island Reef. The outer islands of the Keppel group, particularly Barren Island, have deeper and clearer water than Great Keppel, so larger species of sea life are encountered, like turtles and manta rays.

Heron Island
Heron Island has an area of 19 hectares, and is approximately 72km east of Gladstone and 100km from Rockhampton. It is a true coral cay that sits on the Tropic of Capricorn,

surrounded by 24sq km of reef. It is possible to walk around the island in less than half an hour, and access is by helicopter or a 2-hour catamaran trip. On Heron the reef is at the very foot of the white sandy beaches, and is one of the world's best dive locations with 20 unique dive sites nearby.

Lady Musgrave Island

An unspoilt section of the Great Barrier Reef and a National and Marine Park, Lady Musgrave Island is part of the Capricorn Bunker Group. Around 100km north-east of Bundaberg, Lady Musgrave Island is a true coral cay, around 18 hectares in area and resting on the edge of a huge coral lagoon. The Island is reputedly one of the finest dive sites on the Great Barrier Reef, and the lagoon is reasonably shallow, allowing longer dives to be undertaken.

Lady Elliott Island

The most southerly of the islands of the Great Barrier Reef, Lady Elliot has an area of 0.42 sq km and has been nicknamed Queensland's "Shipwreck Island". This name is not unwarranted, as the wrecks of many ships can be seen littered around the island's shores. It only takes about an hour to walk around the entire island, and it is one of the least commercialised. There are ten excellent diving sites that include Lighthouse Bommie, CoralGardens, Moiri and Shark Pool. Visibility ranges from 80 to 25 to 50 metres.

Mount Morgan

The historic township of Mount Morgan is 40km south-west of Rockhampton, and here visitors can tour through a 100-year-old mining town that is the real thing, not a reconstruction. The Museum on Morgan Street traces the history of the fabulously rich mine. Tours of the historic mine site and dinosaur caves are conducted daily by Mount Morgan Experience Tours.

Capricorn Highlands

The highlands stretch from Carnarvon to Clermont (the Gregory Highway), and from Blackwater to Jericho (Capricorn Highway). The region is one of the most diverse and productive areas in the country. Coal, sapphires, cattle, sheep, wheat, sunflower, sorghum and cotton are but a few of the riches produced from around here. A visit to the Higlands is a rewarding experience.

The Carnarvon Gorge offers breathtaking views with lush vegetation and Aboriginal stencil art. The town of Springsure has the famous Virgin Rock and the Federation Arcturus Woolshed with Old Rainworth Fort located 10kms south of the town. At Emerald, the hub of the Central Highlands, the history of the Pioneer cottage can be absorbed, or watch a cattle sale at the saleyards complex.

The Central Queensland Gemfields are a popular tourist spot in the Capricorn Region, and visitors come for a chance to stub their toe on a sapphire. Towns such as Anakie, Sapphire, Rubyvale and the Willows Gemfields must be experienced to

Carnarvon Gorge

be fully appreciated. Travelling through Capella brings you to the township of Clermont, which was almost completely destroyed by a flood in 1916, and was moved to its present location with the aid of a huge steam engine. The engine has been preserved as a memorial in the centre of the town.

A National Park at Blackdown Tablelands offers camping facilities and spectacular views. After crossing the Drummond Range, the country opens out into Queensland's vast grazing lands, and towns like Alpha and Jericho are becoming increasingly popular stopovers for people visiting this outback area.

Monto

Located 203km south-west of Bundaberg, Monto is the largest town of the North Burnett district, and the service centre for the surrounding dairy industry. 24km north-east of Monto is Cania Gorge, with its spectacular sandstone formations and crystal pools. 8km further on is the massive Cania Dam, where there are attractive picnic areas.

QLD

The Mackay Region & The Whitsundays

The Mackay Region is located in the centre of Queensland and stretches westwards from the Great Barrier Reef, over tropical lowlands and across the green mountain ranges, and west into the outback.

Mackay   Population: 80,000. Climate: Average temperatures: January max 33°C - min 22°C; July max 25°C - min 10°C. Average annual rainfall - 1672mm.

Located 975 km north of Brisbane, the city of Mackay is known as the "Sugar Capital of Australia". Surrounded by miles and miles of sugarcane fields, the district is responsible for producing around one-third of Australia's total sugar crop. Minature trams meander through the fields and transport the cane to one of the seven sugar mills in the area, when it is then exported to the rest of Australia through the Port of Mackay. The city contains all of the necessary facilites for those wishing to visit: restaurants, accomodation, fantastic boating facilites, not to mention the beautiful beaches which have become synonomous with Queensland.

Captain James Cook was the first European to pass by Mackay in 1770, though the area remained untouched until Captain John Mackay entered the area in 1860. Cattle and horses were brought from Armidale the following year, before a settlement was eventually established in 1862. While it initially seemed likely that cattle would be the town's major industry, the first sugar was planted in Mackay in 1865. John Spiller, T. Henry Fitzgerald and John Ewen Davidson were

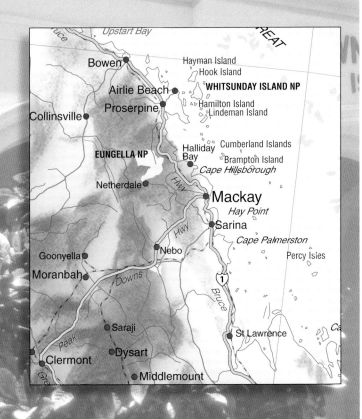

Mackay

Mackay Marina

responsible for pioneering the sugar industry, and from this point the town never looked back. Sugar mills were built in the area in 1867 and and led to the first exports, and Mackay is now home to the world's largest bulk sugar terminal.

A number of tours which can be taken in Mackay for those wishing to observe the local sugar industry. Tourism Mackay have put also together a City Walking Tour that takes in many of the city's historic buildings: some of the most notable include the Police Station which was built in 1885, and the Court House and Commonwealth Bank which were built in 1880. There is also the Holy Trinity Church, Masonic Temple, National Bank, Mercury Building, Pioneer Shire Chambers, Post Office and Customs House – all built in 1901. Harbour Beach is the closest spot for swimming or surfing, and can be found on the southern side of the outer harbour wall. It has plenty of facilities and is patrolled during summer by the Mackay Surf Club. For a great panoramic view of the city and the surrounding countryside, visit the Mt Oscar Lookout in Norris Road, North Mackay.

Visitor Information:

Mackay Tourism can be found at 320 Nebo Road, *(07) 4944 5888*. Their email is *info@mackayregion.com*.

Points of Interest:

The Illawong Fauna Sanctuary is a beachfront family recreation area amid tropical landscaping, and can be found at 4km from the centre of Mackay at Illawong Beach. There are kangaroos roaming free, a swimming pool, trampoline, video games and full catering facilities. For further information call *(07) 4959 1777*.

The Farleigh Sugar Mill can be toured during the crushing season from July to November. The mill is located on Chidlow Street, call *(07) 4963 2700* for more information.

The Polstone Sugar Farm conduct a two hour tour that covers the history, equipment and process of growing and preparing sugar cane for the mill. They are found on Masotti's Road in Homebush, adjacent to Orchid Way, and can be called on *(07) 4959 7298*.

The Dalrymple Bay Coal Terminal Complex is the largest coal export facility in the southern hemisphere. The wharves stretch 3.8km out to sea, and coal trains up to 2km long arrive at the port daily. It can be found twenty-five kilometres south of Mackay at Hay Point, and the Port Administration Building has a viewing platform, call *(07) 4943 8444*.

Forest Flying is an eco-educational flying fox cableway that is suspended 25 metres above the ground, and is 350 metres long. It provides visitors with a bird's eye view of the canopy.

Located at Finch Hatton Gorge, call *(07) 4958 3359.*

The Cape Palmerston National Park is 80km south of Mackay and has 4WD access. It offers sandy beaches, exposed headlands, palm forests, expansive melaleuca headlands and an abundance of wildlife. Attractions include Ince Bay to the north, Temple Island and the volcanic plug of Mt Funnel. Camping is available at Windmill or Clarke Bay. Contact Australian 4 x 4 Adventures for tours, *(07) 4955 5011.*

The Whitsundays **Population: Estimated at 6,000 – 8,000.**

The Whitsundays consist of 74 islands from the Cumberland and Northumberland Island groups, and they form the largest offshore island chain on Australia's east coast. The islands are the remains of a mountain range that was drowned when sea levels rose at the end of the last ice age. Most of them have National Park status, and all are situated in the marine park. There are basic camping facilities on Hook, North Molle, Whitsunday, Henning, Border, Haslewood, Shaw, Thomas and Repulse Islands. Permits can be obtained by calling the Naturally Queensland Information Centre in Brisbane on *(07) 3227 8197,* or by emailing *nqic@epa.qld.gov.au.*

Visitor Information:

Tourism Whitsunday can be found 1/5 Carlo Drive at Cannonbale. Their phone number is *(07) 4948 3333,* and they can be emailed at *tw@whitsundaytourism.com.* Their website address is *www.whitsundaytourism.com.*

The Whitsunday Information Centre is on the Bruce Highway in Proserpine, *(07) 4945 3711.*

Whitsunday Island

Although Whitsunday is the largest of the island in the Whitsunday Group, it does not have a resort. But it does have Whitehaven Beach, the longest and best beach in the whole group, and the destination of many cruises. There is good snorkelling off the southern end of the beach. There are several camping sites on the island.

Lindeman Island

The island has six beaches and 20km of walking tracks that lead through 500 hectares of National Park. There are seven secluded beaches, and at dusk from the top of Mt Oldfield there can seen the sun setting over islands stretching to the horizon in every direction. passages through the Whitsunday

Hill Inlet and Whitehaven Beach, Whitsunday Island

Islands. Its highest point is Mt Oldfield, 210m. The resort's website can be viewed at *www.clubmed.com.au*.

South Molle Island

The island covers 405 hectares, and is 4km long and 2.4km wide. It is situated in the heart of Whitsunday Passage, and offers fishing, golf, tennis, water skiing, coral viewing, scuba diving, para-sailing and bushwalking. The oldest of the resorts in the Whitsunday Group, South Molle is mostly national park and offers some good, if short, walks. The highest point is Mt Jeffreys (198m), and from it there are great views of the surrounding islands. Balancing Rock and Spion Kop also allows visitors to take in breathtaking vistas. Accommodation is available at South Molle Island Resort, *(07) 4946 9433*.

Long Island

The island is directly off the coast of Shute Harbour, and adjoins the Whitsunday Passage. It is deliberately underdeveloped, and the untamed tropical rainforest and protected Palm Bay Lagoon make for a very informal holiday. Long Island is separated from the mainland by a channel that is only 500m wide, making it the closest resort island to the Queensland coast. There are 20km of bush walks through the National Park, and there are some nice sandy beaches on its western side, but the beaches on the eastern side tend to be rocky and usually windy. The Club Crocodile Resort can be contacted on *(07) 4946 9400*. and for a preliminary look at what the island has to offer, follow the links to Long Island at www.clubcrocodile.com.au.

Hayman Island

The island is a resort offering a balance between luxury living and natural beauty. Curving around the sandy shoreline of the blue lagoon on the south-western side of the island, Hayman looks out toward Langford Reef and an island called Bali Hai. All sports, both on land and water, are catered for at the resort. Hayman Island has an area of 4sq km, and is the most northerly of the Whitsunday resort islands. Its resort is one of the most luxurious on the Great Barrier Reef, and in fact is widely considered to be one of the top ten resorts in the world. Thirty kilometres north-east of Hayman are the Hardy and Black Reefs.

Hamilton Island

Hamilton has an area of 6sq km, and is home to the largest resort in the South Pacific with its own jet airport. The resort is actually a small town with shops, restaurants and a 135-berth marina. There are a few walking tracks on the undeveloped parts of the island, and the main one leads up to Passage Peak (230m), the highest point on the island. Hamilton even has island bus tours that operate daily. The Hamilton Island Resort can be contacted on *(07) 4946 9999*.

Hook Island

Hook Island has an area of 53sq km, some great beaches and some of the best diving sites in the Whitsundays, but it has one of the smallest resorts. The focus here is on the budget market, with a choice between camping sites, beachfront cabins and backpacker dorms. Hook Island has two long, narrow bays on its southern end – Macona Inlet and Nara Inlet. The northern end of Hook Island has some good diving and snorkelling sites - Pinnacle Point, Manta Ray Bay, Butterfly Bay and Alcyonaria Point. The Wilderness Resort can answer any further enquiries, *(07) 4946 9380*.

Daydream Island

Daydream is a small island with an area of just 17 hectares. It is a little over 1km long and no more than a couple of hundred

Brampton Island

metres at its widest point, but it has one of the largest resorts. Originally known as West Molle, the island is the closest resort island to Shute Harbour. Sunlover's Beach, at the north eastern end of the island, behind the resort, has a 50m strip of sand and some good coral offshore for snorkellers. The Resort dive shop offers courses, and day cruises to Hardy Reef, about 50km offshore. Contact the resort on *(07) 4948 8488* or *1800 075 040* for reservations.

Brampton Island

Brampton is not strictly in the Whitsunday region. It is part of the Cumberland Group of Islands about 32km north-east of Mackay, at the entrance to the Whitsunday Passage. The island is a National Park, with an area of 4.6 sq km, and has unspoilt bush, lush tropical foliage, swaying coconut palms and many stunning and secluded beaches. It is connected to Carlisle Island and to Pelican Island by sand bars that can be crossed at low tide. A mountainous island with lush forests, nature trails, kangaroos and emus, Brampton also has seven sandy beaches and is surrounded by coral reefs.

Proserpine

Proserpine, 127km north of Mackay, is mainly a sugar cane town. It serves as the centre of the Whitsunday region, in administrative terms, but most visitors by-pass its scenic charm on their way to the more seductive coastline. The town has full facilities and a good range of accommodation. West of the town is Lake Proserpine, where waterskiing is a popular sport. The Whitsunday Information Centre on the Bruce Highway is in Proserpine, *(07) 4945 3711*.

Shute Harbour

Shute Harbour is the focal point for departure of many tourist vessels cruising to the Whitsunday Islands. Not only is it the second busiest passenger port in Australia, it boasts the second largest bareboat industry in the world (a bareboat is a boat hired without a crew). Shute Harbour is mostly a gateway for cruises out to the islands, and is one of the smaller satellite areas for Proserpine, as well as being superceded by Airlie Beach as an accommodation centre. Nevertheless, there are a couple of places to stay here. Use the contact details for

Around Airlie Beach

Whitsunday Tourism, or visit the Tourist Information Centre at Airlie Beach, *(07) 4946 6665*.

Airlie Beach

Airlie Beach, the main resort town on the Whitsunday coast, has a relaxed atmosphere, and is 8km from Shute Harbour, and 24km from Proserpine. The town borders the 20,000 hectare Conway National Park, and is the mainland centre for the Whitsundays. Airlie Beach is a picturesque village and offers a lot to the holiday-maker on its own account, but when the close proximity of the Reef islands is taken into consideration, it is not hard to figure out why some people choose to stay at Airlie and take day trips to the islands. It is a haven for young backpackers, which makes for interesting nightlife. The Airlie Tourist Information Centre is at 277 Shute Harbour Road, Airlie Beach, *(07) 4946 6665*.

Outlying Towns in the Region

Sarina

The town of Sarina is 37km south of Mackay, and 296km north of Rockhampton, on the Bruce Highway. It is yet

Broken River, Eungella National Park

another sugar town in the area, cradled by rainforest and the Conners Range mountains. 13km to the north east is the sleepy seaside community of Sarina Beach. Fishing, and snorkelling are popular pastimes here. Broad Street, the main street of the town, is indeed broad with a median strip in the centre offering tables, park benches, public amenities, and best of all, shade. Helpful local information is provided by the Sarina Tourist Art & Craft Centre, *(07) 4956 2251*.

Eungella National Park

This stunning National Park is an 80km drive west of Mackay. Eungella Road takes you through the the Pioneer River and its tributaries up the valley past Finch Hatton, and through to the Eungella township at the top of the range. Finch Hatton Gorge has attractive mountain-fed waterfalls, a natural swimming pool and good walking tracks. The Broken River area provides shady pools for swimming, and well marked bush walking tracks are a feature of the Park. Those who are lucky may spot a platypus near the bridge. For information on the parks, contact the Mackay Office of the Queensland Parks and Wildlife Service on *(07) 4944 7800*.

Cape Hillsborough

Located 47km north of Mackay, the Cape Hillsborough National Park provides a beachfront picnic area with barbecue facilities. The park is relatively small (830 hectares), but it is typical of the best of North Queensland, with rainforests, beaches and abundant wildlife. Walking tracks travel to billabongs, great lookouts and unusual volcanic formations. Fishing in the park is excellent.

Halliday Bay

Situated north of Mackay, near the town of Seaforth, Halliday Bay is noted for its white sandy beach and safe swimming enclosure. The bay adjoins McBride's Point National Park, and has a shop and boat hire facilities. The Bay is named after Captain Halliday, whose century-old stone cottage is still standing.

QLD

North Queensland Region

North Queensland has a lot to offer visitors to the region, including, World Heritage tropical rainforests, and wide areas of outback. The region is known for its tropical weather conditions. The major city of the region, Townsville, is the second largest city in Queensland.

Townsville
Population: 150,000. Climate: Average temperature: January max 31°C – min 24°C; July max 25°C – min 15°C. Average annual rainfall is 1194mm.

Situated on the eastern coast of Australia and 1443km north of Brisbane, the city of Townsville is the perfect place to experience a taste of "Life in the Tropics". Located right in the thick of the dry tropics, Townsville enjoys more than 300 dry, sunny days every year. Sprawling along the shores of Cleveland Bay and around the foot of Castle Hill, it is the second largest city in Queensland and main commercial centre of the region. Attractions like the Magnetic North and the Great Barrier Reef can be easily accessed, but all the facilities of a major city can also be found in the city. There are four inner city "precincts" for shopping, dining and entertainment, while heritage has been retained in the form of well-preserved civic, commercial and domestic buildings that date back to early European settlement.

Anzac Park, Townsville

Captain Cook was the first to explore the area, reaching Cleveland Bay upon which the city was built in 1770. While a number of other pioneers explored the surrounding areas over the next several decades, none of them seemed to believe that Townsville showed any potential promise as a settlement. It wasn't until 1861 that Robert Towns decided the area could serve as a port for the whole region. As he already owned significant sections of land in the North Queensland region, he chose a site on the shores of Cleveland Bay that he hoped would be able to service his investments. With the town named after its founder, Townsville had been declared a port by 1865.

Townsville is famous for its relaxed tropical lifestyle and perfect weather. Old wooden highset houses known as "Queenslanders" stand everywhere, built to allow cooling breezes under the house and provide a refuge during the heat of the day. In the gardens, mango, paw paw and banana trees seem exotic to the visitor, but are the normal homegrown product of the Townsville backyard. Townsville remains a

busy port and the town has a number of other industrial enterprises. The city's excellent facilities also make it a good starting point to explore the surrounding locations. Magnetic Island is only 30 minutes from the city centre by ferry, and other interesting regions include the Burdekin Shire, northern centres such as Ingham and the tropical playground of Mission Beach.

Visitor Information:
The Townsville Enterprise can be called on *(07) 4726 2728*, or *1800 801 902*. Their online address is *www.townsvilleonline.com.au*.

Points of Interest:
Castle Hill offers a panoramic view of the city of Townsville, and is 286m high. It is topped by an octagonal restaurant which commands a 260 degree view of the city and the bay. The nearby Mount Stuart is also an excellent vantage point.

The Strand was named Queensland's Cleanest Beach in

Magnetic Island off Townsville

2003, and is situated in the heart of the city. The beachfront boulevard is 2.5km long, and can boast views that sweep across Cleveland Bay and Magnetic Island.

Flinders Mall can be found right at the centre of the city, and offers plenty of shopping opportunites for visitors. In addition to the many shops, Flinders Mall is also home to the Perc Tucker Regional Gallery, *(07) 4727 9011*. The Cotters Markets are also held there every Sunday, and include an assortment of local foods, arts, crafts and entertainment.

The Museum of Tropical Queensland provides a good way for visitors to soak in the history of the area. Along with a new range of galleries and exhibitions, the museum is also home to relics from the wreck of the *HMS Pandora* and a replica of the hull of the famous *SS Pandora*. Located at 70-102 Flinders Street, call *(07) 4726 0600*.

The Reef HQ is the world's largest living coral reef aquarium, and allows visitors to come face to face with the wonders of the Great Barrier Reef. Also home to the Great Barrier Reef national education centre, they are located at 2-68 Flinders Street East, and can be phoned on *(07) 4750 0800*.

The SS Yongala is one of the top dive sites in the world, and can be found off the coast of Townsville. The *Yongala* was a steel passenger and freight steamer owned by the Adelaide Steamship Company, and all 124 people onboard drowned when it sank in 1911. The wreck of the *Yongala* is 109 metres long and has become an esstablished artificial reef, and dive operators run expeditions to the site from Townsville.

Outlying Towns and Features

Fitzroy Island

Fitzroy has an area of 4 square km, and is situated 26km south-east of Cairns, only 6km from the mainland. There are a few walking trails - the round trip to the lighthouse; a short rainforest walk to the Secret Garden; and the walk to Nudey Beach. Canoes and catamarans are available for use, and sailing is popular. Contact the Fitzroy Island Resort on *(07) 4051 9588*.

Mission Beach

At Mission Beach, about halfway between Townsville and Cairns, a chain of Mountains runs down to the sea, and surrounds the small coastal settlements. Offshore lie the North and South Barnard, Dunk and Bedarra Islands, and beyond them, the Great Barrier Reef. Mission Beach is set on a stretch of 14km of coastline that includes Garners Beach, Bingil Bay, Narragon Beach, Clump Point and Wongaling Beach.

Four villages comprise the Mission Beach area: South Mission Beach, Bingil Bay, Wongaling Beach and Mission Beach. The region's attractions include 14km of pristine beaches, Dunk Island, the offshore Reef, rainforests, and rafting on the Tully River. The main activities in Mission Beach involve water sports and reef viewing. Trips can also be taken to these popular environmental destinations: Tully Gorge, Hinchinbrook Island, Murray Falls and the Atherton Tablelands. Mission Beach Tourism can be found at Porter Promenade, and they can be called on (07) 4068 7066.

Tully

With a population of around 3000, Tully is set at the foot of

Mt Tyson and is the centre of a large sugar cane and banana growing region. The Tully River rapids provide some very fine whitewater rafting and canoeing, and there is plenty of fishing for enthusiasts. There is a definite Wet Season which begins in December and peaks in March. During this period it can rain every day, and sometimes all day. The Kareeya State Forest is accessible via a spectacular drive up the Tully River gorge. The Tully Visitor and Heritage Centre is on the Bruce Highway in Tully, *(07) 4068 2288*.

Cardwell

Cardwell is a fishing village situated between the mountains and the sea. It is in the middle of a natural wonderland, with world heritage rainforests, waterfalls, swimming holes, wilderness tracks, white-water rafting, canoeing, crabbing, fishing and prawning. The Cardwell lookout offers panoramic coastal views and there are very scenic drives to Murray Falls, Blencoe Falls, the Edmund Kennedy National Park, Dalrymple's Gap Track and Cardwell Forest.

Cardwell is also the gateway to Hinchinbrook Island, the world's largest Island National Park. Edmund Kennedy National Park nestles into the coastline about 4km north of the township. Its features a range from mangrove swamps to open woodland to pristine rainforest. Nearby natural wonders also include Tully Gorge, Dalrymple's Gap, and Murray, Blencoe and Wallaman Falls (Australia's highest single-drop falls at 305m).

Paluma

Located 61km north of Townsville and 40km south of Ingham on the Bruce Highway, the Paluma Range is the rainforest capital of the region. The Mount Spec Road turns towards the mountains of the Paluma Range, following the southern boundary of Mount Spec National Park. The road was built mainly by hand during the Great Depression.

Dunk Island

Dunk Island, across the bay from Mission Beach, is mostly National Park land, but there is one luxury resort. The island is shaped by rolling hills and deep valleys. Dunk Island is also part of the Family Group of Islands, and is very much a family resort. There are 13km of walking tracks, and the 10km walk around the island rates among the best of any on the Barrier Reef islands.

The Great Barrier Reef is an hour away by Quickcat, the high-speed catamaran, and there are four reefs to dive: Beaver, Farquharson, Yamacutta and Potter. Trips to Beaver Reef include glass bottom boat, semi-submersible rides, lunch and onboard dive instruction. Contact the Dunk Island Resort directly on *(07) 4068 8199*.

Bedarra Island

Part of the Family Group of Islands, Bedarra lies about 6km south of Dunk Island and about 5km offshore. It is privately-owned and is shown on marine charts as Richards Island. Bedarra has an area of one square kilometre, and is a rain-forest with natural springs and plenty of water. It has some very good sandy beaches, and trips can be made to the Great Barrier Reef. The Bedarra Island Resort can be contacted on *(07) 4068 8233*.

Hinchinbrook Island

Hinchinbrook is the world's largest island national park, with over 45,000 hectares of tropical rainforests, mountains, gorges, valleys, waterfalls and sandy beaches. It is one of the most beautiful tropical islands in the world and offers some of the best bushwalking in Australia. A magnificent jagged mountain range drops to warm seas and coral reefs, dominating the skyline. The rainforests offer spectacular views. The island is separated from the mainland by Hinchinbrook Channel, a narrow mangrove-fringed strip of water that is very deep. Information be obtained from the National Parks and Wildlife Service in Cardwell (near the jetty), *(07) 4066 8601*. Or alternatively, call the Island Resort on *(07) 4066 8585*.

Orpheus Island

This island is mostly national park, but has a secluded resort at one end. Encircled by wide beaches and a warm shallow sea, Orpheus Island has an area of 14sq km and is the second largest in the Palm Island group. There are a few beaches on the island, although some, such as Hazard Bay and Pioneer Bay, are only suitable for swimming at high tide. Mangrove Bay and Yankee Bay are good places to swim at low tide. Good reefs are found off Pelorus Island to the north and Fantome Island to the south. The Orpheus Island Resort can be called on *(07) 4777 7377*.

Magnetic Island

Magnetic lies 8km across Cleveland Bay from Townsville,

Sunset over the Whitsunday Islands

Charters Towers

fifteen minutes by catamaran. It is roughly triangular in shape and has an area of 52 sq km. With 16 beaches, plenty of reasonably-priced places to stay, and an ideal climate, this is one of the most popular islands on the Reef. It is one of the largest islands on the Great Barrier Reef and draws millions of holiday-makers, with 70 percent of it National Park.

A high spine of mountains covered by forests of eucalypts and wattles, and strewn with granite boulders, runs across the island. Below the peaks lie sheltered white beaches, rocky coves and coral reefs. The four small settlements of Picnic Bay, Nelly Bay, Arcadia and Horseshoe Bay offer a plentiful range of services for the visitor. Contact the Magnetic Harbour Accommodation and Tours, Shop 1 Nelly Bay Ferry Terminal, *(07) 4758 1862.*

Home Hill and Ayr

The twin towns of Home Hill and Ayr are 90km south of Townsville on the Bruce Highway, and sit either side of the delta of the Burdekin River, slightly inland from the coast. The Burdekin is the main waterway of the Magnetic North, and its catchment area includes the mountains to the north and the goldfields to the west. Cape Upstart National Park, some 70km from town, is an imposing granite headland rising from the sea. The Burdekin Tourist Information Centre is in Plantation Park, on the Bruce Highway, Ayr, *(07) 4783 5988.*

Charters Towers

The Outback is just on the other side of the mountains. If wishing to divert from a coastal holiday for a while, the old gold rush town of Charters Towers can be reached 135km south-west of Townsville on the Flinders Highway. Historic buildings line the streets and remnants of the gold mining era dot the surrounding countryside. Ravenswood is about 60km east of Charters Towers, and is another heritage gold rush town. Contact the Charters Towers Information Centre, 74 Mosman Street, Charters Towers, *(07) 4752 0314.*

The Hinterland

The Hinterland is to the north, sweeping towards the Gulf. Volcanoes once peppered the area, and the vast underground Undara Lava Tubes have become a notable attraction. The Undara Lava Lodge is available for accomodation, call *(07) 4097 1411* or *1800 990 992.* The website *www.undara-experience.com.au,* can also be visited.

Bowen

Situated just north of the Whitsunday Islands, Bowen is a town where the ocean laps the edges of the main street. It is 210km south of Townsville on the Bruce Highway, and has one of the best climates in Australia. Bowen's stunning coastline encapsulates its attraction for visitors, and of particular note are the idyllic Horseshoe and Murray bays. Queens Beach is also a popular haven. Inland, Don River Plain is a fruit growing region. The Bowen Visitor Information Centre is at Mount Bowen, *(07) 4786 4222.*

QLD
Tropical North Queensland Region

The Tropical North Queensland region is a vast area that stretches from reefs and islands through to coastal wetlands and mountains, tablelands and Gulf Savannah grasslands. The tropical city of Cairns is the main location in the region.

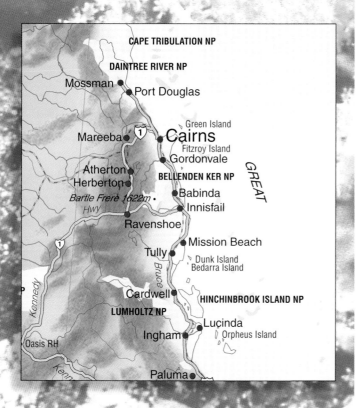

Cairns   Population: 123,760. Climate: Average temperature: January max 32°C - min 24°C; July max 25°C - min 16°C.

The main city in the far north of Queensland and 1757km from Brisbane, Cairns was named as the nation's most livable regional centre in 1995. The consistently warm weather has meant that Cairns has grown popular with tourists over the last 20 years, and it proclaims itself to be the safest tropical city in the world. Cairns has recorded the second highest rate of population growth of any Australian city since 1979, and is a major service centre for the surrounding areas. The physical surroundings of Cairns could be appropriately described as tropical: situated on the shores of the Trinity Inlet, the backdrop is a magnificent collection of rugged mountains and thick tropical rainforests. There are a number of different ways that visitors can enjoy the tropical surrounds of the area – deep-sea fishing, reef tours and snorkelling, indigenous culture, as well as visits to nearby locations like Kuranda and the Atherton Tablelands.

Captain Cook was the first to discover Cairns in 1770, sailing into the inlet on Trinity Sunday. Yet it wasn't until a good 100 years later that the area was finally settled by Europeans, with the discovery of gold at Palmer River meaning that port facilities were required at Cooktown. As gold discoveries continued far north Queensland it became obvious that a more efficient route to the coast was necessary. A prospector named Bill Smith had in the past worked as a fisherman at Trinity Bay, and was convinced it could offer sufficient port facilities. Smith cut a path from the Bay to the Hodgkinson River goldfields in 1876, and was rewarded for his pioneering ways when the town of Smithfield was named after him.

Trinity Bay was declared a port later that same year, but was quickly renamed in honour of the Queensland Governor William Cairns. While the new settlement was somewhat dwarfed by the success of the nearby Smithfield, that settlement was actually destroyed by a flood on the Barron River in 1867. With its pesky neigbouring settlement out of the way, Cairns still took a while to establish itself – most of the population from the destroyed Smithfield chose to resettle in Port Douglas, taking in effect all the maritime business away from Cairns. Things were rough for residents over the next several years, yet the town was revived by the establishment of nearby sugar plantations in the early 1880's.

A portion of the Great Barrier Reef

Cairns became a city in 1923, but it was the building of an international airport in 1984 that established it as a major tourist destination.

The city's International Airport is now the nation's sixth busiest in terms of passenger movements, and Cairns is also rated the third most popular tourist destination in Australia after Sydney and Melbourne. As a reflection of this, more than 3 million international and domestic pasenger movements occurred during 2002 and 2003. The nightlife of Cairns comes alive after dark with nightclubs, restaurants, night markets and the casino merely some of the attractions on offer. Some of the best places to soak up the tropical weather of Cairns include the white sands of Palm Cove, Clifton Beach, Kewarra Beach and Trinity Beach. Cairns also considers itself to be the unnofficial custodian of two of Australia's most famous World Heritage listed attractions, the Great Barrier Reef and the Wet Tropics Rainforest.

Visitor Information:
The Cairns Visitors Information Centre is at 51 The Esplanade, near the pier complex. Their phone number is *(07) 4051 3588*, and the email address is *info@tropicalaustralia.com.au*. Visit the website at *www.tropicalaustralia.com.au*.

Points of Interest:
The Flecker Botanical Gardens are open daily and feature graded walking tracks through natural rainforest to Mount Whitfield. From here there are excellent views of the city and coastline. The gardens can be found on Collins Avenue in Edge Hill, *(07) 4044 3398*.

The Centenary Lakes are an extension of Flecker Botanic Gardens, and were created to mark the city's centenary in 1976. There are two lakes – one fresh water, the other salt. Bird life abounds and barbecue facilities have been provided. The 610 metre high Mount Mooroobool in the background is the city's highest peak. The Centenary Lakes can be found at Greenslopes Street in Cairns North.

The Esplanade is 5km long and runs along the side of the bay. This park-like area is a very pleasant place to relax in.

Cairns - View of Trinity Bay

The Mount Whitfield Conservation Park is one of the highest points in the surrounding areas, at a height of 364 metres. Located near the Cairns Botanic Gardens, the park consists of rainforest and open eucalypt areas, as well as native birds. Call Queensland Parks and Wildlife for more information, *(07) 4046 6600.*

The Pier Marketplace hosts live entertainment daily, and is the departure point for most reef cruises and fishing boat charters. Sit on the verandah for a quick snack or a delicious meal from one of the many food outlets, while checking out the magnificent views over the Trinity Inlet.

The Reef Hotel Casino offers a ritzy and entertaining (as well as potentially expensive) experience for visitors. Situated right in the centre of the city with picturesque views of the surrounds, the casino has a 128 room capacity. The casino is located at 35-41 Wharf Street, and can be called on *(07) 4030 8888.*

The Cairns Regional Gallery is the largest gallery of its type in Queensland, and is located in one of the city's historic buildings. With a diverse range of artworks from local, national, international and indigenous artists on display, the gallery can be found on the corner of Abbott and Shield Street, *(07) 4031 6865.*

The Cairns Convention Centre on the corner of Wharf & Sheridan Streets may be hosting a function at the time of visiting, and can be called on *(07) 4042 4200.*

The Royal Flying Doctor Visitor Centre has fully guided tours, film shows, and displays of the history and present operations of this legendary service. Located at 1 Junction Street in Edge Hill, Call *(07) 4053 5687.*

Outlying Towns and Features

Green Island

The island has an area of 15 hectares and is 27km north-east of Cairns. It is a true coral cay surrounded by coral reefs, and has the only 5-star resort on a coral cay in Great Barrier Reef Marine Park. The waters abound with sea life, and the beach is quite beautiful. It only takes about 20 minutes to walk around the island, passing tropical vegetation, fringing casuarinas and pandanus. The Green Island Resort can be contacted on *(07) 4031 3300*.

Marlin Coast - Northern Beaches

The Marlin Coast area extends from Machans Beach, at the mouth of the Barron River 13km north of Cairns to Ellis Beach, passing by Holloways Beach, Yorkeys Knob, Clifton Beach, Palm Cove and Kewarra Beach. Trinity Beach and Clifton Beach are popular holiday destinations, and Palm Cove and Kewarra Beach have international resorts. Water-sporters can hire catamarans, windsurfers and surf skis at most of the major beaches in the area. The Tourist Information Centre for Cairns should be contacted for information on the Marlin Coast.

Port Douglas

The 83km drive north from Cairns to Port Douglas covers some of the most spectacular coastal strips and beaches in

Australia. The Captain Cook Highway is wedged between towering, lush forest-covered mountains and the Coral Sea. Situated 6km east of the highway, Port Douglas is one of the closest towns to the Great Barrier Reef. It has all the charm of a fishing port tastefully combined with modern tourism facilities. The Port Douglas Tourist Information Centre is in 23 Macrossan Street, *(07) 4099 5599*, and the website is *www.portdouglas.com*.

Mossman

171km south of Cooktown and only 20km north of Port Douglas, Mossman is in the heart of the Mossman Valley. It is a sugar town surrounded by green mountains (highest is Mt Demi, 1159 metres) and fields of sugar cane. Mossman is fast becoming well-known as a centre for exotic tropical fruit growing, and a number of farms conduct tours and offer their products for sale. The business centre of the Douglas Shire, Mossman has wide tree-lined streets, colourful gardens and a large sugar mill.

A few minutes' drive from the township, a sealed road leads to the Mossman Gorge in Daintree National Park. This is a wilderness area of 56,000 hectares, with crystal clear

Treks to the north can only be done by 4WD

running streams, waterfalls, walking tracks through towering rainforest, barbecue picnic sites and a unique suspension bridge over a steep ravine.

Daintree and Cape Tribulation

25km north of Mossman and about 146km south of Cooktown lies the township of Daintree, nestled in the heart of the Daintree River catchment basin, surrounded entirely by the rainforest-clad McDowall Ranges. The Daintree National Park lies to the west and Cape Tribulation National Park to the east; both have flourished largely unspoilt for millions of years. Cape Tribulation, where the rainforest meets the reef, is an increasingly popular tourist area for both camping and day visits. Crystal clear creeks and forests festooned with creepers and vines, palm trees, orchids, butterflies and cassowaries, are part of the Cape Tribulation experience in one of the country's finest rainforest areas.

There are several resorts, hostels and camping grounds. The atmosphere is relaxed and 'alternative' in this tropical rainforest retreat. It is a very popular haven for backpackers. The real attraction, however, is the National Park itself. Given the majestic quality of the natural environment, the emphasis here is on eco-touring. Several cruises operate on the Daintree River. offering passengers a leisurely tour observing the beauty of the river and rainforest, and enjoying morning or afternoon tea. The Daintree Tourist Information Centre is located at 5 Stewart Street, *(07) 4098 6120.*

Cooktown

Cooktown is 246km north of Cairns. Its close proximity to Aboriginal culture, diverse wildlife, rainforests, unique land formations and extensive surrounding savannah, means that it can be described as the geographical intersection of Reef and Outback. The town is clustered on the banks of the scenic Endeavour River. Apart from the picturesque surrounds, it is worth exploring the historical buildings in Cooktown, including the old Post Office, Westpac Bank and the Sovereign Hotel. The Cooktown Tourism Association can be contacted on *(07) 4069 5381.*

Lizard Island

With an international reputation as the place for big game fishing, Lizard Island is 97km north-east of Cooktown and is basically a 1000 hectare National Park boasting pristine natural beauty. It has an area of 21 square kilometres, and is the most northerly of the Barrier Reef resort islands. It is 240km from Cairns, but close to the outer Barrier Reef, and has 23 beaches that are good for swimming and snorkelling, and a superb coral lagoon.

The Island is very remote and exclusive, with access only via a scenic air one-hour flight from Cairns Airport. Some believe that Lizard Island has the best diving along the Great Barrier Reef, and in fact it is surrounded by excellent coral reefs. The Ribbon Reefs lie only a 20 minute boat ride from the island. These are comprised of a string of ten coral ramparts that support an immense undersea world of living coral and sea animals, and the most spectacular underwater scenery.

Cape York

Located 2753km north of Brisbane at the northernmost tip of Australia, Cape York is a remote mainland area that is almost 1000km from Cairns. Like an outstretched finger the peninsula points towards the south coast of Papua New Guinea, just over 100km away on the other side of the Torres Strait. The Jardine National Park hugs the eastern portion of the Peninsula about 50km south of the Cape. Crocodile farming, pearl farming, black boar hunting, barramundi fishing, and Aboriginal Corroborees at Bamaga Mission are just a few of the unique attractions Cape York has to offer. The web pages to explore are *www.tnq.org.au* and *www.visitcapeyork.com*, or call the Cooktown Tourism Association on *(07) 4069 5381.*

One view of the Cape York area

QLD
Outback Queensland Region

The Outback Queensland region is an expansive area that begins to extend north from where the state borders on New South Wales, and stretches all the way to Gulf country.

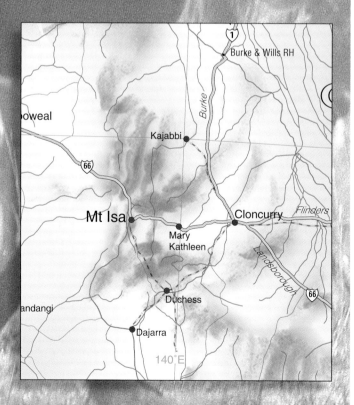

Mount Isa Population: 20,000. Climate: Mount Isa has two distinct seasons - The Wet and The Dry. The Wet lasts from December to March with an average rainfall of 250mm. Average temperatures: January max 37°C - min 24°C; July max 24°C - min 10°C.

Situated in the Selwyn Range and 1829 km from Brisbane, the city of Mount Isa is the region's only relief from the unending flatness of the surrounding outback. A modern mining town with Australia's largest underground mine, the mining industry dominates both the local economy and the city skyline. As the area is one of the few places in the world were silver, lead, copper and zinc can be found in close proximity, Mount Isa Mines Ltd is considered one of the world's most cost efficient and smoothly run source of resources. Around 350,000 tonnes are extracted from the mines every day, and Mount Isa is the world's biggest single source of silver and lead, as well as being amongst the top ten producers of copper and zinc.

The Kalkadoon were the first to exploit the rich resources of the area, producing a large number of axes and other tools to use in trade. With the site of Mount Isa located in an isolated area of the Queensland outback, it wasn't until 1923 that any Europeans showed any interest in settlement. A prospector by the name of John Campbell Miles uncovered the vast ore deposits at the site, a spot which is now marked by an obelisk. Claims from prospectors began to pile in not long after that, but by 1925 they had all been amalgamated into Mount Isa Mines Ltd, the company which still controls the resources to this day. While the site's remote isolation and lack of facilities proved a problem during early settlement, MIM arrived to address these issues in 1927. The construction of a rail link to Townsville two years later provided further assistance, and the resources continued to drive the town's economy for the rest of the twentieth century. Mount Isa was eventually declared a city in 1968.

Though associated with a "tougher" atmosphere than coastal cities due to the harshness of the surrounding outback, the people of Mount Isa have endeavoured to provide themselves with as many of the necessary facilities as possible. The focal point of the town is the mine and the stacks – the lead smelter stack is 266m high, and can be seen for miles around. With Mount Isa Mines Limited being Queensland's largest single industrial enterprise, they are responsible for employing one in five of the city's population. Mount Isa is also the point from which to access the spectacular Lawn Hill Gorge National Park and the world-heritage listed Riversleigh Fossil Fields. One of the most scenic parks in Queensland, the Lawn Hill National Park is comprised of spectacular gorge country and sandstone ranges.

Visitor Information:

Outback at Mount Isa is located at 19 Marian Street, *(07) 4749 1555*. There is a website at *www.outbackatisa.com.au*, or email the centre at *admin@outbackatisa.com.au*.

Points of Interest:

The Mount Isa Mines can be toured by those wishing to have a look at what has sustained the town's economy. Surface tours of the Isa Mines show travel through mine shafts, workshops, mills, smelters and past those huge stacks that dominate the skyline, giving an insight into some of the processes of the industry and the equipment used. Underground tours can no longer be taken, except for the purpose built Hard Times Mine within Outback at Mount Isa. Call *(07) 4749 1555* for more information.

Mt Isa at night

The City Lookout in Hilary Street offers a 360 degree panoramic view of the city and mine area. It is worth a second visit at sunset or later, when the lights of the mine are a spectacle in themselves. The lookout has a global signpost, with distances to cities all over the world, further proof that Mount Isa is a long way from everywhere.

The Royal Flying Doctor Service Base has a display and film of the Service's history to the present day. The School of the Air in the RFDS Base complex also gives visitors an insight into radio and telephone use that augments correspondence education for primary school children of the Outback. The base is located at 11 Barkly Highway, they can be called on *(07) 4743 2800*.

Lake Moondarra is a sanctuary and the regular water storage for Mount Isa. There are barbecue facilities, children's play area, safe swimming, canoeing, sailing, water-skiing and a kiosk. The lake can be found 15.5km north of the city off the Barkly Highway.

The Riversleigh Fossils Display is an award winning attraction that has amazing fossil discoveries of World Heritage listing significance. Some of the specimens date back

Stockman's Hall of Fame, Longreach

30 million years. The display can be found within Outback at Mount Isa on West Street, call *(07) 4749 1555*.

The Kalkadoon Tribal Centre and Cultural Keeping Place has artefacts of the fierce fighting tribe indigenous to this area. They are located in Marian Street next to the Tourist Information Centre.

Longreach Population: 3,800

Located 1181km north west of Brisbane and 687km west from Rockhampton, the town of Longreach is at the centre of one of Queensland's biggest beef and wool areas. The focus on grazing can be traced right back to the beginning of the town's history, but the town is particularly remembered for being one of the original headquarters of QANTAS. Celebrating this heritage is the QANTAS Founders Outback Museum, *(07) 4658 3737*, which traces the history of the famous Australian airline.

Another attraction in Longreach is The Australian Stockman's Hall of Fame and Outback Heritage Centre, *(07) 4658*

2166, which is dedicated to the story of Australia's unsung heroes, the men and women who opened up the outback. With a statue of a stockman located right outside, $12.5 million was spent establishing the centre and it has become a premier tourist destination for the town.

Visitor Information:
The Longreach Visitor Information Centre can be found in Qantas Park on Eagle Street, and they can be phoned on *(07) 4658 3555*.

Outlying Towns

Camooweal

Situated 188km west of Mount Isa, Camooweal is only a few kilometres from the Northern Territory border. It is a supply town for large cattle stations in the vast outback border area. During the 1880's it was an important stop on the great cattle droves, and today the road trains, which transport the cattle to the coast, still stop at Camooweal.

Lawn Hill National Park

Also known as Boodjamulla, this fertile National Park has a spectacular gorge, scenic sandstone ranges, thriving vegetetation and freshwater springs. The main activities are canoeing and walking. A number of rewarding walking trails, from 2-7km in distance, are outlined on a detailed pamphlet by Queensland Parks & Wildlife, available from the Visitor Centre in Mt Isa. To book camp sites, *(07) 4748 5572*.

Mary Kathleen

The now deserted town of Mary Kathleen is 60km east of Mount Isa. It was established in the 1950s to mine the then largest known deposit of uranium in Australia. The mine was closed in 1963, reopened in 1976 and modernised, then finally closed again in 1982.

Cloncurry

Locally known as 'The Curry', Cloncurry is 124km east of Mount Isa. The surrounding hills hide many old ghost towns, and ruins of early copper mines. The area was a big copper producer until Mount Isa was developed. It was here in 1928 that the Flying Doctor Service had its beginnings, and a Cloister of Plaques has been erected to commemorate its pioneers on the site where the first pedal wireless call for help was received

On the Burke Development Road, 378km north of Cloncurry, is Normanton, the main centre for the Carpentaria Shire. The town was established in 1868, and has a population around 930. It is situated on the Norman River, 50km from the coast as the crow flies, and was once an important port. The wharf has long since rotted away, and the cattle are now transported to the eastern seaboard by cattle trains. Here is found the only rail line not linked to the main system in Queensland, and once a week there is a service between Glenore and Croydon, a distance of 132km.

Winton

Situated 343km south-east of Cloncurry on the Landsborough Highway, Winton was the birthplace of QANTAS. The Queensland and Northern Territory Air Service had its first registered office in Winton in 1920, but moved to Longreach, 180km south-east. Winton is synonymous with sheep, and there is a cairn on Winton's town common that commemorates the Great Shearers' Strike of 1891-4. In nearby Elderslie Street is Herb Young's wagon, the last horse drawn wagon to bring wool to Winton's railhead. Road trains now bring cattle from the Channel Country and the Northern Territory to the railway.

Banjo Paterson wrote "Waltzing Matilda" at Dagworth Station in the Winton area in 1895, and a statue of a swagman has been erected in commemoration near the swimming pool. In Elderslie Street is the Waltzing Matilda Centre, *(07) 4657 1466*, a large complex housing Station Store, the Billabong Complex, the Home of the Legend exhibition, the Qantilda Museum, the Outback Regional Art Gallery, and the Coolibah Country Kitchen Restaurant. Contact the Centre for further information on the town.

Karumba

Situated on the mouth of the Norman River and 2,501 km from Brisbane, Karumba is at the centre of a $10 million prawning industry. The trawlers bring the prawns to Karumba, and there they are snap frozen and air freighted to the southern states and overseas.

A buckjumper at a local Rodeo

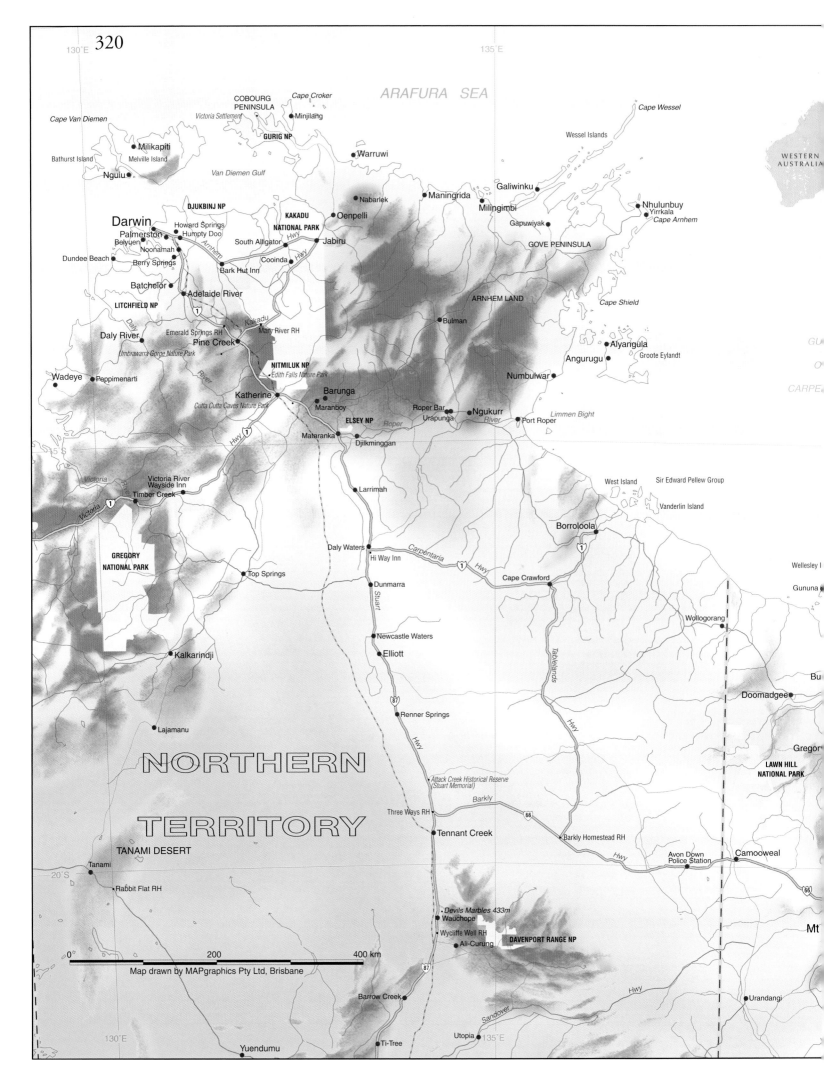

130°E 135°E

ARAFURA SEA

Cape Van Diemen
Cape Croker
COBOURG PENINSULA
Victoria Settlement
GURIG NP
Minjilang
Cape Wessel
Wessel Islands
Milikapiti
Melville Island
Bathurst Island
Warruwi
Nguiu
Van Diemen Gulf
Galiwinku
Maningrida
Milingimbi
Nhulunbuy
Yirrkala
Cape Arnhem
DJUKBINJ NP
Nabarlek
Darwin
Howard Springs
Palmerston
Humpty Doo
KAKADU NATIONAL PARK
Oenpelli
Gapuwiyak
GOVE PENINSULA
Belyuen
Noonamah
South Alligator
Jabiru
Dundee Beach
Berry Springs
Cooinda
Bark Hut Inn
Batchelor
Adelaide River
ARNHEM LAND
Cape Shield
LITCHFIELD NP
Bulman
Daly River
Emerald Springs RH
Mary River RH
Pine Creek
Alyangula
Angurugu
Groote Eylandt
Umbrawarra Gorge Nature Park
NITMILUK NP
Edith Falls Nature Park
Numbulwar
Wadeye
Peppimenarti
Katherine
Barunga
Cutta Cutta Caves Nature Park
Maranboy
Roper Bar
Ngukurr
Urapunga
Port Roper
Limmen Bight
ELSEY NP
Roper River
Mataranka
Djilkminggan
West Island
Sir Edward Pellew Group
Larrimah
Vanderlin Island
Victoria River Wayside Inn
Timber Creek
Borroloola
Daly Waters
Hi Way Inn
Carpentaria Hwy
Cape Crawford
Wellesley I
Gununa
GREGORY NATIONAL PARK
Top Springs
Dunmarra
Newcastle Waters
Wollogorang
Elliott
Doomadgee
Kalkarindji
NORTHERN
Lajamanu
Renner Springs
LAWN HILL NATIONAL PARK
Gregor
TERRITORY
Attack Creek Historical Reserve (Stuart Memorial)
Barkly Hwy
Three Ways RH
TANAMI DESERT
Tennant Creek
Barkly Homestead RH
Avon Down Police Station
Camooweal
Tanami
Rabbit Flat RH
Devils Marbles 433m
Wauchope
Wycliffe Well RH
Ali-Curung
DAVENPORT RANGE NP
Mt
20°S
Barrow Creek
Sandover
Urandangi
Utopia
Yuendumu
Ti-Tree

0 200 400 km

Map drawn by MAPgraphics Pty Ltd, Brisbane

WESTERN AUSTRALIA

130°E 135°E

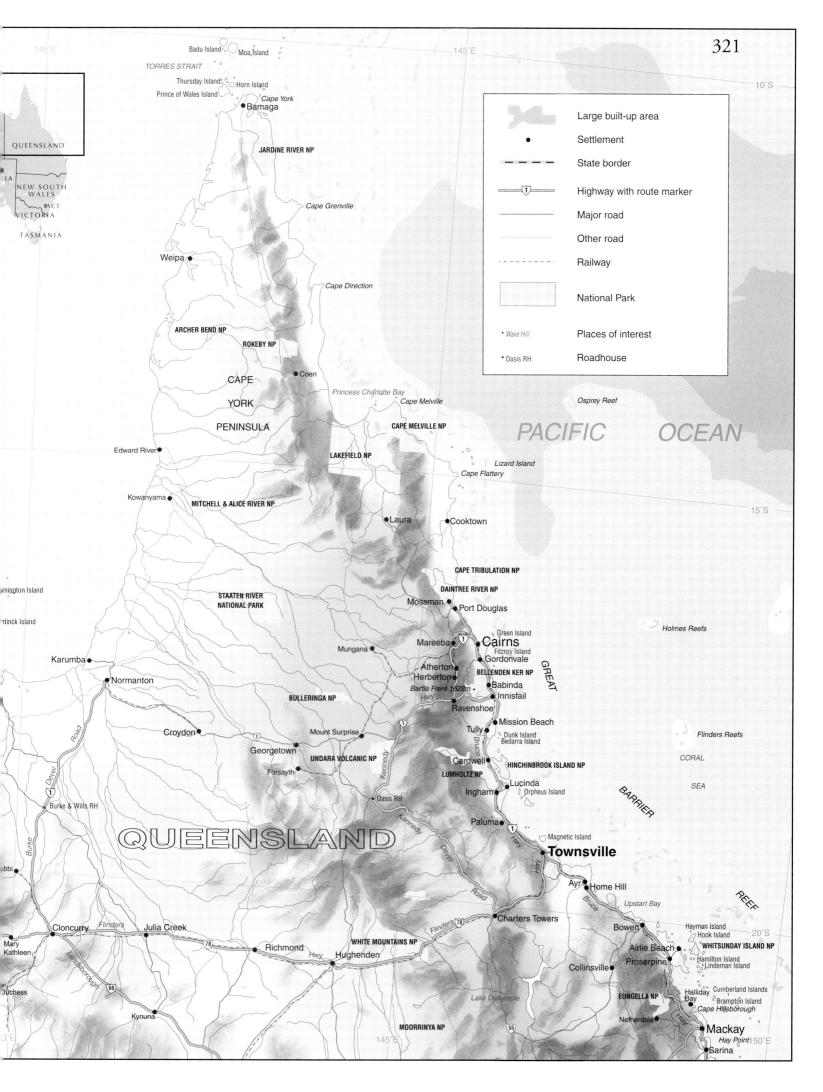

TORRES STRAIT

Badu Island   Moa Island

Thursday Island   Horn Island
Prince of Wales Island

Cape York
Bamaga

QUEENSLAND

NEW SOUTH
WALES
ACT
VICTORIA

TASMANIA

JARDINE RIVER NP

Cape Grenville

Weipa

Cape Direction

ARCHER BEND NP

ROKEBY NP

CAPE

YORK

PENINSULA

Coen

Princess Charlotte Bay

Cape Melville

Osprey Reef

CAPE MELVILLE NP

PACIFIC   OCEAN

Edward River

LAKEFIELD NP

Kowanyama

Cape Flattery
Lizard Island

15'S

MITCHELL & ALICE RIVER NP

Laura   Cooktown

rnington Island

CAPE TRIBULATION NP

DAINTREE RIVER NP

STAATEN RIVER
NATIONAL PARK

Mossman
Port Douglas

ntinck Island

Green Island
Mareeba   Cairns
Fitzroy Island
Gordonvale

Karumba   Mungana

Atherton
Herberton   BELLENDEN KER NP
Bartle Frere 1622m   Babinda
Hwy   Innisfail

Normanton

BULLERINGA NP

GREAT

Holmes Reefs

Ravenshoe

Croydon   Mount Surprise

Tully   Mission Beach
Dunk Island
Bedarra Island

Flinders Reefs

Georgetown

Cardwell   HINCHINBROOK ISLAND NP

CORAL

Forsayth   UNDARA VOLCANIC NP

LUMHOLTZ NP
Lucinda
Ingham   Orpheus Island

SEA

Oasis RH

Burke & Wills RH

Paluma

BARRIER

QUEENSLAND

Magnetic Island

Townsville

REEF

Ayr   Home Hill

Upstart Bay

bbi

Cloncurry   Flinders   Julia Creek

Charters Towers

Bowen

Hayman Island
Hook Island

20'S

Mary
Kathleen

Richmond   Hughenden

WHITE MOUNTAINS NP

Airlie Beach   WHITSUNDAY ISLAND NP

Hamilton Island
Lindeman Island

Collinsville   Proserpine

uchess

66

EUNGELLA NP

Halliday
Bay   Cumberland Islands
Brampton Island
Cape Hillsborough

Kynuna

MOORRINYA NP

55

Netherdale

Mackay
Hay Point

145'E   150'E

Sarina

Legend

	Large built-up area
●	Settlement
– – –	State border
—①—	Highway with route marker
——	Major road
—	Other road
- - -	Railway
▭	National Park
• Wave Hill	Places of interest
• Oasis RH	Roadhouse

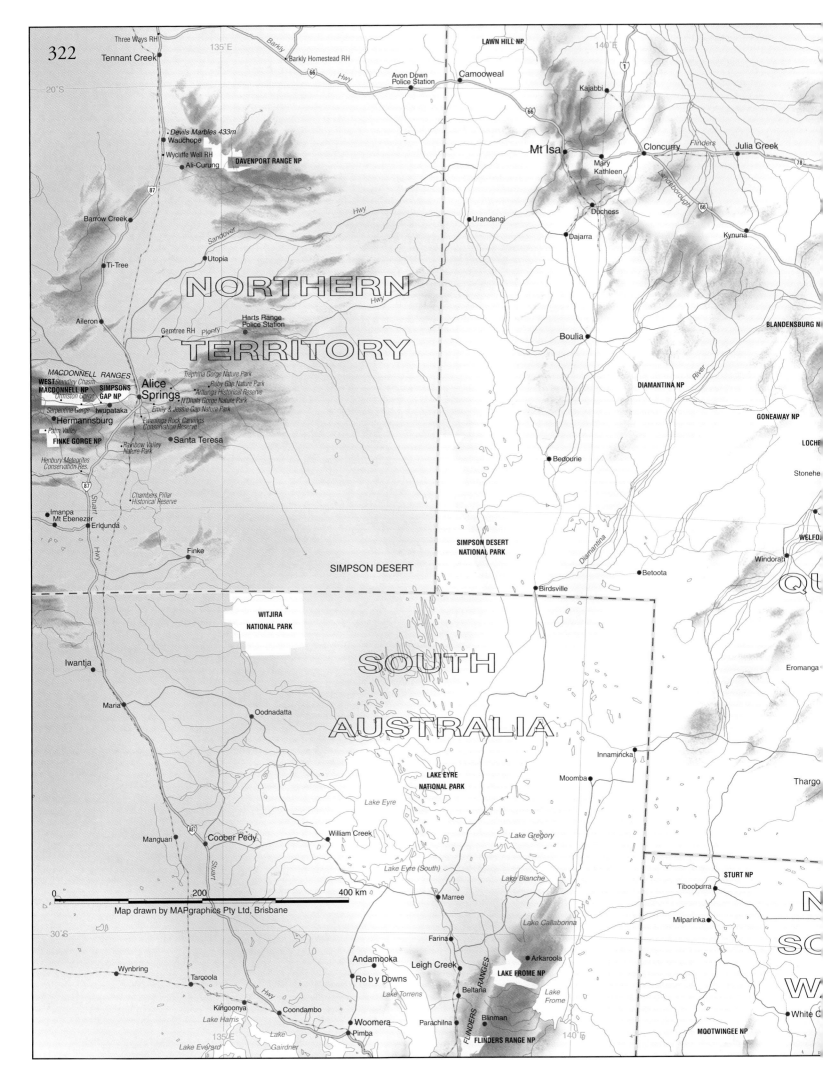

Three Ways RH
135°E
20°S
Tennant Creek
Barkly
Barkly Homestead RH
LAWN HILL NP
140°E
66
Hwy
Avon Down
Police Station
Camooweal
Mt Isa
Kajabbi
Cloncurry
Flinders
Julia Creek
66
78
Devils Marbles 433m
Wauchope
Wycliffe Well RH
Ali-Curung
DAVENPORT RANGE NP
Mary
Kathleen
Duchess
87
Barrow Creek
Urandangi
Dajarra
Kynuna
Ti-Tree
Sandover
Utopia
Boulia
BLANDENSBURG N
NORTHERN
Aileron
Harts Range
Police Station
Gemtree RH Plenty
Hwy
TERRITORY
DIAMANTINA NP
River
MACDONNELL RANGES
Trephina Gorge Nature Park
WEST Standley Chasm
MACDONNELL NP SIMPSONS
Ormiston Gorge GAP NP
Alice
Springs
Ruby Gap Nature Park
Artlunga Historical Reserve
N'Dhala Gorge Nature Park
GONEAWAY NP
Serpentine Gorge Iwupataka
Hermannsburg
Emily & Jessie Gap Nature Park
Ewaninga Rock Carvings
Conservation Reserve
Santa Teresa
LOCHE
Palm Valley
FINKE GORGE NP
Rainbow Valley
Nature Park
Bedourie
Stonehe
Henbury Meteorites
Conservation Res.
87
Chambers Pillar
Historical Reserve
Imanpa
Mt Ebenezer
Erldunda
Stuart
Finke
SIMPSON DESERT
NATIONAL PARK
Diamantina
WELFO
Windorah
QU
Betoota
SIMPSON DESERT
Birdsville
WITJIRA
NATIONAL PARK
Iwantja
SOUTH
Eromanga
Maria
Oodnadatta
AUSTRALIA
Innamincka
Thargo
Moomba
LAKE EYRE
NATIONAL PARK
Manguari
A87
Coober Pedy
William Creek
Lake Eyre
Lake Gregory
Stuart
Lake Eyre (South)
Lake Blanche
STURT NP
0
200
400 km
Marree
Lake Callabonna
Tibooburra
Map drawn by MAPgraphics Pty Ltd, Brisbane
30°S
Milparinka
Farina
N
Wynbring
Andamooka
Leigh Creek
Arkaroola
SO
Tarcoola
Ro b y Downs
RANGES
LAKE FROME NP
Beltana
Lake Torrens
Lake
Frome
W
Kingoonya
Coondambo
135°E
Hwy
Parachilna Blinman
140°E
White C
Lake Harris
Woomera
Pimba
FLINDERS
RANGES
FLINDERS RANGE NP
MOOTWINGEE NP
Lake Everard
Lake
Gairdner

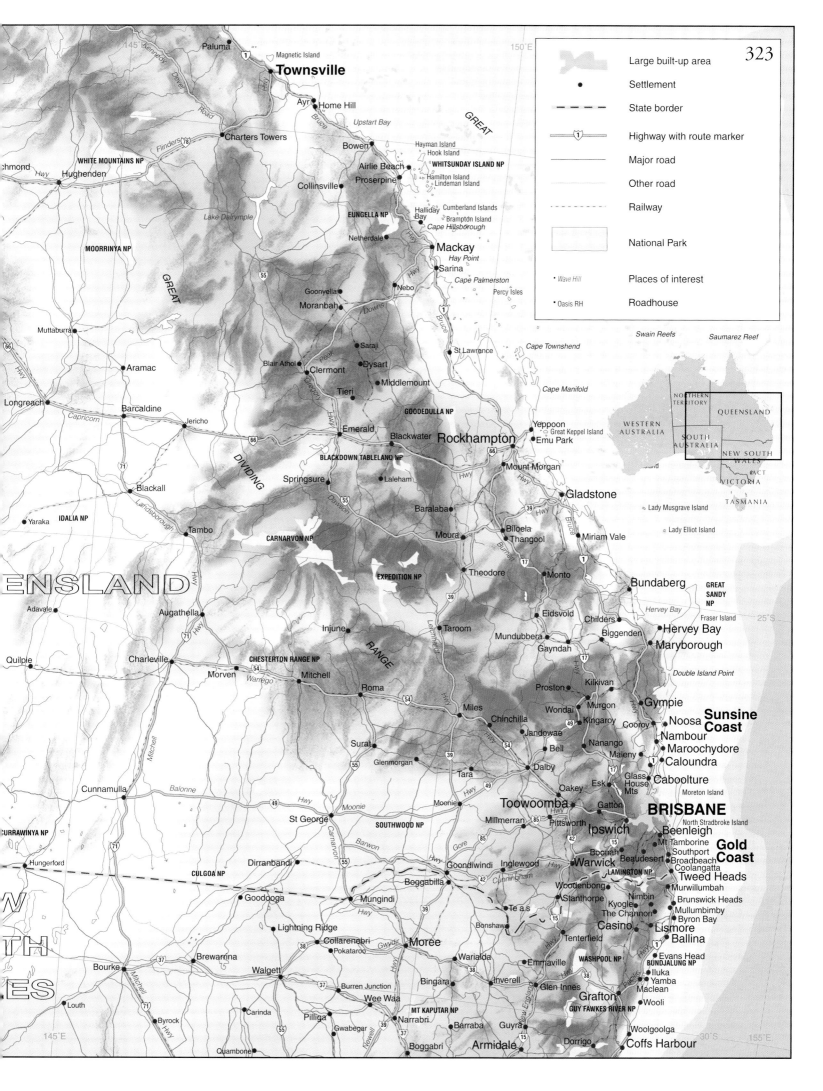

Map legend:

- Large built-up area
- Settlement
- State border
- ① Highway with route marker
- Major road
- Other road
- Railway
- National Park
- • *Wave Hill* — Places of interest
- • *Oasis RH* — Roadhouse

Paluma
Townsville
Magnetic Island
Ayr
Home Hill
Upstart Bay
Charters Towers
Bowen
Hayman Island
Hook Island
WHITE MOUNTAINS NP
Hughenden
Richmond
Airlie Beach
WHITSUNDAY ISLAND NP
Collinsville
Proserpine
Hamilton Island
Lindeman Island
MOORRINYA NP
EUNGELLA NP
Halliday Bay
Cumberland Islands
Brampton Island
Netherdale
Cape Hillsborough
Lake Dairymple
Mackay
Hay Point
Sarina
Cape Palmerston
Goonyella
Nebo
Percy Isles
Moranbah
Muttaburra
Aramac
Saraji
St Lawrence
Cape Townshend
Blair Athol
Dysart
Clermont
Middlemount
Cape Manifold
Tieri
Longreach
Barcaldine
Jericho
GOODEDULLA NP
Emerald
Blackwater
Rockhampton
Yeppoon
Great Keppel Island
Emu Park
BLACKDOWN TABLELAND NP
Springsure
Laleham
Mount Morgan
Blackall
Gladstone
Tambo
Baralaba
Yaraka
IDIALA NP
CARNARVON NP
Biloela
Thangool
Moura
Miriam Vale
Lady Musgrave Island
EXPEDITION NP
Theodore
Monto
Lady Elliot Island
Adavale
Bundaberg
GREAT SANDY NP
Augathella
Injune
Taroom
Eidsvold
Childers
Hervey Bay
Quilpie
Mundubbera
Biggenden
Maryborough
Gayndah
Charleville
Morven
Mitchell
CHESTERTON RANGE NP
Proston
Kilkivan
Double Island Point
Roma
Wondai
Murgon
Gympie
Surat
Chinchilla
Kingaroy
Cooroy
Noosa
Sunsine Coast
Jandowae
Nanango
Nambour
Glenmorgan
Bell
Maleny
Maroochydore
Cunnamulla
Tara
Dalby
Caloundra
Oakey
Esk
Glass House Mts
Caboolture
Moonie
Gatton
Moreton Island
St George
Toowoomba
BRISBANE
Millmerran
Pittsworth
Ipswich
Beenleigh
SOUTHWOOD NP
North Stradbroke Island
Goondiwindi
Inglewood
Mt Tamborine
Gold Coast
Dirranbandi
Boonah
Warwick
Beaudesert
Southport
Broadbeach
Coolangatta
Hungerford
CULGOA NP
Boggabilla
LAMINGTON NP
Tweed Heads
Woodenbong
Murwillumbah
Goodooga
Mungindi
Stanthorpe
Nimbin
Brunswick Heads
Kyogle
Mullumbimby
Te as
The Channon
Byron Bay
Lightning Ridge
Bonshaw
Casino
Lismore
Ballina
Collarenebri
Moree
Tenterfield
Pokataroo
Warialda
Evans Head
Bourke
Brewarrina
Emmaville
WASHPOOL NP
BUNDJALUNG NP
Iluka
Walgett
Bingara
Inverell
Yamba
Louth
Burren Junction
Glen Innes
Maclean
Byrock
Carinda
Wee Waa
Grafton
Wooli
GUY FAWKES RIVER NP
Pilliga
Narrabri
MT KAPUTAR NP
Barraba
Guyra
Woolgoolga
Gwabegar
Dorrigo
Quambone
Boggabri
Armidale
Coffs Harbour

ENSLAND

NORTHERN TERRITORY
WESTERN AUSTRALIA
QUEENSLAND
SOUTH AUSTRALIA
NEW SOUTH WALES
ACT
VICTORIA
TASMANIA

Swain Reefs
Saumarez Reef
Hervey Bay
Fraser Island

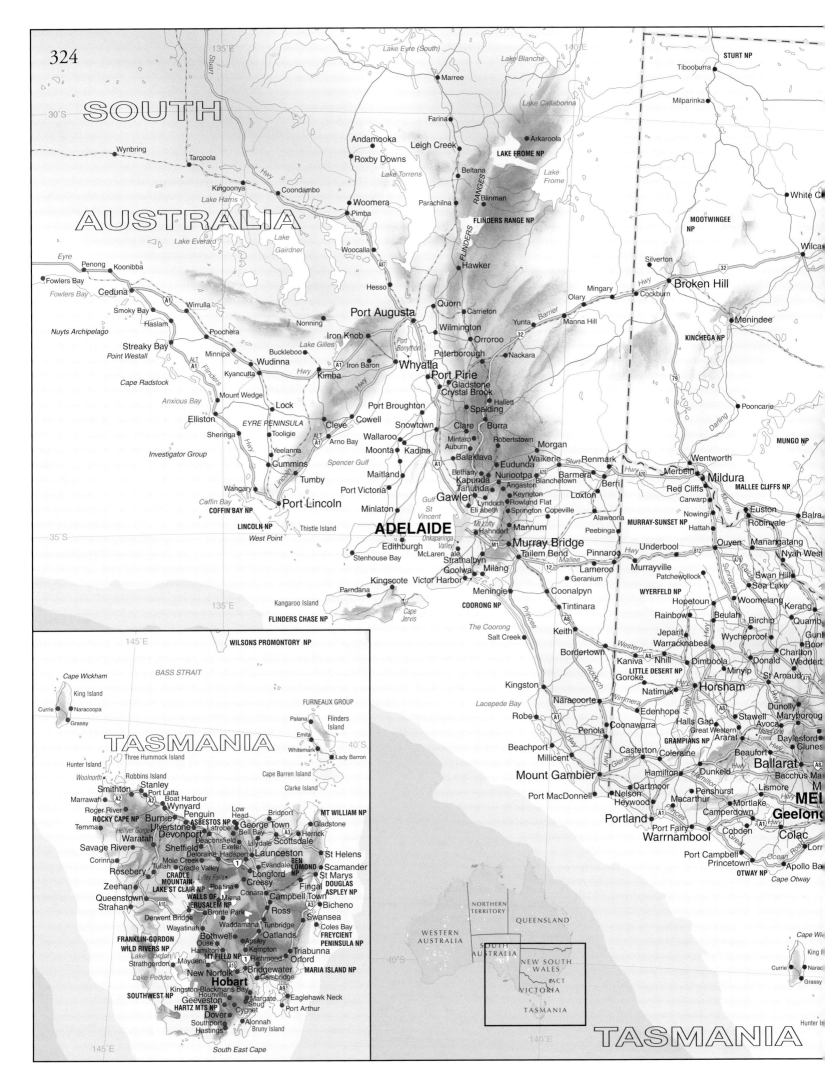

QUEENSLAND Dirranbandi
CULGOA NP

Goondiwindi Inglewood Warwick LAMINGTON NP **Gold Coast**
Boggabilla Woodenbong Stanthorpe Nimbin **Tweed Heads**
Texas Kyogle The Channon Murwillumbah
Bonshaw Nimbin Brunswick Heads
Goodooga Lightning Ridge Casino Mullumbimby
Collarenebri Tenterfield **Lismore** Byron Bay
Pokataroo Moree **Ballina**
Brewarrina Warialda Evans Head
Bourke Emmaville Glen Innes WASHPOOL NP Iluka
Walgett Bingara Inverell BUNDJALUNG NP Yamba
Burren Junction Maclean
Byrock Wee Waa **Grafton** Wooli
Louth Carinda Narrabri MT KAPUTAR NP Dorrigo GUY FAWKES RIVER NP
Pilliga Barraba Guyra Woolgoolga
Nyngan Gwabegar Manilla Uralla **Coffs Harbour**
Warren Coonamble Boggabri Hillgrove OXLEY WILD Sawtell
Quambone Baradine **Armidale** RIVERS NP Nambucca Heads
NEW Coonabarabran Gunnedah Macksville
Cobar WARRUMBUNGL NP **Tamworth** Walcha South West Rocks
SOUTH Gilgandra Werris Creek Kempsey
Warren Binnaway Quirindi Nundle Wauchope
WALES Tottenham Coolah Murrurundi Nowendoc **Port Mac uar ie**
Narromine **Dubbo** LIVERPOOL RANGE Camden Haven
Trangie Scone Wingham
Talleburg Wellington Merriwa Taree
Roto Fifield Yeoval Gulgong Denman Muswellbrook Gloucester Tuncurry
Peak Hill Mudgee Singleton Dungog **Forster**
WILLANDRA NP Euabalong Trundle WOLLEMI NP Maitland Bulahdelah
Lake Cargelligo Derriwong Yarrabandai Rylstone Kurri Kurri Nelson Bay
Hillston Condobolin Tichborne Hill End Kandos Cessnock Port Stephens
Tullibigeal Burcher Parkes Molong Sofala **Newcastle**
Naradhan Rankins Springs Forbes Manildra Ophir Portland Wyong Budgewoi
Eugowra Orange Lithgow Tuggerah Lakes
West Wyalong Weethalle Alleena Gooloogong Bathurst Blayney Richmond The Entrance
Griffith Whitton Ardlethan Barmedman Cargo Lyndhurst **Gosford**
Tabbita Grenfell Cowra Katoomba Leura **SYDNEY**
Hay Darlington Point Leeton Young Koorawatha Bigga BLUE MTS NP Broken Bay
Narrandera Temora Murringo Camden Port Jackson
Booligal Booroorban Coolamon Boorowa Crookwell Picton
Wanganella Morundah Cootamundra Murrumburrah Helensburgh
Junee Bethungra Murrumbateman Mittagong **Wollongong**
Jerilderie Lockhart **Wagga Wagga** Yass Bowral Shellharbour
Finley The Rock Gundagai Moss Vale **Kiama**
Mathoura Urana Oaklands Henty Tumut Goulburn Berry
Berrigan Culcairn Tumut Bomaderry **Nowra**
Tocumwal Mulwala Holbrook Tumbarumba MORTON NP Huskisson
Cobram Corowa **Albury** Jindera Adaminaby Tarago Jervis Bay
Kyabram Numurkah Chiltern **Wodonga** Khancoban **Canberra** Queanbeyan Ulladulla
Dookie Beechworth Mt Kosciuszko **ACT** Bredbo
Shepparton **Wangaratta** 2228m Batemans Bay
Violet Town Benalla Bright Perisher Valley Cooma Moruya
Euroa Myrtleford MT BUFFALO NP Thredbo Jindabyne Central Tilba Tuross Head
Mount Beauty Mt Bogong Cobargo Narooma
Seymour Mansfield 1986m KOSCIUSZKO NP Bega Bermagui
Alexandra Falls Creek Bombala Tathra
Yea Mount Buller Mt Hotham Omeo Delegate Merimbula
Eildon ALPINE NP Dargo Eden
Marysville GREAT Buchan
Craigieburn Healesville Warburton Bairnsdale Nowa Nowa Cann River
Cranbourne Dandenong Ranges Stratford Orbost Mallacoota
Drouin Maffra Lakes Entrance CROAJINGALONG NP
Hastings Tynong Sale Paynesville
Morwell Moe Traralgon Eagle Point **VICTORIA**
Bass Leongatha Seaspray
Wonthaggi Inverloch Foster Yarram

PACIFIC OCEAN

WILSONS PROMONTORY NP

TASMAN SEA

BASS STRAIT

FURNEAUX GROUP
Palana Flinders
Emita Island
Whitemark Lady Barron

ree Hummock Island

Stanley Cape Barren Island
Clarke Island

	Large built-up area
•	Settlement
– – –	State border
1	Highway with route marker
	Major road
	Other road
– · – · –	Railway
	National Park
• Wave Hill	Places of interest
• Oasis RH	Roadhouse

0   200   400 km

Map drawn by MAPgraphics Pty Ltd, Brisbane

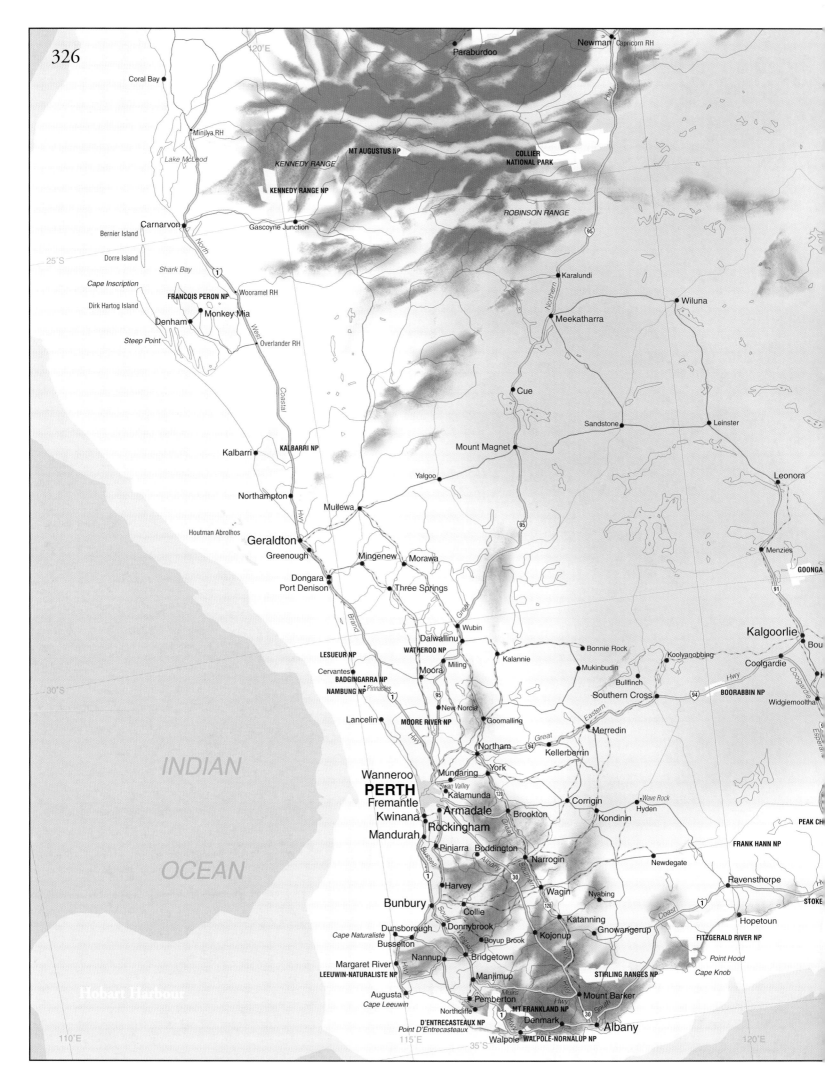

Coral Bay

Minilya RH

Lake McLeod

Paraburdoo

Newman Capricorn RH

MT AUGUSTUS NP

KENNEDY RANGE

COLLIER NATIONAL PARK

KENNEDY RANGE NP

ROBINSON RANGE

Carnarvon

Gascoyne Junction

Bernier Island

95

25°S

Dorre Island

Shark Bay

Karalundi

Cape Inscription

Wooramel RH

Wiluna

FRANCOIS PERON NP

Dirk Hartog Island

Meekatharra

Denham Monkey Mia

Steep Point

Overlander RH

Northern

Cue

Sandstone

Leinster

Kalbarri **KALBARRI NP**

Mount Magnet

Northampton

Yalgoo

Leonora

Houtman Abrolhos

Mullewa

95

Menzies

Geraldton

Greenough

Mingenew Morawa

GOONGA

Dongara
Port Denison

Three Springs

91

Great

Wubin

Kalgoorlie

Dalwallinu

Bonnie Rock

Koolyanobbing

Bou

LESUEUR NP

WATHEROO NP

Kalannie

Coolgardie

Cervantes

Moora Miling

Mukinbudin

Hwy

30°S

BADGINGARRA NP

Pinnacles

NAMBUNG NP

Bullfinch

Southern Cross

94

BOORABBIN NP

Widgiemooltha

New Norcia

Eastern

Coolgardie

Lancelin

MOORE RIVER NP

Goomalling

Merredin

Great

Northam

94 Kellerberrin

Wanneroo

Mundaring York

Swan Valley

PERTH

Kalamunda

Corrigin *Wave Rock*

Fremantle

120

Hyden

PEAK CH

Kwinana Armadale

Brookton

Kondinin

Rockingham

Great

Mandurah

Pinjarra Boddington

FRANK HANN NP

Narrogin

Newdegate

Albany

Harvey

30

Wagin

Nyabing

Ravensthorpe

Bunbury

Collie

Katanning

Coast

Hopetoun

Dunsborough Donnybrook

120

Gnowangerup

FITZGERALD RIVER NP

Cape Naturaliste

Busselton

Boyup Brook

Kojonup

Point Hood

Nannup Bridgetown

STIRLING RANGES NP

Cape Knob

Margaret River

Manjimup

LEEUWIN-NATURALISTE NP

Muirs

Mount Barker

MT FRANKLAND NP

Augusta

Pemberton

Cape Leeuwin

Northcliffe

Denmark

Albany

D'ENTRECASTEAUX NP

1

30

Point D'Entrecasteaux

Walpole **WALPOLE-NORNALUP NP**

35°S

INDIAN

OCEAN

Brand

North

West

Coastal

Hwy

Brand

1

95

1

120

Southern

Albany

South Western

Busselton

South

1

110°E 115°E 120°E

Hobart Harbour

STOKE

120°E

STOKE

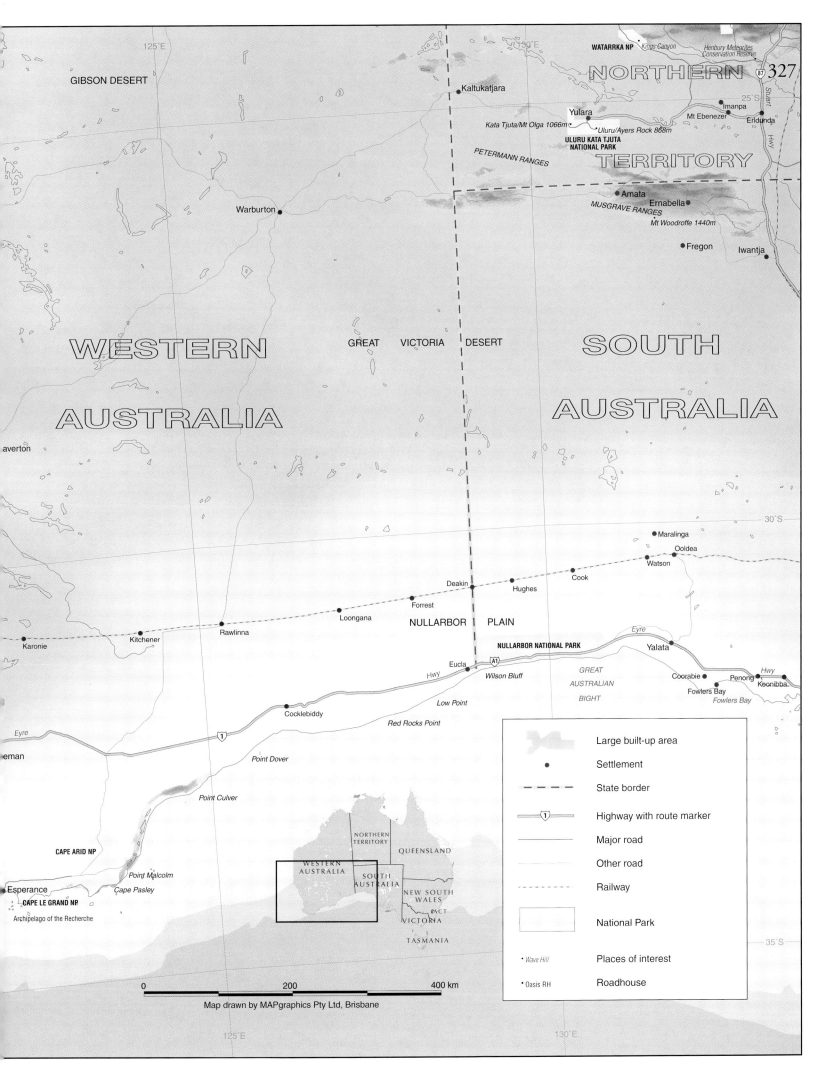

GIBSON DESERT

WATARRKA NP *Kings Canyon*   *Henbury Meteorites Conservation Reserve*

NORTHERN

Kaltukatjara

•Imanpa

Yulara
•Mt Ebenezer   •Erldunda
Kata Tjuta/Mt Olga 1066m   •*Uluru/Ayers Rock 868m*

ULURU KATA TJUTA NATIONAL PARK

PETERMANN RANGES

TERRITORY

•Amata   Ernabella•
MUSGRAVE RANGES

Warburton•

Mt Woodroffe 1440m

•Fregon   Iwantja•

WESTERN

GREAT   VICTORIA   DESERT

SOUTH

AUSTRALIA

AUSTRALIA

averton

•Maralinga
Ooldea•
Watson•

Deakin•
Hughes   Cook•

Forrest•

Loongana•   **NULLARBOR   PLAIN**

Eyre

Rawlinna•   **NULLARBOR NATIONAL PARK**   Yalata•

•Karonie
Kitchener•   Eucla•   *(A1)*
Wilson Bluff   Coorabie•   *Hwy*   Penong•
GREAT   Fowlers Bay•   Keonibba•
Cocklebiddy•   *Low Point*   *AUSTRALIAN*   *Fowlers Bay*
Hwy   *BIGHT*
Red Rocks Point

Eyre

Point Dover

eman

Point Culver

CAPE ARID NP

Esperance•   *Point Malcolm*
•   *Cape Pasley*
CAPE LE GRAND NP
Archipelago of the Recherche

NORTHERN TERRITORY   QUEENSLAND

WESTERN AUSTRALIA   SOUTH AUSTRALIA
NEW SOUTH WALES
ACT
VICTORIA
TASMANIA

	Large built-up area
•	Settlement
– – –	State border
①	Highway with route marker
—	Major road
—	Other road
· · · · ·	Railway
☐	National Park
• *Wave Hill*	Places of interest
• *Oasis RH*	Roadhouse

0   200   400 km

Map drawn by MAPgraphics Pty Ltd, Brisbane

115°E

120°E

INDIAN   OCEAN

0   200   400 km

Map drawn by MAPgraphics Pty Ltd, Brisbane

Legend

Large built-up area

• Settlement

State border

Highway with route marker

Major road

Other road

Railway

National Park

• *Wave Hill*   Places of interest

• *Oasis RH*   Roadhouse

NORTHERN TERRITORY

QUEENSLAND

WESTERN AUSTRALIA

SOUTH AUSTRALIA

NEW SOUTH WALES

ACT

VICTORIA

TASMANIA

15°S

Buccaneer Archipelago

Cape Leveque

Lombadina •

Cape Baskerville

DAMPIER LAND

Roebuck RH •

Broome •

Roebuck Bay

Cape Bossut

Northern

20°S

North West Shelf

Dampier Archipelago

Monte Bello Islands

Point Samson

Dampier •   Cossack

Karratha   Roebourne

Barrow Island

Eighty Mile Beach

Sandfire RH

Cape Keraudren

Poissonnier Point   Pardo RH

Port Hedland •

Cape Thouin   *Great*

Shay Gap •

Marble Bar •

WES

AUST

Telfer •

Nullagine •

Great

Northern

95

Fortescue RH •

Onslow •

North West Cape

Exmouth

Exmouth •   *Gulf*

CAPE RANGE NP

Learmonth •

Nanutarra RH •

Pannawonica •

MILLSTREAM CHICHESTER NATIONAL PARK

HAMERSLEY

PILBARA

• *Wittenoom*

Auski RH

HAMERSLEY RANGE NATIONAL PARK

Tom Price •

Mt Meharry 1249m   *RANGE*   *Hwy*

Newman •   Capricorn RH

Jiggalong •

RUDALL RIV NATIONAL PA

115°E

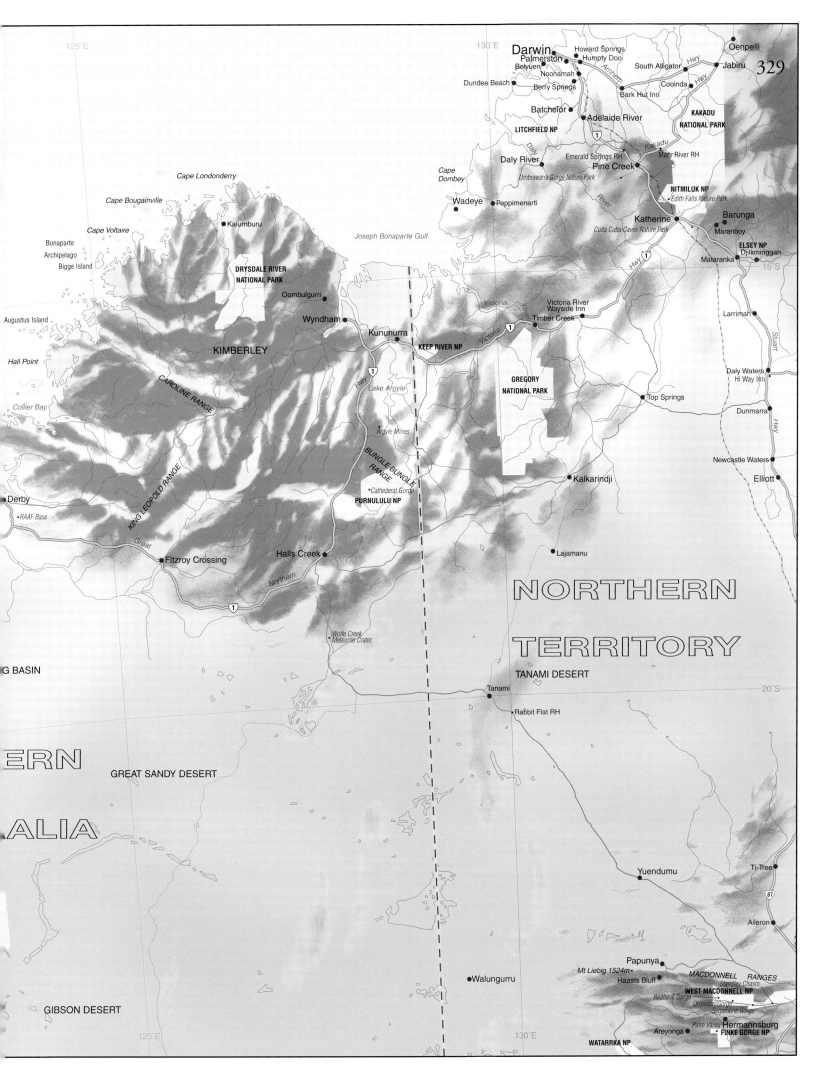

Darwin
Howard Springs
Palmerston
Humpty Doo
Belyuen
Noonamah
Berry Springs
South Alligator
Cooinda
Bark Hut Inn
Dundee Beach
Batchelor
Adelaide River
KAKADU
NATIONAL PARK
LITCHFIELD NP

Oenpelli
Jabiru

Cape
Dombey
Daly River
Emerald Springs RH
Pine Creek
Mary River RH

Umbrawarra Gorge Nature Park
NITMILUK NP
Edith Falls Nature Park

Wadeye
Peppimenarti

Katherine
Cutta Cutta Caves Nature Park
Barunga
Maranboy

ELSEY NP
Djilkminggan
Mataranka

Larrimah

DRYSDALE RIVER
NATIONAL PARK
Cape Londonderry

Cape Bougainville
Oombulgurri

Cape Voltaire
Kalumburu

Bonaparte
Archipelago
Bigge Island

Joseph Bonaparte Gulf

Victoria River
Wayside Inn
Timber Creek

Augustus Island

Wyndham

Kununurra
KEEP RIVER NP

Daly Waters
Hi Way Inn

Hall Point
KIMBERLEY

GREGORY
NATIONAL PARK
Dunmarra

Collier Bay
CAROLINE RANGE

Lake Argyle

Top Springs

Newcastle Waters

Elliott

Argyle Mines
KING LEOPOLD RANGE

BUNGLE BUNGLE
RANGE

Kalkarindji

Derby
RAAF Base
Cathedral Gorge
PURNULULU NP

Lajamanu

Great
Fitzroy Crossing
Halls Creek

Northern
NORTHERN

Wolfe Creek
Meteorite Crater
TERRITORY

G BASIN
TANAMI DESERT

Tanami
20°S

ERN
Rabbit Flat RH

GREAT SANDY DESERT

ALIA

Yuendumu
Ti-Tree

GIBSON DESERT

Walungurru

Papunya
Mt Liebig 1524m
MACDONNELL RANGES
Standley Chasm
Haasts Bluff
WEST MACDONNELL NP
Redbank Gorge
Ormiston Gorge
Serpentine Gorge
Palm Valley
Hermannsburg
Areyonga
FINKE GORGE NP

WATARRKA NP

Aileron

125°E
130°E
15 S
125°E
130°E

ACKNOWLEDGEMENTS

Front Cover: Beach at Noosa Heads with the Sunshine Coast hinterland in the background. (Chris Baker)
Half title Page: Farmland at Maleny, Queensland (Chris Baker)
Title Page: The Glass House Mountains at dusk (Chris Baker)
Back Cover: Hidden Valley, Kununurra (Colin Kerr)

Maps
© MapGraphics, November 2004

Photographs
We are very grateful to the following for their kind assistance in providing photographs for this publication.
© Broken Hill Regional Tourist Association pages 41, 42, 46
© Tourism NSW pages 16-17, 20, 22-23, 23, 24, 25, 26, 27, 34, 35, 36, 38, 39, 40,   44-45, 49, 50, 53r, 54, 56l, 97, 58, 60, 61, 62-63, 66, 68, 71,
© Central Coast Tourism Inc. pages 69, 70
© Colin Kerr pages 43, 100, 156-157, 158, 161, 162, 163, 164, 165, 166, 168, 169, 170, 171, 172-173, 174, 175, 176, 177, 178, 179, 180, 181, 182, 183, 184-185, 186, 187, 188, 189, 190, 191, 198-199, 208-209, 214, 215, 217, 220-221, 222, 223, 224-225, 226, 227, 228, 229, 231, 232, 233, 234, 235,
© Leeton Council 37,
© Dubbo Tourism pages 47, 48,
© Bathurst Visitors Information Centre page 51, 52,
© Hunter Valley Wine Country page 64, 66-67,
© Visions of Victoria pages 80r, 81, 83, 84-85, 86tr, 87br, 88, 89, 90, 91, 92, 93, 94-95, 96, 97, 98, 99, 101, 102, 103, 104, 105, 106, 107, 108-109, 110, 113, 114, 115, 116, 117.
© Tasmania Tourism pages 128, 129, 130, 131, 132, 134, 135, 136, 137, 139, 142, 143, 144, 145, 147, 148, 149, 150, 151, 152l, 153, 154, 155.
© Goldfields Tourism Association, Inc. pages 210-211, 212, 213,
© Northern Territory Tourist Commission pages 236-237, 239, 242-243, 244, 245, 247, 248, 249, 250-251, 253, 255, 256, 260, 261
© Gonzalo de Alvear 246,
© Chris Baker/LHP, Front cover, pages 1, 2-3, 6, 7, 10, 16, 19, 20t, 21, 28, 29, 30-31, 53l, 56l, 59, 65, 69, 70, 72-73, 74, 75, 82, 86bl, 87tr, 111, 112, 118-119, 120, 121, 122, 123, 124-125, 126, 127, 133, 138, 139, 192-193, 194, 195, 196, 197, 200, 201, 202, 203, 204, 205, 206, 207, 217, 218, 219, 264, 265, 267, 268-269, 277, 284, 285,
© Shepparton City Council page 99
© Brisbane Marketing page 266
© Gold Coast Tourism Bureau pages 270-271, 272, 273, 274,
© Toowoomba City Council pages 275, 276
© Tourism Queensland pages 278-279, 281, 285, 286, 287, 304-5, 310, 313, 314, 315, 317, 318, 319
© Bundaberg Region Limited pages 288-289, 290
© Capricorn Central Queensland Tourism pages 292, 293, 294-295, 296, 297
© Mackay Tourism pages 298, 299, 300, 301, 302, 303
© Tourism Whitsundays 308-209,
© LHP Photos by Eduard Domin pages 17, 32, 33, 74, 76, 77, 78-79, 80l, 140-141, 146, 152, 159, 160, 166l, 167, 262-263,
© LHP Photo by Darren Hopton, page 13
© Little Hills Press pages 8-9, 11, 12, 240, 241, 258,

We are very grateful for the invaluable assistance given to us by the following: Colin Kerr, New South Wales Tourism, Dubbo Tourism, Bathurst Tourism Information Centre, Orange City Council, Blue Mountains Tourism, Kim Simpson of Hunter Valley Wine Country Tourism, Amber Cross from Central Coast Tourism Inc, Margaret Mcguire of Cooma Visitors Centre, Southern Highlands Visitor Information Centre, Dinitee Haskard of Broken Hill Regional Tourist Association, Debbra Phillips of Tourism Wollongong, P‰oivi Lindsay of Coonabarabran Visitor Information Centre, Leeton Shire Council, Visions of Victoria Tourism, Christine Celegon, ADC Tourism (Mildura), Liz Dobson of Shepparton City Council, Tasmania Tourism, Regional Tourist Centre - Yorke Peninsula, Tourism Kangaroo Island, Jenny Barnes of the Whyalla Visitor Centre, Lady Nelson Visitor & Discovery Centre ñ Mount Gambier, Sue Finnigan, Sherridan Emery and Phoebe Hain of Brisbane Marketing, Roy Berryman of Goldfields Tourism Association, Esperance Tourism, Devan from Shire of Moora, New Norcia Museums & Art Gallery, Carolyn Bartsch of Cape Naturaliste Tourism Association, Northern Territory Tourist Commission, Allison Forner of Gold Coast Tourism Bureau, Tourism Queensland, Simon Jacobs of Bundaberg Region Limited, Kerry Johnston of Capricorn Tourism, Gladstone Area Promotion and Development Ltd, Brooke Darling of Mackay Tourism, Alison McNamara of Tourism Whitsundays, Outback at Mount Isa and Danielle Bombardieri of Townsville Enterprise Limited.
We have endeavoured to thank all the people who have helped us in this project. Our apologies if we have inadvertently forgotten to mention anyone.

INDEX

A

Adaminaby *33*
Adelaide *158*
Adelaide Hills *160*
Adelaide River *244*
Airlie Beach *302*
Albany *207*
Albury-Wodonga *38*
Alexandra *90*
Alice Springs *256*
Angaston *178*
Apollo Bay *110*
Ararat *115*
Arltunga Historical Reserve *260*
Armadale *202*
Armidale *54*
Arnhem Land *246*
Asbestos Range National Park *137*
Attack Creek Historical Reserve *254*
Auburn *180*
Augusta *206*
Avoca *116*

B

Bairnsdale *93*
Ballarat *113*
Ballina *59*
Barmera *171*
Barossa Valley, The *174*
Barossa Valley Way *177*
Barrow Creek *254*
Bass *87*
Batchelor *244*
Bateman's Bay *24*
Bathurst *50*
Bathurst and Melville Islands *246*
Batman Bridge *137*
Beachport *168*
Beaconsfield *137*
Bedarra Island *307*
Bega *27*
Bell Bay *137*
Benalla *101*
Bendigo *115*

Ben Lomond *136*
Bermagui *27*
Berri *171*
Berrima *29*
Berry *25*
Berry Springs *244*
Bethany *177*
Bicheno *142*
Biggenden *290*
Blackall Range *283*
Blackwood Hills District *161*
Blanchetown *171*
Blinman *191*
Boat Harbour *148*
Bodalla *26*
Bothwell *133*
Bourke *46*
Bowen *310*
Bowral *28*
Brampton Island *302*
Bridgewater *138*
Bridport *143*
Bright *96*
Brighton *138*
Brisbane *264*
Broadbeach *273*
Broken Hill *41*
Broome *231*
Brunswick Heads *61*
Bruny Island *131*
Bruny Island and the D'Entrecasteaux
Channel Kingston–Blackmans Bay *130*
Buchan *93*
Buckland *139*
Bunbury *202*
Bundaberg *288*
Bundanoon *29*
Burleigh Heads *274*
Burnie *146*
Burra *180*
Burrum Heads *287*
Bushy Park *132*
Busselton *205*
Byron Bay *59*

Bywong *29*

C

Cairns *311*
Caloundra *282*
Camooweal *318*
Canberra *74*
Cape Hillsborough *303*
Cape Jervis *162*
Cape York *315*
Capricorn Coast, The *293*
Capricorn Highlands *297*
Cardwell *307*
Carnarvon *220*
Castlemaine *117*
Ceduna *186*
Central Tilba *26*
Cervantes *219*
Chambers Pillar Historical Reserve *260*
Charters Towers *310*
Childers *290*
Clare *179*
Cloncurry *319*
Clunes *116*
Cobar *46*
Cobargo *26*
Cobourg Peninsula/
Victoria Settlement *246*
Cockle Creek *153*
Coffs Harbour *58*
Coles Bay *142*
Collie *207*
Conargo *37*
Coober Pedy *190*
Cooktown *315*
Coolamon Shire *36*
Coolangatta and Tweed Heads *274*
Coolgardie *213*
Cooma *32*
Coonabarabran *51*
Coonawarra *168*
Cootamundra *36*
Coral Bay *226*
Corinna *148*

Corowa *40*
Corroboree Rock Conservation Reserve *260*
Cossack *229*
Cowell *187*
Cradle Mountain *153*
Culcairn *40*
Cutta Cutta Caves Nature Park *248*

D

Daintree and Cape Tribulation *315*
Dalby *277*
Daly Waters *249*
Dampier *229*
Dandenong Ranges *87*
Darwin *238*
Daydream Island *301*
Daylesford *116*
Deloraine *145*
Denham *223*
Deniliquin *37*
Denmark *207*
Derby *143, 234*
Devils Marbles *254*
Devonport *144*
Dongara/Port Denison *217*
Douglas Apsley National Park *142*
Dover *132*
Dubbo *47*
Dunk Island *307*
Dunsborough *205*

E

Eagle Point *93*
East Torren *161*
Echuca-Moama *101*
Eden *27*
Eden Valley, The *178*
Edith Falls Nature Park *248*
Eidsvold *290*
Eildon *90, 115*
Ellery Creek Big Hole Nature Park *259*
Elliott *254*
Elliston *188*
Emily and Jessie Gap Nature Park *260*
Esperance *212*
Eungella National Park *303*
Euroa *102*

Evandale *136*
Ewaninga Rock Carvings Conservation Reserve *260*
Exeter *137*
Exmouth *226*

F

Falls Creek *97*
Fingal *142*
Finke Gorge National Park *259*
Fitzroy Island *306*
Flinders Island *155*
Flinders Ranges *189*
Forbes *51*
Forster & Tuncurry *58*
Franklin *131*
Franklin-Gordon Wild Rivers *153*
Fraser Island *286*
Fremantle *201*
Freycinet Peninsula *142*

G

Gascoyne Junction *223*
Gawler *176*
Gayndah *290*
Geelong *111*
Geeveston *131*
George Town *137*
Geraldton *215*
Gilgandra *51*
Gladstone *293*
Glen Helen Gorge Nature Park *259*
Glen Innis *55*
Goolwa *164*
Gosford *69*
Goulburn *28*
Grafton *58*
Great O cean Road *107*
Greater Port Macquarie *56*
Great Keppel Island *296*
Great Western *117*
Greenock *178*
Greenough *216*
Green Island *313*
Griffith *35*
Grove *131*
Gulgong *52*
Gundagai *36*

Guyra *55*
Gympie *283*

H

Hadspen *138*
Hahndorf *160*
Halliday Bay *303*
Halls Creek *235*
Halls Gap *117*
Hamersley Range National Park *230*
Hamilton *106, 133*
Hamilton Island *301*
Hartz Mountains National Park *152*
Hattah-Hulkyne National Park *105*
Hawker *191*
Hay *37*
Hayman Island *301*
Healesville *88*
Hellyer Gorge *147*
Henbury Meteorites Conservation Reserve *260*
Hepburn Springs *116*
Hermannsburg *259*
Heron Island *296*
Hervey Bay *287*
Heywood *106*
Hillgrove *55*
Hill End *52*
Hinchinbrook Island *307*
Hobart *120*
Holbrook *40*
Home Hill and Ayr *310*
Hook Island *301*
Howard *287*
Howard Springs *241*
Humpty Doo *244*
Hunter Valley Wine Country *66*
Huon Valley *131*
Huonville *131*

I

Iluka *61*
Inverell *55*
Iron Knob *187*

J

Jindabyne *33*
Jindera *40*

John Flynn's Grave Historical Reserve *259*
Junee *36*

K

Kakadu National Park *244*
Kalamunda *202*
Kalbarri *217*
Kalgoorlie-Boulder *210*
Kambalda *214*
Kangaroo Island *165*
Karratha *229*
Karumba *319*
Kataning *207*
Katherine Town *247*
Katoomba *18*
Kempton *138*
Keyneton *178*
Kiama *23*
Kingston *168*
King Island *154*
Kununurra *235*
Kyabram *102*
Kyogle *61*

L

Lady Elliott Island *297*
Lady Musgrave Island *297*
Lakes Entrance *91*
Lake Pedder and Strathgordon *152*
Lake St Clair *153*
Larrimah *248*
Latrobe *146*
Launceston *134*
Laverton *213*
Lawn Hill National Park *319*
Leeton *37*
Leinster *214*
Leonora *213*
Leura *19*
Liffey Falls *137*
Lightning Ridge *46*
Lilydale *137*
Lindeman Island *300*
Lismore *59*
Litchfield National Park *244*
Lithgow *20*
Lizard Island *315*

Lockhart *36*
Longford *136*
Longreach *318*
Long Island *301*
Lord Howe Island *62*
Lorne *109*
Low Head *137*
Loxton *171*
Lyndoch *176*

M

Macarthur *106*
Mackay *298*
Maclean *60*
Macquarie Island *155*
Magnetic Island *307*
Maitland *66*
Mallacoota *92*
Mandurah *202*
Manilla *55*
Manjimup *206*
Mansfield *102*
Marananga *177*
Marble Bar *230*
Margaret River *205*
Margate *130*
Maria Island National Park *139*
Marlin Coast - Northern Beaches *314*
Maroochydore *283*
Marrawah *149*
Maryborough *116, 284*
Marysville *90*
Mary Kathleen *319*
Mataranka *248*
McLaren Vale *163*
Melbourne *80*
Menindee *46*
Menzies *213*
Merimbula *27*
Mildura *103*
Miles, Chinchilla & Boongara *277*
Millicent *168*
Mintaro *180*
Mission Beach *306*
Mittagong *28*
Monkey Mia *223*
Monto *297*
Moora *219*

Morawa *219*
Moree *55*
Moreton Bay and Island *267*
Morgan *171*
Mornington Peninsula *87*
Moruya *26*
Mossman *314*
Moss Vale *28*
Mount Augustus *226*
Mount Buffalo *98*
Mount Buller *102*
Mount Cole Forest *117*
Mount Field National Park *133*
Mount Gambier *166*
Mount Hotham *98*
Mount Isa *316*
Mount Morgan *297*
Mount William National Park *143*
Mt Barker Area *162*
Mt Lofty Area *161*
Mudgee *52*
Mullewa *219*
Mulwala *40*
Mundaring *202*
Munduberra *290*
Mungo National Park *105*
Murray-Kulkyne National Park *105*
Murray Bridge *162*
Murrurundi *68*
Murwillumbah Region *61*
Muswellbrook *68*
Myrtleford *98*

N

N'Dhala Gorge Nature Park *260*
Nagambie *102*
Naracoorte *168*
Narooma *26*
Narrandera *37*
Nelson *106*
Nelson Bay *66*
Newcastle *64*
Newman *230*
New Norcia *217*
New Norfolk *132*
Nimbin *61*
Nitmiluk Katherine Gorge Park *248*
Noonamah *244*

Noosa *280*
Norfolk Island *77*
Norseman *214*
Northampton *217*
North Stradbroke Island *267*
Nowa Nowa *93*
Nowra *26*
Numurkah *101*
Nundle *55*
Nuriootpa *178*

O

Oakey *277*
Oatlands *138*
Omeo *92*
Onkaparinga Valley *161*
Onslow *229*
Ophir *52*
Orange *50*
Orbost *92*
Orford *139*
Ormiston Gorge National Park *259*
Orpheus Island *307*
Ouse *133*
Overland Track *153*

P

Palmerston *241*
Paluma *307*
Parkes *50*
Paynesville *93*
Penguin *146*
Penola *168*
Perth *194*
Peterborough *188*
Phillip Island *92*
Pine Creek *249*
Pontville *138*
Porepunkah *98*
Portland *104*
Port Arthur *128*
Port Augusta *187*
Port Bonython *187*
Port Campbell *110*
Port Campbell National Park *110*
Port Douglas *314*
Port Elliot *162*
Port Hedland *227*

Port Lincoln *186*
Port MacDonnell *167*
Port Pirie *188*
Port Sorell *146*
Port Stephens *66*
Princetown *110*
Proserpine *302*

Q

Queanbeyan *29*
Queenscliff *112*
Queenstown *149*
Quorn *191*

R

Rainbow Valley Nature Park *259*
Redbank Nature Park *259*
Red Cliffs *105*
Renmark *169*
Renner Springs *254*
Richmond *128*
Robe *168*
Robertson *29*
Rochester *102*
Rockhampton *291*
Rockingham *201*
Rocky Cape National Park *148*
Roebourne *229*
Roma *276*
Rosebery *151*
Ross *139*
Rottnest Island *201*
Rowland Flat *176*
Ruby Gap Nature Park *260*

S

Sale *93*
Salmon Ponds *132*
Sarina *302*
Savage River *147*
Scamander *142*
Scone *68*
Scottsdale *143*
Seppeltsfield *177*
Serpentine Gorge Nature Park *259*
Seymour *102*
Shark Bay *222*
Sheffield *146*

Shellharbour *23*
Shepparton *99*
Shute Harbour *302*
Silverton *43*
Simpsons Gap National Park *259*
Singleton *67*
Smithton *148*
Snug *131*
Sofala *52*
Southport *132, 273*
Southwest National Park *152*
South Molle Island *301*
Springton *178*
Standley Chasm *259*
Stanley *148*
Stawell *117*
Stockwell *178*
Strahan *151*
Stratford *93*
St Helens *142*
Surfers Paradise *270*
Swansea *142*
Swan Valley *201*
Sydney *10*

T

Table Cape *147*
Tamworth *53*
Tanunda *177*
Taree *57*
Tathra *27*
Temora *36*
Tennant Creek *252*
Tenterfield *55*
Terrigal *70*
The Channon *61*
The Entrance *71*
The Hinterland *274, 310*
The Rock *36*
Thredbo *33*
Three Ways *254*
Timber Creek *249*
Tocumwal *101*
Tom Price - Paraburdoo *230*
Toogoom *287*
Toowoomba *275*
Torbanlea *287*
Torrens Gorge *160*

Townsville *304*
Trephina Gorge Nature Park *260*
Trevallyn State Recreation Area *137*
Triabunna *139*
Tuggerah Lakes *71*
Tullah *151*
Tully *306*
Tumut *37*
Tynong *87*

U

Ulmarra *60*
Uluru *257*
Ulverstone *146*
Umbrawarra Gorge Nature Park *249*
Uralla *55*

V

Victoria River *249*
Victor Harbour *164*
Violet Town *102*

W

Waddamana *133*
Wagga Wagga *34*
Waikerie *171*
Walgett *46*
Walls of Jerusalem *153*
Waratah *147*
Warburton *90*
Warrnambool *107*
Watarrka National Park *260*
Wauchope *254*
Weldborough *143*
Wellington *51*
Wentworth *106*
Westbury *138*
White Cliffs *46*
Whitsundays *300*
Whitsunday Island *300*
Whyalla *183*
Wilcannia *46*
Wilpena Pound *191*
Winton *319*
Wittenoom *230*
Wollomombi Falls *55*
Wollongong *21*
Wooli *61*

Woolnorth *148*
Wycliffe Well *254*
Wyndham *235*
Wynyard *147*

Y

Yamba *61*
Yeppoon *293*
Yorke Peninsula *181*

Z

Zeehan *151*